# THE BOOK OF THE THAMES.

THE

# BOOK OF THE THAMES,

FROM

## Its Rise to its Fall.

BY

## MR. AND MRS. S. C. HALL.

---

"Though deep, yet clear ; though gentle, yet not dull ;
Strong without rage, without o'erflowing, full."
DENHAM.

---

Published in London by
**Charlotte James Publishers**
45 Heathfield South,
Twickenham, Middlesex

First Published in London
in 1859

First published in London in 1859

Republished as a first new edition in 1975

Second new edition 1976

Third new edition
published in Jubilee Year 1977

**H.M. QUEEN ELIZABETH II
SILVER JUBILEE
1977**

*1952 ~ 1977*

**CHARLOTTE JAMES PUBLISHERS**
45, Heathfield South,
Twickenham, Middx.
England.
(01-892 4656)

Printed in Great Britain by Kingprint Ltd.
Orchard Road, Richmond, Surrey.

Bound by Kemp Hall Bindery, Osney Mead, Oxford.

Paper supplied by Frank Grunfeld Ltd of London
and manufactured by
William Sommerville & Son Ltd. of Edinburgh.

Standard Third Edition                    ISBN 0 9503990 5 1
Leather Bound Limited First New Edition   ISBN 0 9503990 1 9

# PREFACE

(to 1977 edition)

————o O o————

In this Jubilee Year, a year of celebrations, we have much pleasure in producing a third edition of this enormously popular Book of the Thames.

My family and I have indeed come a long way since my original mystery trip down the Thames, which heralded the first new edition. The enthusiasm and help that we have met since its publication has been a continuing delight to us and we should like to thank most sincerely all those concerned.

We are looking forward to all the Jubilee Celebrations that are to take place on or about the river this year and note with pleasure that in our own river town of Richmond we also have the Bicentenary of our Bridge to celebrate.

Our aim in producing this edition is firstly to provide an answer to a popular demand and secondly it allows us to once again indulge in the luxury of following through our original idea of reproducing a quality book of beauty and interest so that many more people can enjoy the pleasures of our greatest of all rivers, the Thames.

R. A. Harris
LONDON
1977

# PREFACE
## (to 1976 edition)

——————oOo——————

In my first preface I described this book as being most beautiful. I now realise, in the light of my experiences during the past year, that it is also considered both interesting and enlightening as well as sometimes controversial, judging from the comments and observations of those many readers whom I have had the pleasure of meeting.

For my family and me it still retains the quality of a magical mystery tour and many weekends during the year have been spent trudging about obscure and inaccessible parts of the river in pursuit of some engraved scene.

It has been an endless source of pleasure to me to think of myself and my family as intrepid explorers retracing the footsteps of the authors, and our habit of reading the text and viewing the scene en route really proves a success. I often wonder how many more will follow the numerous remaining traces of the HOME TOUR as the authors described their adventure.

I am now certain that in reprinting this original edition I really am fulfilling the wishes and ideas of the authors; a feeling which is strengthened when I am brought into personal contact with the pleasure and excitement that the reading public has so often kindly conveyed to me.

R. A. Harris
LONDON
1976

# PREFACE

———o O o———

This is a most beautiful book which relates to views and events which took place some one hundred and twenty years ago.

It is one of those books which has long been around in my family – you know, one of those books that you possibly take for granted.

It wasn't until this year that after having another look at the book I decided to make a similar journey from the source of the Thames to my home in Twickenham. The original aim of the journey was to relate old and new in the form of a children's project guide; however, soon after starting down the river the journey became somewhat of a mystery tour with each turn of the river revealing one of the book's engravings. I took the opportunity to photograph these views as closely as possible to the engraving. This, together with the beautiful text which was easily absorbed en route, provided a wonderful holiday, which was indeed the wish of the authors many years ago.

In reprinting this original I hope that I am fulfilling the original ideas of the authors in allowing a larger audience to enjoy the pleasures of the River Thames, as depicted in this splendid book.

R.A. Harris
LONDON
1975

# THE AUTHORS TO THE PUBLIC

E have the honour to submit to the public a " Book of the Thames," from its Rise to its Fall: hopeful that our readers may share with us the enjoyment we have so long, and so often, derived from the " King of Island Rivers !" We have reprinted it from the Art-Journal, avail- ing ourselves of suggestions, from time to time received, enabling us to correct mistakes, generally to revise it, and to make such additions (neither few nor unimportant) as our own augmented experience, and the advice of competent friends and cor- respondents, have naturally induced.

We have traced the bountiful river from the bubbling well out of which it issues, in the meadow by Trewsbury Mead—its lonely birth- place—through its whole course, gathering tributaries, and passing with them through tranquil villages, populous towns, and crowded cities; ever fertilizing, ever beautifying, ever enriching, until it reaches the most populous city of the modern or the ancient world, forming thence the Great Highway by which a hundred Nations traverse the globe.

Our object will not be answered if we fail to show that, although in landscape beauty it may be inferior to other British rivers, its graces

and its grandeur less, the Thames has attractions of its own which
place it high above all competitors; while it is by no means poor in
natural gifts—of hill and dale, of wood and plain, of all that makes
free Nature a perpetual charm, a never-ending delight. Aided by
several accomplished artists, we have largely illustrated this volume,
not only by engravings of its picturesque scenery, but by introducing
the various objects of interest that are found upon its banks.*

It is a pleasant task, and brings with it a large reward—that
which has for its aim and end to make manifest the advantages
that recompense a HOME TOUR. Any author, no matter how humble,
who writes of England, may show how manifold are its means to
create enjoyment, to convey instruction, and to augment a rational
pride of country—the instinctive patriotism that may exist without
contracting the heart or narrowing the mind.

Several circumstances have of late combined to induce acquaintance
with the charms of scenery, grand or beautiful, which our islands so
plentifully supply. The lovely lakes, the mountain-rocks that guard
our coasts, the rugged mountains, the wood-clad hills, the dense forests,
the delicious dells, the rippling burns and rapid rivers, the spacious

---

* It is a pleasant duty to record our grateful thanks to those by whom we have been thus assisted.
Our esteemed friend and frequent associate, Mr. F. W. FAIRHOLT, F.S.A., has rendered this work of
value by his pen as well as by his pencil : to him we are indebted for many of the " notes," which his
extensive knowledge as an antiquary has enabled him to make both instructive and interesting. To
our friend, Mr. THOMAS WRIGHT, F.S.A., we have also to acknowledge our obligations for his revision of
those parts which involve matters concerning the early people of these kingdoms. To Mr. W. S.
COLEMAN—whose drawings and sketches, made in our company, have supplied us with a large proportion of the engravings—we owe much, not alone because of his great ability as an artist, but for
the zeal and cordiality with which, upon all occasions, he laboured to give value to our undertaking, in
the important part of it that was mainly under his control. And to Commander WALTER W. MAY, R.N.,
our thanks are due for the liberal kindness with which he contributed those pictures of sea-scape
and shipping, the value of which mainly depended on their accuracy, and which his professional
knowledge, combined with his artistic skill, enabled him to give to them. There are other artists whose
aid we gratefully acknowledge.

harbours, the green islets, the rural villages, the luxurious demesnes— these and many other attractions await the traveller who journeys through any of the shires of England, Scotland, Ireland, or Wales.

We shall be, indeed, repaid largely if we are the means of inducing travels AT HOME—to natural beauties, surely not less delightful because of comparatively easy access—to scenes that are associated with glorious memories, and are wholesome and honourable stimulants—to places, such as the banks of the river Thames, where every step is a reminder that we live in a free land, under the sway of a SOVEREIGN to whom every subject of every degree, while rendering obedience as a sacred duty, offers the homage of the heart.

This BOOK OF THE THAMES is full of evidence that justifies all who honour

> " The venerable name
> Of our adored country "

in exclaiming, also with the Poet—

> " Oh, thou Queen,
> Thou delegated Deity of Earth,
> O dear, dear England ! "

S. C. H.
A. M. H.

# BACKGROUND TO THE AUTHORS

———— o O o ————

Samuel Carter Hall (1800–1889), author and editor, was born near Waterford, Ireland, on the 9th of May, 1800, whilst his father was in service with the Devon & Cornwall Forcibles.

Samuel Hall was the fourth son of a family of twelve children. At the age of twenty-one he came to London. Two years later he acted as a Parliamentary reporter in the House of Lords. In 1824 he studied as a student at the Inner Temple and although he was called to the Bar he never practised. He married Anna Maria Fielding in the same year, 1824.

Throughout his life he wrote and edited many, many works and in 1874 he was presented with a testimonial to commemorate his Golden Wedding. The sum of £1,600 was also collected for him and was given as an annuity. In 1880 a Civil List pension of £150 per year was granted to him for his long and valuable services to literature and art.

Throughout his life he was a friend of most of the well-known celebrities of his day and indeed in some of his works he wrote of his experiences with them. Samuel Carter Hall was a most industrious literary man and at the same time he and his wife aided the formation of many charitable institutions.

He died at his home, 24 Stanford Road, Kensington, London, on the 16th March, 1889, and was buried at Addlestone Church, Surrey.

Anna Maria Hall (1800 - 1881), novelist and writer, was born in Anne Street, Dublin, on the 6th January, 1800.

She came to London with her mother in 1815 and on the 20th September, 1824, she married Samuel Carter Hall. In 1826 she lived at 21 Ashley Place, London, with her husband and her mother who died there in 1856, aged 83.

Throughout her life she produced novels and plays, often with an Irish theme. Her books were never popular in Ireland as she saw in the people much to praise and much to blame; thus she failed to please either Orangemen or Catholics.

In 1868 she was granted a Civil List pension of £100 a year.

Throughout her life she and her husband were believers in spiritualism and she was also instrumental in founding the Hospital for Consumption at Brompton, the Governesses' Institute and The Home for Decayed Gentlewomen.

She was a lifelong industrious writer, directing her literary energies in all directions.

She died at Devon Lodge, East Molesey, on the 30th January, 1881, and was buried in Addlestone Churchyard, Surrey.

# LIST OF ILLUSTRATIONS.

# HOW THE ILLUSTRATIONS WERE PRODUCED

———— oOo ————

The illustrations depicted within this book are produced from wood block engravings. The engravings were created by cutting into the end grain of either boxwood or maple with various types and sizes of engraving tools and burins. This process of engraving is carried out firstly by coating the wood block with a thin wash of white water colour, onto which the engraver traces the drawing in reverse. To achieve the engravings in black and white it is necessary to cut away the wood where the paper is to remain unprinted. During the engraving process the block is supported on a small leather sandbag which gives a firm base for the block.

The engravings within this book are to the same size as the engravings produced by the engraver on his wood block. The engravings in the original books were produced by embodying the engraver's wood block within the type face. One can see from the engravings how skilful and fine the work of the engraver was and one can also appreciate the amount of time and effort involved in producing such fine work.

# WAYS IN WHICH TO DERIVE
# PLEASURE AND ACTIVITY FROM THIS BOOK

——— oOo ———

Within this book there is a great deal of interesting information relating to many aspects of the river.

Its engravings range from architectural views to those which show minute details of the plants, flora, animals and fish that abound in, on, or about the river.

The text contains many references to meetings that the authors had with the men and women whose trades and crafts derived from the river and whose trades and crafts have since disappeared.

From this varied information one can seek to construct projects of interest and information which will give a sense of activity and purpose often allowing one to become part of the river's activity rather than just a casual observer watching but not participating.

I would suggest that the projects you devise will often best be orientated around the engravings of the book. Thus one might consider photographic projects: for example, many of the views depicted in the engravings could be photographed as near as is possible to the original engraving. The photographic projects need not be restricted to views; you might also seek out and photograph the plants and insects or the animals and fish that are illustrated. You could also make photographic collections of, for example, the varied and interesting boats and houses upon the river noting their development from the original engravings. Thus the book offers numerous areas of search and activity in the photographic field. To this end I have had all of the three hundred and two engravings within the book copied into 35mm slides, details of which are to be found at the rear of the book.

You could also engage yourself in collecting projects which would involve you in searching and seeking out the various items of plant life and flora illustrated. This could further be extended to the insect life, noting that tabulations and inventories might possibly be more acceptable in these days of conservation.

Rather than travelling the river by boat you might consider exploring the Thames by foot. It should however be noted that the footpath occasionally crosses from one bank to the other at points where there was once a ferry. So to avoid retracing your steps you should carefully plan your journey prior to its start.

From a more general point it is interesting to note from the text how the various towns and villages etc. have changed in character from the original interpretations and observations of the authors. A more adventurous project might involve interviewing and questioning the local people who line the river with a view to seeking out how the original ideas of the authors have changed. When I made my own journey down the Thames I found the people from whom I sought information and to whom I showed the book extremely interested in its contents, and on many occasions they were able to relate the illustrations and text, to the history and association of their families and friends, with the river.

In conclusion I would wish you to consider the ideas that I have out-lined as only a starting point on which to create your own projects and activities. I hope that they might show you how to discover the pleasures and beauties of England's greatest river.

# THE BOOK OF THE THAMES,

## FROM ITS RISE TO ITS FALL.

HE Thames is "the King of Island Rivers;" if deficient in the grander features of landscape, it is rich in pictorial beauty; its associations are closely linked with heroic men and glorious achievements; its antiquities are of the rarest and most instructive order; its natural productions of the highest interest; it wanders through fertile meads and beside pleasant banks, gathering strength from a thousand tributaries; on either side are remains of ancient grandeur, homely villages, retired cottages, palatial dwellings, and populous cities and towns; boats and barges, and the sea-craft of a hundred nations, indicate and enhance its wealth; numerous locks and bridges facilitate its navigation, and promote the traffic that gives it fame. Its history is that of England: the Britons, the Romans, the Saxons, the Danes, and the Normans, in turn made it their "seat of war," or, settling upon its banks, sought the repose of peace and the blessings of agriculture and commerce. In all the civil contests of centuries it obtained melancholy renown : the intrenched camp, the castle, the baronial hall, the mansion, the villa, occupied adjacent steeps, commanded fords, or adorned its sides, as harmony took the place of discord, and tranquillity succeeded strife. There is scarcely a mile of its borders which may not give birth to some happy thought in association with the past: abbeys, monasteries, and churches exhibit their remains, or rear "the tall spire," consecrated by use and age; the better parts of their structures having endured with the purer portions of the ancient faith. Sites and memorials of famous battles—king with baron, lord with serf, ancient owners of the soil with its invaders, those who warred for despotism or fought for liberty, for feudal rights or freedom; the cromlech of the Briton, the tumulus of the Roman, the barrow of the Saxon, the sculptured tomb of the knight, and the simple monument of the gentleman;—these are to be found, in numbers, on its banks. The names of very many of the great men of England—who "penned" or "uttered wisdom"—are nearly or remotely connected with this river: in its "fields beloved" their "careless childhood stray'd;" in its city of colleges, "for meditation apt," their youth gathered strength for the strife of manhood. To its banks full often came the soldier, the statesman, the scholar, and the poet, "after life's fitful fever," to seek that rest from labour which is labour's best recompence—to enjoy alike

> "The solid pomp of prosperous days,
> The peace and shelter of adversity."

Flowing through rich alluvial soil, that is never sterile, during the whole of its course it meets not an acre of unmanageable bog, and hardly a square yard that does not produce pasture or foliage, except where it refreshes and prospers active villages, busy towns, or crowded cities—venerable Oxford, regal Windsor, "mighty London," and a hundred places, wealthy and famous. It would be indeed impossible to over-estimate the value of the Thames to the British capital. It is said that when one of our sovereigns, angry with the chief magistrate of the metropolis, threatened to ruin it by removing the court, he received the memorable answer, "But your Majesty cannot remove the Thames!"

It will require no very great stretch of imagination to pass from the little streamlet in Trewsbury Mead to "the Pool" below the Tower. The river, born in a sequestered nook, grows and gathers strength until it bears on its bosom " a forest of masts ;" enriches the greatest and most populous city of any age ; ministers to the wants and luxuries of two millions of people—there alone ; becomes the mainstay of commerce, and the missionary of civilization to mankind, carrying their innumerable blessings throughout the Old World and the New ; yet ever the active auxiliary, and never the dangerous ally—keeping from its birth to its close the character so happily conveyed by the famous lines of the poet :—

> " Though deep, yet clear; though gentle, yet not dull ;
> Strong without rage; without o'erflowing, full."

Few, therefore, are the poets of England who have no word for " Old Father Thames !" Even its minor enjoyments have been fertile themes for the muse ; and numerous are they who laud the " gentle craft " of the angler, whose " idle time is never idly spent" beside the river which, above all others, invites to contemplation, and promotes familiar intercourse with Nature. Here, too, the botanist and the entomologist gather a rich harvest of instruction ; while to the landscape painter, wander where he will—

> "By hedgerow elms, on hillocks green :
> \*　　\*　　\*　　\*
> While the ploughman, near at hand,
> Whistles o'er the furrow'd land,
> And the milkmaid singeth blithe,
> And the mower whets his scythe "—

it is ever an open volume of natural beauties, which are the only veritable teachers of art.

To this River—the King of Island Rivers—we dedicate this Book.

Before we ask the reader to accompany us on our tour, we require him to pause awhile, and consider two essential points—its source, and the name under which it is rightly to be recognised and known.

Both are in dispute. The Churn, which rises at " Seven Springs," about three miles from Cheltenham, and joins the Thames at Cricklade, is sometimes described as the source of the great river. Generally speaking, the source of a river is the spring farthest from its mouth ; and the head of the Churn is farther from the Nore than Thames Head by perhaps fifteen miles. But old writers, old maps, and old documents, unite in representing " Thames Head," near Cirencester, as the head of

the river Thames.  Leland (temp. Henry VIII.) tells us that " Isis
riseth at three myles from Cirencestre, not far from a village cawlled
Kemble, within half a mile of the Fosseway, wher the very head of
Isis is ; " Stow, that " the most excellent and goodly river beginneth in
Coteswold, about a mile from Titbury, and as much from the hie way
called Fosse ; " Camden, that " it riseth not far from Tarlton, hard by
the famous Foss-way ; " Atkins (1712), that " it riseth in the parish of
Cotes ; " Rudder (1779), that " it has been reputed to rise in the parish
of Cotes, out of a well."  These authorities might be multiplied ; and
although Atkins and Rudder (the earliest historians of Gloucestershire)
both write of the Churn, and its claim to be considered the head of the
Thames, " being the highest source from whence it derives its water "—
and no doubt such claim will have many advocates—we have treated the
river Thames as rising at Thames Head, near " a village cawlled Kemble," hard by the " famous Foss-way."

With respect to the name, it is derived directly from that by which it
was known in the time of Julius Cæsar, *Tameses*, which, as well as its
Anglo-Saxon representative, *Temese*, is sufficiently near the modern
*Thames* to be considered as identical with it.  Lhwyd, the learned
Welsh scholar, believes it to be identical also with the Taf—the name
of several rivers in Wales.  But there are other English rivers bearing
names almost the same.  In Staffordshire we have the nearest resemblance in the Tame ; in Shropshire is the Teme ; and in Cornwall is the
Tamar.  There are minor streams in other counties bearing similar
designations, which appear to be derived from one root, and the signi-
fication of all to imply " a gentle stream."  " This," writes Camden, " is
that Isis, which afterwards joining with Tame, by adding the names
together is called Tamisis, chief of the British rivers, of which we may
truly say, as ancient writers did of Euphrates in the East, that it both
plants and waters Britain."  Camden thus speaks of the river as " the
Isis " until it mingles with the Tame—with which it is joined between
Abingdon and Wallingford—about a mile from Dorchester.  But there
is just ground to believe that this is merely a fanciful designation, to
which currency was given by Camden, who is said by his biographer,

Bishop Gibson, to be the author of that Latin poem, introduced into the "Britannia," which commemorates "the marriage of the Tame and Isis." * Stow, Speed, and Hollinshed, his contemporaries, follow in his wake. But Bishop Gibson effectually dispels the illusion, and shows that from a very remote period—certainly anterior to the Conquest—the name of the river was the Thames (*cujus vocabulum Temis, juxta vadum quod appellatur Somerford*); thus confirming not only the fact that the Isis was a name given to it long afterwards, but that the Thames "near Somerford" is that Thames which rises near Cirencester, and not the Churn, which has its birthplace near Cheltenham. "The same appears from several charters to the Abbeys of Malmesbury and Evesham, and from old deeds relating to Cricklade; and perhaps it may be with safety affirmed that it never occurs in any charter or authentic history under the name of Isis." By the Saxons it was undoubtedly called the Thames : † on all ancient maps and documents it is marked as "Thamesis Fluvius." One of the oldest streets of Oxford was Thames Street (now George Street), anciently "Platea Thamesina." The term "Isis" was certainly unknown to our remote ancestors ; its use is opposed to every principle of the English language ; while it appears contrary to common sense to call a continuous stream by one name in the first half, and by another name in the other half, its channel being in no way changed, and its character in no degree altered. The error, however (for so, after the testimony of Bishop Gibson and others, we must consider it), has largely prevailed. It is traceable, no doubt, to the fancy which tempted the separation of the single Latin word

---

* Some writers concerning the Thames have given to Camden the credit of *inventing* the name Isis ; but it is clear that it is older than his time. Leland, who preceded Camden by thirty or forty years, distinctly refers to the Thames as the Isis, and quotes from an authority yet older—" Isa nascitur à quodam fonticulo juxta Tetbiriam prope Circestriam—*ortus Isidas fu.*"—(Joannis Lelandi de rebus Britan. Collect.)

† The name of the river at its highest point, and forty miles above its junction with the Tame, near Dorchester, is given in the Saxon Chronicle almost as it is spelt in the present day—that is, " Temese." The following are two literal translations from this curious record :—

" A.D. 905.—This year Æthelwold enticed the army in East Anglia to break the peace, so that they ravaged over all the land of Mercia, until they came to Cricklade, and then went over the Thames."

" A.D. 1016.—In this year came Canute with his army, and Eadric the Ældorman with him, over Thames into Mercia at Cricklade."

It is also called Thames in the Anglo-Saxon charters relating to Eynsham, in Oxfordshire.

"Tamesis" into two words, *Tame esis* or *Tame isis*—suggested by the fact that another Tame did arise in Buckinghamshire, and pour its waters into the great river, midway in its course between its source and London. There has been much consequent confusion; sometimes Oxford is described "on the Thames," and sometimes "on the Isis." Even in the Ordnance Map it is called in one place the Thames, in another the Isis, and in another "the Thames or Isis," above the junction. The Tame is among the least important of its tributaries; yielding in importance to many streams, above and below, which "run to the embraces" of the venerable Father. We consider, therefore, the Thames to be the traditional, the geographical, and the legal title of the river, and shall give to it only that name throughout this work.*

The field in which the Thames rises is called Trewsbury Mead, and adjoins a Roman encampment that has long borne, and still bears the name of Trewsbury Castle; this "castle" is a large mound, now covered by trees, the Severn and Thames Canal separating it from a fountain that, born in this secluded spot, becomes the great river that "both plants and waters Britain." The birthplace of the Thames is in the parish of Cotes, in Gloucestershire, but close to the borders of Wiltshire, into which it soon passes. The district is usually described as "at the foot of the Cotswold hills;" but these hills are nowhere seen from the dell, and are, indeed, several miles distant.†

---

* The Town Clerk of Oxford courteously submitted to us a list of several hundred documents he had examined; in no one of which was "the Thames" ever recognised as "the Isis." We state, therefore, on his authority, that in no ancient record of the city of Oxford is the name Isis to be found; from the time of Domesday to the present time, it is not recognised by that name, but always as "the Thames."

An additional authority has just been published, namely, the first vol. of the "Chronicon Monasterii de Abingdon," in which (p. 9), in the very first charter—that of Ina, King of Wessex—occurs the following passage :—"In super et de orientali parte fluminis Tamisa, xx. cassatos quos mihi Cuthredus regulus et Merciorum Rex Ethelredus necnon et Ini rex Saxonum tradiderunt adjiciam x. quoque cassatos secus vadum Bestlesford," &c. (A.D. 699.) The river is mentioned in many places in this book, and is written Tamisa (as above), Tamesa, Thamisia, Tamesis, and always in Saxon, Temese. The charters relate to many places near Abingdon, above the river Tame (which is also mentioned *sub voce* by Cuddesdon, p. 200), and there are also charters relating to Whitchurch and Kingston below. The name of Isis occurs nowhere.

† This chain of gently-rising downs formed a territorial boundary to the early British tribes; and many of the camps on the ridge are probably their work. But the Romans, fully aware of the import- ance of this line of demarkation, kept up the old landmarks and added others. In later times the

The ancient Roman way—called Aceman or Akeman Street *—crosses the country within half a mile of the source, and connects Cirencester with Bath. The source is about three miles south-west of Cirencester—a famous city in old times, and still a town of some importance, its church and town-hall being fine examples of the architecture of the fifteenth century: its Roman name was derived from the British Caer Corin; Ptolemy calls it Corinium Dobunorum; Antoninus, Duro-Cornovium—most probably from *dior*, the British name for water. Cirencester was strongly fortified, to protect its inhabitants from "the fierce Silures," and appears to have enjoyed considerable wealth and importance; these intrenchments were exclusively of earthwork, and remains of them may still be seen, stretching across from the Cotswolds to the Severn, on the heights forming the boundary of the vale of Gloucester. The town of Cirencester—which name is derived from the Saxon Cyren-ceaster—still shows many remains of Roman greatness, and some fine tesselated pavements have been discovered, one of which is still preserved in Lord Bathurst's park; the Museum also exhibits relics of the same ancient people, including various memorials of the Roman soldiery. Few English towns have afforded so rich a field for the antiquary;† but the whole district to Woodchester and Gloucester abounds in such records; they furnished Lysons with some of the most important plates to his great work on Roman remains in Britain. Several great roads branched across England from this city, and all may yet be traced in its immediate neighbourhood. They were known as the Irmin Street (north and south), the Akeman Street,

Cotswolds were almost exclusively celebrated for their pastoral character, and the fine breed of sheep there reared. New celebrity was given to them in the reign of Queen Elizabeth as hunting and coursing grounds, and Shakspere has immortalized the fact in his "Merry Wives of Windsor." Subsequently Mr. Robert Dovor, an attorney of Warwickshire, obtained licence from James I. to institute country sports of all kinds there, and he for forty years presided over them in person, "habited in a suit of his Majesty's old clothes." These games have been celebrated in the poems of Ben Jonson, Randolph, and Drayton.

* Acman, in Anglo-Saxon, would mean an oak-man or forester. The Akeman Street would, therefore, be the Forester's Pathway, if translated literally.

† Corinium was certainly an important city in the Roman time; Richard of Monmouth concludes that it was built by a Roman general in the time of Claudius (probably by Plautius), to whom the Boduni first surrendered; and that it had walls and a castle in the time of Constantine, and was strongly fortified. The coins so frequently found, of the reign of Constantine, may be accepted as evidence of the importance of the place at the period.

the Ickenild Street, and the Fossway.* So admirably were they constructed by the Romans, that to this hour they are used, having retained their solidity for centuries.

But the spot to which we direct the more immediate attention of our readers—Trewsbury Castle, a tree-covered mound, at the foot of which is the cradle of the Thames—retains nothing to indicate its long-ago importance; in the silence and solitude of the place, and looking across the valley towards the great city of which this was an outpost, we recalled the lines of the poet—

> " I was that city, which the garland wore
> Of Britain's pride, delivered unto me
> By Roman victors, which it won of yore,
> Though nought at all but ruins now I be,
> And lie in my own ashes, as ye see."

Having journeyed about three miles from Cirencester, along the Akeman Street of the Romans, crossed the Thames and Severn Canal, and arrived in sight of a railway, the shrill whistle of which broke the solitude of the place, and sadly jarred upon the mind at the moment, we reached a small valley, in which we had reason to believe we should find Thames Head. But neither maps nor books gave us any aid as guides. We naturally expected to trace the river to its source by tracking the signs that water almost invariably leaves on the line through which it passes along the meadow—

> " Which, with a livelier green,
> Betrays the secret of its silent course."

But for such water-marks we sought in vain; there were neither alders, nor osiers, nor rushes to be seen; we observed nothing that could in any degree indicate the infant meanderings of a river. Fortunately,

---

* The Fossway receives its name from the intrenchment which runs parallel to it, on one side or 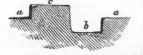 other of its course, and which will be more perfectly understood by the aid of the appended diagram : *a a* is the level traversed by the road ; *b* represents the foss or dry ditch beside it. The earth thus dug out was thrown up to raise the road above the ordinary level, as seen at *c*. The Roman roads are generally raised higher than the ordinary level of the land, but there is no other instance of the intrenchment, as in this Fossway. This is one of the most perfect of our Roman roads, and traverses the Cotswold range in a direct line.

however, we encountered a venerable shepherd of the plain, who conducted us at once to the birthplace of the more venerable father. This is a well, which, when Boydell published his History, in 1794, was "enclosed within a circular wall of stone, raised about eight feet from the surface of the meadow;" the stones have fallen, the well is now filled in; it was with difficulty we could ascertain that it contained

THE SOURCE OF THE THAMES.

water—that water being in the sunny month of June many feet below the surface; but in winter it rises, forces itself through all impediments, ascends in thick jets, and overflows the valley, making its way to greet those earlier tributaries that await its coming to mingle with it and journey to the sea—"most loved of all the ocean's sons." "THAMES HEAD" is therefore pictured, in the accompanying engraving, merely as a heap of stones, overshadowed by trees of no great size. There is not, as we have said, a single water-plant in its vicinity; the bank of the canal forms its background; the dell is a perfect solitude, no dwelling is near, the foot-path is seldom trodden—for, although there still exists "a right of way" through the meadows which lead from the village of Kemble below to that of Cotes above, it is rarely used; but its loneliness is tranquillity, and its silence peace. The fields are fertile, and all things indicate that unobtrusive prosperity which suggests ideas of "contentment, parent of delight." It is still termed "Yeoing Field," and is a part of the parish of Ewelme, of which that name presents the corrupted form; the parish of Ewelme, in Oxford-shire, is in old writing styled "New Elme," but Æwilme is its proper Saxon designation, *i. e.* a spring. It thus obviously derives its name from one of the springs which rises in the neighbourhood, and this must be the one known as "Thames Head." THE HOAR STONE, here pictured, is a venerable relic of antiquity near it: it is named in a grant of lands here by King Athelstan in the year

THE HOAR STONE.

931. This stone, in accordance with the most ancient usage, was an important boundary. Mr. Akerman (in "Archæologia," vol. xxxvii.) thus describes it :—"The Hoar Stone stands, and appears to have stood since the day on which the charter was subscribed by Æthelstan and his court, a few yards above the spring, just within the boundary wall of the Fossway. Of its antiquity there can be no doubt. It will be seen that it has been adapted to the purposes of a horse-block, or 'upping-stock.'" Here, doubtless, travellers in the olden time halted to refresh themselves and their beasts, the Fossway not being then enclosed. When Leland took his journey from Cirencester to Malmes-bury, he passed the spring. In his "Itinerary" he says,—"First I rode about a mile on Fosse, then I turned on the left hand, and came all by

champain ground, fruitful of corn and grass, but very little wood."
Drayton, in his curious topographical poem, "The Poly-Olbion," speaks
of the Thames Head as the chief glory of the district, adopting,
however, the fanciful name of Isis for the upper part of the river.
He says :—

> " But, Cotswold, be this spoke to th' only praise of thee,
>   That thou, of all the rest, the chosen soyle should'st bee,
>   Dame Isis to bring forth (the mother of great Thames),
>   With whose delicious brooks, by whose immortal streams,
>   Her greatnesse is begun : so that our river's king,
>   When he his long descent shall from his Bel-sires bring,
>   Must needs, great pasture's prince, derive his stem by thee
>   From kingly Cotswold's selfe, sprung of the third degree—
>   As the old world's hero's wont, that in the times of yore,
>   On Neptune, Jove, and Mars, themselves so highly bore."

Poetry and prose have laboured from age to age to describe the
pictorial beauty and the moral power of what may be termed the
"church-landscape" of England ; yet no description can adequately
convey an idea of its "pleasantness," or of its elevating influence over a
"people." The first sight of the spire of his native village after years,
long years of wandering, has shaken many a high and firm heart ; and
tears of repentance, and hope, and good resolves, have been often called
forth from comparatively hardened sinners by a sound of the church-
bell—first heard in the days of innocence and youth. There can be
no loneliness, even in imagination, equal to that which the poet pictures
in " Juan Fernandez :"—

> " But the sound of the church-going bell
>   These valleys and rocks never heard ;
>   Never sigh'd at the sound of a knell,
>   Or smiled when a sabbath appear'd."

In foreign countries, the richly-elaborated cathedral in the great square
commands our admiration ; but what can we say of the meagre-looking
church, with its few trees, its rampant weeds, its neglected graveyard,
its dreary interior, its dismal pictures and painted effigies, making
sometimes a feature in the scenery—but how rarely, as with us, being
the sentiment, the centre, the crown and beauty of a whole? Whatever
may be our feelings on certain points—with which this, our chronicle
of the royal English river, has happily nothing whatever to do—we

cannot withhold our tribute of gratitude to the spirit that has rightly
restored and fitly adorned so many of our parish churches, whether
in the crowded city, in the village, or amid the genial solitudes of our
country.

Standing beside the cradle of mighty Thames, and looking forth upon
a landscape wealthy in the gifts of tranquillity and hope, and in the
varied beauty of sunshine and shade, there rises the tower of the
village-church—the CHURCH OF COTES.* Solemn and yet pleasing
associations crowd upon us; for centuries it has been the beacon to

THE CHURCH AND VILLAGE OF COTES.

thousands whose graves are at its base,—they may not have been
" village Hampdens," but they have fulfilled the mission allotted to them
by Providence, and sleep—these

" Rude forefathers of the hamlet "—

beside the homes in which they lived, and under the shadow of the

* The cut exhibits the Church of Cotes on the rising hill in the distance: to prevent any erroneous
mpression of our pictured scene, it is necessary to remind the reader that the stream is not the Thames,
but the Thames and Severn Canal, which is upon a raised embankment, above Ewen field.  The source
of the Thames lies in that field to the left, amid the trees that hang over the stone wall bounding the
towing-path.

church in which they prayed. What scenes of love and life, of joy and sorrow, have alternated here—come and gone!—as time ceaselessly passed onward! Generations after generations have seen the soft cheeks of youth wither into the wrinkles of age, and the step so light and elastic over moss and harebell, become slow and heavy, then feeble and uncertain, tottering at last from the supporting crutch into the quiet grave! Surely are those village spires the lights of our land: come and gone! come and gone! are all around; yet ever enduring, ever inviting, ever rewarding, they continue! Age after age passes, their peaceful bells are heard above. the "crash of empires;" while fears of change alarm the world, "perplexing monarchs," they discharge their mighty yet simple task—

> "Invite to heaven, and point the way."

A walk along the first meadow brings us to the great Bath Road, under which there is a TUNNEL formed to give passage to the Thames

THE FIRST TUNNEL.

when "the waters are out." In June it was dry, sheep were feeding at its entrance; but in winter it is too narrow for the rush of the stream that has then gathered in force.

Close by this tunnel, and about half a mile from Thames Head, is the engine-house of the Thames and Severn Canal, which, by continual working to supply water to the canal, drains all the adjacent springs, and is no doubt the main cause of absorbing the spring-head of the river. This engine-house is an ungainly structure, which the lover of the picturesque may well wish away; but although a blot upon the landscape, it is happily hidden from the valley in which the Thames has its birth. The course of this canal we shall describe when we reach its terminus at Lechlade.

Half a mile further, perhaps, and the burns begin to gather into a common channel; little trickling rills, clear as crystal, rippling by hedge-sides, make their way among sedges, the water-plants appear, and the Thames assumes the aspect of a perennial stream : so it runs on its course, and brings us to the village of Kemble, which occupies a hillock about half a mile from the bank; its church-spire, forming a charming feature in the landscape, standing on a gentle acclivity, and rising above a bower of trees ;—the railroad is previously encountered, the river flowing underneath. This church we shall visit before we resume our tour.

At that part of the field where the railway-arch crosses the Thames, a cemetery of the early Saxon settlers was discovered in 1855. There were found spear-heads and fragments of shields, hair-pins, brooches, and rings, indicating the last resting-places of the warriors and ladies of that powerful race, destined lords of the future greatness of England, though at this time the hated interlopers amid the old Britannic settlements. The district was the stronghold of British and Roman rule, and coins of the successful usurper, Cavausius, were found mingled with the Saxon relics exhumed.

The earliest mention of this parish is in the charters of the Anglo-Saxon kings ;* it is also mentioned in that most venerable record of our country, the "Domesday Book"—the inventory of England made for William the Conqueror. In both it is named *Kemele*—sufficiently close

* The earliest is printed by Kemble in his " Codex Diplomaticus ;" it is a charter of Caedwealha of Wessex, bearing date A.D. 682.

to the familiar pronunciation of its name adopted by the country-folks of the present day. The monks of Malmesbury were possessed of this rich manor in the olden time, it being about six miles from their chief seat. The church is a large structure, still preserving many features of remote antiquity, but they occur only in that fragmentary form which too frequently characterizes such relics. The parts which first strike the eye are of early English architecture,* the best portion being the large PORCH we have pictured, which, however, forms a case, or shrine, to the Norman door, with its chevron ornament decorating the arch.

THE PORCH: KEMBLE CHURCH.

At a little distance from the church are the remains of

---

* Mr. Akerman, secretary to the Society of Antiquaries, read at one of the meetings a paper which contained some interesting and valuable information on this subject:—"Mr. Akerman discovered two Anglo-Saxon cemeteries in the village of Kemble, and this had led him to attempt the identification of the land limits, mentioned in grants of Ewen and Kemble to the Abbey of Malmesbury, by the Anglo-Saxon kings. His researches have been amply repaid, and he exhibited a map of the district, upon which he had marked the ancient and modern names. Among these is the spring known as 'Thames Head,' or the source of the Thames, and the 'hoar stone,' mentioned in the charter of King Æthelstan, as standing near it. This object has hitherto escaped the notice of topographers and tourists, owing probably to its being concealed from the view of persons who pass along the Roman Fossway. Our brethren on the other side of the Atlantic recognise the charms in our local epithets. 'The names are excellent,' observes an American essayist; 'an atmosphere of legendary melody spreads over the land.' In early times there was a chapel at Ewen, but it appears to have been demolished when the church of Kemble was built, as the north side of that edifice is still called 'Ewen Aisle.' The locality of Kemble, its springs, and its lofty situation, favour the inference that it was an early Saxon settlement, and the scene of the peculiar sacrificial rites of that race. The discovery of two distinct burial-places of people who had not abandoned the pagan mode of sepulture favours this inference." A tradition exists in the neighbourhood, that the "chapel" referred to by Mr. Akerman was destroyed beyond the memory of man, and that the materials contributed to form the south aisle of Kemble Church, which is still called "the Ewen Aisle." Near it rises a most beautiful spring of water. Here, doubtless, was celebrated the heathen rites of the first Anglo-Saxon settlers, until the Christian priest-hood consecrated the spot, when a chapel was founded, and the spring dedicated to a saint.

a grove or wood, mentioned in the early charters we have just named. It was probably the sacred grove of our heathen Saxon forefathers, and the scene of human sacrifices to Woden. This grove probably extended as far as the village of Poole, where the remains of a cross stand at the intersection of the roads; though comparatively modern, it probably succeeded a more ancient erection, which obliterated while it interdicted the observance of unhallowed rites.

The water-foliage here commences to encroach upon the stream, giving to it interest and beauty, transparency and health. Among the

WATER CROWFOOT.

earliest of the aqueous plants—and that which is seldom out of sight until the Thames loses somewhat of its purity—is the water Crow-foot (*Ranunculus aquatilis*), the large white flowers of which rise in sparkling profusion above the surface; and at this point the curious variety in the floating and submerged leaves is very apparent—the former being broadly lobed, while the latter are cut into minute thread-like divisions, somewhat resembling the leaves of fennel, as shown in the accompanying figure. Further down the river, where the stream acquires increased depth and velocity, the plant assumes a different character—the flat leaves entirely disappear, both stems and leaves being drawn out by the current into mere bundles of cords, often of great length; in this case the flowers are only produced at occasional intervals.

Resuming our walk by the river-bank, we reach THE FIRST BRIDGE which crosses the Thames—all previous passages having been made by stepping-stones, laid across in winter and removed in summer. This bridge, which leads from the village of Kemble to that of Ewen, is level with the road, the river flowing through three narrow arches; it is without parapet. Hence, along the banks for a considerable distance, there is no foot-path of any kind; the traveller who would explore its

course must cross hedges and ditches, and avoid the main road to Ewen
—an assemblage of cottages and farm-houses. And a delicious walk it
was, to us, beside the river,—pleasure being augmented by difficulties
in the way; the birds were singing blithely in small wood-tufts; the
chirp of the grasshopper was gleeful in the meadows; cattle ruminated,
standing knee-deep in adjacent pools; the bee was busy among the

THE FIRST BRIDGE ON THE THAMES.

clover, and, ever and anon, darted across the stream the rapid kingfisher, the sun gleaming upon his garb of brilliant hues.

> " The softly-warbled song
> Comes from the pleasant woods, and coloured wings
> Glance quick in the bright sun, that moves along
> The forest openings."

Perched on an overhanging branch, the Kingfisher (*Alcedo Ispida*)
quietly surveys the motions of his finny prey in the stream beneath,
waiting with patience the moment for a favourable plunge; down then
descends, " like an arrow," the glittering bird, and in an instant he is
on his perch again, bearing the fish in his beak; quieting his prey by a
few smart raps against the branch, it soon vanishes down his capacious
throat.*

---

* A few years ago we had the satisfaction to find that which is seldom found—a kingfisher's nest;
and our pleasure at the discovery was enhanced by our being able to present it to Mr. Jesse, who had

The Thames here, in its entire loneliness, is precisely that which " most the poet loves :"—

> " The rivulet, delighting in its strength,
> Ran with a young man's speed."

So quiet are its nooks, into which the whirling eddies run, that it would seem a very paradise of the angler; it is not so, however—bait and fly will be alike unproductive here; although an adventurous trout will sometimes make a journey hither, he soon seeks his way back again, for instinct tells him that during the summer months the sources of these pleasant streams are dry. There are no fish to be found, therefore, except the stickleback and minnow; and these may be properly introduced here as the river's earliest produce of animated life.

THE KINGFISHER.

The Minnow (*Leuciscus phoxinus*), called also the Minim and the Pink, is one of the smallest of fresh-water fish, rarely exceeding three inches in length, and not often above two; it is common in rivers and

never until then seen one.  The place of incubation is a burrow in the river-bank, two or three feet in extent, bearing diagonally upwards, at the end of which is a little chamber, in which, without making any nest, the female deposits from five to seven eggs, of a clear pinky white.  The female, while sitting, is supplied by her mate with fish, the indigestible parts of which, the bones and scales, are disgorged, so that the eggs are soon surrounded by a circle of these *rejectanea*, giving rise to the erroneous supposition that the nest is composed of fishbones.  The bones, however, assume a compact character, and are arranged in a concave form; they become so closely knit by pressure as to be easily removed in the mass.  The colouring of this beautiful bird is as follows :—Bill blackish brown, reddish at the base; behind each eye is a patch of light orange-brown, succeeded by a white one.  From each corner of the under mandible proceeds a streak of verditer-blue, tinged with verdigris-green ; crown of the head deep olive-green, the feathers tipped with verdigris-green ; down the back is a stripe of verditer blue feathers, tinged in some shades with verdigris-green ; chin and throat yellowish-white ; breast and under parts orange-brown ; tail greenish blue ; the feather-shafts black ; legs pale tile-red.  Length seven inches ; thick and compact body, large head ; the bill long, straight, and sharp.

streams, preferring gravelly bottoms, and usually swimming in shoals; it lives on aquatic plants, worms, and small portions of any animal substance. The top of the head and back are of a dusky olive, the belly white, and in summer of a rosy or pink tint, whence one of the names by which it is known; its fins are of pale brown. It is a gracefully-formed and remarkably active fish, and feeds greedily—as the Thames angler well knows, for in fishing for gudgeon he is frequently compelled to leave "the pitch," because the minnows take the bait every time it is let down. We have the authority of Izaak Walton for believing that "being fried with yolks of eggs, the flowers of cowslips and of primroses, and a little tansie, they make a dainty dish."

THE MINNOW AND STICKLEBACK.

The Stickleback (*Gasterosteus leiurus*), the common or rough-backed stickleback (for there are several varieties, distinguished by the number of spines, the common being the three-spined), is found in all our rivers ponds, lakes, brooks, and canals, and inhabits both salt and fresh-water. They are active and peculiarly pugnacious—fighting for supremacy as fiercely as game-cocks, and rarely terminating a duel till one of the combatants is either slain or has made off rapidly. They are seldom longer than three inches, and not often so long. The fish derives its name from the sharpness of its spines; its body is without scales; the colour of the back is green; the cheeks, sides, and belly, are of silvery white ; "the sides are defended throughout their whole length by a series of elongated bony plates, arranged vertically ; a small fold of skin forms a horizontal crest on each side of the tail." If this little creature, pugnacious, ravenous, with natural armour offensive and defensive, were of size proportionate to his vigour and power, he would soon depopulate the stream, of which he would be the despot. Old Izaak says of this little fish, " I know not where he dwells in winter, nor what he is good for in summer." A curious and very interesting statement, however, printed by Mr. Warington, exhibits the stickleback as a devoted husband and father, constantly protecting his mate and her progeny, and actually building a nest for her comfort and accommodation—a peculiarity which distinguishes him from all others of the " finny tribe." *

Among the many agreeable sights presented by the river " hereabouts " are large wooden tanks, formed to aid the annual process of sheep-washing ; these are for the most part situate in sequestered nooks, and are usually connected with the opposite shore by rustic bridges, composed of large branches of trees, with a sort of hand-rail to conduct the wayfarer across.

It is rarely we can tread these solitary paths without the occurrence of some simple incident worthy of record for those who love nature. We seek it sometimes, but often it comes when least looked for and expected. While our artist was sketching this rustic bridge a little lad bounded from the thicket, and danced along the plank until he reached the opposite bank; then, pausing, he shouted, " Emmy, come, Emmy ;

---

* " The day after they had been placed in their new domain, the strongest of the male fish was observed most busily employed gathering small ligneous fibres, and carrying them in its mouth to one particular spot, where he appeared to force them into the sand and gravel with his nose. Being perfectly unacquainted at the time with the fact of this little creature building a nest, I watched him more attentively. He had selected a spot behind a piece of rock-work, almost hidden from view; but on looking down from the top of the water I could perceive that he had already constructed a small hole as round as a ring, and with a good broad margin to it, formed of the materials he had been so industriously collecting, and on which he appeared to have placed numerous particles of sand and small pebbles. This spot he guarded with the utmost jealousy, continually starting forth from his position and attacking the other fish with most extraordinary fury."—( *Vide* a paper by Robert Warington, in the " Annals and Magazine of Natural History," October, 1852.)

now don't be a fool, Emmy!"   While speaking he returned midway on
the bridge, and made a deliberate stand; a little girl then moved out of
the thicket which her brother had quitted at a bound, and cautiously
put one foot, and then another, on the quivering plank, while the boy
see-sawed backward and forward, first on one leg, then on another, to
keep up the motion of the bridge.   Poor Emmy screamed; the little
fellow repeated, "Come, come at once; you know you must come—you
can't get home unless you do come;" but "Emmy" held fast by the
rail, and would not "come."   Screaming at every fresh spring of the
plank, every second moment the child looked over the bridge, where—

> "The water-lily to the light
> Her chalice reared of silver bright,"

and we saw her little chest heave with suppressed sobs: this was cause
for inquiry, "Why will you not cross the bridge, Emmy?"

THE RUSTIC BRIDGE.

"I be afeered."

"What do you fear, Emmy? it is quite safe."

"Will you take me across?"—the child looked up with the sweet
confidence of childhood on her tear-washed face.

"Mother said she was to come over by herself, because it was growing
on her," interposed the boy, with the determination of young manhood.

"What is growing on her?"

"Please, I do try to help it," said the girl, timidly; "but every time I look over the rail I see it!"

"But, Emmy, mother told you *not* to look over the rail," persisted the boy.

"If you'd only give me your hand and walk this side, I couldn't, you know."

"Then it grows on you, Emmy, and you'll be a crazy Jane some day—father said so."

This brought a fresh gush of tears, more abundant than the last, from Emmy's large blue eyes.

"Emmy, what do you see when you look over the rail? *We* see the broad green leaves, and white shining cups of the water-lilies, and floating plaits of duck weed, and tall waving rushes, and bright little fish darting here and there, their quick eyes turning upwards as they vanish: you can see nothing else—except, indeed, the dazzling skimmer of the dragon-fly, and the gentle ripple of that little tide-stream, trying to keep its own pathway amid the waters of the Thames—you *can* see nothing else." The child drew closer, and clenching her little hand over ours, trembling and white, she whispered—

"I see her face down there—down!"

"Mother would be very angry at your telling that nonsense to strangers."

"No, not at all angry," we replied; "but look steadily, Emmy, there is no face—that is simply a line of sunbeam on the water. Stay—if we throw in this stone, you will see how the rays divide—the sunbeams will dance merrily then."

The child shrieked, "No, no, no! you would hurt her—you would kill her. Oh! no, no, no—don't!"

We turned to the boy, who looked with softened eyes at his sister—"It's only a notion she has. There, Emmy, they won't throw stones or anything." He was no longer a boy-bully, but a sympathising brother: he attempted to dry her eyes with the sleeve of his jacket tenderly, even while he told her she ought not to be a fool. "There now, don't cry, and I'll take you over the bridge." The two went on, hand in hand, together; but curiosity obliged us to recall the boy; he came, and told us the cause of his sister's agitation :—" Mother does not know rightly what to do with her; some says she must be made to cross the bridge, and so get used to it; others advise sending her away to gran'-mother's for a year or two, till she forgets it. She did so doat on Nanny Green, and took such care of her! And last winter the two were coming over the bridge from school, as it might be now; the plank was thick with snow, and slippery: Emmy held Nanny fast, but she was a wild little thing, springing about like a kid, and all at once Nanny slipt in, and we boys behind heard her crash through the ice, but before we got up, Emmy was over after her. We dragged Emmy out all cut and bleeding, but poor Nance was drawn under the ice, and men had to look for her, and at last she was found. I never like to think of it, she was such a fat, merry little thing, and Emmy did love her so; and she don't understand death, and won't believe she lies under the churchyard grass, because she saw her go under the water; she won't believe mother no more than she will me; only everything she sees bright on the water she says is Nanny's face—Nanny's face looking up at her! I wish there was another road to school."

Soon after we leave the valley in which the Thames is born, and where its infant wanderings are but promises of strength, the river becomes well defined, and of no inconsiderable breadth and depth; its waters have gathered force, and are turned to profitable uses. A mile or so of pleasant walk along its banks, and we reach THE FIRST MILL ON THE THAMES—the earliest effort to render it subservient to the wants of man, ministering to industry and producing wealth. The mill is suffi-ciently rude in character to be picturesque: it is in an open court, fronted by an old pigeon-house, and occupied by a pleasant and kindly miller, who reasonably complains that the engine of the canal frequently leaves him without water to move his wheel. He was, however, busy during our visit, and seemed well pleased to aid the artist in his efforts, apparently much interested in the progress of his work.

While the artist was thus employed, we had leisure to rove about the adjacent meadows, and to examine the numerous wild flowers and water

plants which, in this vicinity, assume forms more than usually large.
Among the most prominent was the Comfrey (*Symphytum officinale*),
which appears in great abundance on the river-bank, rearing its bold
form above the lowlier herbage.   When in blossom — every branch
decorated with clusters of pendant bell-shaped flowers, varying in every

THE FIRST MILL.

shade of colour from white to deep purple—the comfrey is one of the
most ornamental among the many floral beauties that grace the water-
side ; and it once held a high place in the herbal of our forefathers for
its great healing virtues : but its reputation for these qualities, whether
deserved or not, has passed away, in common with that of most of our
native medicinal herbs, to make way for the drugs of foreign lands,
which, if sometimes less efficacious, are at least more novel and costly.

Hence a turn in the road (or through a pleasant meadow, if we prefer to cross it) leads to the village of Somerford Keynes, with its beau-tiful and graceful little church. It is covered with flowers—roses and honeysuckle intertwined with green ivy—from the base to the roof; and is lovingly cared for by its present incumbent: it is a model of cheerful aspect and simple beauty. It consists only of a nave and chancel, with a small side chapel. There is a small piscina by the altar; but the most curious features within are the fragments of paintings that once decorated its walls, and portray legendary histories of the Romish church. Thus, opposite the door is a gigantic figure of St. Christopher bearing the Saviour across an arm of the

THE COMFREY.

sea, his passage being assisted by the lantern held by a monk. So great a value was attached to the intercession of this saint in former times, that it was believed no peril could happen to him who during the day had offered a prayer before his image. Erasmus alludes to this superstition in his " Praise of Folly." *

---

* His legendary history declares him to have been a pagan giant of evil propensities, who used to destroy travellers by pretending to carry them across a river; but the Saviour appearing to him as a little child, miraculously surprised him by the almost immovable weight he was upon his shoulder. Christopher, astonished, inquired of him the reason, and was answered, " You bear now the whole world, and also its Creator." With much difficulty and fear he crossed the water ; and, being christianised, performed as many good deeds as he had previously done evil. Our little engraving displays the ordinary manner in which this very popular saint was represented by mediæval artists, who in all instances worked to conventional rule ; hence in England or upon the Continent there is a complete similarity of treatment for this saintly legend; in the same way the Greek Church at the present day preserves in its pictures the conventional forms of the tenth century unaltered. We constantly find traces of similar representations of the saint in old English churches ; but in continental ones they abound : nor is it unusual to encounter gigantic statues of him at the gates of cities (as at Treves, on the Moselle), as if to cheer the parting traveller, or welcome him home on his return.

From the church we traverse the river-bank, again through meadows, until we arrive at a graceful gravel walk overarched by trees, in the grounds of the ancient manor-house ; and soon we reach the village of Asheton Keynes. The river here obtains a picturesque character by being arched over in numerous instances, forming footways to the various pretty cottages that skirt its bank. The church is old, but by no means picturesque—the interior being thoroughly modernized, and thus form-ing a contrast to the CHURCH OF SOMERFORD KEYNES. There are in this village the sockets of three ancient crosses.

THE CHURCH, SOMERFORD KEYNES.

Thence our path lay to Waterhay Bridge, and then across several sloping fields laden with corn, from the elevations of which, above the river, are obtained many fine views ;—and so we enter the ancient mar-ket town of Cricklade, in Wiltshire. It presents no feature of interest, except that at the bridge—a new bridge outside the town—the rivers Churn and Rey * meet, and mingle their waters with the Thames. Its

* The river Rey is of small account, although of some importance as one of the earliest tributaries of the Thames: it rises below Swindon, in Wilts. The Churn, however, demands especial notice,

church-tower is, however, a "landmark" for many miles round. It was a famous town in old times, and is said to have been inhabited by learned monks, from whom it derived its name of *Greeklade*, corrupted into *Creeklade*—another fanciful invention of the poets; and Drayton, following ancient historians, makes this town the predecessor of Oxford, where—

"To Great Britain first the sacred Muses sung."

It has two churches, dedicated to St. Sampson and St. Mary; neither, however, advance any pretensions to architectural grace or beauty. The two CROSSES still preserved in Cricklade are unusually fine specimens of those sacred mementoes in England. That in our first engraving now stands beside an avenue of trees in the churchyard of St. Sampson's, but it formerly stood in the High Street of the little town.* The finial has been broken, and the figures which once occupied the canopied niches have disappeared. Our second engraving exhibits the more perfect cross in St. Mary's churchyard, nearer the Thames. This remarkably graceful example has figures of saints in the niches, as well as a representation of the Crucifixion. Both appear to be works of the fourteenth century—a period when religious foundations flourished. It was at this time the custom in England (as it still is upon the Continent) to erect these sacred emblems not only near churches and in cemeteries, but by the road-side, to aid the devotions of the traveller, or ask his prayers for some other wayfarer who may have met death by accident or violence. They were also occasionally used to mark great events: such were the crosses erected to commemorate the places where the body of Queen Eleanor rested; or to signify where important battles had been fought.

---

inasmuch as it advances claims to the honour of being the source, and not a tributary, of the great river. It has its rise at "Seven Springs," about three miles south of Cheltenham, and its course is above twenty miles before it loses itself in the Thames—"Thames Head" being not more than ten miles from the junction of the two waters. The Churn has changed its name but little: it is the *Chwyrn* of the British, signifying rapid. Drayton calls it "the nimble-footed." It passes through the villages of Cowley, Colesbourne, North Cerney, and Baunton; then waters Cirencester, passes through Siddington and South Cerney, and so joins the Thames at Cricklade.

* It probably occupied the site of the old cross, which is named as a boundary mark in the reign of Henry III.

The town of Cricklade is about ten miles from the source of the Thames. "Thames Head," though in the county of Gloucester, is so near to its southern border that the river, after meandering a mile or two, enters Wiltshire—the village of Kemble being in that county: and it is in Wiltshire the great river first assumes the character of a

CROSS AT CRICKLADE.

perennial stream—for the meadows between that village and the source are, as we have intimated, usually dry during the summer months; soon, however, the river re-enters its native county, which it continues to fertilize during many an after mile of busy toil and tranquil beauty.

Having rested awhile at Cricklade, we pursue the river on its course, and arrive at Eisey Bridge.* At this bridge the traveller will pause awhile to examine the church, which, standing on a gentle acclivity, overlooks the stream, that here assumes a bolder aspect, and is navigable at all seasons for boats of small draught. A mile or two farther along its banks, and we reach Castle Eaton—a village now, but once a place of size and strength: "the grete ruines of the Lord Zouche's castelle" exist no more; but, here and there, some venerable walls bear records of "hoar antiquitie." A school, so aged as to have been the seat of learning of the great-great-grandfathers of the urchins we found within; and a

* The Thames at this part anciently formed the boundary of the old Forest of Braden. It was one of the earliest appanages of the Crown, and was perhaps augmented by Canute, who enacted some severe forest laws for the preservation of the game therein. On the opposite sides the forest extended to Wootton Bassett and Malmesbury.

church, very old and very curious; with a pretty bridge, more than sufficient for its traffic,—these are the only points that demand notice in this secluded and most pleasantly situated spot, where the "busy hum" is rarely heard.

The church is picturesque, but exceedingly simple in plan, consisting merely of a nave and chancel. The chancel arch is Early English; but the general structure and the prin- cipal doors are Norman. The walls have recently been denuded of a thick coat of whitewash, and many of the ancient paintings that once covered them are again brought to light. They appear to be works of the fourteenth century, and to illustrate scripture history or saintly legends. The FONT is early Eng- lish, with a simple wreath of foliage boldly carved around the basin, which is supported on a central pillar of carved stone. The church has boasted a fine cross at one period, but only the stone grooves now remain. Upon one of the bells is inscribed, "God prosper this place." The BELL-TOWER is the most remarkable feature of the ex- terior; it stands upon the junction of the roofs of nave and chancel,

CROSS AT CRICKLADE.

and is entirely constructed of thick slabs of stone, the bell swinging on a massive beam withinside.

Our readers will have perceived that while we conduct them on their voyage down the Thames, we desire to "gossip" with them now and then, believing that "matters of fact" are rendered more impressive by indulgence in those "fancies" which are suggested by scenes and

incidents described.    Our visit to the school at Castle Eaton naturally
suggested a comparison between the venerable adjunct of the village in
old times, and that by which it is now-a-days usually "adorned."

There are few things so changed in character throughout England,
both internally and externally, as its village schools, which, in days not
long gone by, were nearest in picturesque effect to the village church—
simple, contemplative dwellings, covered with climbers, coroneted with
flowers, a many-paned win-
dow at either side of the door,
which was shaded by a covered porch, sometimes solid
and thatched, or else open and
matted with woodbine—this
terminated the path whose line
was carefully marked out, and
guarded by a border of thrift
or a box edging; while within the sanctuary flourished all
kinds of " poseys " — wall-
flowers, and stocks, and sweet-
williams, and riband-grass, a
white rose, and a red rose-
bush, and, mayhap, a flaunting York-and-Lancaster, or
tower of white lilies—the gift

FONT AT CASTLE EATON.

of sweet "Miss Mary," who married, and had children five, and now is
in the churchyard underneath a marble tomb; " herb rosemary" grew
there, and woody lavender, and lavender cotton--

> " The tufted basil, pun-provoking thyme,
> Fresh baum, and marigold of cheerful hue,"

and streaky pinks, and rich crimson cloves; and sage (a leaf in tea to
make it wholesome), and feathery fennel, and such hot turnip-radishes,
and little onions, whose silver bulbs disdained the earth, and shot their
waving green and narrow leaves above their heads; the row of double

parsley was a green banquet to the eye;—all was in harmony with the
sweet low-roofed house, from which came the hum of young voices,
sometimes low and sweet, sometimes shrill and troubled.  The low
palings, which divided the garden from the road, were green from age,
and had, as it were, taken root and grown their own way, some remaining upright in their rectitude of purpose, others, like weak-minded
persons, leaning to the right
or left, and having no will of
their own.  Often a blackbird
or a thrush hung in a wicker
cage beneath the porch; an
old cat on the window-sill
winked at the sunbeams; and
beyond, close to the yew
hedge, whose centre was clipped into some monstrosity
called a "peacock," or "flow-
er-pot," lay a shelf of bee-
hives, more than half concealed from public gaze by a
row of broad-beans, or blos-
soming peas, upon which the
bees under the straw thatch
came to banquet.  *Now* the
school-house is generally a

BELL TOWER, CASTLE EATON.

new, clean, trim two-storied house, of no particular order of architecture;
but upon the external ornamentation of which enough has been spent to
clothe, as well as educate, a rising generation.  Money, it has been said,
is not wealth; neither is size or elaboration beauty—and as yet our
National Schools look hard and dictatorial.  When the softening hand of
Time passes over those seats of embryo learning—when the bright red
brick, or the pure white stone, is toned down by the weather, and ivy
and Virginia-creeper clasp the gables, and take off the sharpness of
those corners—when, in fact, the new becomes old—the schools of the

present time will better harmonize with the character of our beloved English scenery.

But, if the change is so apparent in the schools, what is it in the teachers ?  Shenstone has drawn with fidelity the picture of the "dame," in the old times of dames' schools—

> " Her cap, far whiter than the driven snow,
>   Emblem right meet of decency does yield ;
>   Her apron dyed in grain—as blue, I trow,
>   As in the harebell that adorns the field ;
>   And in her hand, for sceptre, she does wield
>   Tway birchen sprays."

She was old, and mild but firm ; the nod was her help, the rod was her argument ; the shake was her warning, the fool's-cap her disgrace ; a kind smile or word, accompanied by a ginger-bread nut on rare occasions, her reward.  We cannot but wonder how those bright, clever-looking women, sent from normal schools to diffuse education in our country parishes, would look in close mob-caps, " whiter than the driven snow," linsey aprons, and "russet stoles and kirtles !"  Alas ! for the back-headed bonnets and gay muslin—or *mousseline*—dresses, that sweep the school-room floor, and the air of superiority with which our simple questions, born of domestic wants, are often answered—making us sigh for the days when girls were taught by dames to mend stockings, darn invisibly, sew on buttons to remain on, and piece linen or broadcloth so that the rent became a myth.

Some twenty summers have come and gone since we were much interested by an aged woman, who for many years had kept a dame's school in a quaint little village not a long way from the Thames— indeed, you could see its placid waters from the school-house door, shining and shimmering through the trees.  She was called " Dame Madam," or, sometimes, " Madam "—people said that was not her real name, but the "real name" nobody knew.  She combined the calling of nurse with that of schoolmistress ; but she would only engage to "nurse " at night, as nothing could prevail on her to neglect the charge of " her children."  The school outside was like a garland, a tangled mass of clematis and all kinds of climbers ; it was built on a knoll facing the south; the ground had never been levelled, so the school-room stood on an inclined plane—the "top" form being considerably elevated over the rest. The dame said that was an advantage, as, her seat being on high ground, she could at a glance overlook every little urchin, creep he where he might. The children, and, indeed, the villagers, held "Dame Madam" in great respect. There had been a rumour, when she first took the little cottage—consisting of two rooms and a shed—a quarter of a century before our acquaintance with her—that she had been "somebody," who was "whispered about and watched;" but the rumour faded away. She would rise in the night to attend the sick poor,—if they could pay her, well; if they could not, that was well also; and the most incorrigible of village children did her bidding without birching. The time of her coming seemed so long past that it had become a legend; and although her delicate frame was worn and bent, and the dimples round her sweet placid mouth had grown into wrinkles, no one ever thought the time of her going was drawing near. She never had much to give, and yet, when in the summer's evening she sat knitting under her great rose-tree, the labourers or wayfarers never passed her door without a greeting or a blessing. She said she liked that seat in the gloaming, when there was no call for her elsewhere, because she could hear the children's voices, as they played and shouted to each other on the green: one would have thought she had had enough of those "sweet voices" during the day; but no, she would listen and exclaim, "There, that's Jimmy Grey; what lungs he has! and that's Peggy Lloyd; how she screams—she will hurt herself by screaming; and that's Bat Thompson's growl—Bat is *so* like a lion!" The cottagers declared that Madam, under the rose-tree, was "quite a picture" —and so she was. Her mob-cap, of spotless white, was tied beneath her chin with a bow of soft white muslin, a white "Rockspun" shawl folded over her bosom, the ends concealed by a white muslin apron; she wore an open dress of brown stuff, and a quilted black petticoat: there was certainly vanity in those neat-fitting Spanish-leather shoes, peeping out daintily on the straw stool. One thing I had nearly forgotten to mention—the dame always wore a green silk over her eyes, like a penthouse; so that, between the shade, and the wide border of her mob-cap, and the great soft bow under her chin, you caught only glimpses of her pale face, except her mouth and the dignified tip of a nose decidedly aquiline; yet nobody ever heard her complain that she was short-sighted. For some time past Dame Madam felt the "shadow of coming events," which is surely the shadow of an angel's wing; she became more silent and thoughtful, and the Bible had almost usurped the place of her knitting. Her fame as a nurse continued, and though she was unable to do much, yet the doctor said Dame Madam's head was worth five pair of hands. The first sweet month of summer had passed, the evening of the first of June closed in, and the Dame had vacated her seat under the great rose-tree, and gone into the cottage; the birds had ceased to rustle among the leaves—the stars were made visible by increasing darkness—there were bright phosphoric lights glancing over the placid river, giving an almost unearthly interest to the scene; the ray of Dame Madam's candle threw the shadow of stems, and leaves, and tendrils across the path; she heard her little gate "click" and open, and a step struck upon the pavement of "pretty stones," which her scholars had laid down, that their beloved Madam's path might be always dry. She closed her Bible, repeating the last words she had read therein—"Blessed are the merciful, for they shall obtain mercy."

"Dame Madam," said a rough voice at the window, "a gentleman at the inn be taken bad, and missus says please come up, for doctor wants ye."

"Has the gentleman no servant of his own, Giles?"

"Yes, his wife and a black-a-moor; but missus says they be fools—so come up, Madam, you're bad wanted."

The dame tied on her black hood, threw her scarlet cloak around her, and, having extinguished her candle, hastened to the inn. She found the poor lady-wife nearly as ill and worn out as the sick gentleman. She prevailed on her to go to bed, received the doctor's instructions, and took her seat by the bed-side. The patient slept; when he awoke, his voice shook the dame as if she had been galvanized, and when he asked her to move his pillows, he thought she would have fallen on the bed.

With trembling hand she gave him his medicine—and then some instinct prompted him to ask her name; and that told,—as it never had before been told in the village,—it became his turn to tremble. Excited beyond all power of self-control, he entreated the wife he had married and abandoned in the days of their youth to have mercy on him. He swore that some years after his desertion he sent from India, and heard she had disappeared, believed her dead, and again married. The dame heard him with seeming calmness; she had recovered her composure; she knew his excuses were untrue, but still her heart yearned to the white-headed, attenuated old man who had been the love of her youth. "He would make her rich," he continued, "give her gold"—anything so she would keep silence, and not destroy the mother of his children, and brand his sons with the name that blanches the cheek of honourable manhood. He would have crawled from the bed to her feet for pardon and mercy if he could. All this time she spoke not.

"If their child lived he would provide for it."

Then the mother's indignation burst forth;—if her child *had* lived, she would have broken her vow of secrecy, and spoken out her honour to the world. No; her child watched for her in heaven!

The excitement and alarm were more than he could bear; he lay back gasping on his pillows, face to face with the woman whose peace and happiness he had destroyed; his hands clasped in supplication; every limb quivering with strong emotion. The dame withdrew from beneath the folds of her handkerchief—where they had been concealed day and night during years of anguish—the certificate of her marriage, and sundry letters, yellow from age, and spotted with tears; one by one she opened them, and held them with her small transparent fingers before his bloodshot eyes;—well he knew them; and from his parched lips came the prayer, "Mercy, mercy! for HER and our children!" but he did not dare again to offer her gold. One by one she held those evidences of his dishonour and of her honour—those treasures of her life—over the candle, and saw them flutter and fall, in dark transparent flakes, upon the snowy sheets. She then drew out a riband, which passed round her neck and through a wedding ring; she tried to break

it—it would not yield.    The man's heart was touched,—" Noble, generous woman !" he faltered forth, and tears, hot scalding tears of remorse,
if not of penitence, came from his eyes : " Not that—it is enough !  Not
that !"    She fell on her knees by his bed-side, and her cheek, if not her
lips, was pressed upon those yellow hands !    There were no more
words spoken between them; and when in the grey light of morning
the lady, enveloped in her cashmere dressing-gown, stole gently into
the room, she thought her husband's fever increased, and the old nurse
looking so ill, that she pressed a gold coin into her hand, and entreated
her, in a soft low voice, to go home and sleep.    When she turned from
the bed, a ray of early sunshine was sporting with the coin upon the
floor ; and the nurse was gone.    What power sustained her trembling
steps until she arrived at her fragrant home, where every leaflet bore the
wealth of jewels that Nature pours upon the sleeping earth—who can
tell ?    She never shut the door, but laid her on her bed—and died.    The
" gentleman " recovered, and, much to the amazement of the village,
erected a monument to her memory; the text upon it is there still—
" Blessed are the merciful, for they shall obtain mercy."

THE GREEN FORESTER.

In the meadows that lead by a somewhat steep
ascent to Cricklade, our attention was attracted
by a number of bright green insects flitting
over the long grass : on capturing one, we recognised it as the moth known to entomologists as
the Green Forester (*Ino statices*), by no means a
common species in most localities ; but here were
thousands, either on the wing or at rest among the
grass.    The prevailing colour of this pretty moth
is a very unusual one among the British lepidoptera
—the whole surface, except that of the lower wings,
being of a lustrous golden green, while the body
glitters like a gem.    The caterpillar feeds on the
cardamine, dock, and some other semi-aquatic
plants which everywhere abound in this humid district; we may thus
account for the great abundance of the moth in this locality.

The perfect transparency of the water, with its uniform shallowness, gives great facility for studying the zoological, as well as the botanical curiosities of this well-stocked aquarium. Several species of fresh-water shells (*lymneus, planorbis,* &c.) were plying about in great abundance on the sandy bed, or adhering to the herbage that fringed the water-side.

Again the river flows onward—again waters flat, but fertile fields—again affords a rich supply of water-plants, but undergoes no change of character; yielding no food for thought until re-entering Gloucestershire, the county of its birth, it passes under the beautiful church, and washes the foundations of Kempsford—a palace of the Plantagenets long ago. Of this there are some interesting remains, but of the dwelling of their Saxon predecessors there exists only a vague tradition, confirmed, however, now and then, by evidence gathered from adjacent earth-mounds.

The manor of Kempsford was the property of the great Harold; the Conqueror gave it to one of his Norman soldiers; it passed from him to the family of Chaworth; and from them, by marriage, to Henry Duke of Lancaster, who, in the year 1355, presented it to "the Church;" at the Dissolution, the crown granted it to the Thynnes, ancestors of the marquises of Bath; by whom it was sold to Lord Coleraine,* whose tomb is in the church; by him the ancient mansion, erected by Sir Thomas Thynne in the reign of James I. (a quadrangular structure of large dimensions, of which two engravings exist), was dismantled and sold for the value of the materials, the trees were cut down, and a host of "fair memories" destroyed by the recklessness of one bad man. The place is, notwithstanding, full of rare associations; the foundations of the castle may yet be traced, the battlements being in some places unbroken.

The church is a noble structure, remarkable for the grand windows which light the junction of nave and chancel, and above which rises the

---

* Better known as Colonel Hanger, and an intimate associate of George IV. when Prince of Wales. The marble tomb in which he is placed was brought from Rome, and his coffin is placed above ground within it.

tower. It was chiefly erected in the fourteenth century, at the expense of Henry Duke of Lancaster, whose arms, and those of other noble
families, are conspicuously displayed amid the spandrels within.    There
are many fragments of fine painted glass in the windows, one of the
most perfect delineating St. Anne teaching the Virgin to read.    There
is also a characteristic altar-tomb of a priest in the chancel, upon which

THE CHURCH AT KEMPSFORD: AND THE GUNNER'S ROOM.

is sculptured the Rood, and the Virgin in glory; but they have been
grievously injured by the hands of iconoclasts.    The floor is remarkable
for its early English tiles, and the roof for its timber-work.    The porch
is Early English, forming a framework for the earlier Norman door
within it.

The vicar's garden, adjoining, was originally known as the Provost's
Garden (probably the garden of the provost-marshal), and, until the

year 1800, the road went to the ford across it.  The level field on the opposite side is still known as "the Butts," * and marks the site of the ground appropriated to the military exercises of the soldiery who once garrisoned the castle.  "The Butts" were mounds of earth, marked with a ring like a target, and were used in practising archery.  A strong arrow with a broad feather was necessary to be used; such bows and arrows as gave "immortal fame" to the archers of the English army at Crecy and at Poictiers.

Of the castle itself but a few fragmentary walls remain, and a portion of a tower, which is traditionally known as "the Gunner's Room."  The windows command the river, and the embrasures defend the castle at an exposed angle, which seems to have received an additional amount of attention from the architect.  The walls are very massive, and now afford abundant room for wild plants and bushes, overshadowed by patrician trees.  We may almost imagine we are in the gloomy room of him who guarded the approaches in days long past, when security depended more upon stone walls than on "even-handed justice." A horse-shoe nailed to the church-door continues to sustain the legend that when Henry Duke of Lancaster was quitting it for ever, his steed cast a shoe, which the villagers retained as a memorial, and placed where it is found to-day.  However much we may lament over scenes of grandeur passed away, it is a rare consolation to see the church, the rectory, the grounds, and the whole neighbourhood kindly thought of, and well

---

* Butts, or "dead-marks," as they were sometimes called, were embankments of earth having marks, or "bull's eyes," upon the flat face, for practising soldiers in archery.  They were in constant use in the middle ages, and erected near great towns, or where soldiers were stationed—hence the constant occurrence of the term "Butts," appended to names of streets and places near old cities.  One of the most ancient pictures of the exercise is copied on a reduced scale in our woodcut.  The original is a drawing in the famous psalter executed for Sir Geoffrey Louterell, who died in 1345.  It exhibits an archer aiming at the butts, his arrow  drawn to the head; several others are stuck in his girdle.  His companion points triumphantly to an arrow fixed in the bull's-eye, and awaits the prowess of his companion previous to trying again, for which purpose he already holds his bow and arrow.

cared for, by the incumbent, who preserves what time has left, and restores where restoration is desirable.

A few miles further, but with little to detain the traveller,—unless he linger awhile at Hannington Bridge, and hence obtain a view of the distant church of Highworth,—and we approach Lechlade ; but, within a mile or so of the town, we pause at a place of much interest ; for here the Coln contributes its waters to the Thames, and here terminates that gigantic undertaking—the canal which unites the Severn with the Thames, and which, when steam was thought to be a day-dream of insanity, poured the wealth of many rich districts into the channel that carried it through London to the world.

The Coln—a river which the angler loves, for its yield of trout is abundant—rises near Withington, in Gloucestershire, and, passing by Foss Bridge, Bibury, Coln St. Aldwin, and Fairford—a town rendered famous by the painted windows in its church *—runs its course of twenty-three miles, and finishes by joining the Thames at the place we have pictured, the terminus of the canal being close to " the meeting." The nearest village, that of Inglesham, has a very ancient church, small and rude in character, and strangely isolated in position, being at a considerable distance from any cluster of houses. It consists of a simple nave and chancel, a bell-tower crowning the roof, somewhat similar to that we have already pictured at Castle Eaton. Beside the porch there is inserted in the wall the very curious piece of sculpture we here engrave. It represents the Virgin seated, and holding in her lap the Infant Saviour, who rests his left hand upon a book, while his right is extended, giving the benediction, as still practised in the Latin church. A similar benediction is given by a hand above, which is evidently intended for that of the first person of the Trinity. It is surprising

---

* Fairford is but three miles from Lechlade, and will amply repay a visit. The windows are in number twenty-eight, and are said to have been painted from the designs of Albert Durer ; they are certainly of his period, and are not unworthy of so illustrious a parentage. They are all allegoric, the more remarkable of them exhibiting the persecutors of the Church, surmounted by dæmons ; and its upholders and protectors associating with angels. Although some of them are much injured, chiefly by hail-storms, they are for the most part in a good state of preservation. The history of these windows is curious: a sea-captain, named Tame, took them on one of his piratical voyages, and, his conscience not permitting their personal appropriation, he built this church for their reception.

how this sculpture (which may be a work of the thirteenth century, or earlier) has escaped the destruction to which so many monuments of early faith have been subjected; but it is worthy of observation that these old villages on the Thames banks retain many vestiges of a past age still unmolested: thus the steps and shaft of an old stone cross stand close to the porch at Inglesham, and we have already noted several such relics of the Romish faith in the earlier part of our tour.

The Thames and Severn Canal was commenced in 1782, and opened in 1789; but, so far back as the time of Charles II., the scheme of thus uniting the two great rivers of England had been entertained; and Pope mentions that to effect this object was a cherished thought of Lord Bathurst, " when he had finer dreams than ordinary." In 1782 Mr. Robert Whitworth, an eminent engineer, " formed plans and estimates," and, in the following year, an act was

CARVED STONE AT INGLESHAM.

passed for carrying them into operation; it was completed within seven years, the first boat passing through on the 19th of November, 1789. " This navigable canal [we quote from Boydell] begins at Wallbridge, where the Stroud navigation ends, and proceeds to the immediate vicinity of Lechlade, where it joins the Thames, taking a course of thirty miles seven chains and a half. From Stroud to Sapperton comprehends a length of seven miles and three furlongs, with a rise of two hundred and forty-one feet three inches; from Sapperton to Upper Siddington, including the branch to Cirencester, nine miles eight chains and a half, and is perfectly level; and from Upper Siddington to the Thames near Lechlade it continues a course of thirteen miles four fur-

longs and nine chains, with a fall of one hundred and thirty feet six
inches; the general breadth of the canal is forty-two feet at the top,
and thirty feet at the bottom."

"The Round House,"—for so the lock-house is named from its form,
—the lock, and the two rivers, at their "meeting," are pictured in the
appended cut.

JUNCTION OF THE THAMES, THE COLN, AND THE CANAL.

We have now arrived at that point in the Thames where it becomes
navigable for boats of burthen; the canal conveys in barges, each from
thirty to sixty tons, the produce of the four quarters of the globe into
several parts of England; the port of Bristol is thus united with that of
London; other canals are combined with this: and so an internal communication was formed, the value of which may be readily estimated
before the introduction of steam. But the railways have placed this
mode of traffic almost in abeyance,—the canals are comparatively idle,
and ere long, perhaps, will be altogether deserted. The passage of a

boat through the lock is now an event of rare occurrence : it is seldom
opened more than once or twice in a week. Greater speed is obtained
by the railway, of course, but the chief impediment arises from the cost
incurred in passing through the locks and weirs along the Thames,—
strange as it may seem, the expense hence arising to a laden boat of
sixty tons burthen, between Teddington, where the locks begin, and
Lechlade, where they terminate, is not less than thirty pounds. The
natural consequence is, that steam absorbs all the traffic, except to places
remote from stations ; and then boats are in use only for heavy cargoes,
chiefly timber and coal. The barges here used are necessarily long and
narrow,—the appended engraving will convey an accurate notion of
their form ;—they are generally drawn up the river by two horses, and

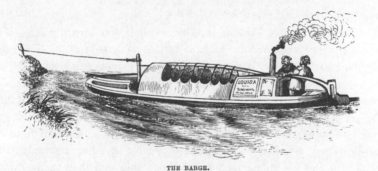

THE BARGE.

down the river by one, along the " towing-path "—a footpath by the
river-side. The towing-paths between Lechlade and Oxford, in consequence of the causes we have observed upon, are so little disturbed as
to be scarcely perceptible : they are for the most part so " grass-
o'ergrown " as to be distinguished from the meadow only after a careful
search. Indeed, all along the Thames bank to Lechlade, and much
lower, almost until we approach Oxford, there is everywhere a singular
and impressive solitude : of traffic there is little or none ; the fields are
almost exclusively pasture-land ; the villages are usually distant ; of
gentlemen's seats there are few, and these are generally afar off; the
mills are principally situated on " back-water ;" and but for the pleasant

cottages, nearly all of which are peasant hostelries, which, in their immediate relation to the locks and weirs, necessarily stand on the river-bank, with now and then a ferry-house, the whole of the landscape for nearly forty miles from the river-source would seem as completely denuded of population as an African desert. Between Kemble and Lechlade we did not meet two boats of any kind, and only at the lock-houses did we encounter a dozen people—except at the few villages of which we have taken note. This loneliness has its peculiar charm to the wayfarer ;—it will be long ere we lose remembrance of the enjoyment we derived from a reflective saunter beside the banks of the grand old river, where solitude invites to thought—

> " The blackbird's note comes mellower from the dale,
> And sweeter from the sky the gladsome lark
> Warbles his heaven-tuned song."

The moorhen revels here in security, for it is her own domain,—if a footstep shake the shelving bank, it is that of a peasant, of whom the shy bird has no fear. It was a rare pleasure to note this liveliest of all our water-fowl darting from side to side, or plunging midway in the channels, to rise in still greater security among the reeds and rushes farther off.

The Moorhen (*Gallinula chloropus*) is commonly seen not far from its reedy haunts, swimming along with a peculiar nodding motion of the head, and picking up its food first on one side and then on the other. It feeds generally on aquatic plants, insects, and small fishes. Mr. Selby mentions that he has frequently known this bird to have been taken on a line baited with an earth-worm, intended for catching eels or trout,—from which he infers that it is by diving it obtains the larger water beetles and the larvæ of dragon-flies, &c., upon which it is known to feed. Shenstone refers to the recluse habits of the moorhen, and its frequent associate, the coot,—

> " To lurk the lake beside,
> Where coots in rushy dingles hide,
> And moorcocks shun the day."

The colouring of the moorhen, quoting from Yarrell, is as follows :—" The beak yellowish-green ; the base of it, and patch on the forehead, red; eyes reddish-hazel; the back, wings, and tail, rich, dark olive-brown; head, neck, breast, and sides, uniform dark slate-grey; under tail-coverts white; legs and toes green, with a garter of red above the tarsal joint. Contrary to the almost universal rule among birds, the female is frequently more richly coloured than the male. The length of the moorhen is usually about thirteen inches."

We are, however, now at Lechlade, where the Thames is a navigable river, and a sense of loneliness in some degree ceases; — effectually so, as far as Lechlade is concerned, for, as the reader will perceive, its aspect is an antidote to gloom. Lechlade is a very ancient town. It de-

THE MOORHEN.

rives its name from a small river that joins the Thames about a mile below its bridge. The Lech is little more than a streamlet, rising in the parish of Hampnot, in the Cotswold district, and passing by Northleach and Eastleach. The proofs of its antiquity are now limited to its fair and interesting church, dedicated to St. Laurence. It is very plain within-inside, but stately-looking. It contains no old monuments, with the exception of a brass of a gentleman and lady of the time of Henry VI., and another of a man of the time of Henry VII. Close to the north porch is an interesting relic of the olden time—" a penance stone," on which formerly offenders against the discipline of the church stood enshrouded in a white sheet to do penance. The spire is a pleasant landmark all about. It is now, as it was when Leland wrote, two hundred years ago, " a praty old toune," where those who love quiet may be happy. It is clean and neat, and has a well-ordered inn, where

a "neat-handed Phillis" strives to make the way-worn traveller at ease
and in comfort. The priory of "Blake Chanons, at the very end of
St. John's Bridge," is gone; of "the chapelle in a medow" no stone
remains; the bold barons—from Baron Siward, who slew Tofte, Earl of
Huntingdon, to Ferrers, Earl of Derby, and Roger Mortimer, the
Talbots, Spensers, and Hollands—who once lorded over the district, are

LECHLADE BRIDGE AND CHURCH.

forgotten there; but the Thames still rolls its waters round the town,
and blesses a generation to whom rumours of war are but far-off
sounds—

"All glory to the stern old times,
But leave them to their minstrel rhymes."

A mile from the town—much less to the pedestrian—and another
and much older. bridge is reached—St. John's Bridge, beside which is
"The Angler's Inn;" and here "a hop, step, and jump" will lead from
Gloucester into Berkshire, and from Berkshire into Oxfordshire. But
bridges are now becoming numerous. It is here we first meet a point
of greater interest—THE FIRST LOCK on the river Thames. It is rude

enough to be picturesque. This lock occurs, however, in a back-water, or rather an artificial cut, the main branch of the river flowing through the arches of St. John's Bridge, and passing the village of Buscot, where is found the first example of the lock and weir in combination. Buscot has a very plain old church, with no other feature to notice but a Norman chancel arch. The vicarage is a large mansion of the time of William III., and the garden has cut trees and fir bowers in the semi-Dutch taste of that era. We continue our voyage to the pretty villages of Kelmscott and Eaton Hastings, and continue still by the river-side, by green meadows, which, in their solitude, seem to progress

THE FIRST LOCK.

unaided by the art of man. Kelmscott has a small cruciform church. The arches, which occupy the centre, are supported by early foliated capitals. In the chancel window is an old piece of painted glass, representing St. George and the Dragon. It may be of the time of Edward III. Eaton Hastings church is a mile and a half from the weir. It consists of a plain nave and chancel, without a tower, and is situated on a slight eminence. The scenery around is picturesque, and most perfectly pastoral. At Buscot "the river quits the open meads for a more secluded progress, and, having been from Inglesham a boundary of Berkshire, it now leaves for ever its native Gloucestershire, and begins

to mark the limits of the county of Oxford." Our next point of interest
is a venerable relic of antiquity—RADCOT BRIDGE. This bridge, built
entirely of stone, is one of the oldest on the Thames, bearing unmistakeable marks of early construction. The arches are ribbed internally ;
the ascent is very steep ; and over the centre arch is the socket of a
cross which once towered above the primitive structure, in accordance
with the old custom which invested bridges with a sacred character, and
beside, or upon which, it was once usual to construct wayside chapels,
for the purpose of affording the weary traveller repose while performing
his religious duties.

RADCOT BRIDGE.

The towing-path, which keeps on the Gloucestershire side to Radcot
Bridge, now crosses the bridge to the Berkshire side of the stream,
which here divides, and forms an island.

We have leisure, however, just now to ask the reader's attention to
circumstances and objects that will have occurred to him, or have been
presented to him on his journey. After passing Lechlade, thousands of
glittering Dragon-flies, of the species figured (*Calepteryx virgo*), kept
up an incessant fluttering over the water-side herbage. Their graceful

and rapid movements, with the metallic brilliancy of their green and azure colouring, gave an unwonted vivacity to the scene. It is to these insects, the *demoiselles* of the French, that Moore alludes— though in reference to a far different scene—

" Chasing with eager hands and eyes
    The beautiful blue damsel-flies,
    That flutter'd round the jasmine stems,
    Like winged flowers or flying gems."

The Pike (*Esox Lucius*) is abundant in this neighbourhood, and the troller may have ample sport. It is the wolf of pond, lake, and river; and any mode by which he can be taken is considered right. The longest lived of all the fish of freshwater, he is the largest and the most ravenous, growing sometimes to enormous size—

THE DRAGON-FLY.

often to fifty, sixty, or seventy pounds; in the Thames, we believe, none have been caught of greater weight than thirty-five pounds. The body of the pike is elongated, nearly uniform in depth from the head to the commencement of the dorsal fin, then becoming narrower; "the head is elongated, depressed, wide;" the colour dusky olive-brown, lighter and mottled with green and yellow on the sides, and passing into silvery white on the belly. The angler takes this fish by trolling; but sometimes also with "live bait;" in the latter case a gudgeon, a small dace, or, better still, a small trout, is placed on a double hook; the pike seizes it sideways between his jaws, and makes off to his lair; time must be given him to "gorge" it before the strike. But trolling is the more common practice, on the Thames especially; in this case, a dead fish is impaled on a "trace" of hooks—*i. e.* six hooks so arranged as to embrace the bait from the head to the tail, the mount

being gimp wire, for gut would be instantly snapt in twain—nay, it is
by no means rare for the pike to snap the gimp asunder, and make off
with the six hooks; but so voracious is the fish, and so insensible
to pain, that frequently another trace of hooks will be immediately
taken by it, and the lost trace be thus recovered. We have known
instances in which two traces have been thus expended, a third
being successful. When the troller sets to work, he usually lets his
boat glide gently with the tide, or impels it very gradually; the bait
having been dropt overboard, is drawn quietly through the water at a
distance of between fifteen and twenty yards. When the pike is

THE PIKE.

hooked, and the angler has what is called "a run," it is not easily
taken, but makes a bold struggle for life. The trace of hooks must,
however, be mounted with a swivel, in order that, by frequently turning in the water, it may more nearly imitate the motions of the living
fish; artificial, or imitation fish, are in frequent use, and are of very
ingenious make—they are sometimes good substitutes, but anglers well
know that the actual fish is *the* thing. Unless a breeze ruffles the
surface of the water there is but little chance of a run. The pike is
also called the *luce* (it is the lucie of heraldry), and in Scotland its name
is the *gedd*. The jack is, properly, a young pike. The pike is a

solitary fish—even two of them are rarely seen together; his usual haunt is a dark and comparatively still nook, thick with rushes or close water-plants; here he remains, seldom moving an inch until his eye fixes on his prey, when a sudden rush is made, and back again to consume it at ease and leisure. Some startling anecdotes are told of his voracity—he will swallow a fish of nearly his own weight. The pike is said to be a good fish for eating, and many are fond of it; the flesh is certainly hard and sound; much, however, depends upon the skill of the cook—old Izaak gives a receipt for its dressing, which he says "makes a dish of meat too good for any but anglers or very honest men."

We have delayed the tourist too long. At Radcot Bridge he has a view on the right of Faringdon Hill, and on the left of BAMPTON CHURCH SPIRE; either place may lure him awhile from the river-bank—each being distant between one and two miles. The wood-crowned heights above Faringdon have, indeed, been pleasantly in our sight for a long time along our course. Faringdon is well entitled to a pilgrimage; although the house is gone which so bravely withstood the army of

SPIRE OF BAMPTON CHURCH.

Cromwell, when the assailants were led to the attack by the owner of the mansion himself—Sir Robert Pye, who had married a daughter of the patriot, John Hampden. Of a far older castle, which " the favourers of Empress Matilda erected, and King Stephen pull'd down," there remains nothing but tradition. There sleeps, however, in the village church a brave knight, whom England chronicles among the worthiest of her worthies—that Sir Edward Unton, who, while Queen Elizabeth's ambassador to France, upheld her honour and that of his country by sending a challenge, couched in memorable words, to the Duke of Guise, who had slandered the fair fame of his adored queen and mistress, and who, in speaking basely of her, had "most shamefully and wickedly lied."

Bampton, in Oxfordshire, on the left bank of the river, but distant about a mile, is a pretty village town,* remarkable for its interesting church, which has the singular peculiarity that it has three rectors, who are all presented by the Church of Exeter—"to which certain lands were given by Leofric, chaplain to Edward the Confessor, and first bishop of the see, about the year 1046." Bampton steeple is so very conspicuous for many miles on this part of the river that we have deemed it right to delineate its features, which are in themselves sufficiently remarkable to warrant their introduction. The tower is square, from which rises an octangular steeple with four belfry windows. Pinnacles are at each corner, supported by slabs resting against the steeple, and forming basements for statues which surmount them. This unique arrangement is very striking; the church is well worthy a visit, as, in the characteristic language of Skelton, it is affirmed to contain "examples of almost every period of architecture, from the Conquest to the reign of King George III.;" it has, among other "noticeable" features, a fine Norman porch, and an equally fine arch withinside, of the same early date, some good brasses of priests, and a very curious series of sculptures of the Saviour and the Apostles—a work of the fifteenth century, highly enriched by colour.

At Radcot Bridge the Thames is divided—a circumstance of frequent occurrence in the course of the river—a new cut and a "short cut" having been made to facilitate navigation—thus also deepening the

---

* Its name is probably derived from the Anglo-Saxon *beam*, a tree, and *tun*, an enclosure, and it is still sometimes called Bampton-in-bush.

channel. The tourist will take the old stream,—which passes under three venerable arches,—although it is considerably choked up with weeds, and closely overhung with branches of the water-willow. He will here have occasion to pause and admire the foliage that adorns the banks, or rises from the bottom of the slow current : a nosegay of wild flowers may be gathered here, such as might deck a maiden's brow, and vie in beauty with the rare exotics of the conservatory. We direct attention to some of them—first asking observation to the Great Water Dock (*Rumex aquaticus*), the luxurious growth of whose flamboyant foliage gives to it a gigantic character among its lighter and more graceful neighbours. The astringent root of this plant formerly had a considerable reputation as a medicine, but its use is now almost obsolete.

THE DOCK.

Our course may be rapid between Radcot Bridge and New Bridge, although the distance is some ten miles; for there is no village along its banks, but one small bridge— Tadpole Bridge—and but one ferry. There are, however, several weirs that act as pathways for foot-passengers ; and these weirs break the monotony of the river, afford " rests " to the voyager, and add materially to the picturesque of the scenery— nearly all of them being old and somewhat dilapidated. These are Old Man's weir, Old Nan's weir, Rushy weir, Kent's weir, Ten-foot weir, and Shefford weir : they occur during the first half of the voyage, Rushy weir being the only one that has the adjunct of a lock. A stone's throw from the river, a small cluster of houses, scarcely to be called a village, points out the site of ancient Siford, or Shefford ; yet, on this lonely and isolated spot, now apparently far removed from human intercourse, the great Alfred held one of his earliest parliaments. "There sate, at Siford, many thanes, many bishops, and many learned men, proud earls and awful knights. There was Earl Alfric, very learned in the law, and Alfred, England's herdsman—England's darling. He was king in England : he began to teach them, as we may hear (*i. e.* as we shall hear in what follows), how they should live." * What a dream might have been enjoyed, resting under a hayrick the mowers had raised in a corner of the meadow in which this memorable event is said to have taken place !

Arrived at NEW BRIDGE, we again pause awhile to look around us— to ponder and reflect. The neighbourhood is unchanged since Leland

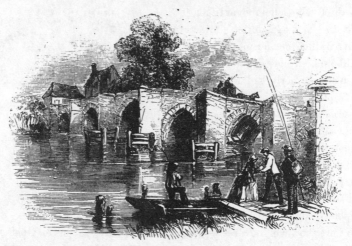

NEW BRIDGE.

described it as "lying in low meadows, often overflown by rage of rain :" a small inn stands on the Berkshire side, and a busy mill on that of Oxfordshire ; in the time of the venerable historian, there was here "a fayre mylle a prow lengthe of ;" and it is probable a hostel also entertained the wayfarer. Age has preserved only the bridge, which

* The poem, of which this is the commencement, has been printed in the "Reliquiæ Antiquæ," vol. i. p. 170.

was "new" six centuries ago, and is now, we believe, the oldest of all that span the river.* A short distance below, the Windrush contributes its waters to the Thames,—one of the prettiest and most pleasant of English rivers; it rises among the hills of Cotswold, near Guiting, and, passing through Bourton-on-the-Water, Burford, Minster-Lovel, Witney (so long and still famous for its blankets), fertilizes and flourishes rich vales, quiet villages, and prosperous towns; having done its duty, and received grateful homage on its way, it is lost for ever—absorbed into the bosom of the great father.

Drayton, in his "Poly-Olbion," tells, in his own peculiar manner, the tale of these small rivers which swell the infant stream, describing them as handmaidens, anxious—

> " ————— to guide
> Queen Isis on her way, ere she receive her traine.
> Clear *Colne* and lively *Leech* have down from Cotswold's plain,
> At Lechlade linking hands, come likewise to support
> The mother of great Thames. When, seeing the resort,
> From Cotswold *Windrush* scowres; and with herself doth cast
> The train to overtake; and therefore hies her fast
> Through the Oxfordian fields; when (as the last of all
> Those floods that into Thames out of our Cotswold fall,
> And farthest unto the north) bright *Elnlode* forth doth beare."

Again the locks and weirs pleasantly and profitably bar our progress —the principal of these are Langley's weir and the Ark weir—until we reach the ferry, which continues the road between the village of Cumnor and that of Stanton Harcourt—the former in Berkshire, the latter in Oxfordshire—each being distant about two miles from the river-side. To visit one of these weirs—HART'S WEIR—we must ask the reader's company before we proceed farther on our route. In describing this, we shall make him sufficiently familiar with an object, to which it will be requisite frequently to direct his attention during his progress.

Sometimes the weir is associated with the lock; but, generally, far up the river, where the stream is neither broad nor deep, the weir stands

---

* Its construction is worth noting, as it is a good example of ancient bridge building, with its groined arches and its projecting piers, which not only give strength to the structure, but protection to the traveller, who could shelter in their angles while the roadway was occupied by passing waggons. As a breakwater these piers had an additional value.

alone.   We shall have occasion hereafter to picture them in combination.   The weirs are artificial dams, or banks, carried across the river in
order to pen up the water to a certain height, for the services of the
mill, the fishery, and the navigation.   A large range of framework rises
from the bed of the river; this supports a number of flood-gates sliding
in grooves, and connected with a sill in the bottom.   Our engraving
represents a group of these flood-gates as they were drawn upon land,
and resting against the support rudely constructed for them beside Hart's
weir.   They are thus used :—The square piles in the foreground are

HART'S WEIR.

first struck at regular distances in the sill under water : between each of
these one of the gates is placed by means of the pole attached to it—the
boards completely stopping the space, and forming a dam across the
river.   Two forms of dams are used : one with the board full upon the
centre of the piles, and secured to them by strong plugs, over which the
boat-hook is sometimes passed to aid lifting ; the other has the water-
board on one side, with a groove attached to it.   Both of these are
shown in the cut, as well as the rude stay for the rope of a barge to pass

through, and which is generally formed of the branch of a tree. Such are the usual accompaniments of a weir in the upper Thames. When these dams, or paddles, are drawn up, the whole body of the stream, being collected into a narrow space, rushes through with great rapidity, and gives a temporary depth to the shallows, or, by the power of the current, forces the barges over them. It is obvious that care is required to prepare the boat for the descent; for there is some danger to be encountered.

The weir is ever picturesque, for the water is always forcing its way through or over it—sometimes in a huge sheet, forming a striking cascade, at other times dribbling through with a not unpleasing melody.

WEIR PADDLES.

As we have elsewhere observed, there is usually a cottage close beside the weir, for the accommodation of the weir-keeper; generally this is a public-house, pleasantly diversifying the scenery, and not the less so because often rugged and old.

The tourist, to visit either Cumnor or Stanton Harcourt, must moor his boat at the very pretty ferry of Bablock Hithe. He will turn to the right on his way to Cumnor, and to the left on his road to Stanton Harcourt; the latter, especially, will amply recompense him for an hour's

delay in the progress of his voyage. Cumnor has been made famous by
the novel of "Kenilworth," the scene of which is here principally laid;
but neither history nor tradition do more than supply a few dry bones,
to which the great magician gave life. A few vestiges only indicate
the site of Cumnor Place; the "haunted towers" are down; a "Black
Bear" still exists; and it is not likely that Cumnor will ever be
without a village hostelry so named. In the church is the tomb of
Anthony Forster, who has been condemned to an unenviable notoriety

STANTON HARCOURT: FROM THE MEADOWS.

by Scott, but is lauded in his epitaph as a man of honour and integrity.
The tomb is an altar tomb within the chancel railing, and has a
highly enriched canopy. A brass is inserted with figures of Anthony
and his family.

STANTON HARCOURT, the old seat of one of the most ancient and honourable families of the kingdom,—a family with much to dignify and less to
discredit it than perhaps any other of which England boasts,—is but
a relic of its former magnificence; but that relic suffices to indicate its
early grandeur, and retains much that cannot fail to create deep and
absorbing interest. The Harcourts have possessed this manor of

Stanton for more than six hundred years; the original grant was from
Henry I. to "Milicent, the kinswoman of the Queen," whose daughter
Isabel, marrying Roland de Harcourt, the deed of gift was confirmed by
the kings Stephen and the second Henry.   It ceased to be their dwelling
in 1688, and fell gradually to decay, until, in 1770, it was taken down—
all except the porter's lodge, now the residence of the rector, the
"kitchen," and one of the towers—the tower some time the residence
of the poet Alexander Pope, and where (as he has himself recorded) he

STANTON HARCOURT.

translated the fifth book of Homer.   On the ground floor of this tower
is a private chapel, the walls still bearing indications of painted story;
the small room on the second floor, to which ascent is gained by a
narrow stone staircase, is called, and will ever be called, "Pope's study;"
it commands a fine view, and must have given to the poet that happiest
of all enjoyments—quiet in the country.   On a pane of glass in one of
the windows he wrote an inscription, recording the fact and date that here

he "finished the fifth book of Homer." *    The kitchen is best described
by Dr. Plot, the old historian of Oxford county :—" It is so strangely
unusual that, by way of riddle, one may truly call it either a kitchen
within a chimney, or a kitchen without one ; for below it is nothing but
a large square, and octangular above, ascending like a tower, the fires
being made against the walls, and the smoke climbing up them without
any tunnels or disturbance to the cooks, which, being stopped by a
large conical roof at the top, goes out at loop-holes on every side,

POPE'S STUDY, STANTON HARCOURT.

according as the wind sets, the loop-holes at the side next the wind
being shut with folding doors, the adverse side open." This description is accurate now, as it was then ; it is still used by the gentleman
who farms the estate, whose dwelling-house, formed of the old materials,

---

* This pane has been removed to Nuneham Courteney, the seat the Harcourts now occupy, a few
miles below Oxford, and which we shall visit on our voyage from that city down the Thames. The pane measures about six inches by two ; it is of red stained glass. We append a copy of the inscription, taken from "Ireland's Picturesque Views," and which we compared with the original, courteously shown to us by Mr. Granville Harcourt.  Of the authenticity of this rare and curious relic there can be no doubt.

*In the year 1718 ALEXANDER POPE finish'd here the Fifth Volume of HOMER* adjoins the kitchen. It is surmounted by a vane, the crest of the Harcourts.

The church is a fine and very interesting structure : much of it is of Norman architecture : it is among the most beautiful of the many beautiful churches of Oxfordshire. Through one of the doors the men have entrance, while the women enter by another, in accordance with "a custom established there from time immemorial." The decorations of the interior are of very early date : the oak wood-screen being considered the oldest, of wood, in England. A small chapel contains the dust of many of the Harcourts*—a race honoured and esteemed, always and without exception, from the founder of the family to its present representative. It is surely something to be a gentleman of six hundred years ! In the churchyard is a monument to the memory of an affianced pair who were struck dead by lightning : the epitaph is from the pen of Pope ; so also is an epitaph to the only son of the Lord Chancellor Harcourt—the good

THE VANE.

and learned peer who was the friend of Pope and the other poets of the age. This epitaph contains the touching lines of lament—

> "How vain is reason—eloquence how weak!
> That Pope must tell what Harcourt cannot speak!"

We crept up the narrow stairs which led from the chapel, with its remnants of adornments and painted glass,—where the poet, no doubt, worshipped according to his faith,—and entered the little turret room, a shrine where numbers, "past, present, and to come," have recalled, or will recall, the memory of Pope, not only as a poet and a deep earnest thinker, but as one who proved the English language as susceptible of

---

* The most interesting of these monuments are those which contain the effigies of Sir Robert Harcourt, and Margaret Byron, his wife. The knight received the Order of the Garter about the year 1463. His lady, who reposes by his side, is also, like her husband, adorned with the mantle of the order, and has the garter on her left arm, just above the elbow. This is one of only three examples of female sepulchral effigies thus decorated.

grace as of dignity of expression; and though "pure Doric," in our "slang" days, has fallen into contempt, and it may be that even those who cherish "good English" may consider his prose somewhat "stilted," yet it was pleasant to find ourselves within the sanctuary of the narrow chamber where, in "the year 1718, Alexander Pope finished the fifth volume of Homer." Pope's attachment to, and subsequent hatred of, Lady Mary Wortley Montagu, are matters of history: his first letter to this remarkable woman, commencing their correspondence, held during the "embassy," is dated Twickenham, 1716; and we find in a letter, undated, that he sends his fair correspondent the *third* volume of the "Iliad," saying, "I make not the least question but you could give me great *éclaircissements* upon many passages in Homer, since you have been enlightened by the same sun that inspired the father of poetry. You are now glowing under the climate that animated him; you may see his image rising more boldly about you, in the very scenes of his story and action; you may lay the immortal work on some broken column of a hero's sepulchre, and read the fall of Troy in the shade of a Trojan ruin." As Lady Mary's reply is dated 1717, it is not unfair to infer that this, and other more impassioned epistles from the poet to the lady, were written within these walls. One, in particular, bearing date September the 1st, is so interwoven with his residence at Stanton Harcourt, that we cannot refrain from copying it on this page.

"I have a mind," he writes to the lady, "to fill the rest of this paper with an accident that happened just under my eyes, and has made a great impression upon me. I have just passed part of this summer at an old romantic seat of my Lord Harcourt's, which he has lent me; it overlooks a common field, where, under the shade of a haycock, sat two lovers, as constant as ever were found in romance, beneath a spreading beech. The name of the one, let it sound as it will, was John Hewett, the other Sarah Drew. John was a well-set man, about five-and-twenty; Sarah a brown woman of eighteen. John had for several months borne the labour of the day in the same field with Sarah; when she milked, it was his morning and evening charge to bring the cows to her pail. *Their love was the talk, but not the scandal of the neighbour-*

*hood*, for all they aimed at was the blameless possession of each other in marriage. It was but this very morning that he obtained her parents' consent, and it was but till the next week that they were to wait to be happy. Perhaps this very day, in the intervals of their work, they were talking of their wedding clothes, and John was now matching several kinds of poppies and field-flowers to her complexion, to make her a present of knots for the day. While they were thus employed (it was on the last day of July), a terrible storm of thunder and lightning arose, and drove the labourers to what shelter the trees or hedges afforded. Sarah, frightened and out of breath, sunk on a haycock, and John (who never separated from her) sat by her side, having raked two or three heaps together to secure her. Immediately there was heard so loud a crack as if heaven had burst asunder. The labourers, all solicitous for each other's safety, called to one another; those who were nearest our lovers, hearing no answer, stepped to the place where they lay. They first saw a little smoke, and after, this faithful pair—John with one arm about his Sarah's neck, and the other held over her face, as if to screen her from the lightning. They were dead. There was no mark or discolouring on their bodies, only that Sarah's eyebrow was a little singed, and a small spot between her breasts. They were buried the next day in one grave, in the parish of Stanton Harcourt, in Oxfordshire, where my Lord Harcourt, at my request, has erected a monument over them." The poet then quotes the epitaph he had written to their memory—lines not worthy of him, and which still stand in the churchyard just above their grave. A few words more and our quotation is at an end. "Upon the whole, I cannot think these people unhappy; the greatest happiness, next to living as they would have done, was to die as they did. The greatest honour people of this low degree could have was to be remembered on a little monument, unless you will give them another—that of being honoured with a tear from the finest eyes in the world. I know you have tenderness; you must have it; it is the very emanation of good sense and virtue; *the finest minds, like the finest metals, dissolve the easiest.*" Lady Mary's reply, unfortunately, proved how little she deserved this charming compliment. She had neither faith in, nor comprehension of, the nature and virtues of humble life; she tries her skill on the epitaph Pope half requested, and it lives as a record of her want of sympathy in the pure and delicate—a coarse lampoon.*

There is not much standing of the "old romantic seat," save the spacious and stately kitchen (how important were those kitchens of old times, both for domestic and social purposes!) and Pope's little tower; but we fancy the real scene, the *locale* is very little changed from what it was one hundred and thirty-five years ago; the "common field," immediately round the "remains," is now a kitchen garden; and there is a bewildering labyrinth of paths and rugged old trees, and somewhat extensive "stews" or fish-ponds, beside whose tangled banks we saw several "spotted snakes" in full enjoyment of land and water, literally basking in sunshine on the stagnant pool; they looked so happy and inoffensive, that fear of their poison was removed by their beauty. The tower of the venerable church, the ruin of the dwelling, the heavy and massive foliage of the noble trees, through which the sunbeams struggled to obtain entrance, now glaring full upon an impenetrable oak, then glancing through the spines of a fir, or beneath the silver arm of a beech, formed a rich sylvan scene, which, even without the kindly hospitality at the vicarage, and the full memories of Pope, would not have been easily forgotten.

In the immediate neighbourhood of Stanton Harcourt are two large stones, popularly known as "the Devil's Quoits:" all earlier writers mention three; there are now but two, and these are distant nearly a quarter of a mile from each other. They are said to commemorate a battle fought at Bampton, between the British and the Saxons, A.D. 614; but this is little more than a village tradition; they are most probably ancient boundary stones.

We rejoin the Thames at the Ferry of BABLOCK HITHE; it is a horse-ferry, as will be observed by the appended engraving. The river is

---

* Mrs. Sarah Josepha Hale, of Philadelphia, has published a very comprehensive and interesting memoir of Lady Mary Wortley Montagu, accompanied by some of her best correspondence.

narrow here, and for some distance, above and below, it passes by the sides of low meadows—famous pasture land for cattle, though occasionally under water in winter, and when there have been heavy and continuous falls of rain. We keep in view, as we descend the stream, the pleasant hills—those of Witham—which environ Oxford, distant about five miles ; but the distance is doubled to those who make "the voyage" in boats—so continually does the river "wind."

BABLOCK HITHE FERRY.

The better dressed, the more comfortable and "respectable," are our peasantry, the less interesting and picturesque they become as subjects for the pen or pencil of the tourist. We so seldom meet on our journeyings any one who looks, or does, or says, what can be called "original," that we have a delightful sensation of "freshness" when we encounter aught that promises a departure from "every-day" existence. While crossing the Thames in the primitive "horse-boat," at Bablock Hithe, our attention was attracted by an unusually tall man, who was leaning, in an attitude at once careless and graceful, against the door of the ferry-house ; his smockfrock, of some grey material, was elaborately

K

pleated and worked on the shoulders; and his heavy, but handsome, Saxon features were expressive of the most intense melancholy. On the ground beside him was what looked like the foundation of an arm-chair, crossed and recrossed by wicker-work, round which various long grasses in seed and flower were twisted, every passing breeze bending their heads or rustling among their stems. The chair was divided into three or four compartments, overarched by these grasses—bower-fashion—and we imagined we saw something moving within each recess. We inquired who the stranger was.

"That!" replied the boatman; "oh, that is Tom Hirsell, the owl-finder."

"Owl-finder!—what do you mean?"

"Why, he travels the country, from one end to the other, looking for owls and bats: owls, especially, he catches, or steals from their nests, and tames, and then sells them to the gentry, or may be to gardeners. Many a one likes them in barns and granaries better than cats; and Tom is a man of his word—if he promises an owl he'll be sure to bring it, and for the price he named, even if some one else offered him twice the sum. He don't matter a walk of thirty mile to get the owlets, and he's as true as a sun-dial."

We asked "Tom Hirsell" if he had any owls for sale.

"None fit," he replied—none that he could recommend.

There was a sleepiness in the man's look; his eyes winked in the sun, as if light were disagreeable to him; he moved his head, too, slowly, in a sort of half-circle, while he spoke, and we fancied he had imbibed some of the owl-nature—

"Our nature is subdued to what it works in."

One of our party laughingly observed, that in a former state of existence he must have been the bird of night. Certainly, there was much about him unlike any other person we had ever noted; he seemed hardly awake, and yet it was evident he saw and observed us. We inquired if there was an owl under shelter of those long grasses? "Yes, there was, a fine tame one. He had a deal of trouble training that owl; it was such a sulky! he had taken it at Farnham; but it was promised to a lord's gardener near Marlow; he couldn't sell it—it was promised." He pulled the bird out; it fluttered, and winked, and twisted on his hand, and shook its feathers, and its eyes dilated and contracted while creeping up his sleeve, gently, and hiding its great full head in the neck of his smockfrock. He drew out another—a fierce, spiteful little bird—who hissed like a serpent, and chattered, and clapped its beak, and tried to bite, though it evidently did not see what to bite at.

"It will take another month or two to tame this one," he said.

"Had you ever one you could not tame?"

The owl-finder gave a grim, solemn smile, while a sort of phosphoric light glittered in his eyes. "One I could not tame?" he repeated : "they're all awhiles stubborn—it's their nature; they take different training from other birds—not at all the same; the younger they be the better; but I'd be sorry to find one I couldn't tame."

"Do you find them at night?"

"Night and day is all the same to me; day and night—all one. Glow-worms, owls, bats, night-hawks, snakes, fish, flesh, and fowl—all the same. I can catch anything I like; tame anything I like; but the owls are my favourites—I know them best, and they know me." The peculiar light that glittered in the eyes of the "owl-finder" was anything but pleasant, and the more he talked (his talk was decidedly an undertoned graveyard whisper), the more he blinked his eyes and moved his head. "I've a young one here," he continued, "Pope I call it; it came from the tower where the pope lived once; they call it Pope's Tower." He pulled it out of its appropriate cage, and held it up : the bird hooted and hissed, and the others took up the inharmonious notes, and hissed in concert, flapping their wings. "Here is a thing," said the man, "I don't understand, though I've been among them, man and boy, these many years, for my father was grave-digger to an old church, and so I may say I grew up among them. I used to climb the ivy when I was a little chap—so high—in twilight, or moonlight, or dead darkness—all one. I knew well the two great nests of the big buff owl, and the horned owl, at different sides of the old clock-tower; and I used to take up bits of meat or mice, and lay em on the edge of the nest; and the great buff owl, or the horned owl, would come and take up the things, and feed the little muffy owlets; and at last they came to know me, and would coo like doves when they heard me coming. And I had, like many another boy, a mother-in-law—step-mother some call it—who had no feeling for the child of the dead bones that were in the churchyard; and she'd often, when my father was abed and asleep, turn me out in the shiny snow or the bitter rain, and I'd away, and just climb up and shelter under the nest of the great buff owl in the angle of the tower, warm and dry; and the old owls would come and coo at me as they did to their young ones, but never seek to hurt me; and many's the star we've seen shining and falling through that darkness, and many a blink of the moon I've got that never reached the earth; and seen and heard much through the broad leaves of the ivy that nobody would believe if I was to tell it. There's more roams the skies a' nights than we think of. I shall never on this earth have the happy time again I had under the buff owl's nest." He raised his dreamy eyes, but their brightness was gone; they looked dim and heavy, and the poor fellow sighed.

We reminded him he had said there was something he did not understand about that particular owl he called "Pope."

"Oh, yes; day or night, night or day, whenever Pope hisses all the rest hiss; and if he hoots they all hoot; he seems like a master among them—they have their masters; *he* never minds *their* hooting."

"Is Pope bespoke?"

"Yes. I've only three with me; they're all bespoke."

"Have you any at home?"

"At home?" he repeated, then moved his head in that strange half-circling way, and added, "home! I have no home; but I have two or three sets to take from different parts of the country. You're from the town, I think. I shall be on Waterloo Bridge on the 12th of November, and if you want an owl by then, I'll keep one for you; I rest there for a couple of hours between two and four."

We bespoke an owl. Tom Hirsell replaced his birds, tying all to their perches, except the senior, who seemed to have an affection for his master, and a desire to nestle about his person, rather than to return into the shadows of the long grass. There was something strange and mysterious about the "owl-finder." He did not seek even to dispose of his game. What an unchildish childhood must his have been!—escaping from the brutality of a cruel step-mother to shelter under an owl's nest in the tower of an old church—finding a forbearance in those savage birds that was denied him in his father's house—hanging like a bat from the ivied tower above the mouldering graves—watching the stars, and peering through the ivy at the moonbeams—wondering if the shooting stars were angels—wondering and feeling, rather than thinking —alone! alone! in the mysterious universe of night, when the animate and inanimate assume shapes, and sounds, and shadows all unlike themselves. If the young and the brave—the strong-hearted and strong-minded, knowing as much of causes and effects as it is given us to know—become superstitious in the darkness, and often quail and quake with undefined sensations they shame to confess, it is no subject of astonishment if the mind of the poor ill-used child was so shaken in his youth as to grow up morbid and melancholy, deriving a species of pleasure and excitement from the companionship of the unearthly birds with whom he associated during those lonely hours.

It was a rude and evil thing of one of our friends, after we had left the "owl-finder," to suggest that the stalwart fellow was a "Detective" in disguise. The months passed on; we had forgotten our *tryst* on Waterloo Bridge, and were crossing it on the 12th of January—two months after the appointed day—with no memory of Tom Hirsell in our minds, when a soft, quiet, clear voice, heard amid the din of traffic, said—

"Will you please to have your owl?"

And we did have it, and brought it home, and it was put in a parrot's cage; but it seemed so unhappy, both by day and night, that we sent it to the country, where it has already established a good mousing reputation.

From Bablock Hithe we encounter no object of interest (excepting the broad reach, and the quaint old "public" at Skinner's weir) until

we arrive at ENSHAM—or, as it is called in the Ordnance map, SWIN-
FORD—BRIDGE.

ENSHAM BRIDGE.   a.

Ensham, Eynesham, or Einsham, was a place of note before the
Conquest: so early as 1005 an abbey was founded here by Ethelmar,

ENSHAM CROSS.

Earl of Cornwall, in the reign of Ethelred,
the king " who signed the privilege of
liberty with the sign of the Holy Cross;"
and here he held a general council in
1009.   At the dissolution, the abbey and
its site became the property of the Earl
of Derby.   None of its remains can now
be found : a few stones here and there
indicate its site.   A venerable CROSS stands
in the market-place, opposite the church ;
but its date is not very remote, although
time has much defaced its beauty.

It is in this neighbourhood we begin
to perceive the dangerous results of the
recent and rapid growth of the weed,
*Anacharis alsinastrum,* commonly called

"the American weed." It has not been known in England more than ten years; but during that brief period it has spread so extensively—almost universally—through every district of our island, as very frequently to affect the traffic of rivers and canals, to impede the currents of minor streams, and even to fill up isolated ponds. It has already rendered the Thames, in some parts, almost impassable without difficulty. A small pamphlet, written by William Marshall, Esq., of Ely, gives its history as far as it can be given. "The intruder is so unlike any other water-plant, that it may be at once recognised by its leaves growing *in threes*, round a slender stringy stem. The colour of the plant is a deep green; the leaves are about half an inch long, by an eighth wide, egg-shaped at the point, and *beset with minute teeth, which cause them to cling.* The stems are *very brittle,* so that whenever the plant is disturbed, fragments are broken off. Although, at present, it cannot propagate itself by seed (all the flowers being male) its powers of increase are prodigious, as every fragment is capable of becoming an independent plant, producing roots and stems, and extending itself indefinitely in every direction. Most of our water-plants require, in order to their increase, to be rooted in the bottom or sides of the river or drain in which they are found; but *this* is independent alto-

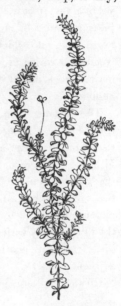

AMERICAN WEED.

gether of that condition, and *actually grows as it travels* slowly down the stream, *after being cut."* That this weed is "a foreigner" there can be no doubt. Weeds very closely resembling, if not identical with it, are found in American rivers. Mr. Marshall is of opinion that it is an importation from North America, and that, probably, its first visit was paid to us in a load of American timber. He considers that all attempts to "get rid of it" must be futile: *that it never can be eradicated;* and that all we shall be able to do is to "keep it down." Its rapid spread is one of the marvels of nature. It is becoming a serious evil : the Commissioners of the Thames should lose no time in grappling with the common enemy.

Immediately below Ensham Bridge we made the somewhat dangerous passage of the weir, close to which, on the north side, is the site of " The Burnt Tree," dear to Oxford citizens as the scene of many a merry picnic. This tree was struck by lightning, and formed for many years a very picturesque object, and an excellent excuse for making a pleasant water excursion. We soon arrive at Canott's Ham, on the north side, into which many a pheasant strays from the neighbouring wood, and where in winter the snipe and wild duck abound. It is also noticeable as one of the few places on the river where the tench is to be found.

The distance from Ensham to Godstow Bridge is about three miles; between these bridges we meet the Evenlode, a pleasant river, which, rising on the edge of Worcestershire, and passing by Moreton-in-the-Marsh, Charlbury, and Combe, and refreshing Blenheim Park, here joins the Thames, and proceeds with it to Oxford.* All along to the right of the river highway, we keep in sight the wooded heights of Witham—a pleasure enhanced by the numerous windings of the river, which exhibit the hill in every variety of form. This " bit" is the more valuable because of its rarity, as contrasting with the ordinary flatness and sameness of adjacent lands.†

On the opposite side of the river is seen the tall spire of CASSINGTON

---

* The Evenlode receives the Glyme, and conveys it to the Thames; the Glyme takes it course through Blenheim Park, and waters the ancient town of Woodstock. The palace built by Henry II. is entirely gone, but " Rosamond's Well " still yields delicious draughts to the wayfarer. Several naiads of various ages are in attendance to welcome visitors. Of the house in which Chaucer lived and wrote, a few fragments remain in the garden of a modern dwelling. Of the manor-house, where Queen Elizabeth was some [time imprisoned by her sister Mary, nothing now exists. Blenheim, however, takes the place of Woodstock " unsurpassed in clumsy magnificence and untruthful grandeur." The mansion contains many good pictures, which are heir-looms; the library is extensive, but unavailable for any useful purpose. Nature and Art have combined to make the grounds and gardens beautiful.

† There is a tradition that King Otta had a castle on Witham Hill, which is confirmed by the Chronicle of the Monastery of Abingdon, as appears by the following extract, p. 8 :—" Bellum—inter Offam regem Merciorum et Kinewolfum regem Westsaxonum, tunc temporis factum erat castellum super montem de Witham." The Chronicle adds that this war had the effect of driving from Witham a colony of nuns just settled there.

CHURCH; it is in view all the way to Oxford, and is ever a pleasant sight, refreshing to the eye and cheering to the heart.

On the same side of the river a building has been recently erected, which may be accepted as evidence of the progress of the age, in the midst of so much that is eloquent of "hoar antiquitie;" it is the new PAPER-MILL of the University. All makers of books are well aware that of late years the manufacture of paper has not been what it was a

CASSINGTON CHURCH.

century since, or, rather, three centuries ago: while the leaves of our great-great-grandfathers are as fresh and fair as on the day they issued from the press, modern books, and illustrated books especially, are often full of unsightly and diseased marks, that mar the beauty of the volumes. The University, having experienced this evil, resolved to make its own paper; it is a boon which claims public gratitude. The manufactory has a picturesque character seen from the Thames—not the less valuable because of the purposes to which it is dedicated.

L

GODSTOW BRIDGE is highly picturesque; the river divides here, and at the brink of the older and more shallow channel is a pleasant inn—"The Trout," well known to anglers, but better to the "Oxford scholar," as a place accessible to the rower, who here seeks refreshment after toil, and finds the homeward voyage with the current an agreeable and easy

THE UNIVERSITY PAPER-MILL.

evening task. At this spot commences the meadow—"Port Meadow," which, containing 439 acres, reaches almost to the city, whose property it is, and has been from time immemorial, as recorded in Domesday. Every citizen has the right of free pasturage for cattle, or, rather, a right for which he pays the annual tribute of two pence for each horse or cow found there on the day upon which the city authorities meet for inspection—a day of which, of course, no previous notice has been given. It is usually overflowed in winter, and has thus time for repose.

The story of "Fair Rosamond" has been told in a hundred ways: the "fair and comely dame" who was loved by Henry II. was, according to the legend, concealed by the king in a bower at Woodstock from the jealous eyes of his queen, Eleanor. The theme was in high favour with the early minstrels, and historians have not disdained to preserve the memory of her surpassing beauty and her sad fate.* She was, according

---

\* " Her crispèd lockes like threads of golde
    Appeared to each man's sight;
    Her sparkling eyes, like orient pearles,
    Did cast a heaven!ye light.

" The blood within her crystal cheekes
    Did such a colour drive,
    As though the lillye and the rose
    For mastership did strive."

to Stow, who follows Higden, the monk of Chester, the daughter of
Walter Lord Clifford, became the "lemman" of Henry II., and died at
Woodstock A. D. 1177, "poisoned by Queen Eleanor, as some thought." *

GODSTOW BRIDGE.

Stow proceeds to relate that her royal lover had made for her a house of
wonderful working, so that no man or woman might come to her but he
that was instructed by the king, or such as were right secret with him
touching the matter. This house, after some, was named Labyrinthus,
or "Dædalus' worke, which was wrought like unto a knot, in a garden
called a maze." Drayton, using the poet's licence, describes it as "consisting of vaults underground, arched and walled." And, in the famous
ballad of "Fair Rosamond," it is more minutely pictured as "a bower,"

* Lord Lyttleton tells us that Henry II. met Rosamund de Clifford at Godstow, in 1149, on his return
from Carlisle. She was at that time, in accordance with the custom of the age, a resident among the
nuns here for educational purposes. She had two sons by the king: one the famous Earl of Salisbury,
whose effigy is still to be seen in Salisbury Cathedral; the other was educated for the Church, and
became Bishop of Lincoln, and ultimately Chancellor of England.

curiously built of "stone and timber strong," having no fewer than one hundred and fifty doors, and so cunningly contrived with turnings round about, that none could obtain access to it except by "a clue of thread." But jealousy is proverbially quick-sighted : Queen Eleanor discovered the secret, possessed herself of "the clue of thriddle, or silk," and so dealt with her rival that "she lived not long." Authorities differ as to the mode by which the queen obtained the necessary guide. Hollinshed seriously states that "the king had drawn it after him out of her chamber with his foot ;" and Speed, that "it fell from Rosamond's lappe as she sate to take ayre, and, suddenly fleeing from the sight of the searcher, the end of her silk fastened to her foote, and the clue, still unwinding, remained behind." But historians content themselves with informing us that the lady "lived not long after," and do not insinuate that she was wounded with other weapons than sharp words, although tradition and the ballad-makers unite in charging the queen with the murder of Fair Rosamond by compelling her to drink poison. She was buried at "Godstow, in a house of nunnes beside Oxford," according to Stow, and "with these verses carved upon her tomb :"—

> " Hic jacet in tumba Rosa mundi, non Rosamunda!
> Non redolet, sed olet, quæ redolere solet."

Her royal lover expended large sums in adorning her tomb. But, in the year 1191, Hugh, Bishop of Lincoln, ordered the removal of her remains "without the church ;" he was obeyed, but after his departure her bones were gathered in a perfumed bag, and laid again in their resting-place, "under a fayre large grave-stone, about whose edges a fillet of brass was inlaid, and thereon written her name and praise." This tomb was partially existing in the last century, and "from the remains of the inscription it appears that she lived to a considerable age," setting aside the popular tale ; the most probable account of the close of her life is, that she broke off her connexion with the king, and retired to Godstow, spending there the remainder of her days in religious duties—a theory quite in accordance with the usages of the times in which she lived, and of which there are abundant examples.

Of " THE HOUSE OF NUNNES" there now exist but a few ivy-clad walls;
it was consecrated for Benedictine nuns A. D. 1138, in the presence of
King Stephen and his queen; seven hundred years and more have passed
since then, and three hundred years since the last abbess resigned her
home to the physician, Dr. George Owen, to whom Henry VIII. had

RUINS OF GODSTOW NUNNERY.

given it; still the river rolls by its rugged courtyard and dilapidated
gables, recalling to mind the story of the fair and frail beauty who gives
the ruin a special place in history.

At the foot of Witham Hill—the hill that has so cheerful and fair an
aspect from all points of the river within a range of several miles, and
so agreeably enlivens the view from Oxford—is the ancient village of
Witteham, or Wighthham, where a nunnery existed in the year 690.
Here the Earls of Abingdon have now their seat, partly built, it is said,
with the stones of Godstow.

The Eel (*Anguilla acutirostris*) "sharp-nosed," is that which chiefly abounds in the Thames, and the other rivers of England, although the broad-nosed eel (*Anguilla latirostris*) is almost as common; the names sufficiently indicate the distinction. The Thames eel is the eel *par excellence*; in consequence, perhaps, of its cleaner feeding, it is far more delicate and yet much richer than the fish found elsewhere; but it is not easily obtained, and is seldom offered for sale. In the Thames, the eel is

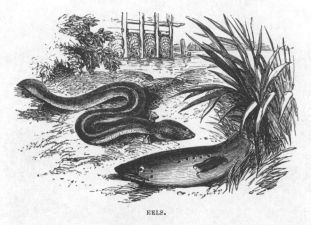

EELS.

rarely caught by the angler, although in ponds, and lakes, and other rivers it is freely taken with hook and line. "Eel-pots" made of wicker-work, which are sunk "over-night," baited within with any sort of animal matter, or eel-baskets, which are fixed in convenient places across by-currents of the river, are the "traps" by which they are secured in the Thames.

The Thames eel seldom grows to a very large size; it is not often obtained of a weight greater than three pounds, although occasionally one is found to weigh as much as seven pounds; about seven or eight years ago, an eel was caught in a trap at Hart's weir that weighed eleven pounds: we had some doubts as to the statement given to us by the weir-keeper, by whom it had been caught, but it received confirmation from a fishmonger at Oxford, to whom he had disposed of it, and who kept it for some time as "a show." During last year, a fisherman brought to us, while angling on the river, a *lusus naturæ*—a yellow eel, entirely and purely yellow, from head to tail inclusive. We recommended him to offer it for sale to the Zoological Society; but, by some accident, it was lost. Subsequently, we communicated the fact to Professor Owen, who informed us that, though very uncommon, it was by no means a solitary instance. The fish was remarkably beautiful, as well as curious.

The form and character of the eel are so well known as to render description unnecessary; its great characteristic is its tenacity of life—it is almost impossible to kill it, as the cook knows, to her great discomfort. It is certain that the eel can move about freely on land, travelling through the dewy grass for miles from one pond or river to another. It has long been in dispute whether the eel is oviparous or viviparous. Mr. Yarrell seems, however, to have set the question at rest—he considers it "oviparous, producing young like other true bony fishes;" and it is stated by Mr. Jesse that "they have been bred artificially from spawn."

All readers are aware that for ages there existed a strong prejudice against this fish, originating, probably, in its general resemblance to the serpent; the popular belief was that they were created out of decomposed animal matter—"sprang from mud"—were produced by horse-hairs generated in water, and so forth; and in many places even now people will starve rather than eat them. Perhaps, of all the fish of the fresh-water, they form the most delicious food: a Thames eel of two pounds weight is a dainty dish to set before the Queen.

When the eel is fished for with the hook, it is generally with the night line, for they prowl only by night; a line with perhaps forty or fifty hooks, baited with lob-worms, is thrown into the river to take its chance, and it is usually successful when the water is "coloured," or after a flood; but this is, of course, a practice to which the angler does not condescend: the Thames angler can rarely obtain an eel, except by means of "a silver hook."

One of the handsomest of British aquatics is the Arrow-head (*Sagittaria sagittæfolia*), whether as regards the elegant spear-shaped leaves

of glossiest green, or the flower-spikes rising in pyramidical form from
the water with strong fluted stems, and presenting altogether a striking

resemblance to a highly-decorated gothic
finial; the flowers are three-petaled, white,
with a flush of violet towards the centre, from
which rises a granulated boss of green, that
adds much to the beauty of the flower. This
plant is extensively cultivated among the
Chinese—not for its beauty, but for the sake
of the bulb, which fixes itself in the solid
earth below the mud, and constitutes an article
of food. The roots attain a larger size in
China, it appears, than they do with us; but
still we should think that, even in this country,
their cultivation might be attempted with success in very watery localities, where other

THE ARROW-HEAD.

esculent plants are not grown; and a little attention to its culture
might produce the same improvement in the size and quality of the
root, as has been the case with most of our garden vegetables. This
very graceful plant is found in great abundance in this neighbourhood;
but there are few parts of the upper Thames which it does not enliven
by its luxuriant foliage.

Having passed through Godstow Lock, Oxford City comes in sight;
the village of Wolvercot is passed, but that of Binsey claims a moment's
thought. The voyager will pause at Binsey weir, for here a charming
view is obtained of ancient and venerable Oxford—its pinnacles, and
towers, and church spires rising proudly above surrounding domiciles.
Nowhere do we obtain a more striking view, and here especially do we
recall the expressive lines of the poet :—

> " Like a rich gem, in circling gold enshrined,
>   Where Isis' waters wind
>     Along the sweetest shore
>   That ever felt fair culture's hands,
>     Or spring's embroidered mantle wore—
>   Lo ! where majestic Oxford stands."

We step ashore awhile to visit the little village, and to walk to its church, half a mile or so distant from the river-bank. At Binsey, A. D. 730, the holy virgin Frideswide had a chapel constructed of "wallyns and rough-hewn timber;" * hither were sent of her nuns "the most stubborn sort," to be confined in a dark room, and to be deprived of their usual repast; and here, too, was the famous well of St. Margaret, which St. Frides-wide, "by her prayers, caused to be opened;" here came the people to ease their burthened souls, and to be rid of their diseases; consequently the adjoining village of Seckworth became a large town, containing

OXFORD, FROM NEAR BINSEY.

twenty-four inns,—the dwellings chiefly of the priests appointed by the prior of Binsey to confess and absolve the penitents. Binsey has now but a dozen poor houses; its church has a heart-broken look; and of the well there is but an indication—a large earth-mound in a corner of the

---

* The little chapel thus constructed by the saint was evidently one of those wooden buildings, dedi-cated to ecclesiastical services, which were not uncommon in the Saxon era. The "wallyns" used by Frideswide were the timbers which formed the mainstay of the building, and were such as we still find in old timber houses; the "rough-hewn timber" was fastened on them, and so made the outer walls. The Saxon chronicles give many notices of similar buildings. Thus, when Edwin was converted to Christianity in 627, he was baptized in a wooden church, on the spot where York Cathedral now stands. The famous church of Lindisfarne was first constructed, in 652, of sawn oak, and thatched. The most extraordinary existing instance of such a primitive English church is at Greensted, in Essex, which is thought to have been originally erected in haste to receive the body of the martyr king, St. Edmund, in its passage from Suffolk to London. The body of the church is formed by a series of split trees, the flat side inward, and the rough bark outward; they fit in sockets above and below, also formed of timber: and this is doubtless the sort of erection Frideswide constructed, after the Saxon fashion.

graveyard completely dried up, there being no sign of water; the spring is lost; and so, indeed, is its memory—for we inquired in vain among the neighbouring peasantry for St. Margaret's Well, of which they had heard and knew nothing—*sic transit!* *

The ancient farm of Medley, which adjoins Binsey weir, is still a farm, as it was before the Norman conquest.

Shortly before Oxford is reached, at a point called the Four Streams, the river separates into two channels, its "divided flood" meeting again just below the city, at the foot of Folly Bridge, at the commencement of Christ Church meadow.† Our course takes us by the right-hand stream, the only navigable one, under a bridge on the highroad leading from Oxford to the west—a road which numbers seven bridges within a mile, and illustrates somewhat expensively the divided character of the Thames at this part of its course.

A cluster of old houses points out the site of Osney; we first pass, however, through OSNEY LOCK, one of the most picturesque locks on the river; although its accessories are only low houses and broken walls, they are such as the painter loves, and to our friend, Mr. E. W. Cooke, we are indebted for the sketch of which we append an engraving.

Osney, or Ouseney, Abbey, once rivalled in extent and architectural beauty the grandest of the colleges that now adorn and dignify the proud city. It was "seated on a flat or low ground, but for the grove, and trees, and rivulets that encompassed it not a little pleasant." It received

---

* A superstitious belief in the efficacy of holy wells was one of the most characteristic features of the middle ages, and to them pilgrimages were made from great distances. Some religious establishment was generally near them, which profited by the devout. There is scarcely a large town in England without a record of some holy well near, and London had several—the most famous being that of Clerkenwell, which takes its name from it, and the holy well in the Strand, which still designates the street there. The most famous of all these mediæval wells is that still remaining in Flintshire, and known as St. Winifred. The marvels told of the miraculous cures here effected obtained such renown for the waters, that a gothic chapel of singular beauty was erected over them. But it was not curative properties alone they possessed—they had other virtues. Thus the well at the far-famed Abbey of Walsingham gave success to the "wishes" of the pilgrim who drank of it devoutly. Other instances of "wishing-wells" might be quoted, and superstitious observances noted, more akin to fortune-telling than medicine.

† The Thames, at and about Oxford, forms a complete network of streams—so much so as to be puzzling even to the surveyor. Our Oxford readers will recollect the various names of "Seckworth," "the Reach," "the Dunge," "Pot Stream," "the Wyke Stream," "the Four Streams," and many others.

its first erection in 1129, by the donation of Robert D'Oyly, at the instance
of his wife Edith; and the legend is, that often, when walking out of
Oxford Castle by the river-side, she observed magpies chattering on a
certain tree, "as it wer to speke to her;" much marvelling at this, she
asked of her confessor the meaning thereof, who told her they were not
pies, but so many poor souls in purgatory, who were complaining to her,
and entreating of her some good. Thereupon, and for their relief, she
procured the building of the abbey where the tree stood; her "confessor,"
of course, becoming its abbot. During after-times, it was enriched by

OSNEY LOCK.

other donors, until it became "one of the first ornaments and wonders of
this place, or nation;" to the great hall would often come, as guests,
kings, prelates, and nobles of the first rank; whatever heart could wish
the monks enjoyed, "by means of the generosity of their founders and
succeeding benefactors;" the church was adorned by the gifts of the
pious—all who contributed something towards the building being entitled to "forty days' indulgence and forgiveness from sin"—hence it
became "the envy of other religious houses in England and beyond sea;"
of architecture exquisite and full of variety; with hangings of most

excellent work, windows of famous painting; with pillars elegant and uniform, each bearing a statue; with wonderful variety of carvings and paintings, "that not only fed the eye with delight, but struck the spectator with surprise and admiration." Of this grand and glorious work there is now not one stone remaining upon another; "it suffered not a little from the Rump Parliament,"—Time did the rest, and—

> " Of it there now remains no memory,
> Nor any little monument to see."

The abbots of Osney were peers of parliament. The last abbot was Robert King, who, in 1539, " surrendered" the abbey to Henry VIII.— who, in 1542, made it the see of a bishop, assigning Gloucester Hall, now Worcester College, Oxford, for his residence. In 1546 the episcopal chair was transferred to the conventual church of St. Frideswide, which was then constituted the cathedral of the see, and called Christ Church, and the last abbot and only bishop of Osney became the first bishop of Oxford. Of Dr. King there is a portrait in the library at Christ Church, the background of which is a picture of the abbey. Others of its treasures are also in that college—" Old Tom," the famous Oxford bell, being one of them. Standing upon the site it occupied in the days of its power and grandeur, and searching in vain for a few stones to indicate its splendour, the mind is absolutely forced to ponder and reflect.

Although, no doubt, much was gained to religion and liberty by the suppression of monasteries, and we may rejoice that we no longer hear in our "schools"

> " The harsh jargon of contentious monks,"

something was surely lost of intellectual supremacy. Osney shared the fate of so many wealthy establishments, which the cupidity, and not the piety, of Henry VIII. caused him to suppress. Although the friaries and the lesser monasteries were destroyed by law, the more powerful establishments were ruined by "surrender." By threats, cajolery, or bribery, the abbacies came into the king's hands, or under his control. Untractable abbots were summarily disposed of by easily sustained charges of high-treason, and the monks were "sent adrift to dig, or beg, or starve." Osney revived somewhat in the days of Queen Mary, masses were again chanted within its walls; but during the Commonwealth its ruin was completed, and of its remains there is now nothing but the site, which the Thames waters as freely and abundantly as it did three centuries ago.

In the still recesses of the river we found that queen of water-nymphs, the White Water-Lily (*Nymphæa alba*) in the greatest luxuriance, both in number and in the extraordinary size of the flowers and leaves; on dragging some of these into the boat, we found that the stems were from eight to ten feet in length, and the leaves were of immense breadth; the flowers also were unusually developed, and some specimens were suffused with a blush of roseate tint that contrasted delight-

THE WATER-LILY.

fully with the rich green of the calyx and leaves. It is in our aquatic flora, certainly, that we can vie with the richness of tropical regions; and we should wish to see our ornamental waters better stocked with these native beauties than, with few exceptions, is the case. What more lovely decoration could a small piece of water receive than a group of Water-lilies, white and yellow, the elegant Frog-bit, and the princely Flowering-rush, with its crown of purple and white blossoms, with a number of other charming plants either growing in the water or fringing its edge?

On the current which runs to the left are the few indications which still exist to point out the locality of another abbey—that of Rewley. Rewley Abbey, "sometime seated within pleasant groves, and environed within clear streams," with its twenty-one elm-trees, and a tree by itself, to represent the abbot and situated on this branch of the river; its

PORCH AT RAWLEY ABBEY.

the number of its monks, was former splendour is, however, indicated only by a doorway, and a wall which now incloses part of the North-Western Railway.

The left stream is the course that is most picturesque; but there is no exit, as the current is arrested to turn the mill which still works there, where, by itself and its predecessors, it has worked since the castle first reared its strong and stately towers and battlements by the river's side; indeed, there is evidence that the miller had precedence of the chatelain. We pass under a new railway bridge, close to the opening of the Oxford and Coventry Canal; and, at the entrance to the city on this side, as we near one of the most ancient of its bridges—Hithe, or Hythe, Bridge—we observe a small cluster of rude and primitive houses, the small dwellings of a race of fishermen, who have followed that calling from father to son, in unbroken succession, for several hundred years.

It was in this neighbourhood we heard an anecdote, to listen to which we ask the reader a brief delay "*en route.*"

Years many and long must pass before "cemeteries," with their cold marble monuments, and hard-hearted catacombs, their vaults, and gravelled walks, and slender trees—rational, and well-ordered, and necessary as they are—can become a natural feature in our English landscape. The village churchyard was and is a sanctuary,—however neglected, however over-crowded, it is sanctified to us by that strong English bond, "old association:" it has formed for centuries the link between the living and the dead—the present and the past.  The church has been deprived, by modern innovation, of a most imposing and attractive ceremony, which the law of man has changed from a religious compact to a civil contract—thus breaking with a rude and coarse hand a tie that was hitherto so sacred; but the old English churchyard is still with us, and still bears the hallowed fruitage of abundant memories : it is one of the evidences of the

"Immortality that stirs within us,"

this craving to perpetuate the remembrance of what was dearly loved in life.  The sentiment is as strong in the lowly, when they mark a resting-place by a simple head-stone, as in the rich when they erect the costly cenotaph.  This

"Keeping the memory green in our souls,"

is one of the dearest of all hopes and all duties, and the humblest natures cling to it as closely as do the highest.

Within sight of our noble river, some ten years ago, a man named Jabez Lloyd was considered as treading the path to independence : he was growing from a village carpenter into a boat-builder.  He was a courteous, frank, and kindly fellow, becoming famous for launching those canoes in which "Oxford men" skim the surface of the Thames.  Jabez was married to a meek, dove-eyed little woman—one of those who continue to work on silently through the world, attracting very little attention while they are with us, but if laid up by illness, or called home by death, leave a blank which, because we find it impossible to fill up, we know how well it must have been filled.  In this instance, however, it was not the meek little creature—never happy but in the sunshine of her husband's presence—who was taken, but the strong-handed Jabez ; he was trying one of those painted skimmers of the Thames, and had just got free of the reeds and weeds and rushes that weave a leafy barrier at a particular bend of the river, when, leaning incautiously a little on one side to disentangle his oar from the tough fibres of some water-plants, he went over, right into a bed of lilies, and was drowned before he could be extricated from the meshes of the golden-chaliced

flowers and their broad leaves. Jabez left absolutely nothing, or " less
than nothing," to his widow. After the sale of spars, and paint, and
fishing-tackle, and household goods, there was barely enough to pay
the funeral expenses, and to purchase unpretending mourning. And in
the overwhelming and miserable loneliness of her first widowhood, the
little creature was forced to think of what she should, or could, do, to
keep from out the workhouse. She was quite uneducated ; he married
her when she was but sixteen, just learning to be a dressmaker. What
could she do ? She could sew, and attend to a cottage home ; she could
be a farm servant—that little delicate pet of a woman, whom the great
boatman cherished and watched over, and tended as if she were his one
darling child—poor Mrs. Lloyd a farm servant ! She tried it ! She
hired herself out at three shillings a week at the farm,—you can see the
ricks and trees of that large farmhouse from where we stood,—and the
farmer's wife—a great glory of a woman, as far as size and good-nature
goes—trained her voice to speak gently, and abandoned altogether the
tone of an ill-used woman she was wont to assume when addressing her
domestics, saying "Thank you" to Mrs. Lloyd for every service, useless though she thought it, which the poor little woman rendered. She
washed and she ironed, and she took most loving care of the poultry ;
chickens grew rapidly under her superintendence, and young turkeys
" cut " their red heads—as children do their teeth sometimes—with very
little difficulty. She worked too at her needle. She did all she could ;
but she was so neat and exact, so fond of doing everything she knew
how to do in the best manner, that the farmer's wife considered her
" slow." She preferred her " helps " to be quick and slatternly ; she
could not bear them to be slow. The little widow felt this, but what
could she do more than she did ? and despite the sympathy of the
farmer's wife, her quick temper overcame her humanity, and she gave
the widow warning. Just at this time the curate of the village wanted
a housekeeper, and with a belief in her being quite unfit for such a post,
Mrs. Lloyd still felt it a duty to " try ;" and so, with a trembling hand,
she raised the garden latch, and presented herself as a candidate. The
curate, besides being the earnest, hard-working minister so suited to a

country parish, was just the person to inspire poets with a subject, and young ladies with the enthusiasm that leads to the manufacture and presentation of pen-wipers, slippers, and footstools : he was pale and thin, with a clear soft voice, and such truthful eyes! Well, he told Mrs. Lloyd that he was too poor, he feared, to offer her sufficient remuneration : he could not afford to pay a good servant. And Mrs. Lloyd assured him she was *not* a good servant, and if he would try her, very moderate wages would be more than she deserved : indeed, she feared she was hardly worth wages, but she had something to do before she died, and she could not be happy until it was done. Accordingly that evening she brought a bundle, and the clerk carried her box. She was installed in the smallest of all kitchens, and had even a smaller bedroom ; but there was room on the white wall for a portrait of her husband, which some Oxford youth had painted, and though a dreadful daub, it was a likeness. Before *that* she knelt, and before *that* she prayed ; and at the end of the week the curate thought—such was the peace, and comfort, and quiet, and neatness of his cottage—that he must be entertaining an angel unawares. The curate had £80 a year, and the rector, who had £800, cautioned him, when he first came, in a fatherly sort of way, not to be extravagant. The advice was very good, and the young man profited by it, for he kept out of debt, and often sent his sister, who was a governess, small sums in postage stamps. All he could pay the little widow was about two and sixpence a week, and she had to find her tea and sugar and " beer " out of that. Do not pity her ! She was bright and cheerful ; she could do very well without sugar, and as her master could not afford " beer," surely she was better without it. She was her own mistress—never found fault with ; her black dresses (she had two) wore to a miracle, but she was forced to buy another, because she must look respectable : that took away the savings of more than six months. Yet she went on saving, adding halfpence to halfpence, denying herself everything almost which the humblest servant considers she wants ; sitting up at night when the moon was at full (for she would not waste her master's candle), making her caps " do," and ironing out her cap-strings—darning, turning, trimming, all to save perhaps twopence ;

but she had a purpose to work out.   She rarely opened the garden gate
except to go to church or to do the small marketings.   On Sunday
evenings she indulged in the luxury of tears over her husband's grave ;
and returning from market, she always paused at the stone-cutter's yard,
eyeing the tombstones.   Once she entered timidly—she was timid in all
things—and inquired the various prices ;  and the stone-cutter, when he
saw her threadbare but neat dress, and observed the fluttering of the
washed-out crape curtains on her bonnet, and noted how limp and poor
she looked, wondered why she troubled him : but he was a kind man,
and did not say so.   Time wore on : the curate had an ever-accumu-
lating stock of pen-wipers, slippers, and footstools ;  sometimes went out
to dinner, but more frequently to tea ;  and still more frequently visited
the poor and the schools, and lectured, or stayed at home ;  or, as a great
luxury at Midsummer, when there was not much sickness in the parish,
and it was holiday time in the school, took his rod to wander beside the
queenly river he loved so well.   The rod was simply an excuse for
loitering, though he did sometimes bring home some little fish that
would have formed good subjects for the microscope.   Time wore on,
and some people wondered that the curate permitted his little servant to
wear such threadbare black ;  but others—the majority—only saw the
widow's meek thankful face, and her soft hopeful eyes, and marvelled,
with more reason, how neat and pleasant she made all things in her
master's house.   How different are the meanings different people draw
from the same readings !

Time again passed on, and it was now three years since the strong
boat-builder had found his death in the Thames, when the "widow"
again entered the stone-cutter's yard ;  she placed a slip of paper in his
hand, and he read,—

SACRED TO THE MEMORY OF
JABEZ LLOYD,
AGED TWENTY-EIGHT, BOAT-BUILDER,
WHO WAS DROWNED IN THE SUNSHINE OF THE 24TH OF JUNE, 18——,
AMONG THE WATER-LILIES OF THE THAMES.
HE WAS BELOVED BY GOD AND MAN.

She pointed to a tombstone, the one upon which her heart had long
been fixed.

"But who will pay for this?" inquired the stone-cutter.

The little widow put the money into his hand. The man looked at her with astonishment, and involuntarily lifted his hat while he spoke.

"It is a very humble stone," she said, "and no one can think I have taken a liberty in putting it up. I have worked and saved for it day and night. I shall be able to see it every Sunday. You will put it up at once, sir?"

"God bless the woman!" exclaimed the stone-cutter; "I would have done it long ago if I had given it a thought. I loved Jabez; and as to your money, I'll not touch it. You shall see the stone in its place next Sunday."

Such a warm colour as came to the widow's cheeks—such brightness as flashed from the widow's eyes! and how she trembled beneath her threadbare drapery!

"You *must* take the money," she said, firmly; "it *must* be my doing. Take the money, sir, or else I must go elsewhere; only thank you for your offer—you meant it in kindness."

The following Sunday it *was* in its place, and the stone-cutter told the story over and over again, interrupted occasionally by a guttural sort of sound in his throat. The only one who did not appreciate this woman's offering was the churchwarden, who stoutly contended that the poor had no business with such fine feelings, and grew very red, and looked very indignantly at the tombstone. Nevertheless, it excited a good deal of interest; after evening service, even the little children retired from the corner of the churchyard in which it is placed, knowing who had a right to kneel there in solitude and silence.

Of OXFORD CASTLE there remains only a solitary tower; but the mound, planted with evergreens, still rises at its northern side. As will be seen in our engraving (for the sketch we are indebted to Mr. Harvey, of Oxford), the old mill and its dependant dwellings are in harmony with the old walls with which they have been so long associated. The castle was begun by Robert D'Oyly* in 1071, and finished in 1073, "to keep in

* There are several persons bearing this name residing in the north of Oxfordshire at the present time, and reputed to be descendants of Robert D'Oyly.

order the neighbouring parts, especially the city of Oxford, which gave great affronts and proved troublesome to King William." It was famous from that time to the Civil Wars, when it had lost much of its strength and value; afterwards it gradually became a ruin, which ranks among the most interesting relics of the venerable city.

> " Time's gradual touch
> Has moulder'd into beauty many a tower,
> Which, when it frown'd with all its battlements,
> Was only terrible."

The old castle could tell many strange stories from its palmy days, immediately following the Conquest, to the commencement of the present century, when this tower was the jail of the county. Perhaps the most

OXFORD CASTLE.

remarkable of its incidents is that which relates to the Empress Maud, who, being besieged there by the army of King Stephen, contrived to escape thence into Abingdon. The river was frozen over, and, accompanied by three trusty knights, all clad in ghostly white, she issued from its postern gate at dead midnight, and, crossing the ice, passed the sentinels of the enemy unobserved.

There is little doubt, however, that a castle, a residence of some kind or other, existed at Oxford long prior to the Conquest, and, probably, on the site which the castle now occupies, and also that it was a royal dwelling, in which Offa, and Alfred and his sons resided; indeed, many Saxon remains have been from time to time discovered by digging in the immediate neighbourhood, and it is clearly ascertained by ancient records that a tower was standing in the time of King Ethelred.

We bring together, in the appended engraving, the Roach and Dace, for, as all Thames anglers know, they are generally found together, and caught with the same bait—the gentle. These fish supply the principal sport of the angler during the summer months, the dace being more abundant in June and July, and the roach in autumn; biting most freely, and being in best condition, in September and October. It is only the skilful angler who can fill his basket with these fish, although they abound in all parts of the Thames.

The Roach (*Leuciscus rutilus*) is found in nearly all English rivers, preferring, however, those which are comparatively slow; and living freely in lakes, ponds, and pools, where the water has no egress. According to Yarrell, " the colour of the upper part of the head and back is dusky green, with blue reflections, becoming lighter on the sides, and passing into silvery white on the belly; the irides yellow, cheeks and gill-covers silvery white; dorsal and caudal fins pale brown, tinged with red; pectoral fins orange red; ventral and anal fins bright red; the scales are rather large, marked with consecutive and radiating lines." The roach is a handsome fish, and is known at once by his bright red colour, and especially by the marked redness of the eye. It is frequently caught of about six or eight inches in length, and weighing between half-a-pound and a pound. It is not uncommon to catch four or five dozen of that size as the result of a day's sport; particularly in the neighbourhood of Marlow, where perhaps the largest roach are found in greatest abundance, especially during the autumn months, and when the water has been somewhat " coloured" by rain. It is rare to find a roach in the Thames

weighing more than two pounds.   Mr. Jesse speaks of one that weighed
three pounds; we have ourselves caught one, but only one, that weighed
a pound and three quarters.

The Dace (*Leuciscus vulgaris*) is like the roach, gregarious—roaming
and feeding in shoals; it is found in all parts of the Thames; it bears a
resemblance to the roach, except that its body is more taper and graceful,
the scales are much smaller, and its hue is silvery without any admixture
of red.   It prefers the more rapid to the quieter current; and, although,
as we have stated, these fish are usually found together, the angler knows
by experience where the one will be found more abundantly than the

THE ROACH AND DACE.

other.   The dace seldom measures more than six inches in length, and
rarely weighs more than half-a-pound; but it is by no means uncommon
for a skilful angler to kill twenty dozen of them in the course of a day.
The dace is frequently caught with the fly, for it will rise freely.

The usual mode of angling for roach and dace is, however, by
"bottom-fishing," in a depth of water about six feet.   The angler
moors his punt in some well-known "pitch," where the fish are known
to congregate; it must be free from weed, and the current neither too
rapid nor too slow.   He fishes with a very small hook, baited with a
single gentle, or it may be two gentles; his bait should lie as near the

ground as it can be without actually touching it; his bottom line is of
horse-hair, or, at all events, the lower portion of his line—not plaited,
but single; and he soon finds that, if his strike is sharp and sudden, he
loses both hook and fish; good hair, however, will last a whole day, if
properly used, and be of sufficient strength to land a heavier fish than
any roach or dace in the Thames. Many anglers prefer to fish with fine
gut; but no matter how fine it may be, it is never so efficacious as the
single hair: the gut will always "magnify" in water, and usually raises
bubbles, so small as to be imperceptible to the human eye, but which the
fish see well enough to have warning of danger. The hair has not these
disadvantages. In using either, care is taken that the colour is of a
pale tint—as near as may be to the colour of the water. It is obvious
that the angler who fishes with hair must be more skilful and experienced than he who trusts to gut; but we answer for it, that he who
uses the one will be twice as successful as he who depends on the other.
"When you fish for roach or dace," as honest Izaak says, "you must
have a small hook, a quick eye, and a nimble hand." And let the fly-
fisher say what he will—and he does say a deal to lower the craft of the
bottom-fisher—the skill required to secure sport is at least equal to that
which is demanded by him who throws the mimic insect under a bough
across a river fifty feet wide. The ire of the fly-fisher, however, is
chiefly induced by a common practice of the bait-fisher, who, in order
to draw the fish to his vicinage, is continually throwing in ground-bait—
*i. e.* balls composed of bread and bran mixed up with clay, which, dis-
solving and separating, attract the fish to the source from whence food
has proceeded. It must be confessed that this practice does look
unseemly, and goes far to justify the sneers which the more ambitious
anglers of the Scotch and Irish lakes so frequently aim at the simple
joys of those who are content with such pleasures as are supplied by the
venerable river which gladdens and glorifies the great capital of the
world.*

---

* Not very long ago, roach and dace were valuable chiefly for their scales, which were used in the
manufacture of artificial pearls; this trade has, however, now altogether ceased. Neither of these fish
is desirable for the table, although some persons profess to be fond of them, and they may be good
enough when nothing better is to be had.

Leaving to the left the rugged island, once the site of Osney, and now covered with houses of a low grade, with rough gardens, inclosed by dilapidated walls or broken palisades, and to the right the fertile meadows around which winds the ancient bed of the river, we arrive at Folly Bridge,* but must previously pass through a lock, the river here having a fall of about three feet. At the extremity of the little island we have described, was the famous tower with which for centuries was associated the once dreaded, but now venerated, name of Friar Bacon.

"FRIAR BACON'S STUDY," which formerly stood on this bridge, "near the end next the city," was taken down in the year 1779; and the prophecy thus failed, that "when a man more learned than he passed under it the tower would fall,"—hence the old warning, when a youth was sent to the University, "Beware of walking near the Friar's Tower!" It is traditionally narrated that to this tower the great Roger Bacon, one of the greatest luminaries of the middle ages, used to resort at night "to take the altitude and distance of the stars." Popular prejudice accused him of practising magic, and, according to the legend, he was cited to Rome on this charge by the general of his order (he was a Franciscan friar); but having cleared himself, he was sent back to England. The tower was said to have been built in King Stephen's time, as "a Pharos or high watch-tower for the defence of the city."

FRIAR BACON'S STUDY.

* The bridge at which the several branches of the Thames unite was anciently called Grand Pont and South Bridge; it is now named "Folly Bridge."

We have been passing for some time through the lower parts and the outer side of Oxford; for these picturesque houses and gardens that skirt the bank of the river are its lanes and alleys. Into Oxford, however, it is not our design to enter with a view to describe the city; to do so at all adequately is impossible within the space to which we

OXFORD.

are limited. The visitor will readily lay his hand on one of the many books in which it is illustrated largely and described fully.

We will only, therefore, ask the reader to "step" with us into Oxford before we rejoin the river, and resume our voyage between its banks.* Its antiquity (according to legendary lore) is as remote as that of any existing English city. The earlier chroniclers, in the absence of fact, had recourse to fiction; and finding the early history of the city

* The distance from London to Oxford by water is understood to be 116½ miles; by land it is 52. "The Oarsman's Guide" calculates the water distance at 115¾ miles.

depended on tradition only, gave these traditions a lasting form in monkish history. Of these the most amusing, but the most fanciful, is the work of Geoffrey of Monmouth, an ecclesiastic who lived in the twelfth century, and whose industry and credulity were both equally remarkable. He declares Oxford to have been originally built one thousand and nine years before Christ, by Memphric, King of the Britons, when it was called Caer-Memphricii, or as some write it, Memphritii, "upon the ryver Temes," and therefore "deserves to be reckoned not only amongst the first and most antient cities of Britain, but of all Europe and of the world." More correct chroniclers come to our aid, and we know from authentic history that the Saxons "much affected this city with hurt." It was burnt by the Danes, and suffered in a hundred ways during the wars and civil contests that followed—from the Conquest to the struggles of Charles I. and his parliament.

At the Conquest the citizens numbered twelve hundred. It is stated in Domesday Book that in Oxeneford " are two hundred and forty-three houses, as well within as without the wall, that pay or yield geld; and five hundred and twenty-two more, at least, which are so wasted and destroyed that they cannot pay geld." *

Commentators differ, without any reason, as to the derivation of the name. There can be no doubt that Oxenford, by which it was called in early time, means neither more nor less than a ford for oxen; much useless controversy has been expended on this point, which might, it would seem, be at once determined by common sense : Domesday, the old Saxon chronicles, and the city seals,† confirm the Ford. It was called Oxford probably from the king's oxen being driven thither (for

---

* Domesday Book is the most important and valuable monument of its kind possessed by any nation. It was compiled under the direction of William the Conqueror, and in accordance with the resolution passed at the council held in Gloucester, A.D. 1085. It contains a survey of all England, and minutely specifies the extent of lands in every county, and who they are held by. It also gives the various tenures under which they are held, and notes whether they are meadow, pasture, or woody districts. In some instances it gives the number of persons living on them, and notes if they be bond or free. To the historian and topographer this work is invaluable ; and it aids us in the darker times of Saxon rule, by incidentally narrating its grants.

† The old city seal represents an ox crossing a ford.

it was a royal demesne under the care of a bailiff) from the royal forests, in the summer, to pasture on the luxuriant grasses of the meadows, which were flooded and inaccessible to them in winter. In the time of Harold the walls were so ruinous that the rents of several houses were allotted for their repair. It is certain that it was a walled town in the time of the Confessor : King Alfred is stated, on very suspicious authority, to have set his halls *infra muros Oxoniæ;* and it is said that long previously the city had both walls and gates. Of these walls there are several interesting remains, the best preserved being in the gardens of New College. The Mayor and Aldermen, accompanied by the city officers, and preceded by the beautiful silver-gilt mace of Charles II., have an annual ceremony of going in procession to trace these walls, and demanding the right of entry into any garden or house that occupies the site of any portion of them. This perambulation still bears the title of "the reparation view," and was doubtless instituted for the purpose of seeing that the walls were kept in good repair. It forms, at the present time, an interesting memorial of the boundaries of the "old citie within the walles." The moat and trenches may be still accurately traced,* and are generally clothed with ivy—

> " To gild destruction with a smile,
> And beautify decay."

It is to the University, however, that Oxford mainly owes its fame ; for centuries it has been—

> " That faire citie, wherein make abode
> So many learned impes, that shoote abrode,
> And with their branches spreade all Brittany."

Walking through its lanes, and courts, and streets, and reminded at every turn of the sacredness of its history, associated with so much that is great and good—of learning, piety, patriotism, and true courage— the enthusiast is almost tempted to cast his shoes from off his feet, for

---

* The Corporation claim a right to refreshment at certain places on the route,—commencing with crawfish and sops in ale at the starting-point, a house in St. Aldate Street, and ending with " Canary wine " at the lodgings of the President of Corpus.

the ground on which he treads is holy : while it is impossible for the mind least instructed or inspired to withhold homage, or to avoid exclaiming with the poet—

> " Ye spires of Oxford ! domes and towers !
> Gardens and groves ! Your presence overpowers
> The soberness of reason."

The High Street, from the bridge which crosses the Cherwell—the Botanic Gardens on the left, and the fair and honoured college, Magdalen, on the right—to the Carfax Church, at its extremity, is said to be the most beautiful street in Europe ; and, surely, with truth, for the very inequalities of the later-built houses aid the picturesque ; while, on either side, are the interesting and time-honoured structures— University College, Queen's College, All Souls' College, and the richly-adorned Church of St. Mary ; down narrow alleys glimpses are caught, at brief intervals, of New College, St. Peter's Church, St. Mary's Hall, Oriel College, of Corpus, also, and Brazen Nose, the Radcliffe and Bodleian Libraries, "the Schools," Lincoln College, and the great college, Christ Church, in St. Aldate's.

The most important and the most interesting of the "new" buildings at Oxford is the Museum ; the necessity of such an addition to the city, and especially to the University, had long been felt—the want was increasing from year to year ; the valuable geological collection of Dr. Buckland, and the entomological collection of Mr. Hope, were acquisitions that imperatively demanded some fitting accommodation. The work was therefore commenced ; and it was thought desirable to introduce a novelty in architecture. It was determined that, as Oxford is a " Gothic " city, the new building ought to be Gothic, and yet the new style introduced by the Crystal Palace was to be taken advantage of. This has been successfully accomplished by the shell of the building —built in a square—being " English Gothic," while the inner court is glazed over, and converted into a museum. The corridor which runs round this square has the columns made of various English granites, syenites, and other stones likely to be useful in building ; and it is to be ornamented likewise by statues of men distinguished in physical science, five of which have been contributed by Her Majesty. Most probably the books from the Radcliffe Library connected with the physical sciences will be transferred to the new building, so that there will be accumulated an almost unique collection of books on these subjects in close proximity to the objects which they describe and illustrate.

Without dating the commencement of learning in Oxford so far back as did Geoffrey of Monmouth—a thousand years before the commencement of the Christian era—it is asserted that in the ninth century it had become the fountain whence issued many learned clerks, and that among the earliest to endow it was the king *par excellence*—King Alfred,* " whose memory shall be always sweeter than honey." The erection of colleges, or houses set apart for students, and for their special accommodation, did not, however, commence until the middle of the thirteenth century—students having been previously lodged in various houses of the town. Merton College, Balliol College, and University College, were founded about the same time, between the years 1264 and 1300; Exeter College, Oriel College, Queen's College, and New College, between 1314 and 1386; Lincoln College, All Souls' College, and Magdalen College, between the years 1430 and 1460; Brazen Nose College, Corpus Christi College, and Christ Church, between the years 1507 and 1532; St. John's College, Trinity College, Jesus' College, and Wadham College, between the years 1555 and 1610; Pembroke College in 1620; and Worcester College in 1714. There are thus in Oxford nineteen Colleges, and five " Halls," which differ from the colleges only in some unessential forms and privileges. These halls are

---

* The curious little silver penny here engraved, from the rare original in the Bodleian Library, was coined by King Alfred in the city of Oxford. The letters exhibit all that irregularity which characterizes the early Saxon coinage of England, many of them being upside down, while the O looks more like an ornament than a letter. On one side is the king's name, ÆLFRED, and above and below it the name of the town, spelt ORSNAFORDA. The other side contains the name of the " moneyer," or person who struck the coin.

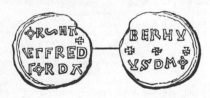

St. Alban, St. Edmund, St. Mary, New Inn Hall, and Magdalen Hall.*

The Bodleian Library owes its foundation to the munificence of Sir Thomas Bodley, by whom it was commenced at the close of the sixteenth century; it has been increased by the gifts and bequests of many other benefactors, and also by annual grants of the University. But its principal augmentation was by an act of parliament, which ordains that a copy of every new book shall be contributed by the publisher. The library was first opened to the public on the 8th of November, 1602. Its management is creditable to the liberality of the University; it is freely opened to all applicants who desire its use, and are properly introduced; and it has thus been made available to men of letters, not only of England, but of all other countries.†

---

* "The University is a corporate body, 'styled and to be styled by none other name than the Chancellor, Masters, and Scholars of the University of Oxford.' It is not, as is often supposed, a mere collection of colleges, nor do the colleges form part of the corporation, though its existence may be said to depend on a union of them. The business of the University is carried on in the two houses of Congregation and Convocation, which are made up of members of the University who have obtained the degree of M.A. The duty of the upper house, or Congregation, is principally to pass graces and dispensations, and grant degrees. The power of Convocation reaches to all the affairs of the University, though it can only entertain questions sent to it from the Hebdomadal Council, elected by Convocation, and so named from their meetings being held weekly; and its power is limited with regard to matters regarding the statutes of the University. Yet, while these houses are entrusted with such authority, their measures are subject to an absolute veto by the chancellor or vice-chancellor singly, and by the two proctors jointly. The chief officer of the University is the chancellor, who is elected for life, and holds, nominally at least, high powers; but, actually, these are delegated to the vice-chancellor. According to Oxford etiquette the chancellor, after his installation, never enters the University, except when he is called upon to receive or accompany any royal visitants. The office is now an honorary one, and is always conferred upon some eminent nobleman who is already a member of the University. The resident head of the University is the vice-chancellor, who is chosen in rotation from the heads of houses, and holds his appointment for four consecutive years. He is the chief executive officer of the University, and his position is one of much dignity as well as importance. His immediate deputies are the two proctors, also officers of importance. The other University officers are the professors, and such as are required for carrying out its educational purposes, with those necessary for the enforcement of discipline, and the management of its pecuniary concerns. The chief distinction in the members of the University is into those ' on the foundation,' and those 'not on the foundation;' the former consisting of the heads of houses, or persons holding college fellowships or scholarships, and receiving from them a certain income; those not on the foundation being, on the other hand, such as maintain themselves, while at the University, wholly at their own expense. The distinction is pointed out in the term applied officially to the two classes, the one being styled ' dependent,' the other ' independent' members. There is no difference in their privileges. All students who matriculate at the University are required to belong to some college."

† Sir Thomas Bodley was born at Exeter, in 1544-5, and is, therefore, one of the "worthies of Devon." While yet a child his family removed to Geneva, to avoid the persecutions of Queen Mary's reign; but on the accession of Elizabeth they returned to England and settled in London. The youth, who was to be hereafter the illustrious benefactor of Oxford, studied much under the great

The Radcliffe Library was founded by the eminent physician, Dr. Radcliffe, about the middle of the eighteenth century.*

The lovers of Art have always a special treat at Oxford : the "University Galleries"—erected by C. R. Cockerell, R.A.—contain treasures of rare interest and value—chiefly the drawings of Michael Angelo and Raffaelle, collected by Sir Thomas Lawrence; and the gift of the widow of Sir Francis Chantrey of the busts and monumental figures which were the original models of the accomplished sculptor.† This is a new building—and by no means the only one by which modern architecture preserves the supremacy of the city; while, from time to time, " restorations" are effected judiciously and liberally. Oxford to the Future will, therefore, be as grand and beautiful as it has been to the Past.

Of the once famous Beaumont Palace, built by Henry I., nothing now remains ; its site, however, is indicated by a new street, to which it gives a name. Of ancient structures—made venerable by time and holy by uses—Oxford has, of course, many besides her colleges ; the most interesting of these are the several parish churches, all of them containing venerable relics of times long gone by. Two or three days may be profitably spent in visiting these parish churches. The Church of St. Peter's in the East " lays claim to a higher antiquity than that of

---

early reformers of the Continent; at the age of fourteen or fifteen he was admitted at Magdalen College, becoming Master of Arts in 1566. In the meantime he was elected fellow of Merton College. In 1569 he served the office of Minor Proctor. In maturer age he was employed by Queen Elizabeth in various important offices at home and abroad. In 1597 he "set himself a task," says Camden, " which would have suited the character of a crowned head." He died in London, in 1612-13, in the sixty-eighth year of his age, not having lived to see his great project entirely carried out, but having seen " the whole design in a fair way to be fulfilled."

* Dr. John Radcliffe was born at Wakefield, in Yorkshire, in 1650, and was admitted a member of University College at the age of fifteen. Though by no means deficient in classical attainments, he "recommended himself more by ready wit and vivacity than by any extraordinary acquisitions in learning." In 1682, he took his doctor's degree in medicine, and in 1684 settled in London, in Bow Street, Covent Garden. He acquired wealth rapidly. Several singular anecdotes are recorded of him : when William III. consulted him, a short time before his death, he showed him his swelled legs and ankles, and asked what he thought of them ; " Why," replied the physician, " I would not have your majesty's two legs for your three kingdoms."

† " The Taylor Building," as it is generally styled, originated in a large bequest of Sir Robert Taylor, in 1788, " for the erecting a proper edifice, and for establishing therein a foundation for the teaching and improving the European languages." The legacy of Dr. Randolph was to the effect that " a building should be erected for the reception of the Pomfret statues, belonging to the University of Oxford." The two objects were combined in one edifice.

almost any other ecclesiastical edifice in England:" that of St. Mary the Virgin stands on the site of an ancient chapel of King Alfred; it contains a fine monument by Flaxman to the memory of Sir William Jones. In St. Michael's Church may be observed "seven or eight different periods of construction, though nearly the whole of it is of considerable antiquity," the tower being of the eleventh century. All Saints' Church dates no longer ago than 1708, but it occupies the site of one which flourished early in the twelfth century. Of St. Martin's, or Carfax, Church, dedicated to the famous Bishop of Tours, the foundation is of great antiquity—according to Anthony Wood, "beyond all record;" the old tower remains, and is said to have been lowered by command of Edward III., "because upon the complaints of the scholars, the townsmen would in time of combat with them retire there, as to their castle, and from thence gall and annoy them with arrows and stones." St. Peter le Baily was rebuilt in 1740, on the site of a church that is "beyond the reach of any records," and which fell down in 1726. Of St. Aldate's Church the foundation is very remote; it is supposed to have been British before the settlement of the Saxons or the Danes, the saint whose name it bears being a Briton, who lived about 450. Speed says it was founded or restored, probably rebuilt of stone, being previously of wood, in 1004. "The present fabric is composed of many different styles and dates, but is on the whole a venerable structure, deriving additional interest from the comparatively perfect state in which it remains, and the satisfactory account that has been preserved of most parts of the building." St. Ebbe's Church is dedicated to one of the Saxon saints, Ebba, daughter of Ethelfred, King of Northumberland, who died 685. It was rebuilt 1814, the only remaining part of the old building being the tower, which is of great antiquity, being built of rubble, very massive, and having no staircase. St. Mary Magdalen is said to have been erected before the Norman Conquest; but of the original church the only portion remaining at all perfect is a semicircular arch, with the zigzag mouldings which divided the nave from the chancel. The Church of St. Giles is among the most interesting churches of the city; its nave, chancel, and aisles are of fine architectural character. The Church of Holywell, that of St. Clement, and that of St. Thomas, though less striking and important than those previously referred to, have each their peculiar attractions, and, as will be readily supposed, the visitor to these interesting churches will be recompensed in many ways; they are crowded with "memorials," all of which speak eloquently of the past, and are suggestive of thoughts in keeping with the impressive solemnity of the venerable city. In several of the streets, also, there are singular relics of old houses.

But, as we have stated, to convey anything like a reasonable idea of the attractions of this great city would be to fill a volume of more than "goodly size." For this reason, also—because it would be impossible to do justice to the theme within limited space—we have given fewer illustrations than usual to this part of our work. The establishment of Messrs. J. H. and J. Parker will, however, supply all the information the tourist can need, upon every subject concerning which he will require knowledge.

We have but named the several colleges and public structures which have made, and make Oxford famous throughout the world; and give to it importance next to London, and interest second only to that of regal Windsor :—

> " Leaving us heirs to amplest heritages
> Of all the best thoughts of the greatest sages,
> And giving tongues unto the silent dead."

The visitor who goes through and about them will have days of enjoyment, not alone because of "old renown," and the memories associated with every step he treads, but as the great intellectual hereafter of the nation. The names that will occur to him are those of England's loftiest worthies : here, apart "from the bustle of resort," they girded on their armour to battle against ignorance, superstition, infidelity; here, great men of the past, who best "penn'd or uttered wisdom"—

> " Their spirits, troubled with tumultuous hope,
> Toil'd with futurity "—

drank deep of that holy fountain which gave them strength for life. Here the aristocracy have their full share of glory; but here the people

P

have just right to pride;—for high among the highest of their country's benefactors are, and ever have been, those who "achieved greatness" unaided and alone.* Rare delight, and ample food for thought, will he obtain who wanders through the streets—where Wolsey walked in triumph, and Shakspere housed in obscurity; where Laud and Wesley taught; where liberty inspired Hampden; where Wicliff planned for his country freedom of conscience, achieved and kept; where was the chief battle-field of that great contest which threw from England an intolerable burthen; whence the Reformation spread its light; and where perished the great THREE, who, by their deaths, " lit such a candle in England as, by God's grace, hath never since been put out."

Here have gathered, fraternized, or fought, great men—from the age of Alfred to the reign of Victoria: men hostile in politics, opposed in religion, often zealous over much, but earnest, faithful, and unflinching; however separated by opinion, all labouring in the great cause of human progress—differing only as " one star differeth from another star in glory "—

> " their names
> In Fame's eternal volume live for aye! "

But chiefly the visitor will pause and ponder beside the iron cross which, in the middle of a causeway, marks the spot where bigotry consumed three prelates—Cranmer, Latimer, and Ridley; and he will thence make pilgrimage to the " Martyrs' Memorial," which a grateful posterity raised as a perpetual reminder that by their heroic deaths they gave vigorous life to that purer faith, which, far above all other things—kings, principalities, and powers—makes England a land of liberty.† The " Martyrs'

---

* As old Fuller quaintly says, " It is not the least part of Oxford's happiness that a moiety of her founders were prelates who had an experimental knowledge of what belonged to the necessities and conveniences of scholars, and therefore have accommodated them accordingly; principally in providing them the patronage of many good benefices, whereby the fellows of those colleges are plentifully maintained after their leaving the University."

† It has been ascertained that the burning took place a few yards from the spot indicated by the iron cross in Broad Street. Mr. Parker, whose numerous publications have given to Oxford a renown akin to that which it derives from its University, has instituted a close research into the facts connected with this deeply interesting subject, the result of which has been to demonstrate that the fire was lit immediately opposite the gateway of Balliol College, over which at that time the master's lodgings were situated.

Memorial" was erected in 1841, and stands in St. Giles'. It is the work
of Messrs. Scott and Moffat; the statues of "The Great Three" having
been sculptured by Weekes. It is a fine work of Art, and worthy of the
city. It was resolved that, as "a general idea," the plan of the "Eleanor
Crosses" should be followed; and of the proffered designs, that of Messrs.
Scott and Moffat was selected. The first stone was laid on the 19th of
May, 1841—"the third centenary from that same month in which the
whole Bible in English—and that Bible Cranmer's—was first authorized
and appointed to be frequented and used in every parish church in
England." The purpose of the erection was to "testify a grateful
admiration of the pious martyrs who preferred the endurance of a most
cruel death to a sacrifice of principle." The following is the inscription
on the memorial :—

TO THE GLORY OF GOD,
AND IN GRATEFUL COMMEMORATION OF HIS SERVANTS,

THOMAS CRANMER,

NICHOLAS RIDLEY,

HUGH LATIMER,

PRELATES OF THE CHURCH OF ENGLAND,
WHO NEAR THIS SPOT
YIELDED THEIR BODIES TO BE BURNED,
BEARING WITNESS
TO THE SACRED TRUTHS
WHICH THEY HAD AFFIRMED AND MAINTAINED
AGAINST THE ERRORS OF THE CHURCH OF ROME,
AND REJOICING
THAT TO THEM IT WAS GIVEN
NOT ONLY TO BELIEVE IN CHRIST,
BUT ALSO TO SUFFER FOR HIS SAKE,
THIS MONUMENT
WAS ERECTED BY PUBLIC SUBSCRIPTION
IN THE YEAR OF OUR LORD
M DCCC XLI.

It is, indeed, impossible to exaggerate the claims to consideration of
stately and learned Oxford; such is its solemn and impressive grandeur,
that even in walking its streets laughter seems desecration, and haste
unnatural. Its very atmosphere is a lure to study; the "mossy vest
of time" is everywhere instructive; the crumblings of its ancient
walls tempt to thoughtful repose : even the waters of the Thames
are calmer here than elsewhere; while its many spires are closely,

and in true glory, linked in happy association with the memorable past :—

> " Amid th' august and never-dying light
> Of constellated spirits, who have gained
> A name in heaven by power of heavenly deeds."

In cloisters pale, in venerable halls, beneath stately porticoes, in silent galleries, in sombre quadrangles, by solemn altars, in neatly-trimmed gardens, in umbrageous walks,—the students think and work : its rare libraries, enriched by the wisdom of ages ; its large assemblages of Art-wonders ; its vast resources of science,—are their daily teachers. Lessons still more valuable are taught by tombs and tablets in their chapel courts ; by quaint windows, that let in "religious light ;" and by statues of pious founders and canonized saints, still speaking from niches they have occupied for centuries, giving emphasis to that memorable text, more impressive here than elsewhere, commingling piety with loyalty—" Fear God ! Honour the king !" Move where we will in this fair and holy city, we think and feel as of a higher and a better race than the world's ordinary denizens ; while

> " The attentive mind,
> By this harmonious action on her powers,
> Becomes herself harmonious."

We must resume our course ; and, making our way again to Folly Bridge, bid adieu to the fair city, quoting, as we enter our boat, the quaint and homely couplet of the old poet :—

> " He that hath Oxford seen, for beauty, grace,
> And healthinesse ne'er saw a better place."

FOLLY BRIDGE was anciently called Grand Pont. Its modern name (modern, although dating back 200 years) is derived from the following circumstance. The tower, which stood on the bridge, and had been so long known as " Friar Bacon's Study," being much dilapidated, the city leased it to a citizen named " Welcome," who repaired the lower part, and added to it a story, which appears in our engraving. This was called by the neighbours " Welcome's Folly ; " and thus the bridge acquired its new title of " Folly Bridge." The present bridge was built in 1825-7 : the architect was Ebenezer Perry. The first erection of a bridge on this spot is "beyond all authentic record;" but it is the opinion of our best antiquaries that here a bridge existed so early as the Saxon times.

We are below Folly Bridge, having passed through the lock, which, as we have intimated, terminates the right branch of the river : there is a fall here of about three feet. The bridge is seen in the annexed view. A tavern, situate on a sort of quay, and a block of warehouses, suffi-

FOLLY BRIDGE.

ciently mark the locality, but the latter unfortunately interrupts the passage into the street from the beautiful grounds of Christ Church. Christ Church Meadow, with its embowered "walks," has been famous for ages; it is the public promenade; and necessarily here, or at the quay alluded to, boats are always numerous, for this is almost the only place in the vicinity in which there are conveniences for boating.

As will be supposed, the boats are of all sorts and sizes, from the huge and elaborately decorated pleasure-barge, to the thin, light rowing boat, that looks like a line upon the water. We must pause awhile to give some description of these conveyances upon the great highway of the Thames, for, from Oxford, the river is of value for passage and traffic. The engraving exhibits two large boats, one of which (that nearest) was originally the barge of the Stationers' Company of London; * it was sold some years ago to Exeter College Club; the other belongs to the Oxford University Boat Club, and was built expressly for them, from the design of Mr. E. G. Bruton, a distinguished architect of the city. Both are of costly workmanship, the latter being somewhat sombre in style when we saw it, but now, as we learn, richly decorated with colour, and displaying the armorial bearings of all the colleges: the former still flaunting in

STATE BARGES.

scarlet and gold, although age and use have somewhat tarnished its brilliancy. These "vessels" serve as floating club-houses, and are well supplied with newspapers, periodicals, and writing materials, and have dressing-rooms for members. They are not calculated for making voyages, and are rarely released from their moorings.

---

* This barge used regularly to proceed as far as Lambeth Palace on the 9th of November, when the Lord Mayor took the oaths at Westminster, and it was the custom for the Archbishop to send out wine and refreshments to the members of the Company within it. The custom originated at the beginning of the last century, when a relation of Archbishop Tenison's, being the master of the Stationers' Company, thought it would be an acceptable compliment to call at the palace in full state. The archbishop sent out a pint of wine to each of the thirty-two gentlemen who came; and so originated the annual custom of calling there, and receiving sixteen bottles of wine from the palace—the Company returning the civility by the presentation of the various Almanacks they publish.

For smaller parties, of about twenty or thirty, Oxford is abundantly supplied with boats, such as that pictured in the accompanying engraving, and which are known by the name of "HOUSE-BOATS." The interior is a spacious room; while "the deck" affords opportunities for viewing the scenery and enjoying the pleasant breezes of the river—being furnished with benches for the convenience of such as prefer the

THE HOUSE-BOAT.

open air, and having a light iron balustrade around. These boats are leisurely towed up and down the river by horses, and are, in fact, large and broad barges, within which the "house" is constructed, with its windows and gaily painted or gilded panels. Seats surround the interior, and a table, generally bountifully spread, occupies the centre.

The traffic barges encountered in this locality are much narrower and more "shapely" than those to be met lower down; necessarily so, to pass through the locks * and weirs, and over parts where the stream is

---

* The old locks were much less navigable than those that have been constructed within the last thirty or forty years. In old times it was no uncommon case to be compelled to *drag* the barge through one of them, for which purpose a winch was used. These winches are still found occasionally on the banks of the river, and we thought it worth while to picture one of them. It is of rude construction, with four hands, the rope rolling round the centre as the boat progressed. We believe they are now entirely disused, and are only found in the immediate vicinage of deserted locks. They certainly add to the picturesque of the scenery, especially as they are usually found in quiet and retired nooks on the river's banks.

shallow.* The "barge-walk," or towing-path, is, as we have elsewhere
intimated, a path made by the tread of horses, sometimes at one side of
the river and sometimes at the other,† according as fewer obstructions
occur in the passage. The barges usually carry between thirty and
forty tons, and are generally navigated by two men and a boy, a man
on shore governing the horses; two horses are usually employed to draw
the barge up the stream, while one suffices for the downward voyage.
These barges are usually gaily painted, with a variety of colour and
ornament; beside the steersman is a little cabin, in which he sleeps or
cooks his food. The smoke of the fire is frequently seen ascending the
small iron funnel in the roof, and occasionally the wives of the bargemen
peep forth from the little room where they perform the duties of house-
wife; in some instances linen may be seen hanging to dry, in return
boats, in the space occupied by luggage. The latter is generally protected by a canvas awning drawn over a pole along the boat. At sharp
turns in the river, the towing-rope is passed round a post, and the man
manages the rudder so that when the turn is making the rope is slipped,
and the boat pulled as before. The Thames barge, such as we see it
near London, is very different: this we shall describe hereafter. The
tax paid by these barges in passing through a lock varies from 7s. to
10s., and there are nearly fifty such tolls to pay from London to the
entrance of the Thames and Severn Canal, including the weirs, for which
1s. 6d. or 2s. each is charged.

At the termination of Christ Church Meadow occurs the junction of
the Cherwell and the Thames: the river so dear to Alma Mater has its

---

* The larger barges, sometimes carrying ninety tons, are still used in the district above Oxford,
although rarely, and are called "West-country barges;" the next size are called "trows," and average
fifty or sixty tons; and the least, called "worsers," are of thirty, or rather less; these small boats
were first introduced from the Oxford Canal. The antiquity of the West-country barges appears by
the following extract from "The Voyage of Mr. John Eldred to Tripoli, &c., in 1583," in which he
says—"Having completed all our business at Basora, I and my companion, William Shales, embarked
in company with seventy barks, all laden with merchandize, every bark having fourteen men to drag
it up the river, like our West-country barges on the river Thames, and we were forty-four days in
going up against the stream to Bagdat." It also appears, from the Thames Acts, that the navigation
upwards from Oxford had existed from time immemorial, notwithstanding the great difficulties to be
encountered.

† When the towing-path changes its side (for instance, just this side of Abingdon, at the Poplars), a
ferry-boat conveys the horses to the opposite side.

source in the Arbury Hills, near Daventry, in Northamptonshire : it enters Oxfordshire near Claydon, flows past the town of Banbury, through Islip and several other villages, runs its course of about forty miles (but nowhere navigable), and on its arrival at Oxford surrounds an island appertaining to Magdalen College (where it is crossed by a bridge of great beauty), running beside "Addison's Walk," waters the banks of the Botanic Garden, passing by the side of Christ Church Meadow and its tree-embowered walks, and loses itself in the great river in

JUNCTION OF THE CHERWELL AND THE THAMES.

whose company it journeys to the sea. Our noble old topographer, Camden, takes the opportunity of this locality for an eloquent praise of the city in his "Britannia." He says, "Where Cherwell is confluent with Isis, and pleasant aits, or islets, lye dispersed by the sundry dissevering of waters, there the most famous University of Oxford sheweth itself aloft in a champion plaine. Oxford, I say, our most noble Athens, the muses-seate, and one of England's stays—nay, the sun, the eye, and the soul thereof, from whence religion, civility, and learning, are spread most plenteously into all parts of the realm. A fair and goodly city, whether a man respect the seemly beauty of private houses, or the stately

Q

magnificence of public buildings, together with the wholesome site or pleasant prospect thereof. Whence it came to pass that of this situation it was (as writers record) in ancient times called *Bellositum*." *

The current carries us gently to Iffley lock, distant about two miles— rich flat meadows on either side; but the landscape receiving grace and beauty from the hills of Shotover, Bagley Wood, and the slope on which stands the fine and very venerable church. The voyager, however, will often look back, for gradually, as we remove from the city, the view gains in interest; the lower houses disappear, while towers, and domes, and spires of churches and colleges rise above the trees, standing out in high relief, backed by the sky. IFFLEY is justly considered "one

IFFLEY CHURCH.

of the finest and most beautiful examples in England of an Anglo-Norman parochial church." It consists of a nave and chancel divided by a tower, forming, indeed, "an interesting school of ancient architecture," affording a series of examples of almost every age and style, and being "accepted" as high and pure "authority" by church architects.

The date of its foundation is probably as far back as the reign of King Stephen, when it was built by the monks of Kenilworth; authentic records prove it to have been in existence at the end of the twelfth

---

* Camden's "Britannia," as translated by Holland, 1637.

century; it has endured with very little change from that far-off period to this; and many of its elaborate and beautiful decorations, exterior as well as interior, are now as perfect as they were when they left the hands of the sculptor-artizan.

The churchyard contains an aged yew-tree—so aged that no stretch of fancy is required to believe it was planted when the first stone of the sacred structure was laid.* The rectory is in admirable keeping with the church, although of a much later date: also at the adjacent weir is a venerable mill, the successor of that which flourished here so far back as the time of the first Edward.

There are consequently few places on the banks of the Thames with so many attractions for the tourist, and its value is enhanced by immediate vicinage to Oxford. The river between Oxford and Iffley is very deep, and there are dangerous eddies, where bathers have been sacrificed. It is shallower towards Nuneham; from whence it is much deeper in its course to Abingdon.

Resuming our voyage, we pass through Sandford lock,—one of the most picturesque of the many combinations of lock, weir, and mill,—and keeping in view the mansion of Nuneham Courtenay, which crowns the summit of the nearest hill, our boat is soon moored at the pretty landing-place which the artist has pictured on the succeeding page.

The interest of these pretty and graceful cottages is enhanced by the knowledge that they exist for the comfort and convenience of pleasure-seekers. Nuneham Courtenay has long been a famous resort of Oxford students and Oxford citizens; and seldom does a summer-day go by without a pleasant " pic-nic" upon one of its slopes, amid its umbrageous woods, or within the graceful domicile, erected and furnished, literally, for " public accommodation."

---

* It has been generally stated that yew-trees were planted near churches to supply bow-staves for archers, at a time when archery was much practised, and enforced by law. But the custom is now believed to be much older, and to be a relic of paganism; these trees, being sacred to the dead from a very early period, and therefore especially venerated by the Druids, were adopted by the Romans and Saxons; hence " the church was brought to the tree, and not the tree to the church," for the eminent botanist, Decandolle, notes that the yews at Fountains and Crowhurst are 1200 years old, while that at Fortingale, in Scotland, is believed to be 1400 years of age.

There are few "homes" in England more auspiciously located; and happily it has ever been the wish of its successive lords to share, as widely as possible, with "their neighbours" the bounties which Nature and Art have here associated to bestow upon "house and lands." Long may the present estimable gentleman who owns the fair mansion and

COTTAGES AT NUNEHAM COURTENAY.

beautiful demesne find imitators in his successors! for the example of his illustrious predecessors has been continued during his honourable life. It is not too much to say that Mr. Harcourt and his lady * make annually

---

* Frances, Countess of Waldegrave, the charming and accomplished daughter of the late John Braham, Esq. Mr. Harcourt is the son of the late Archbishop of York, who succeeded to the Harcourt estates, and assumed the name of Harcourt—Vernon-Harcourt—on failure of the male line. At the Domesday survey, Nuneham Courtenay belonged to Richard de Curci; it afterwards passed to the Riparys or Redvers. Mary, youngest daughter of William de Redvers, Earl of Devon (surnamed de Vernon), married Robert de Courtenay, Baron of Okenhampton, in Devon. Probably by this marriage the manor of Nuneham passed into the family of Courtenay. The Pollards, of Devonshire, next succeeded to the possession; from them it passed to Audley, of the Court of Wards, called "the rich Audley." From him it passed to Robert Wright, Bishop of Lichfield, whose son, Calvert Wright, sold it to John Robinson, merchant of London, in the time of Oliver Cromwell. From the Robinsons it descended to David, Earl of Wemyss, who married Mary, daughter and co-heir of Sir John Robinson, Bart., of whom it was purchased, in the year 1710, by Simon, first Lord Harcourt, Lord High Chancellor of England. We have shown, in treating of Stanton Harcourt, that the seat of this ancient family was changed at the period of this purchase.

tens of thousands of persons happy, and hence derive their own chief happiness.

To describe the house and grounds of Nuneham Courtenay would demand a volume, and to do so is foreign to our purpose. The former is full of interesting portraits, with many fine pictures by the great old masters. The portraits are principally those of the personal friends of the Chancellor Harcourt—the poets of his time, who were his frequent guests and companions.

The house is, however, less conspicuous for architectural display than for domestic quiet. It is upon the grounds that taste and wealth have been expended; and they combine, in the happiest manner, beauty with grandeur. While Nature has been lavish of her bounties, Art has been employed everywhere to give them due effect. Open glades, solitary walks, graceful slopes, a spacious park, fruitful gardens—in short, all that can attract and charm in English scenery is here gathered; and it is scarcely too much to say that the demesne—taken altogether—is unsurpassed in England.*

From the heights there is an extensive view of the adjacent country for many miles around. Oxford, with its domes and spires, and the venerable church of Iffley, the woods of Blenheim, the town of Abingdon, the hills of Buckinghamshire, the green hill-downs of Berkshire, the historic Chilterns,† Faringdon Hill, with its dark crown of trees, which gives it the local name of "Faringdon Clump;" in short, on all

---

* In the grounds is a "new" church, built in a style semi-Greek, by no means agreeable or impressive. The old church was taken down by Simon Lord Harcourt, and the present structure erected in 1764 after a design of his own, which was slightly corrected by Stuart. "It affords a memorable instance of the taste of that age, of which it was the misfortune that those persons who were the most liberal and desirous to serve the church, and who, for their private virtues, were most worthy of praise, were precisely those who did the most mischief. The fault was that of the age, not of the individual." Happily, in our own times, a far better and holier spirit prevails: our new churches have generally all the advantages they can receive from Art, rightly directed and rightly applied.

† These hills are a chalky range, which cross Buckinghamshire, and reach from Tring in Hertfordshire to Henley in Oxfordshire. The district is crown land, and the steward is consequently an officer under the crown; but the position gives neither honour nor emolument, and is assigned to members of Parliament who wish to vacate their seats. In this way the stewardship has been granted to several members in one week; and the position is understood on all sides as a legal fiction, and one of the curiosities of our old parliamentary system.

sides are presented objects that add value to the fair demesne, while the winding Thames is ever present to refresh the eye that, withdrawn from distance, seeks the beauty that is more immediately at hand.

CARFAX CONDUIT.

On one of the slopes that ascend directly from the river stands the ancient and far-famed "CARFAX CONDUIT," which formerly stood as "a kind of central point" to the four principal streets of Oxford. Certain alterations requiring its removal, it was, with "most perfect propriety,"

presented to the Earl Harcourt. It was built, in 1610, by Otho
Nicholson,—a liberal and enterprising gentleman,—in order to supply
the city with pure water, brought from a hill above North Hinxsey; and
although the conduit is removed the pipes still remain, and afford a
partial supply, likely to be superseded by the new City Waterworks.
It is a square, decorated in accordance with the taste of the time
—mermaids, "holding combs and mirrors," and dragons, antelopes,
unicorns, being scattered about; while the Empress Maud is introduced
riding an ox over a ford—"in allusion to the name of the city." The
letters O. N., the initials of the founder, are conspicuous; while above
the centres of the four arches are the cardinal virtues—Justice,
Temperance, Fortitude, and Prudence.

It is, however, we repeat, from the spacious grounds of Nuneham that
the visitor will derive especial enjoyment :—

> " Society is all too rude
> To this delicious solitude;
> Where all the flowers and trees do close
> To weave the garland of repose,"—

so says one of the many tablets scattered lavishly about the park,
gardens, and walks; they were written " for the occasion," chiefly by
the poets Mason and Whitehead—poets famous in their day, and for a
day. The lines we quote, however, are borrowed from a loftier spirit—
Andrew Marvel : happily, as we have intimated, the sentiment is not
altogether adopted by the generous owner of these beauties, who
gives liberal ingress to all comers, to whom " society" seems ever
welcome, when it comes on holiday from thought and toil, and who has
learned from a hundred brave and honourable ancestors, that the surest
way to be happy is to make others happy.

The fine trees of Nuneham hang luxuriantly over the river—it is a
perfect wealth of foliage piled on the rising banks. This scenery continues until we reach the modern railway bridge, when, on the right
bank of the stream, Radley House is descried : another turn of the
river, past this demesne, and the spire of Abingdon comes in view.
Between Nuneham Courtenay and Abingdon the river winds so much,

that when we reach this ancient town we are nearly opposite to Oxford, distant about six miles.

About half a mile from Abingdon the Thames divides into two parts, the eastern portion leaving the main stream at right angles, and going to Culham Bridge, and the western going to Abingdon; the eastern part was the navigable stream from Oxford to London in the time of James I., and the old lock is still remaining, but blocked up. We have already quoted an extract from "The Chronicon" relating to the eastern part; and the following, relating to the western, occurs at the commencement of the volume. :—"Mons Abbendone ad septeutrionalem plagam Tamese fluvii, ubi prætermeat pontem Oxenefordis urbis situs est; a quo monasterio non longe posito idem nomen inditum."

Abingdon is one of the most ancient towns of the kingdom; it stands near the junction of the little river Ocke (which rises in the Vale of

DISTANT VIEW OF ABINGDON CHURCH.

White Horse)* with the Thames, and although now a place of small importance, has played a conspicuous part in many of the most stirring events of British history. A legendary tale thus describes its origin :—

* This vale takes its name from an enormous representation of a horse cut in the side of the chalk hills. This singular figure has existed there from time immemorial. It is rude in character; but, inasmuch as that character is precisely similar to the figures of horses on ancient British coins, it is believed to be equally ancient. It has long been the custom of the peasantry to clear it of weeds, and generally to restore it, at certain seasons of the year.

"At a time when the wretched pagan Hengist basely murdered 460 noblemen and barons at Stonhengest, or Stonehenge, Aben, a nobleman's son, escaped into a wood, on the south side of Oxfordshire, where, leading a most holy life, the inhabitants of the country flocking to him to hear the word of God, built him a dwelling-house and a chapel in honour of the Holy Virgin; but he, disliking their resort, stole away to Ireland, and from him the place where he dwelt is called Abingdon."* It is hardly necessary to state that this derivation is incorrect, and that the name is purely Anglo-Saxon. We give the legend as an example of the fanciful interpolations in early history by the elder chroniclers.

The old hospital at Abingdon is founded on the site of the monastery dedicated to the Holy Cross and St. Helena, by Cisa, sister of the king of the West Saxons, in the seventh century: this religious foundation having gone to decay, a hospital was erected in its place by a rich merchant, in the reign of Henry V., named Geoffry Barbour: in the reign of Henry VIII. this and other charitable institutions in connexion with the church were forfeited to the Crown; and the Abbot of Abingdon, being one of the first to acknowledge the king's supremacy, was rewarded for such subserviency by the gift of the Manor of Cumnor, and a pension of £200 a year for his life. Sir John Mason, in the reign of Edward VI., bestirred himself to restore the charity, and in the year 1553 it was re-endowed, and named Christ's Hospital. It then accommodated thirteen poor men and women; the number is now thirty-two.

The old almshouses partially surround the churchyard of Abingdon. They are provided with a covered cloister, leading to each door. Our engraving exhibits the central entrance, with the cupola above the old hall. Over this gate are a series of old paintings, all allusive to works of charity; and in the hall are many curious portraits of benefactors, the principal being the youthful Edward VI. holding a

---

* "Abingdone" (says Leland in his "Itinerary") "stands on the right side of the Isis, and was of very old time called Seukesham, since Abendune."

R

charter with the great seal appended, by which the hospital was
founded.    There is also a painting of the building of the bridges over
the Thames, which first gave Abingdon importance, as they occasioned
the high road from Gloucester to London to be turned through this

town.    Burford Bridge was
near the town, and Culham
Bridge about half a mile to
the east of it.    Before they
were erected, in 1416, the fords
here were very dangerous, and
the road turned to Wallingford
to avoid them.    The merchant
Barbour, feeling the importance of these bridges to the
town, gave one hundred marks
toward them;    and Leland
says three hundred men were
employed at once upon them
at the rate of a penny per
day; which Hearne the an-
tiquary observes was " an extraordinary price in these
times, when the best wheat

THE ALMSHOUSES AT ABINGDON.

was sold for twelvepence per quarter."    Another curious picture of
a local antiquity is painted on the exterior wall of the hospital, opposite
the Thames: it is a view of the cross which formerly stood in the town,
and was destroyed by Waller's army in May, 1644, in revenge for his
repulse at Newbridge.

Holy things are these almshouses—holy and beautiful records of the
thoughtful royal heart of one who, young in years, seemed aged in
wisdom and goodness.    We looked on them with more than common
interest, having heard of them in our childhood; they had been, indeed,
long associated with one of the happiest of our "memories."    In very
early life we knew a kind and beautiful French woman, who, in her full

soft voice—her French accent lingering round the vowels—told us a story of an inmate of one of those very cottages, which bound them by romance, as well as reality, to our heart.

Now this is her story :—During the reign of terror in France, one of the first lady-refugees who sought shelter in London we shall call Madame la Marquise de Riordeau. She had contrived to bring over to England a large sum in jewels and valuables as well as in money ; she was neither old nor young, but handsome, and a widow. Madame la Marquise was very proud, and very benevolent; she was proud even among the proud : she could not bear to abate one jot or tittle of her state,—she exacted a deference of word and manner from all around her, which acted as a perpetual restraint on her dearest and most intimate friends. She would have servants and liveries exactly as she had them when resident in Paris ; and yet she was perpetually receiving and relieving those less fortunate emigrants who had literally nothing, and many of whom on their first arrival were found fainting from hunger on the door-steps of our English homes.

Madame's hand never seemed weary of giving—it was outstretched continually and liberally ; people began to speculate as to what her income really was ; for to live and act *en prince,* as regarded personal expenditure, and at the same time to relieve the needy numbers who came to her for aid, required the produce of a golden mine. There were one or two of Madame's intimate friends as stately, but not as charitable,—and more wise than herself,—who remonstrated, and told her that in time she would be obliged either to give up her . domestic expenditure, or to "cease to do good." She told them somewhat hotly, and with an increased elevation of her superb head, that she could not forget the duty she owed her buried lord ; that while she bore his honoured name, she *must* maintain its dignity; and that as to giving, she could never see her countrymen in want, and not share with them the last crumb of bread she had in the world.

All her friends were thus discouraged from further counsel ; all save one—a little earnest, honest banker (bankers in those days *were* honest and of good repute) ; he placed before her in black and white the state of her affairs, telling her plainly that if she did not give less, or expend less, she would soon be ruined—be perfectly and entirely unable to do either the one or the other. More than once, when she urged that it was from respect to her husband's memory alone she maintained her state, the straightforward man of business told her she was self-deceived, that she herself delighted in the splendid show; that it was a source of intense gratification to her; that if it were not so, she would soon change her plan; that she imagined she was devoted to *two* duties, whereas it was simply a *fancy* and a duty; that if her love of her desolate and heart-broken countrymen were sincere, she would sacrifice her pomp to a stronger and more elevated feeling. Everybody wondered how the Englishman had mustered sufficient courage to speak in such a way to Madame, and still more wondered how or why she endured it—she, so haughty, so resolved, yet so generous, so warm-hearted, so sympathising.

The cry was still, "they come!"—emigrants swarmed everywhere! Madame felt herself overwhelmed. There were the footman, the groom of the chambers, the page—such a delicious imp! all embroidery, and satin, and curls, and perfume—so different from the boots and broadcloth of a modern "buttons,"—there were the companion and the *bon père*,— all that Madame had enjoyed in her own land—*except* the *income*. She was living, and causing others to live, upon her goods and chattels. The banker entreated her to *think*. Now, Madame encouraged feeling more than thinking; but it became evident to her friends that frequently and painfully thoughts would force themselves upon her. On one side was the expenditure necessary, she honestly believed, to do honour to her husband's memory as long as she bore his name;—and there were her fellow-emigrants! It was observed that the banker called more often upon Madame, and that Madame daily and hourly became more thoughtful. He was heard more than once, as he descended the stairs, muttering to himself, "Noble woman! noble woman!" Madame's *jour de fête* was at hand: numerous presents were prepared for her, and scores of emigrants whom she had succoured made ready their little gifts as tokens of their gratitude and love. On the eve of the day, both the banker and the *bon père* spent many hours with Madame, and when they left, she desired to remain alone during the remainder of the evening.

My friend remembered being taken by her mother that very evening to visit her beloved countrywoman; she also remembered being sorely disappointed at not seeing her—Madame was so lavish to her young visitors of caresses and *bon-bons*. Her mother promised to take her the next morning, that she might have the honour to present to Madame a bouquet of pure white lilies. Betimes in the morning, my old friend was up, hoping she might be the first to offer the lilies of France to her mother's countrywoman. How beautiful they looked! how delicious their perfume! how often her handsome nose was tipped with orange from the farina of the flowers! and how often her mamma scolded her in pure French and broken English, because she was stealing the fragrance from Madame's lilies! It was a beautiful morning towards the middle of June when they reached the corner of the street in which Madame resided; they saw a crowd on the pavement, and my friend remembered that she burst into tears, because even the milk-girl had brought a bouquet of lilies to Madame!—every third or fourth hand grasped a bunch of lilies; but as they drew nearer, they saw that dismay, astonishment, and disappointment were painted on every face!

Madame was gone! they should see her no more!—nobody would see her any more! She was gone for ever! She had left all she possessed in the world—except the smallest possible sum, which some said she would soon bury with herself in a convent—to be divided among the emigrants according to the judgment of the banker and the *bon père*.

Poor lady! she could resign, but not diminish, her pomp. She resolved to gild her husband's name even at the last with the refined gold of charity; and when she had no longer means to keep up state, and minister to those who needed, she made her choice, leaving "all her goods to feed the poor!" It made a great sensation at the time. Everything was sold—turned into gold; and the sum so realized was something fabulous—at all events, it saved hundreds from misery, and gave them the happy feeling that one of their own people had done this!

My friend grew from a child into a girl, and was married, and, soon after the birth of a daughter, went abroad with her husband, who was killed by an accident. She returned to England, and after the lapse of five or six years married again. Her second wedding tour was taken along the banks of the Thames,—there was so much she wanted to see in her own country,—Hampton Court, and Richmond, and Kew, and Windsor, and Runnymede, and Oxford; and King Edward's Almshouses were more talked about, and visited, and sketched then than they are now, for the continent at that time was closed against us. As they drove up to Abingdon, a funeral was in the very act of passing away from one of the dwellings; but it was not like the "removal" of the poor widow of an English tradesman. The coffin had neither name nor ornament, but it was covered with black velvet. There were no pallbearers, but it was lifted into a hearse, and two very old gentlemen—old, feeble men, each tottering, yet each supporting the other—brought a host of bewildering memories to my friend, for she could not tell whence they came, or who they belonged to. The old gentlemen in elaborate mourning cloaks, and scarfs, and hatbands, got into a mourning coach, and the hearse and its attendants disappeared among the trees. The windows of those usually calm almshouses were filled with aged faces, and all wore the expression of intense sorrow. Many were weeping bitterly. An aged woman stood at the door from which the coffin had been removed; she was dressed in well-worn mourning, and looked through floods of tears after the procession—so earnestly, that my friend asked if the departed was to be buried in the churchyard.

"No," she sobbed; "and that's one of our griefs. Not one of us who loved her so, and to whom she was as an angel, shall ever see a blade of grass, or a bud or blossom, on her grave: it would have been some consolation to know that her dust would mingle with ours, and that we should rise together: but she's gone as she came."

A few more words, and the good dame invited the strangers into the house. From nothing, poor soul, could she derive consolation except sympathy: and my friend's tears and smiles ever flowed or beamed with those who wept and those who smiled.

"There's no harm in telling the truth now;" said the woman; "and, indeed, I hope to see it on a tablet in the church some day; thank God, it's a beautiful truth to tell:—and though she *was* a Papist, there's no living soul more sorry for her this blessed day than our own parson. Poor dear lady! she would never go *inside* our church during service, but every summer Sunday, when the sun shone, and the dew was not heavy on the grass, I used to carry a high chair, and place it under the shadow of the ivy, close to the window that's nearest the pulpit, and she would throw her fair white shawl over her snowy cap, and making a trumpet of her hand so,—for latterly she became deaf,—sit with it to her ear; and not a word that passed from our good parson's lips escaped her."

"You call her a lady—and she was a Roman Catholic, I suppose?" observed my friend; "how was that?—This foundation is for the Protestant widows of decayed tradesmen."

"I am a Protestant widow," replied the woman, "and Madame lived chiefly with me. Mr. Gresham, the banker, who knew me and mine all our lives, got me the presentation, and here I have been more than twenty-eight years. One of those gentleman was Mr. Gresham, the other is a M. Mercier, *her clergy*—"

"And her name," exclaimed my friend, "was Riordeau?"

"I did not tell you—how did you know?" inquired the astonished woman.

The long past was soon explained; and then the woman told how that, finding she could not continue to keep up her state and exercise her benevolence, and not having sufficient courage to brave the appearance of changed fortunes, she sacrificed herself and gave up all she possessed, except the pittance we have mentioned, to relieve the distresses of her countrymen.

"Mr. Gresham, who managed all her affairs," continued our informant, "told me that a worthy person (he did not say lady) wished for country air and quiet, and would live with me for a month or two, until arrangements could be made to enable her to go into a convent. When she came—I know what ladies are, and could see she was no 'person'—I loved to tend her, and it was wonderful how, after a week or two, her heart opened, so that everything got into it—children and old people, flowers (how she *did* love them, especially violets and lilies), birds, animals. She would have nothing to do with the gentry, except that she wished me to sell those beautiful artificial flowers and embroideries she used to make; and as fast as the money came (and the gentry would give any price she pleased to ask) it went among the poor. If her purse was empty, her spirits sank directly; if it was full, no bird on a bush was ever happier. I heard nothing of the convent, though the gentleman she called her *bon père* used to come and see her every two or three months. After having been here five or six years, she permitted our parson to call on her, and, according to duty, I know, he offered to read or pray with her; and she told him haughtily she could do the one for herself, and the *bon père* attended to the other. Two or three years elapsed before he saw her again, and then they got on kindly together until the last. She never told any one who she was, or why she came here; she denied herself all earthly pomp and state, and all for charity. God bless her! Oh! how she loved these walls; she loved this little home, so mute and peaceful. She was as humble as a mole with the poor, but, dear lady, if any of the gentry came about her, she would put them away with a bend of her head, as if she was an empress. She sacrificed her all to charity. She had a great idea, I think, of going back to her own land, and thought her estates would be returned; I do not know; and when this illness came on her, she would pray that she might be permitted to see her country before she died. They will carry her there, I know, though I think her spirit, if it is permitted, will often wander about King Edward's Almshouses."

That is our old friend's story.

From Abingdon the Thames pursues its course with little to attract the tourist until we arrive at the ferry of Clifton, over which hangs a small hill, the summit of which is crowned by one of the most graceful and beautiful modern churches in England.

Before we visit it, however, let us pause awhile to enjoy the calm quiet of the scene; to examine the luxuriant water-plants, and listen to the music that issues from every " bush and bosky dell," and not unfrequently from the borders of the stream on which we glide.

The chorus of lively chirpings that greets our ear from the neighbouring reed-beds, proceeds from those little aquatic songsters, the Sedgewarbler (*Salicaria phragmites*), and the Reed-warbler (*Salicaria arundinacea*), two birds closely related in appearance and habits, and generally to be found in company in reedy spots by the water-side, uttering their varied chant, the programme of which comprises imitations of the notes of the swallow, lark, sparrow, and linnet, with some original bits of their own. We append a cut of the Reed-warbler—the larger bird of the two, with its curiously constructed and situated nest, suspended between three or four reed-stems above the water, formed of reeds and grass, wound round and interlaced with the supporting stems, and lined with a little wool, fine grass, and long hairs; it is made of considerable depth—a neces-

THE REED-WARBLER.

sary provision for the safety of the eggs or young, when it is considered that, from its suspended situation, their cradle is rocked by every breeze, and in a high wind the slender reeds that support it bow almost to the surface of the water; yet the mother bird has been seen to sit steadily in her nest when it was swinging and dipping with the violence of the wind-gusts, so as occasionally to be almost immersed in the water. This elegant little warbler is of somewhat sombre colouring, being brown above and buff beneath, with white throat, and is one of our summer visitants only,—remaining in this country from April to September, when it seeks a warmer latitude,—its insect food becoming very scant as winter approaches. Those who row up or down the Thames, or walk along its ever-pleasant banks, have, therefore, a source of enjoyment which inland dells and woods do not afford, for the notes of these birds, even if

" Sounds inharmonious in themselves and harsh,"

8

give exceeding pleasure when in keeping with the character of the scene, and in harmony with those "gentler solitudes" which create tranquil joy—

> " Nor rural sights alone, but rural sounds,
> Exhilarate the spirit, and restore
> The tone of languid nature."

The common river Crayfish (*Astacus fluviatilis*), which abounds in the Thames (and "its tributaries") for the greater part of the course, is

THE CRAYFISH.

frequently brought to market as an article of food, but is not held in much esteem. In general appearance it greatly resembles a small lobster, but on comparing the two together considerable difference in structure will be observed, the body of the crayfish being flatter than that of the lobster, and the claws being rougher, and of a distinct form. The colour of this animal is a dull, dark, greenish grey, and its usual length about three or four inches. The principal food of the crayfish consists of aquatic shell-fish, the grubs of insects, and sometimes even of such small fish as come within their reach. The following amusing and graphic account of the habits of this species in confinement was communicated by Mr. Ball, a naturalist of Dublin, to Professor Bell, from whose work on "British Crustacea" we quote it :—"I once had a domesticated crayfish (*Astacus fluviatilis*), which I kept in a glass pan, in water not more than an inch and a half deep—previous experiments having shown that in deeper water, probably for want of sufficient aeration, this animal would not live long. By degrees my prisoner became very bold, and when I held my fingers at the edge of the vessel he assailed them with promptness and energy. About a year after I had him I perceived, as I thought, a second crayfish with him; on examination I found it to be his old coat, which he had left in a most perfect state. My friend had now lost his heroism, and fluttered about in the greatest agitation.

He was quite soft, and every time I entered the room, during the next two days, he exhibited the wildest terror. On the third he appeared to gain confidence, and ventured to use his nippers, though with some timidity, and he was not yet quite so hard as he had been. In about a week, however, he became bolder than ever; his weapons were sharper, and he appeared stronger, and a nip from him was no joke. He lived in all about two years, during which time his food was a very few worms, at very uncertain times; perhaps he did not get fifty altogether. I presume some person, presuming to poach in his pond, was pinched by him, and plucked him forth, and so, falling, he came by his death." During our visit to Oxford, a thoughtful friend furnished the breakfast-table with the crayfish, which is there considered a luxury "in season"— the season being the autumn of the year. Although frequently eaten on the Continent, it is but seldom used in England, even as the garnish-ing of a dish. Like the lobster, it is dark— almost black—when alive, but becomes red when boiled. In several parts of the river, and especially in the neighbourhood of Binsey, above Oxford, the fish is obtained in large quantities; these are caught in traps resembling the common eel-traps, but much smaller; they are formed of common willow-wands, and are baited with animal matter, or with dead fish.

FLOWERING RUSH.

We were gratified by finding in great profusion near Abingdon that most elegant aquatic, the Flowering Rush (*Butomus umbellatus*), clumps of which were constantly occurring where the water was shallow, either at the river-side, or in spots where the ground approached the surface in mid-stream. It is a lordly plant, with its graceful stem rising from the water some three or four feet, bearing on its head a crown of purple and white flowers—a "bunch" of considerable size. The long grassy leaves, which diverge in sweeping curves from its foot, add greatly to its beauty. Those who have seen this charming plant will agree with the eulogium of quaint old Gerard, who, describing it in his Herbal, saith :—" The Water Gladiole, or Grassie Rush, is of all others the fairest and most pleasant to behold, and serveth very well for the decking and trimming up of houses, because of the beautie and braverie thereof." It is by no means common to all the banks along the Thames. We voyaged many miles on several occasions, and sought for it in vain, finding it in great luxuriance in the river Tame, between Dorchester and the junction. It resembles, however, so nearly the common rush when not in blossom, that the unscientific searcher might easily pass it by without recognition.

It is singular that while so many efforts have been made to transfer to the greenhouse and garden the exotics—weeds—of foreign countries, we have so much neglected the wild graces which await, at our own doors, that removal for culture which expands and extends beauty.

IVY-LEAVED SNAPDRAGON.

Even in the miniature lakes which so often refresh an " elegant demesne," or in the pools that so frequently act as drains to a lawn or plantation, and are made " ornamental," that the eye may be gratified by converting a blot into a grace, we too generally observe that Nature is left to plant as she pleases, while a little aid brought to her from one of her rich stores of fertility and beauty, might essentially add to its other attractions.

The walls and woodwork of the old locks are beautifully decorated with groups of graceful plants that would altogether form choice studies for the Pre-Raphaelite painter. Perhaps the most elegant of these is the Ivy-leafed Snapdragon (*Linaria cymbalaria*), a pendent plant, with glossy, deep green, ivy-like leaves, and quaintly formed flowers of violet colour, with yellow throat. It appears this is not strictly an indigenous plant, but that it was originally introduced from Italy into our gardens, from which it has escaped and naturalised itself through the country, having now become as thoroughly English as any family that came in at the Conquest. From Oxford to Teddington we are continually meeting with the flowery festoons of this pretty plant, wherever old stonework is found in proximity to the water : we may suppose seeds of it have, in old times, escaped from some Oxford garden washed by the Thames, and, having been carried downwards by the stream, were deposited in convenient resting-places along the river's course. This will account for the abundance of the plant on the line of the Thames, while in most other districts it is hardly ever met with.

It will be obvious that from these water-plants the designer of ornament may obtain very valuable lessons ; it is indeed surprising that as yet they have been but little resorted to for the purpose of the manufacturer, or of those artists to whom he gives special employment. He will find within the range of any single mile on the upper Thames a number of valuable suggestions, any one of which would be a "fortunate thought,"—for it would have the value of novelty, inasmuch as subjects to be obtained there have been hitherto made so little available.

On the floating leaves of the water-plants, or among the moist herbage of the river-side, we constantly find a curious little shell—the Amber-shell (*Succinea amphibia*)—tenanted by an odd-looking little creature of amphibious habits, who, though born in the water, and passing much of his existence there, has the faculty of leaving that element at pleasure, and wandering to considerable distances from it

AMBER-SHELL.

without injury : we observed it sometimes high up on the stems of plants, quite removed from the water. The shell is very fragile and transparent, of a clear amber tint, whence its name of "Amber-shell." Many of the fresh-water shells, of which a great number of species inhabit the Thames, are of elegant forms ; and the habits of the animals that occupy them render them extremely interesting objects for the aquarium, where their history may be studied to great advantage; moreover, a collection of these shells would make a pretty addition to the cabinet.

Before we reach the little church of CLIFTON HAMPTON, we pass the village of Sutton Courtenay and Culham—the former with a modern, the latter with an old church; both are towered and embattled, and have a picturesque effect. They are situated about two miles from Abingdon, the river flowing the whole way through meadows of the richest luxuriance, their banks covered with wild flowers. A mile beyond this, the railway crosses the river at the village of Appleford.

CLIFTON HAMPTON CHURCH, AND FERRY.

No part of England can display more secluded pastoral scenery than is here met with; the utmost abundance seems to crown every orchard and garden. The county is agreeably diversified with wood and water; the banks of the river rise to a considerable elevation, and upon their summits many graves of the early Roman and Saxon settlers have been discovered. At Long Whittenham, close by,—a quiet village embosomed in trees,—some fine Anglo-Saxon jewels have been exhumed.* The

* The hill above Long Whittenham has earthworks of an early kind upon it, believed to be the work of the Romans. It is certain that these early conquerors of Britain were located here, inasmuch as

scenery is purely pastoral, but is relieved by gently undulating hills. Upon one of the boldest stands the new church of Clifton—for it is a new church, although externally and internally the architect has followed the best models of the best periods of church architecture : it occupies the site of the ancient structure; indeed, the foundations, and some portions of the walls, have been preserved. It is a most attractive and graceful object seen from the river, and will bear the closest examination, for every part of it has been confided to the care of a competent artist; and all its appurtenances are as perfect as Art can make them. The village, too, is neat, well-ordered, and evidently prosperous. Over the whole district there is evidence of wise and generous superintendence; the clergyman is, we believe, the squire, and it is obvious that the temporal as well as the spiritual wants of the district have a generous and considerate minister.* A handsome LICH-GATE of carved oak has been placed at the entrance

LICH-GATE, CLIFTON.

of the churchyard, adding much to the picturesque beauty of the scene. From the tower of this church, raised as it is so much above the surrounding scenery, we obtain a noble view of now distant Oxford; and here, especially, we are impelled to recall the lines of the poet Warton :—

" Ye fretted pinnacles, ye fanes sublime,
Ye towers that wear the mossy vest of time;

many antiquities, unmistakeably Roman, have been found in the immediate vicinity, and several of their burial-places discovered, from which vases, coins, &c., were obtained.
* " A small church, of mixed styles, beautifully situated on a cliff, at a bend of the river Thames. It has been restored under the direction of Mr. Scott, the architect, in extremely good taste, by the present patron, Mr. Henry Hucks Gibbs, in pursuance of the wishes of his father, the late Mr. George Henry Gibbs, with whom the design of restoring the church originated, and who left by will a considerable sum for this object." (" Guide to the Architectural Antiquities in the neighbourhood of Oxford." Parker.)

> Ye massy piles of old munificence,
> At once the pride of learning and defence ;
> Ye cloisters pale, that, length'ning to the sight,
> To contemplation step by step invite :
> Ye high-arch'd walks, where oft the whispers clear
> Of harps unseen have swept the poet's ear ;
> Ye temples dim, where pious duty pays
> Her holy hymns of ever-echoing praise ;
> Lo ! your loved Isis, from the bord'ring vale,
> With all a mother's fondness bids you hail !
> Hail ! Oxford, hail ! "

After passing Clifton the hills to the right are somewhat bold in character, and we see more distinctly the picturesque formation of the Long Whittenham range : they are round, chalky hills, with clumps of trees on their summits. We now pass by Little Whittenham Church, embosomed in luxurious trees, and the fine, woody hills beside Day's lock, where the river makes a circuit, passing, as usual, between low and luxuriant banks on either side, where the hay harvest is ever abundant, but where the husbandman will rarely look for any other crop, inasmuch as the land is covered with water in winter floods.* We approach Wallingford, but within a mile or two of this town the voyager will pause at a narrow bridge, about twenty feet in length, which crosses a poor and somewhat turgid stream. The tourist would row by it unnoticed, as of "no account," but that he knows this to be the famous river Tame, and that here it joins the Thames—or, if the fanciful will have it so, " the Isis ;" this being the marriage-bed of the two famous rivers, who hence forward become one ; for from this spot, according to the poet,—

> " Straight Tamisis stream,
> Proud of the late addition to its name,
> Flows briskly on, ambitious now to pay
> A larger tribute to the sovereign sea."

Although most of the poets have described " Tame " as of the rougher,

---

* " Tradition has given to this place (Little Whittenham) an intellectual importance which heightens, at least, if it does not transcend, its native beauties. Here an oak had long flourished—and hard was his heart who suffered the axe to strike it—beneath whose shade Prior is said to have composed his poem of ' Henry and Emma.' The poet has described this spot as the scene of his interesting story, and such a tree might surely have been spared for the sake of its traditionary character, when the general ravage was made, by its last possessor, on the sylvan beauties of the place." (Boydell, 1794).

and "Isis" as of the gentler sex, they are not all of one mind on this subject. Camden celebrates the Tame as a female—

> " Now Tame had caught the wish'd-for social flame
> In prospect, as *she* down the mountains came."

With Drayton, Tame is the bridegroom—

> " As we have told how Tame holds on *his* even course,
> Return we to report how Isis from *her* source
> Comes tripping with delight."

He calls her also—"the mother of great Thames." Pope, in allusion to the Thames, makes reference to—

> " The famed authors of his ancient name,
> The winding Isis and the fruitful Thame."

And Warton,—

> " As the smooth surface of the dimpled flood
> The silver-slipper'd virgin lightly trod."

Spenser has this passage :—

> " Him before thee went, as best became
> His ancient *parents*, namely, the ancient Thame
> But much more aged was his wife than he,
> The Ouse, whom men do Isis rightly name."

The Tame rises in the eastern part of the Chiltern Hills, in Buckinghamshire, between the town of Aylesbury and the village of Querendon ; and after winding through the golden vale of Aylesbury, enters the county of Oxford, and soon refreshes the town to which it has given a name. Hence its course is to the very ancient city of Dorchester, from whence by slow progress—and by no means "running to the embraces" of the fair Isis—it paces about two miles to join the Thames beneath the small wooden bridge we have pictured; its whole course, from its rise to its fall, being about thirty-nine miles. Fancy may be permitted full scope and free indulgence while "the voyager" passes underneath the plain rustic bridge that marks the interesting locality. He has visited the scarcely perceptible source of the great river—already seen it fertilize and enrich cities, towns, and villages; but here he will naturally consider in prospect the mighty gifts it presents to the world, between this com-

T

paratively insignificant confluence of "two waters," and the illimitable
sea to which they are together hastening :—

> " Let fancy lead, from Trewsbury mead,
>     With hazel fringed, and copse-wood deep ;
> Where, scarcely seen, through brilliant green,
>     Thy infant waters softly creep,
> To where the wide-expanding Nore
> Beholds thee, with tumultuous roar,
>     Conclude thy devious race ;
> And rush, with Medway's confluent wave,
> To seek, where mightier billows rave,
>     Thy giant Sire's embrace."

The portion of land at the upper part of the Tame, near Dorchester,
is intrenched across to the Thames, and by this means the passages of
both rivers might be commanded.   This ancient military work has been
attributed to the Romans, and by some writers to the Ancient Britons.
The works consist of a dyke, into which the rivers might be turned, and
high embankments are on either side, which are now known as " DYKE
HILLS."   Dr. Plot conjectures that they may be part of the fortifications
still remaining at Long Whittenham, to which we have already directed

DYKE HILLS, DORCHESTER.

attention.   They are similar in structure to the earthwork known as
Grimsdyke, nearer Wallingford; the banks are twenty feet in length;
they illustrate, therefore, the early history of Britain.

A row up the Tame to visit Dorchester will be the duty of those who
have leisure, and desire to examine the several points of interest on or
near our great British river.   He will be amply repaid for a brief delay.
Although the " city " has fallen to the grade of a poor village, the Roman

amphitheatre is an earth-mound, and the cathedral half a ruin, history and tradition supply unquestionable proofs of its former magnificence—proofs which time has been unable altogether to obliterate. On its site was a Roman station of large extent and importance; and the place was famous during the ages that immediately followed. But its high and palmy state was in the seventh century, when Birinus, who was sent from Rome to convert the West Saxons, here first preached to them the Gospel of our Lord. The missionary had baptized Cynegil, the king; and at the ceremony Oswald, King of Northumberland, attended as god-sib; when the two sovereigns, according to Bede (who calls it Civitas Dorcinia), gave the bishop this town for the foundation of an episcopal see in honour of the occasion. The see was for a long period of "gigantic dimensions," comprising the two large kingdoms of the West Saxons and Mercians. Twenty bishops here sate in "papal grandeur;" and, although seven bishoprics were afterwards "taken out of it," the see continued to be the largest in England, until about the year 1086, when Remigius removed it to Lincoln. At the Conquest, however, the town had dwindled; it was "small and ill-peopled," although "the majesty of the church was great, either by the antiquity of the building, or the diligence of such as had lately repaired it."

The old Abbey Church of Dorchester is remarkable for its extreme length, and for some peculiar architectural features. It is now much too large for the wants of the parish, and was, a few years ago, allowed to fall into a lamentable state of decay, from which it has been in a great degree rescued by a general subscription, under the auspices of the Oxford Architectural Society. The portions of Norman architecture now remaining are striking in their solidity and beauty; but the most remarkable feature in the church is the celebrated "Jesse window," which lights the north side of the chancel. At the base lies the figure of Jesse, from whose body rises the tree of the Saviour's genealogy; its stem forms the great centre mullion, the branches from it crossing the other mullions, and forming the intersecting tracery of the window; they are all richly sculptured with foliation, and a figure of one of the tribe of Jesse appears at each intersection. The statue of the Virgin with the Saviour, which once crowned the whole, has been destroyed. The sedilia and piscina opposite this window are highly enriched, and have a peculiarly brilliant effect from the insertion of painted glass

THE FONT, DORCHESTER.

beneath the beautiful canopies that shadow them. The other most noticeable feature in the church is the ancient FONT we here engrave. The upper portion is Norman; but the shaft is much more recent, probably a work of the fifteenth century. The bowl is circular, and exhibits figures of apostles seated in eleven semicircular arches; above and below them is a rich border of foliage. The whole of this portion of the font is of lead, and the rarity of such early work in this material makes this example precious in the eye of the antiquary. It is, moreover, a curious work of Art, inasmuch as it presents the peculiar features which are strongly characteristic of the Byzantine taste, founded on the decadence of the great Roman empire in the East. The richness of detail and abundance of decoration visible in the Norman style may be referred to this influence on European Art. On the whole, perhaps, there are few localities of the kingdom more interesting than those which surround Dorchester: it should be visited by all tourists who traverse this part of the Thames.

From the junction to Wallingford the "united streams"—

> "With friendly and with equal pace they go,
> And in their clear meanderings wandering slow "—

soon pass under the bridge of Shillingford, from whence the tourist may walk some two or three miles to offer homage at that shrine in the grand old church of Ewelme, which contains the dust of Sir Thomas Chaucer, the poet's first-born son.

Shillingford is an antiquated village, with many large farm-houses of red brick and timber, warmly thatched, and with an air of picturesque comfort about them thoroughly characteristic of English rural life of "the better sort." Indeed, this portion of the Thames is as completely rural and unsophisticated as any part of England. The character of the scenery changes completely at the bridge, and we see again the rich level meadows, with the square tower of Bensington Church, and the quiet village of farms and cottages beside it.* A mile further, and we reach another lock, close to the town of Wallingford, which is nearly hidden by the luxurious growth of trees in surrounding meadows.

WALLINGFORD was famous in its day : the British, the Romans, the Saxons, and the Danes, had each and all their settlements there ; it was a borough in the time of the Confessor, and had a mint before the Conquest.† Traces of its ancient walls and castle may still be obtained by the patient searcher ; the latter is described by old historians as "impregnable," but "Time, the destroyer," has effectually removed all its

---

* "West of the church is a bank and trench, of a square form : the north side still retains somewhat of its original appearance ; to the west and south they are readily traced, but to the east it requires a minute examination to discern them. Doctor Plot mentions an angle of King Offa's palace near the church, which must have stood on this spot, where bones of men and horses, as well as old spurs and military weapons, have been dug up. This, being a frontier town, often changed its masters in the contests between the West Saxons and the Mercians. Offa, king of the latter, considering it to be politically necessary to his government that his enemies should hold no place on that side of the Thames, at length possessed himself of it, and finally united it to his own dominions." (Boydell, 1794.)

† We engrave here the silver penny struck at Wallingford by Edward the Confessor. It is a type of the utmost rarity, and is preserved with other scarce Saxon coins in the Bodleian Library. By comparing it with the Oxford coin of Alfred, which we have also engraved, the progressive improvement in the English mintage will be apparent— a neater and truer character prevails in those of the Confessor, indicative of more peaceful times. Indeed, the coinage of England tells in some degree the history of the country. The rude monies of the Heptarchy seem only fitted for barbaric need ; and it is not until the amalgamation of the

Saxon kingdom under one sovereign that a great improvement takes place. The rude heads of early kings on our coins seem scarcely human ; but this of Edward the Confessor exhibits truthful features. In the troublous times which succeeded the death of the Norman Conqueror, the national currency lapsed into its old barbarism, and it was not till the era of Edward I. that it recovered itself. We must refer to the Reading penny, engraved under our notice of that town, as an example, and to the note appended, for a continuation of these remarks.

strength except a few indications, which consist of rubble and stones. In the time of Leland it was "sore in ruines, and for the most part defaced." Camden described it as "environed with a double wall and a double ditch; the citadel standing in the middle on a high artificial hill." It must have been of immense size and strength, and was perhaps, as it was said to have been, "impregnable" before

> " Villanous saltpetre had been dug
> Out of the bowels of the harmless earth."

During the civil wars, when King Stephen and the Empress Maud contended for England, the lady was here besieged by her enemy; but all assaults were vain, until famine came to the aid of the besiegers. Her son, afterwards Henry II., arrived at the seat of war just in time to save his heroic mother; but a conference took place on the river's bank,

WALLINGFORD.

when it was resolved that Stephen should possess the crown during his life, and that Henry should succeed him. Of its "fourteen parish churches" Wallingford retains only three, one of which was "erected at the sole expense of that eminent lawyer and learned judge, Sir William Blackstone." Notwithstanding its comparative decadence, however, Wallingford has the aspect of a cheerful and thriving town.* The approach to it is particularly pleasing—the plainer features of the place

---

* Camden mentions his having frequently visited it in his academic character, and that it then retained a considerable portion of its ancient grandeur.

being happily hidden by a profusion of foliage on the noble trees that line the banks of the stream.

Soon after passing under its bridge we reach the little Norman church of Crowmarsh, and about a mile further, at a lock known as "Chamber Hole," we observe Newnham-Murrell, with an old church on one side of the river, and Winterbrook on the other. A short distance below is Mongewell, a fair mansion, with rich gardens, lawn, and plantations. A small modern Gothic church is erected here. We soon reach Cholsey, where an older church awaits the antiquarian tourist. At Little Stoke, some distance onward, we are again met by a railway-bridge, and notice the high chalk down rising above it. Passing the bridge, the church of Moulsford appears embosomed in trees. Nearly opposite is South Stoke, and, a short distance further, at Cleeve Hill lock, we arrive in view of the Streatly hills, at the foot of which are the twin villages of Streatly and Goring—the former in Berkshire, the latter in Oxfordshire, joined by a long and picturesque bridge, from which a fine view is commanded of the river, with its graceful windings and its pretty "aits" above and below, and especially between the bridge and the lock, distant some half a mile apart. These villages of course contain churches; that of Goring, however, is by far the most interesting; it stands close to the water-side, and beside it are a graceful cottage and a busy mill.*

The church is of Norman foundation, but the tower only preserves the peculiar features of that style. It is very massive in construction, with round-headed windows, divided into two lights by a central pillar; a winding stair to the belfry is formed in a small round tower, appended

---

* Nearly a century has passed since the village of Goring was "famous" " on account of the virtues " of a medicinal spring in its immediate vicinity: it was called " Spring-well," and was situated on the margin of the Thames. It is particularly mentioned by Dr. Plot (in the reign of Charles II.) as celebrated for its efficacy in the cure of cutaneous disorders, and also for ulcers and sore eyes. Much more recently, however, it was considered " a valuable specific;" for its then owner, Richard Lybbe, Esq., published several advertisements, wherein he states " that other water had been substituted and sold for that of Goring spring;" and he informs the public that, to prevent such deception, every bottle or vessel hereafter filled with the genuine water shall be sealed with his arms, of which he gives a particular description ; and that the persons appointed by him to seal and deliver it shall demand nothing for the water, but a penny a quart for attendance and impress of his arms. The value of Spring-well, if it ever had any, has long ceased to be appreciated. The spring now gives its supply to the Thames without fee or reward, and the " penny stamp " is a tradition of the past.

to the north side of this square tower.  The body of the church is much
more modern—a circumstance by no means uncommon in English ecclesiastical architecture.  It has been recently restored in very good taste ;
but while it gratifies the ecclesiologist, it offers few antique features on
which the architectural student can dwell.

GORING CHURCH.

The houses at Goring are excellent examples of those " peasant
homes " which nowhere exist more happily than in our own favoured
isle.  The cottages have that look of comfort so essentially English, and
their little gardens are trim and neat.  Its opposite village has equal
claims to attention, and is more romantically situated on the hill-side.
The scenery is the most striking we have yet met in our downward
course.

Resuming our voyage, we leave to the right, on the slope of one of the
hills which now " accompany " us for several miles, the beautiful mansion
of Basildon.  Hence, until we arrive at the villages of Pangbourne and
Whitchurch, the Thames assumes a new character—high hills, richly
clad in foliage, suspend over us on either side, now and then opening,

occasionally bare, and frequently fringing the banks of the stream with the branches of the best varieties of British trees. The villages of Pangbourne and Whitchurch, like those of Streatly and Goring, are united by a bridge, a little above which are the lock and weir; the scenery all about this neighbourhood is exceedingly interesting and beautiful—the stream is broad, and the wood-crowned heights that arise on either side add to the view that variety which is especially welcome after so much that is tame and flat, with which the upper Thames so continually supplies us. These low lands, however, have their value, not alone as suggestive of fertility—they abound in the picturesque; of such scenes the poet has happily said—

> " Everywhere
> Nature is lovely : on the mountain height,
> Or where the embosom'd mountain glen displays
> Secure sublimity, or where around
> The undulated surface gently slopes
> With mingled hill and valley ;—everywhere
> Nature is lovely ; even in scenes like these,
> Where not a hillock breaks the unvaried plain,
> The eye may find new charms that seeks delight."

The Thames at Pangbourne—above and below it—is, and has long been, a favourite resort of the angler; its sides "hereabouts" are full of water-lilies, and those other aquatic plants which afford the fish shelter and protection; they are especially such as are loved by the perch—and perch-fishing in this vicinity is perhaps as good as it is upon any part of the bountiful river. The Perch is "one of the most beautiful of our fresh-water fish, and when in good condition its colours are brilliant and striking;" according to Yarrell—from whom this passage is borrowed— "the upper part of the body is a rich greenish brown, passing into golden yellowish white below; the sides ornamented with from five to seven dark transverse bands; the irides golden yellow; the fins brown, spotted with black." The scales are rough, hard, and not easily detached; as the angler well knows, the fins are so sharp that those who handle them must be careful of their touch. The fin of the perch is, indeed, a weapon of defence, and is said to protect it against the assaults even of the pike; certain it is that the perch will live and thrive in a pond or lake with pike, while all its other denizens gradually vanish before the tax which the water-wolf perpetually levies.  The perch has been emphatically called "a bold fish :" he is unquestionably, as old Izaak styles him, "a bold biting fish." If one be caught another is pretty sure to follow; and as they usually "march in troops," and are seldom scared by any noise or bustle in the water, the angler, when he encounters a "school" of them, is likely to fill his basket before his prey discovers what he is about.  Again, to quote from Izaak Walton, "they are like the wicked of the world, not afraid, though their fellows and companions perish in their sight."  The perch is fished for in the Thames usually with a "paternoster ;" that is to say, a gut or hair line of about four feet long is mounted on the ordinary running line, and this gut or hair line contains three hooks, mounted on pigs' bristles, placed at intervals a foot or eighteen inches apart, so that different depths are attained.  The usual bait is the minnow, but the fish will eagerly take the brandling, or dew-worm.  The perch is not often taken in the Thames above a pound weight, or above eight inches in length.  They grow, however, to a much larger size, frequently weighing four or five pounds, and occasionally so large as eight or nine pounds.  They breed rapidly : Yarrell states that a perch of half a pound weight has been found to contain 280,000 ova.  Like the pike, it is a fish of prey, and has great tenacity of life; perch have been kept for twenty-four hours out of water without peril to life.  Next to the trout, the pike, and the eel, the perch is perhaps the best fish for the table, its flesh being hard and sound.

The Gudgeon (*Gobio fluviatilis*) is commonly found where the perch luxuriates ; although associates, however, they are by no means friends— on the contrary, the one is the prey of the other.  The gudgeon abounds in the Thames, and to catch them is a favourite sport of the angler—and a pleasant sport it undoubtedly is, inasmuch as it is usually pursued in hot weather, when there is little disposition to exertion, and repose, amounting to indolence, becomes pleasure for a season.  It is in this pursuit especially "the punt" is used, and it is frequent in June and July to see one of these boats moored in the centre of the river, containing three and sometimes four persons, lazily hooking the fish and bringing it to the boat's side, when the fisherman removes it from the hook, sees that the bait is in order, and places it again in the water, to be almost immediately drawn up again for a like operation.

Gudgeons swim in shoals, are always greedy biters, and a very small degree of skill is therefore requisite to catch them; it is the amusement of ladies and boys more frequently than of men; for the fish is sure to hook himself, and little more is required of the angler than to put the bait down and draw it up again as soon as he sees his light float under water. Consequently, "jokes" concerning this easy sort of fishing are very abundant, and it must be confessed they are not unmerited; for neither skill, labour, nor activity are requisite to catch some ten or fifteen dozen of this tiny fish by a single hook in a day; and a boat such as we describe may be pretty sure to contain thirty or forty dozen when a late dinner-bell calls a party home on a summer evening.

PERCH AND GUDGEON.

But let not those who can enjoy no pleasure that is not derived from toil despise the pleasure that is simple and obtained easily. The gudgeon fisher usually seeks a holiday, a quittance from labour, a repose from thought; "his idle time" is, therefore, never "idly spent;" but his amusement is derived from other sources besides those supplied by his rod and line; he moves about from place to place—from "pitch" to "pitch:" the hot sun is rendered not only innocuous, but agreeable, when a gentle breeze passes along the river to cool his brow—look where he will his eye encounters some object of natural beauty, and his ear is regaled by the songs of birds along the banks, and the lark ever rising above some adjacent meadow. He has leisure to enjoy all this and much more—musing and not thinking—reclining rather than sitting—because neither the exercise of skill, neither mental nor bodily exertion, are requisite to secure sport.

For those to whom a full and heavy basket is but a secondary consideration, who covet the many other true enjoyments which a day on the Thames affords, there is, after all, no "pleasure" more truly pleasure than that which may be obtained by the gudgeon-fisher from morn till eve of a bright day in summer.

The gudgeon is invariably fished for with a small hook, baited with a small red worm, or a blood-worm, usually in water about three feet deep, and as close as may be to the bottom; the fisherman always selecting a gravelly bottom, which, every now and then, he "scrapes" with a large iron rake, part of his boat's furniture. The object of the raking is to draw the fish together : they feed on the aquatic insects, and their larvæ, the ova, &c., which the rake thus frees from the gravel ; of course, they seize greedily on the more tempting morsel which conceals the fatal hook. It is not uncommon to catch nine or ten dozen in one "pitch," and, frequently, half-a-dozen will be taken without losing or changing a bait.

The Thames gudgeon seldom exceeds six inches in length, the ordinary size being four inches. The lower jaw is broad, the mouth wide, with a barbul at the angle on each side ; the tail deeply forked ; the scales of the body moderate in size ; the colour of the upper part of the head, back, and sides olive-brown, spotted with black ; irides orange red, pupil large and dark, gill-covers greenish white ; all the under surface of the body white ; pectoral, ventral, and anal fins nearly white, tinged with brown ; dorsal fin and tail pale brown, spotted with darker brown. If people care to eat, as well as catch, fish, there is no fish of the Thames more "palatable" than the gudgeon, fried with a plentiful supply of lard. It is "of excellent taste, and very wholesome," and has been sometimes called "the fresh-water smelt."

From Pangbourne to Reading—or rather to Caversham Bridge—
a distance of six miles, the banks of the river again become more level,
although the hills continue for a short distance, and remain long in
sight, as a fine background to a most beautiful picture.

As we have said, the villages of WHITCHURCH and PANGBOURNE—the
former in Oxfordshire, the latter in Berkshire—are twin villages, united
by a long, narrow, ungainly, yet picturesque wooden bridge, from which
pleasant views are obtained of the river, both above and below.   There

WHITCHURCH.

are, indeed, few prettier localities on the Thames: both have their venerable churches, their homely inns, of which the more "ambitious" is at
Pangbourne; but here the angler may seek and find comforts in the
little way-side "public" introduced into our sketch, which pictures also
the weir-fall, the foreground timber-yard, and the cottage of the fisherman, John Champ, whose "punts" are always ready, and who is in high
favour with the "brethren of the angle," being

"Himself as skilful in that art as any."

As a residence for a time, Pangbourne has many attractions; the scenery
in the neighbourhood is very beautiful; the hills are high and healthful,

and command extensive views; the place is sufficiently retired,—for although the Great Western Railway runs "right through it," visitors are few, except those who take the shortest cut to the river-side, and make the most of a morning "pitch" beside the water-plants, which here grow in rich luxuriance, and where the perch abound.

Pangbourne was held, according to Domesday-book, by Miles Crispin of William the Conqueror. Its manor and church were afterwards granted to the Abbey of Reading, as appears from the confirmations of the charters of Henry II., its founder, by Hubert, Archbishop of Canter-

PANGBOURNE.

bury, and Robert, Bishop of Sarum. Pangbourne afterwards formed a part of the possessions of Edward, Duke of Somerset, who was executed in the year 1553, in the last year of Edward VI. It was then granted to Sir Francis Englefield by Queen Mary; and he, becoming a fugitive, it reverted to the crown, "as appears from an explification of the Inquisition for the finding of him." The reversion of the mansion and manor of Pangbourne was granted by Queen Elizabeth to Thomas Weldon, cofferer of her majesty's household. The house is mentioned by Leland as a fair manor-place, that had belonged to the abbot of Reading. The village, however, has preserved few or none of its antiquities; the visitor will seek in vain for traces of its early renown, although he may pleasantly muse and dream of its former greatness, while lulled to repose by the murmur of the "fall" that now gently, and now angrily, gives voice to the waters as they make their way through the weir.

The floral enrichments of the water-side, which have afforded us so much interest and pleasure during the whole of our river voyage, still maintain their luxuriance. A glow of rich purple greets our eyes even from a considerable distance, wherever the Purple Loosestrife (*Lythrum salicaria*) predominates. The tall spikes of handsome flowers are so large and conspicuous, as to form a prominent feature for the artist to introduce into the foreground of a river-scene, its warm colour rendering it particularly valuable for that purpose. We may not be weary of repeating advice to the artist whose task it is to design for manufacturers, to resort for models to this rich storehouse of natural graces and beauties. The weeds of the field, the lane, and the hedgerow are, indeed, fertile of suggestions; but they

PURPLE LOOSESTRIFE.

are far better known than those of the water-side, which are truly but "flowers out of place:" not only in form, but in colour will they be found practically useful—in bud, in blossom, and especially in leaves; and inasmuch as many of them are climbing or creeping, they may be applied to a hundred purposes of which the ornamentist has hitherto little thought:

"Not a leaf, a flower, but contains a folio volume:
We may read, and read, and still find something new,
Something to please, and something to instruct."

The Yellow Loosestrife (*Lysimachia vulgaris*), which we meet with so abundantly on the banks of the Thames, is interesting for the beauty of its yellow flowers, which have a fine effect when contrasted with its usual companion, the Purple Loosestrife, and also on account of the singular property attributed to it by the ancients of taming ferocious, and reconciling discordant animals, whence they derived its name of *Lysimachia*, of which the English "Loosestrife" is a literal translation. A quotation on this subject from Parkins, the old herbalist, may be amusing to our readers: describing the plant, he speaks of its "taking away strife or debate between beasts, not only those that are yoked together, but even those that are wild also, by making them tame and quiet, which, as they say, this herb will do, if it be either put about their yokes or their necks, which, how true, I leave to them who shall try and find it so." Whether the operation of this invaluable specific be or be not extended to the human race the author does not state; amid the calm and tranquillizing solitudes of the upper Thames it may not be required— but of a surety its application is very often desirable somewhat lower down.

YELLOW LOOSESTRIFE.

Continuing our voyage from Pangbourne—a line of undulating chalk hills on the immediate left, and an uninterrupted tract of flat meadow-land stretching for two or three miles along the opposite bank—we soon arrive opposite Hardwicke House, seated on the slope of a wooded height above the river. It is a large gabled structure of red brick, situated on a terrace of earth raised considerably above the river, upon which are many shady bowers of old yews cut into fanciful arcades. It is so little altered from the time of its erection, that it seems to carry back the spectator to the era of our great civil war. Here Charles I. spent much of his time during the troublous period that preceded his fall, "amusing

himself with bowls," and other sports.*   On the fine lawn between the
house and the river are some noble specimens of cedar, oak, and elm-
trees, that, judging from their great age, must have been witnesses of
the alternate sports and apprehensions of the sovereign.   A little further,
and we arrive at an assemblage of choice picturesque objects, such as are
not often met with even singly, and are very rarely encountered grouped
together into one rich picture as we here find them.   At one view we

MAPLE-DURHAM CHURCH AND MILL.

have MAPLE-DURHAM ferry, lock, and weir—the mossy old mill embosomed in rich foliage, from which again rises the grey church tower,
behind which, though almost hidden by lofty trees, we see the turreted

---

* No nobleman's mansion was considered complete, at this period, if it were not provided with a
bowling-green.  Our little cut exhibits the
game as played in the time of Charles I.,
and is copied from an Italian print, by
Rossi, dated 1647.   The sport is said to
have originated in England ; and the
earliest traces of it are to be found in
manuscripts of the 13th century.   Covered
alleys were afterwards invented for the
enjoyment of the game in winter ; and it
was looked upon as a gentlemanly recrea-

tion, of value for the exercise the players attained in its practice.   The reader will remember Pope's
line :—

" Some Dukes at Marybone bowl time away."

X

outline of MAPLE-DURHAM HOUSE, forming altogether a painter's paradise.* The river here becomes broad and studded with numerous islets,
between which extends a series of weirs, over which the water tumbles
and foams, adding life and variety to the general calmness of the scene.
To obtain a good view of the house, the tourist should land on the right
bank, just below the lock, when, looking across the river, he will see,
between the two tall elms that frame the picture, a matchless pile of

MAPLE-DURHAM HOUSE.

gables, dormers, ornamental chimneys, and all the other elements of " the
Elizabethan style." From the river we have no good view of the principal front of the house, which is towards the east, looking down a
magnificent avenue of elm-trees nearly a mile in length. There are in
the house, it is said, several secret rooms and passages used in the time
of the Commonwealth by the Royalist party for the concealment of

* It was built in 1581 by Sir Michael Blount, then Lieutenant of the Tower of London. In the
church are many interesting memorials of the Blount family. Maple-Durham is a corruption of
Mapulder-ham, literally meaning, the residence or manor among the maple-trees. Mapulder was the
Saxon and early English name for a maple-tree, Apulder for an apple-tree, &c.

troops or priests, as the case might be. Maple Durham has long been the property of the ancient family of the Blounts. " The church is of singular design, having a nave of irregular form, with a south aisle only."

On the opposite side of the river is the village of Purley, the small church of which stands close to the bank, buried in a grove of towering trees. Purley Hall, on the right, on high ground, is a plain, square, modern villa. The towing-path is closed where the grounds of Purley reach the Thames, but is continued on the opposite bank of the stream, so that men and horses have to be ferried across, and continue their journey for about a quarter of a mile, when they reach Purley Ferry, and are again carried across to the right bank, where the ferryman's house is situated, from whence the path continues to Caversham Bridge.

The line of the Great Western Railway is in sight almost all the way between Pangbourne and Reading, and, for the most part, in close proximity to the river. About Purley, the tall wooded banks approach each other, and forming now and then close umbrageous scenes of exquisite beauty. Continuing our journey, no object of particular interest meets us for some distance, until, coming to a turn of the river where the country opens out, we obtain a sight of Caversham, with its old bridge and church, and the large town of Reading. The ground on the right has now sunk to a level; but on the left, chalk-hills, with steep declivities, approach and almost overhang the stream. From these hills beautiful prospects are obtained of the river and surrounding scenery; and, for half a mile before reaching Caversham, the northern bank is adorned by a fine hanging wood of fir-trees, passing which we arrive at Caversham Bridge and village.*

---

* During the civil war, many skirmishes took place in this vicinity. Of one of them, between the troops of the Parliament and those of the king, some records are preserved in the diary of Sir Samuel Luke, said to have been the original of Butler's " Hudibras." He writes:—" Upon Cawsam hill, unexpected to us, came his Majesty's forces, under the command of General Ruven and Prince Rupert, consisting of about forty collours of horse and nine regiments of foot, with ordnance and other ammunition; they fell upon a loose regiment that lay there to keepe the bridge, and gave them a furious assault both with their ordnance and men—one bullet being taken up by our men which weighed twenty-four pounds at the least. This was answered with our musketts, and we made the hill soe hott

CAVERSHAM BRIDGE is an ugly structure, partly of wood and partly of stone. At its foot is a small cottage, where boats are hired, and where the curious may trace some ancient remains, which appear to be those of the wayside chapel noted by Leland in his "Itinerary" (*temp.* Henry VIII.). He tells us—"At the north end of Caversham Bridge, as we come from Reading, there standeth a fair old chapel of stone, on the right hand, piled in the foundation because of the rage of the Thames." In the letters addressed to Hearne, the antiquary, is one dated 1727, from an inquirer, who informs him that "this chapel was dedicated to St. Anne," and that from thence the religious went at certain times to a

CAVERSHAM BRIDGE.

holy well, "between the field called the Mount and a lane called Priest's Lane," from which circumstance it obtained its name; and that there was "in the memory of man a large ancient oak just by this well, which was also had in great veneration."

The lock—Caversham Lock—is distant half a mile from the bridge;

for them that they were forced to retreat, leaving behind seven bodyes of as personable men as ever were seene, and most of their armes; besides others which fell in three or four miles compasse, as they retreated. And it is sayed that within five miles there were five hundred hurt men drest in a barne, besides many prisoners which wee tooke, and many hurt men within our precincts, to which wee sent the next morning our surgeons to dresse, and gave orders to have the dead bodyes buryed by the parishioners where they were slain."

and a small island, containing about four acres, divides the current. A view of the town of Reading would be hence obtained but for the intervening railway. The steeple of St. Lawrence's Church is, however, seen high above surrounding houses ; and so is the red-brick ruin of the Abbey gateway, closely adjoining the modern jail, beside which the ruins of the old abbey have been laid out in shady public walks : they exhibit little remains of distinctive architectural features, inasmuch as the walls have been denuded of the outer squared stone for building purposes, leaving the core of the walls only. A very pretty public garden is in front of this, and a mound, with a fine group of trees, commands a beautiful view of the winding of the Thames, from Purley on the left to Shiplake on the right of the spectator.

The Kennet, which runs through the town, joins the Thames between Caversham Bridge and Sonning. This river rises near the village of East Kennet, on the eastern side of Wiltshire, in the vicinity of Abury, and, "after a sequestered course" of about four miles, reaches Marlborough, afterwards waters the ancient village of Ramsbury, thence visits and refreshes Hungerford, proceeding thence to Newbury, where it becomes navigable ; and during a course of nearly forty miles ministers to the wants and industry of man—aiding the operations of the Thames in producing and distributing wealth. Drayton in his quaint poem, the "Poly-Olbion," thus narrates the junction of the streams :—

> " At Reading once arrived, clear *Kennet* overtakes
> Her lord, the stately *Thames;* which that great flood again
> With many signes of joy doth kindly entertain.
> Then *Loddon* next comes in, contributing her stóre,
> As still we see, the much runs ever to the more."

Reading is the venerable capital of Berkshire. "This little city," say some topographers, "was termed by the Saxons, Rheadyne, from *rhea*, a river ; or the British word *redin*, signifying fern, which Leland mentions as "growing hereabouts in great plenty;" but these are fanciful derivations. In all such names the termination *ing* was the Saxon patronymic. The Rædingas was a family, or, as they would say in Scotland, a clan, whose original head was a chief named Ræda. The name, therefore, simply meant that this was the seat and property of that family. In most parts of England the name of the family is joined with *ham, tun,* &c., meaning a residence, as Birmingham (Beorminga-ham, the home of the Beormingas), Wellington (Wællinga-tun, the tun, or dwelling, of the Wællingas), &c. But in the south, especially in Berkshire, Sussex, and perhaps Surrey, the family name was given to the place without any adjunct; as we have Worthing (the Worthingas), and Reading (the Rædingas), and Sonning (the Sonningas).

A strong castle existed here until the time of Henry II., by whom it was destroyed, as " affording a place of refuge to the adherents of King Stephen." Its site has long been matter of speculation. Its abbey was one of the most considerable in England, " both for the magnitude of its building and the state of its endowments," its abbots being mitred, and enjoying the honour of a seat in Parliament. The structure was commenced by Henry I. " on the site of a small nunnery, said to have been founded by Elfrida, mother-in-law of Edward the Martyr, in order to expiate the murder of that king at Corfe Castle." The active and honourable part which Reading sustained during the war between Charles I. and the Parliament, occupies a prominent page in the history of the period; but Reading, from its proximity to the Thames, being on the high road to London, and from its strength, " though not a walled town, as may be supposed," shared largely in many of the leading events of the country in all ages.* Of " the castle," as we have intimated,

---

\* The town of Reading had the privilege of coining from the early days of the Saxons, and it was continued until the local coinage of England was merged into the metropolitan mint. The penny of Edward I., here engraved, was struck at this town, which is termed " Villa Radingy " on this piece, in

accordance with the Latinized form so constantly adopted in mediæval currency. The great improvement in the coinage at this time is due to the long and prosperous reign of Edward I., who restored the currency to beauty, from a state of barbarism worse than that of the Saxon era, into which it had sunk after the reign of John, and during the troublous times in England. The coinage remained without change until another great monarch had arisen to give peace after intestine wars — Henry VII., who first gave portraiture on our national money; for from the time of Edward III. until his period, one head only was used for the series, like that upon this little coin; and it is not easy to distinguish the particular coins of some sovereigns from others of the series, except by minute peculiarities known to the students of Numismatics, but which would escape the eye of the general observer.

even the site is unknown : Leland conjectures that "a piece of the abbey was built of the ruins of it;" while of the famous abbey itself there are but few remains, the county jail now occupying its place. At the dissolution it was "extremely wealthy," and contained many "valuables." It was peculiarly rich in relics, possessing, among other treasures, "a hand of the Apostle James," and "the principell relik of idolytrie within thys realme, an aungel with oon wyng that brought to Caversham the spere hedde that percyd our Saviour is side upon the crosse." * The town is active and prosperous, although of its once famous woollen manufactories there is but the tradition. The only important manufactory it now possesses is one for the production of "biscuits;" and, strange as it may appear, this is so extensive as to employ several hundred men, aided by large machine power. It is foreign to our purpose, or a very agreeable and interesting paper might be written concerning the several processes in use to create this minor accessory of the table, which is exported—not by thousands, but by millions—and sent to every part of the globe. They have, and deserve, a universal reputation, obtained and sustained by using only the best materials of all descriptions—flour, milk, eggs, sugar, and so forth; and it must be

---

* A curious story is told in Fuller's Church History, which records a memorable visit of "bluff King Hal" to Reading Abbey:—"As King Henry VIII. was hunting in Windsor Forest, he either casually lost, or more probably wilfully losing himself, struck down, about dinner time, to the Abbey of Reading, where, disguising himself (much for delight, more for discovery unseen), he was invited to the abbot's table, and passed for one of the king's guard,—a place to which the proportion of his person might properly entitle him. A sirloin of beef was set before him (so knighted, saith tradition, by this Henry); on which the king laid on lustily, not disgracing one of that place for whom he was mistaken. 'Well fare thy heart (quoth the abbot), and here in a cup of sack I remember the health of his grace your master. I would give an hundred pounds on the condition I could feed so lustily on beef as you do. Alas! my weak and squeezie stomach will hardly digest the wing of a small rabbit or chicken.' The king pleasantly pledged him, and heartily thanked him for his good cheer; after which he departed as undiscovered as he came thither. Some weeks after, the abbot was sent for by a pursuivant, brought up to London, clapt in the Tower, kept close prisoner, and fed for a short time with bread and water ; yet not so empty his body of food, as his mind was filled with fears, creating many suspicions to himself, when and how he had incurred the king's displeasure. At last a sirloin of beef was set before him, of which the abbot fed as the farmer of his grange, and verified the proverb, that two hungry meals make the third a glutton. In springs King Henry out of a private lobby, where he had placed himself, the invisible spectator of the abbot's behaviour. 'My lord (quoth the king), presently deposit your hundred pounds in gold, or else no going hence all the daies of your life. I have been your physician, to cure you of your squeezie stomach, and here, as I deserve, I demand my fee for the same.' The abbot down with his dust, and, glad he had escaped so, returned to Reading, as somewhat lighter in purse, so much more merry in heart, than when he came thence."

recorded as a gratifying fact, that the manufacturers, while making their own fortunes, have contributed very largely to the prosperity of the town.

Reading was the birthplace of Archbishop Laud, and among honourable and happy memories associated with this town, or rather with its vicinity, is that of "THREE MILE CROSS," long the residence of Mary Russell Mitford.

We ask the reader to leave the Thames for awhile, and make with us a pilgrimage to the grave of this admirable woman, whose writings have found their way over the whole civilised world, rendering familiar to all the peculiar traits of English village character, and the graces, so essentially our own, which decorate the lanes, the homesteads, and the cottages of rural England.

Reading is a credit to the beautiful river that sweeps through its valley; neat, active, bustling—a sort of miniature city, with a sprinkling of pretty villas in pleasant suburbs, some more than half concealed at this season by the foliage of close shrubberies, and surrounded by borders and parterres of flowers that would joy Miss Mitford's heart, were she moving among them, instead of resting beneath the granite cross erected to her memory in the homely, yet solemn churchyard of Swallowfield.

Our first object was to visit the humble dwellings, in one of which she lived for more than a quarter of a century, in the other of which she died. To "Three Mile Cross," the "Our Village" of her stories and sketches, we wended our way. It was a day "brimful" of air and sunshine; no dust, no rain; every leaf at maturity; every bird in song; every streamlet musical; the shadows calm, distinct, and still, as if waiting to be painted; our driver intelligent but unobtrusive; our carriage comfortable and not noisy; the "sunny lanes" showing themselves worthy the reputation SHE has given them, and the steady dignified trees proving, if proof were needed, "England before the world" for beauty of upland and lowland, of park and pleasaunce, of wood and water, of cottage and croft, of corn-field and meadow, of all things—every thing that can render life enjoyable, and plenteous, and happy. We were in Mary Russell Mitford's own county, "the sunny Berkshire," made famous in so

many of her bright pages. We fancied we knew the roads and the trees
she wrote about or talked of; the rough-coated elms, standing boldly and
bluntly out from velvet hedge-rows—a slim stick of sprouting foliage
springing here and there from the rugged bark, reminding one of an
old man's child, while the great robust tree-tops were telling of vigorous
old age! The signs of the over-many public-houses, so quaint and
"un-London-like"—"The Four Horse-Shoes," "The Fox and Horn,"
"The Swan," "The George and Dragon," "The Star," were so many
landmarks. There were herds of sheep on the uplands and lowlands,

THREE MILE CROSS.

and lowing cattle under trees; there were children "clapping their
hands, and blooming like roses;" the jobbing gardener, with his rake,
his garland of "bass," and his bundle of "shreds—blue, black, and red;"
the bronzed and muscular village blacksmith; the pale-faced shoemaker;
the ragged, rosy, saucy boys; the fair, delicate "lily-of-the-valley-like"
maidens—the descendants of those who were boys and girls when "Our
Village" was written,—we saw them all, and identified them all with the
painter of "Three Mile Cross." And then we arrived, after delicious
loiterings, at "3 Mile X" itself, as it is described, by itself, on the first
wall to the right: it is a long, lean, straggling hamlet of twenty houses

Y

and a half (we counted them conscientiously), the "half" being the shoe-maker's shop, from whence, in Miss Mitford's time, "an earthquake would hardly have stirred the souter."

The village shop is there still,—"Bromley's shop,"—just as it was in her day, except that the master and mistress are "elderly," and the chil-dren not exactly *young;* but children flourish round *them,* keeping the picture "fresh." The master of the village shop (a handsome old man) was pleased to talk of Miss Mitford, and "the Doctor," and of her good-nature and oddity. "Yes," he said, "that was her house, the very next door; we might call it, as every one did, ugly, and small, and incon-venient; but she liked it. She made herself and everybody else happy in it: he didn't know what visitors expected the house to be; he could repeat every word she had written on 't. 'A cottage—no, a miniature house, with many additions—little odds and ends of places—pantries and what not; a little bricked court before one half, and a little flower-yard before the other; the walls old and weather-stained, covered with holly-hocks, roses, honeysuckles, and a great apricot-tree.'"

"But where are they?"

"Ah! the hollyhocks, the roses, honeysuckles, and great apricot-tree, are destroyed and dead; but there is the window into which the Doctor used to fling apricots to my children."

Yes, the flowers are all gone, and every tree in the garden is gone—all except the old bay and one "fairy rose!"

The house, so far as the bare walls are concerned, is much as she left it: an assemblage of closets ("our landlord," she says, "has the assurance to call them rooms"), full of contrivances and corner-cupboards. "That house," to quote her own words, "was built on purpose to show in what an exceeding small compass comfort may be packed."

Yet when we entered the tiny, low-ceilinged rooms, almost without light or ventilation, and ascended the narrow stairs,—where crinoline could not come,—and saw around us ample evidence of the impossibility to impart to the dwelling anything approaching the picturesque of cottage life, we felt—what?—the most intense admiration and respect for the well-born and once wealthy lady who brought within these "old and weather-stained walls" an atmosphere of happiness, an appreciation of all that is true and beautiful in nature; and sent from out those leaden casements, and that narrow door, such floods of light and sunshine as have brightened the uttermost parts of the earth! Who ever heard her murmur at changed fortunes—when obliged to leave the home, "stately though simple," the home of eighteen years, "surrounded by fine oaks and elms, and tall, massy plantations, shaded down into a beautiful lawn by wild overgrown shrubs!" She confesses, indeed, in her sweet playful way, that at the time it nearly broke her heart to leave it:—"What a tearing up by the root it was! I have pitied cabbage plants, and celery, and all transplantable things ever since; though, in common with them and other vegetables, the first agony of transportation being over, I have taken such firm and tenacious hold of my new soil, that I would not for the world be pulled up again, even to be restored to the beloved ground." What was this? philosophy or heroism? or the perfection of that sweet plastic nature which receives, and retains, and fructifies all happy impressions—which opens to, and cherishes, all natural enjoyments, and adapts itself to circumstances with the true spirit of the practical piety that bends to the blast, and sees sunshine, bright and enduring, beyond the blackest cloud: let the darkness be ever so dense without, the lamp burns calmly and purely within! *

* Mary Russell Mitford was born on the 16th of December, in the year 1786, at the little town of Alresford, in Hampshire. Her father was George Mitford, M.D., the son of a younger branch of the Mitfords of Mitford Castle, Northumberland, and Jane Graham, of Old Wall, Westmoreland, a branch of the Netherby clan. Her mother was Mary Russell, only surviving child and heiress of Richard Russell, D.D., Rector of Ashe and Tadley, and Vicar of Overton, in Hampshire, above sixty years. He died at the age of eighty-eight, before his daughter's marriage, and remembered having seen Pope when at Westminster School. He was intimate with Fielding, and many of the wits of that period; and Miss Mitford had a portrait of him, with a wig, not unlike a judge's wig, hanging over it.

Three or four years after, Dr. Mitford removed from Alresford to Reading; and three or four years after that, again, when his daughter was in her ninth year, he went to reside at Lyme Regis, in Dorsetshire, in a fine old house, previously occupied by the great Lord Chatham, where his two sons frequently spent their holidays. By this time Dr. Mitford had spent between £30,000 and £40,000, and went to London to retrench and determine his future course of life. His daughter, then ten years of age, was his favourite companion; and, lounging about, he one morning strayed into a dingy house, which proved to be a lottery-office; for what follows we are indebted to Miss Mitford's "Recollections of a Literary Life":—

" ' Choose what number you like best,' said dear papa, 'and that shall be your birthday present.'
" I immediately selected and put into his hand No. 2224.
" ' Ah!' said my father, examining it, ' you must choose again. I want to buy a whole ticket, and this is only a quarter. Choose again, my pet.' [" ' No,

Those only who had known the extent and luxury of her former home, and afterwards had the privilege of enjoying her society, in that "scrappy" cupboarded dwelling at "Three Mile Cross," can sufficiently appreciate the fulness, the warmth, the geniality, the strength of her sunshine, which, without effort or exaggeration, made all within and without happy in her happiness. What the worthy shopkeeper, Mr. Bromley said, was quite true—there was nothing exaggerated in her description of that miniature home; if strangers expected the relics of a cottage *ornée*, that was their fault, *not* Miss Mitford's. She had described it as it was, literally; if touched by the *couleur de rose* of her happy mind, *that* she could not help. She could no more avoid enjoying the beauties of nature, than the sun could decline to give heat; and if all people have not the same happy gift, *that* is not the fault of Mary Russell Mitford. Despite the dilapidated condition of the cottage at Three Mile Cross, we fancied much of her genial spirit there; and could, from her descriptions, identify the present race of children with the children of past times. Those villages, which yet continue far away from the contamination of railway stations, are " Old England;" and as her sketches are from nature, they remain true to nature still.

A gentle and kindly young woman, the daughter of "Bromley's shop," who had memories for a hundred gracious and thoughtful words and acts, ran after our carriage with a branch of yellow *japonica*— "There," she said, "that is from Miss Mitford's garden;" we had pre-

---

" ' No, dear papa—I like this one best.'

" ' There is the next number,' interposed the lottery-office keeper, ' No. 2223.'

" ' Aye,' said my father, ' that will do just as well. Will it not, Mary ? We 'll take that.'

" ' No,' returned I, obstinately, ' that won't do. This is my birthday, you know, papa, and I am ten years old. Cast up the figures forming my number, and you will find they make ten—the other is only nine.' "

The father, like all speculators, was superstitious. The argument was irresistible. The ticket was purchased, and a few months afterwards intelligence arrived that No. 2224 had been drawn a prize of £20,000.

"Ah me ! " (reflects Miss Mitford), " in less than twenty years what was left of the produce of that ticket, so strangely chosen? What? except a Wedgwood dinner-service, that my father had made to commemorate the event, with the Irish harp within the border on one side, and his family crest on the other. That fragile and perishable ware long outlasted the more perishable money."

Miss Mitford died at Swallowfield on the 10th of January, 1855, and was buried in the graveyard of the village church, on the 18th of the month of that year.

viously obtained a sprig of bay and a fairy rose from the sanctuary, but her kindness made the yellow branch the sweetest of the three.

The drive to Swallowfield,* about two miles farther from Reading, was a repetition of the scenery from Reading to "Three Mile Cross," with the exception of the common, which Miss Mitford immortalized by the "cricketing"—a sport she enjoyed as much as any youth in the county. One of her great powers was certainly her large sympathy; she threw herself into the joys, sorrows, pastimes, and feelings of young and old. Her extensive poetic, and even classic, reading—the glare and glitter, and town-bred celebrity of her dramas, did not lessen her appreciation of the *true*, and practical, and beautiful, in rural life: if the worldly carry the world within them, so did she bear the joyousness of nature within her heart of hearts. We watched to see a graceful greyhound—"Mayflower"—spring out of the hollow beyond the common; but, alas! in vain; that day there were no cricketers, no sheep—only a few boys, and they were too quiet by half; while a winding flock of sober goslings, with their attendant parents, eyed us without a single hiss. We chatted over the peculiarity which had often amused us in our old favourite and friend; the habit—which had increased with her increasing years, and particularly after her father's death—of seldom rising until long past noon, and walking miles by moonlight, or light of lantern—she did not seem to care which, so long as it was night. In the afternoon she was busied with her flowers, and after sunset she would sally forth with her maid, her lantern, and a long stick, almost, if not quite, as long again as herself, and trot merrily off, rarely returning until late at night: her next door neighbour assured us that more than once,

---

* "The manor of Swallowfield was anciently held as an appendage to Shinfield, by the St. Johns of Legham; and afterwards by the De la Beche family. It subsequently became the property of the celebrated Regent of France, John Duke of Bedford, who, at his death, in 1435, bequeathed it to the King. In 1443 it was presented by the Crown to John Penicoke, groom of the wardrobe; and in process of time came into the family of Backhouse. By marriage with the widow of Sir W. Backhouse, K.B., who died in 1649, Lord Clarendon became lord of the manor, and, if we may believe tradition, wrote at Swallowfield Place, after his retirement from public life, his well-known 'History of the Rebellion.' Edward, grandson of the historian, sold it in 1719 to Governor Pitt, better known as 'Diamond Pitt.' After belonging successively to the Dods and Beavans, it came into the possession of Sir Charles Russell, Bart., the present proprietor," whose estimable mother, the Lady Russell, was the devoted friend and continual comforter of Mary Russell Mitford.

when driving home, he found "the dear little lady" breasting a snow-drift, and this was confirmed by the kindly and benevolent clergyman who now resides at Swallowfield. She loved the stars as well as the sunshine; but it is singular that she has given no record of these wanderings in the dark.

Swallowfield, to which she removed some four years before her death, and where she died, is a delicious wayside cottage, standing on a triangular plot of ground, skirted by roads overarched by magnificent trees; it is the *beau-ideal* of a residence for one who loves the country. She

SWALLOWFIELD.

could chat over the fence with the passing peasant, and see all who drove up either road; but lovely as it is, we think she must have missed the *village*—missed the children—missed the hourly life-interests that clung round her heart at "Three Mile Cross." The aged tree had been transplanted; and, superior as this lovely cottage is in extent, in beauty, in the richness of its close scenery to her first humble dwelling, we believe "the roots" never struck far below the surface. Swallowfield was lovely, but her father had never been there; old familiar faces could not be brought there, as to "Three Mile Cross," by a simple effort of memory; they did not *belong* to Swallowfield; it was lovely, but the well-known voices of village children did not bound in through the open window; it was more beautiful, more commodious, but " pretty May " never " stretched " before that fire; " the dear father " never sate under the shadow of that mantelshelf : to the old, these delicious home-memories are more " life " than the actual life in which others exist; the eye may be closed, and the lip silent, but the *past*—the PAST—is, with the old, ever fresh and young as a " blind man's bride."

The family at Swallowfield respect Miss Mitford's garden, and have not altered the position of a single tree, nor turned a path, nor done aught to disturb that which her hand has " hallowed." The clergyman showed us her favourite rose-tree, and permitted us to visit the room out of which her spirit passed from life's pilgrimage ;—no ! she never felt life to be a " pilgrimage ;" it was rather a ramble through the pleasant paths of a pleasant world ; and though thorns would now and then show their sharp points among the flowers, even to her, yet, despite the sufferings of her latter days, it was with her

" Life to the last enjoyed."

" To the last " she was as fond of green trees and lanes, and the songs of bird and bee, and the " mountain nymph, sweet Liberty," as if she had been born a gipsey queen ; and she herself would sometimes laugh and say, that at best she was but a gipsey lady.

She corresponded more or less with the *literati* of her time, and when she was—as she but rarely was—a " star " in London, her society was much courted ; but she was out of place in the metropolis—the heat and " celebrities," the noise and tramp, the perpetual movement fatigued her. She loved best to be where the affections and sympathies had time to take root, and grow, and fructify ; she was no fine lady, to put out of the sphere of those sympathies and affections such as were not born with a passport to " good society." All were her neighbours, and her poor neighbours knew the value of her regard. It is somewhat singular that, alive as she was to political movements, alive to rural sports, to society, friendships, and affections, she took no interest in education ; had no desire that the Lucys and Tommys, the Janes and Jacks, should

be educated : her mind was, perhaps, too poetic to embrace the business
of education, or to grasp its advantages—she believed more in *inspira-
tion* than in *training.*   The dame-school only interested her because it
was picturesque; like many others of high blood, she believed herself
a liberal, when she was strongly conservative in her opinions and—her
prejudices; she had no love for schools or railroads.   Miss Mitford's
letters were charming; her handwriting stiff and sturdy; quite unlike
the graceful penmanship of Mrs. Hemans, the crabbed strokes of poor
L. E. L., or the style systematic of good Maria Edgeworth.

   In her introduction to her Dramas, dedicated to her long-loved friend,
Francis Bennoch, she expressed a wish to be buried in the churchyard of
Swallowfield : and this excited the surprise, and somewhat of the loving
jealousy, of the dwellers at "Three Mile Cross," who imagined she would
have rested with her beloved parents in *their* churchyard.

THE TOMB OF MISS MITFORD.

   A cross of Aberdeen granite marks her grave in "the beautiful churchyard of Swallowfield."   It may be about a mile from the cottage from
which the spirit of Mary Russell Mitford passed to a world even more
beautiful than hers—to "fresh fields and pastures new "—and joins the
park of one of her latest and truest friends : the breeze sweeps through

the noble trees, and the sunbeams penetrate the foliage, so as to chequer the sward with light; the shadow of the fine old church falls gently over the graves of "the rude forefathers of the hamlet," and the ploughman's whistle mingles with the whistle of the blackbird and the bleating of the sheep: it is an exquisite spot, a fit resting-place for the author of "OUR VILLAGE."

Having rambled through Reading, noted its large capabilities for commerce, visited its principal antiquities, and made our pilgrimage to the home and grave of Mary Russell Mitford, we continue our voyage, entering the boat at Caversham Bridge, previously examining the picturesque and venerable church, and the singular "bit of ruin" that appertains to the boat-house.

The Kennet, close to its junction with the Thames, is crossed by two

SONNING CHURCH.

railway bridges, the South Eastern and the Great Western, the latter being the nearest to the great river into which the tributary runs.

In the immediate neighbourhood of Caversham Lock, there are wooded slopes crowned with villas, which give variety and interest to the

z

scenery; thence the banks are flat and tame, until we come in view of
Sonning Park, and pass underneath the woods which overhang the river.
The church and village of Sonning are very simple, but highly picturesque,—the former is venerable from antiquity, but exceedingly neat
and well kept; the latter is clean, neat, and sufficiently aged to retain
many of the best characteristics of its "order," which, unhappily, are fast
decaying throughout England.  It is described by Leland as "an upland
town, set on fair and commodious ground, beneath which the Tamise
runneth in a pleasant vale."  A handsome bridge of brick connects it

SHIPLAKE CHURCH.

with the opposite side: many of the cottages are covered with climbing
plants—the old honeysuckle, the time-honoured jasmine, and the sweet
clematis, mingled with the more recent acquirements of simple florists of
humble homes.

On the opposite bank, a little above the junction, is the village of
Shiplake, backed by hilly slopes, on one of which is the church, of
which Grainger, author of the "Biographical Dictionary," was the
incumbent; living here "in competency, obscurity, and content"—so

says the tablet which marks his grave; and here dying, in 1776, "as he was officiating at the altar." From the church porch there is a glorious view of the valley of the Thames :—

> " The tranquil cot, the restless mill,
> The lonely hamlet, calm and still;
> The village spire, the busy town,
> The shelving bank, the rising down;
> The fisher's punt, the peasant's home,
> The woodland seat, the regal dome,—
> In quick succession rise to charm
> The mind, with virtuous feelings warm ;
> Till where thy widening current glides
> To mingle with the turbid tides,
> Thy spacious breast displays unfurl'd
> The ensigns of th' assembled world ! "

The lock and mill of **Shiplake** are now reached, just below which the Loddon meets the Thames; the great river being crossed by the railway from Twyford to Henley. The Loddon is " composed of various branches,"— its most distant source being in the vicinity of Basingstoke, one of its accessory rills gliding through a part of Windsor Forest. The village of WARGRAVE is a pretty and long village, with a picturesque church, surrounded by well-grown trees, and environed by productive meadows. In the venerable church is a monument to Thomas Day, the eccentric but amiable author of " Sandford and Merton," who was killed by a fall from his horse on his way from Anningsly, his home, near Chertsey, to the residence of his mother at Bear's Hill, near Wargrave. The monument contains these lines, written by Day as an inscription for the tomb of a friend; but they were well applied to himself :—

WARGRAVE CHURCH.

> " Beneath the reach of time, or fortune's power,
> Remain, cold stone, remain, and mark the hour
> When all the noblest gifts that Heaven e'er gave,
> Were enter'd in a dark, untimely grave !

Oh! taught on reason's boldest wings to rise,
And catch each glimm'ring of the opening skies!
Oh, gentle bosom of unsullied mind!
Oh, friend to truth, to virtue, to mankind
Thy dear remains we trust to this sad shrine,
Secure to feel no second loss like thine."

We now approach one of the cultivated "lions" of the Thames—
"Park Place," famous in the annals of the river for the beauty of its
site, the growth of its trees, and some circumstances which give it
interest beyond that of ordinary demesnes. The house was built by
the Duke of Hamilton: it was some time the residence of Frederick,
Prince of Wales, the father of George III.; but it is mainly indebted
for its many attractions to Marshal Conway, who, towards the close of

THE BOAT-HOUSE AT PARK-PLACE.

the last century, became its possessor, and who "set himself the task"
of giving to Nature all the advantages she could derive from Art. The
grounds have since received the benefit of time; they have not been
neglected by successive lords; and the gentleman who at present owns
them has evidently studied, by all the means at his command, to render
them—what they are—"beautiful exceedingly." Visitors, by whom
access on fixed days is easily obtained, land at the very charming

"BOAT-HOUSE" we have pictured; it is, in reality, a furnished dwelling,
and contains some fine, and several remarkable, works of Art,—statues,
pictures, wood-carvings, and foreign curiosities,—in the examination of
which half an hour may be profitably expended.

A walk through the grounds, however, is a more exquisite treat—hill
and dale, richly-wooded slopes, and shaven lawns, are happily intermixed; while every now and then judicious openings supply views of
the Thames underneath, or the landscape far beyond.

Here and there, on green hillocks or in gloomy dells, mimic ruins have
been introduced; some of them built out of the debris of Reading
Abbey.   In one of them is a long subterraneous passage (cut through a

THE DRUID TEMPLE AT PARK PLACE.

chalk bed), leading to a Roman amphitheatre, the base of which is planted
with the mournful cypress.   This is the work of Marshal Conway; but
there is an object of greater interest in these grounds, although its value
is lessened by the knowledge that this also is "artificial."   Strictly
speaking, however, artificial it is not; for the DRUIDIC TEMPLE which
stands on the summit of one of the small hills, was placed exactly as it
was found, keeping precisely the same form and character it received
from the hands of the "builders," it may be twenty centuries ago.   We

may briefly tell its history. The temple was discovered on the summit of a high hill near the town of St. Helier, in the Isle of Jersey, on the 12th of August, 1785; it was entirely covered with earth, having the appearance of a large tumulus, and was laid bare by workmen employed to level the ground. Fortunately, General Conway was then Governor of Jersey; his attention was at once directed to its preservation; and, on his leaving the island, it was presented to him, and by him removed to Park Place.

"This curious structure is sixty-five feet in circumference, composed of forty-five large stones (measuring, in general, about seven feet in height, from four to six in breadth, one to three in thickness), and contains six perfect lodges, or cells. The supposed entrance, or passage, faces the east, and measures fifteen feet in length, and four feet and upwards in breadth, and about four feet in height, with a covering of rude stones from eighteen inches to two feet thick. In the removal of this curious temple from Jersey, all the parts were marked with such care as to be correctly placed in their original form, and precise direction, when they were re-erected on the charming spot which is distinguished by them. In the eighth volume of the 'Archæologia,' a particular account is given of this venerable antiquity." *

We ask the reader to pause awhile at this pleasant "Place," and give a few moments' consideration to another subject which may be suggested to his thoughts in various parts of the river; and nowhere, perhaps, will it occur to him more forcibly than it does here.

---

* We have retained the popular term "temple," as applied to this antiquity; but it is properly a tomb. Recent researches in Jersey and Guernsey have sufficiently established that fact. The circle of stones formed the wall of a small chamber, which was covered by heavy slabs; the "cells" contained bodies of the dead. A narrow covered passage led to this chamber, and a mound of earth was placed over all. In the thirty-fifth volume of the "Archæologia," Mr. Lukis, of Guernsey, has described several of these burial-places, from his own investigations in these islands. He describes the avenue or entrance to them as rarely more than 3 feet in height by 2 feet in width; the interior chamber of the largest was 8 feet in height, 45 feet in length, and 15 feet in width; the roof stones, of granite, were computed to weigh thirty tons. They appear to have been used for successive interments of the aboriginal chieftains of the islands, and have been found with additional chambers as the original ones became filled with the "great departed." Sometimes in these chambers skeletons are found; sometimes bones, which show that the body was consumed by fire; sometimes the ashes are preserved in urns, rudely decorated with incised ornament. The other articles found in these tombs tell of an early and primitive people, such as spear and arrow-heads of flint, as well as knives of the same material, rudely formed beads of coloured earth, bracelets of jet, &c.

Perhaps every angler may not be aware that the May-fly (*Phryganea*) and the Caddis-worm are but one and the same insect in different stages of development ; such, however, is the case, the caddis-worm being the grub which afterwards changes into the winged fly. The caddis, during his aquatic existence, is a worm of no very prepossessing appearance, but he makes amends for his own want of personal attraction by investing himself with a most picturesque and original garment, which, in its formation, shows among different individuals a curious variety of taste, or instinct we must call it, in the selection and adaptation of the materials employed. Sometimes it is a collection of seeds of various plants that are

THE CADDIS.

cemented together to form the caddis-worm's case ; sometimes a grass-stem is cut into nearly equal lengths, and arranged in a polygonal form of great regularity. One specimen that we fished up had made choice of the clearest crystalline grains of quartz from among the sand, and had built himself a veritable crystal palace. But the oddest and most attractive of these little curiosities, are those composed of fresh-water shells, while still tenanted by their living inhabitants, and arranged together in grotto fashion (as shown in one of the accompanying figures), forming " a covering," as Kirby and Spence remark, " as singular as if a savage, instead of clothing himself with squirrel skins, should sew together into a coat the animals themselves." After a few months spent in these subaqueous operations, the caddis-worm retires into his cell, puts a grating over the aperture, and then shortly emerges in the shape of a large brown fly, to commence his aerial existence, happy while he can avoid the hook of the angler or the gulp of the trout, for now he is a " May-fly."

We constantly meet this insect haunting the water-side, and flitting about with a loose flight over the herbage ; in appearance it greatly resembles a moth, but the wings are semi-transparent, and covered with hairs, not scales, like those of the moth ; the prevailing colours are

various shades of brown. The following note on the proceedings of a
female May-fly is quoted from Patterson's Zoology, to which it was
communicated by Mr. Hyndman of Belfast, and may be of interest to
our readers :—"I first observed the Phryganea on the leaf of an aquatic
plant, from which it crept down along the stem under the water, very
nearly a foot deep ; it appeared then to have been disturbed by some

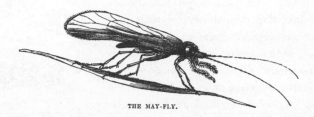

THE MAY-FLY.

sticklebacks, which approached and seemed inclined to attack it, and
swam vigorously and rapidly beneath the water, over to some other
plants. I then took the insect up, and found a large bundle of eggs, of
a green colour, closely enveloped in a strong jelly-like substance,
attached to the extremity of its abdomen." This power of diving and
free movement under water is very remarkable and unusual among
winged insects.

The trout is so well known that a few remarks only are necessary in
reference to this the "best-loved" of all the fish of the river, not by the
epicure so much as by the angler. The trout is, however, not very
often caught in the Thames, there is so much space, and so ample a
supply of food, that he will not often rise to the fly ; on the other hand
he lives, while he does live, in the midst of so many enemies, that his
chances of growth are few. Those who do escape death, however, by
good fortune, vigorous constitution, or peculiar watchfulness, grow to be
aged and very large ; usually every season there are a dozen or twenty
trout caught in the Thames, weighing each between ten and twelve or
fourteen pounds ; but we do not often find them, as we do in other
rivers, weighing between one pound and two pounds ; and the "fish of
size" are usually caught by "spinning," the bait being a bleak, a small

dace, a gudgeon, or a minnow.  The trout fisher, however, should go
" farther a-field" who covets a good day's sport, and loves to walk along
banks, scenting the thousand wild flowers that spring about him, in-
haling the pleasant breeze, and listening to the songs that rise from
meadow, tree, and bush—when

> " The wind from the south
> Drives the hook into the fish's mouth."

The Common Trout (*Salmo fario*) is an inhabitant of most of the
English lakes and rivers, yet varies considerably in appearance in
different localities.   Mr. Yarrell gives the history of several species—

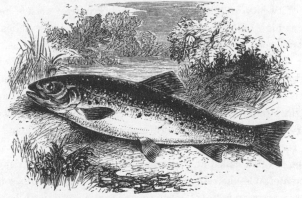

THE TROUT.

the salmon trout, the Great Lake trout, the Lochleven trout, the bull
trout, the Gillaroo trout, the sea trout, and the common trout.  " The
trout"—we quote from Yarrell—" though a voracious feeder, and thus
affording excellent diversion to the experienced angler, is so vigilant,
cautious, and active, that great skill, as well as patience, are required to
ensure success.  During the day the larger sized fish move but little from
their accustomed haunts, but towards evening they rise in search of small
fish, insects, and their various larvæ, upon which they feed with eagerness.  Though vigilant and cautious in the extreme, the trout is also
bold and active."

A A

We never yet knew an ardent fly-fisher who was not also an enthusiastic lover of nature; in truth, it is almost impossible to separate the one from the other. The trout is an inhabitant of the swift, clear, running stream, where the banks are fringed with the tall flag, and the pebbly bottom is half concealed by beds of rushes, often extending many yards of continuous length, and rising to a level with the water. On the top of these beds, or in the narrow spaces between them, the trout lies with his nose against the stream, waiting to rise at any moth or fly that may chance to be floated down on its surface. The experienced angler knows a "likely place" where a fish is to be found, and casts his artificial fly, with wonderful precision, within a few inches of his nose, even at a distance of twenty or thirty yards. Other favourite spots of resort are close under high grassy banks, bushes, overhanging trees, eddies, behind fragments of rock and large stones, at the junction of streams; in fact, wherever it is probable the current of the water will carry or collect such food as the trout prefers to feed on. If the trout be—as he unquestionably is—" a bold and voracious feeder," he is readily alarmed, even by so slight a thing as the shadow of the line or the rod, if it chances to pass over him, and when once frightened away from his home he does not soon return to it.*

Angling is often called an "idle pastime," and we cannot deny that to sit in a comfortable chair in a firmly-moored punt on the bosom of the Thames seems an amusement open to such an imputation; but to walk fifteen or twenty miles in a day, "whipping the water" from sunrise to sunset, during twelve or fourteen hours, is anything but an idle pastime. Whatever fatigue it brings with it, however, it is pleasant, health-giving, and instructive—so far as to make the angler acquainted with much of the science of nature, animate and inanimate, and keenly sen-

---

* A few years ago a trout weighing twenty-two and a half pounds was caught in the Tame, near Tamworth. It was at once forwarded to Sir Robert Peel, who, with his customary courtesy and consideration, immediately ordered it to be sent to Professor Owen. The professor had an accurate portrait of the fish painted—or rather two portraits, one of which he presented to Sir Robert, the other now graces his own cottage in Richmond Park. He then took steps to preserve the skeleton, which is now at the Museum of the College of Surgeons. It was a pure trout, richly spotted, and although very aged, a remarkably beautiful fish.

sitive to the beauties that Providence, with so lavish a hand, spreads out before his gaze as he wanders by the side of the winding, silvery stream—

> " To tempt the trout with well-dissembled fly,
> And rod, fine tapering."

During our rambles in the neighbourhood to which we are now introducing our readers, an incident occurred which we recall to memory with much pleasure, especially as it is associated with the subject we are treating. It was a warm soft evening, and the shadows fell heavily across the green lane, which somewhat diverges from the line of our regal river, yet not *out of sound* of the breeze among its reeds and pollards : we could hear the sudden splash of the water-hen ; and, after a while of loitering and listening, we crossed a stile, and were again on the bank. The swallows were skimming the water, " hawking insects," and so intent on their sport, that they winged close to us in their undulating rounds. But we little heeded the swallows or the insects, our attention being at once attracted by a tall, thin old man, who, attended by a slim, fair-haired boy, was as busily employed with his rod as if the day were but just born ; his face was turned towards the stream, but his silver hair and curved back told that he had passed even the autumn of his days. We saw by the motion of his rod that he had a " bite ; " yet when he drew in his line the little lad seized it, and took the fish off the hook.

" I caught my last trout with a worm," said the old man, " and then we put on a minnow : sure it was a minnow, Alf ? "

" Yes, gran'father, a real minnow ; but this is only a chuckle-headed chub."

" The varlet! let me feel—let me feel," added the old man impatiently. He extended his thin, muscular hand, and the lad placed the fish in it.

" A chub, sure enough,—cat's food! We 'll move on and try another quarter of an hour—trout are so hard to get."

" Gran'father, it grows late, the sun is long down, and the evening grey. Mother will fret,—you promised her you would be early home."

"Not so, Alf, it can't be getting grey yet: we have been such a little time—so few fish! What did the church clock strike last? It can't be sundown yet."

The lad made some reply which we did not catch, and then ran towards us,—"Will you tell me the time, please?"

"Half-past eight."

The old man caught the words and repeated them,—"Ay, I remember, it grows a little grey at half-past eight."

"Is your grandfather blind?"

"He is quite blind," answered the boy; "he was once a great fisherman, and it amuses him still, so mother often sends me with him in the afternoons; he takes such delight in it that he will never believe the night is at hand."

We had heard of the "blind angler!" and were not a little pleased at the meeting.

In a few minutes the old man warmed to a brother of the angle; he sat beside us on the stile, and talked of the past,—old age loves to recall "the past," whether painful or pleasant. He had been a fisher in his youth, a sailor in his manhood, and returned to his old haunts in the autumn of his days, incapacitated for active service by a severe wound in his knee. He "whipped the river" with a "loving rod," until a flash of lightning deprived him of sight. "More than ten years have passed," said the old man, "since I have seen sunlight or moonlight on the waters; never, never shall I see fin of fish again—never see the flutter or the rise! but I can feel them and hear them. When his mother cannot spare the lad to stay with me, my little gran'daughter leads me to the bank, and while she chases butterflies and gathers flowers—the sweet lamb!—I listen to the fish—I do, indeed! I can tell the short quick turn of the bleak in the water; I know the heavy scud of the barbel in the deeps; and what column of soldiers ever marched more closely than the young eels in *eel-fare* time? I know all the points and turns of the river so well—God bless it!—that I say, Lead me to such a turn or under such a tree; and if they tell me the hour, I know which way the shadows lie, and what sport I shall have. I can still teach a youngster how to fish for roach in winter, with paste and gentles, and in April with worms; many a roach have I 'ticed to the top of the water, just by that old pollard yon—"

"I have told gran'father the pollard is gone," interrupted the boy.

"Ay, ay, my lad, *but not the roach*," said the blind man, turning his head quickly. "I could teach any youngster, sir, to make the best ground paste for roach and dace; but he must have a small hook, a quick eye, and a nimble hand to catch them. Angling comes by nature—it can be improved, but it's a gift, a wonderful gift: it's more soothing than all the 'bacca that was ever grow'd in Virginia. Lord, sir, I could love a Frenchman while I'm angling! This lad here is not a bad lad, though somewhat of a scoffer at angling. I thought to make him eyes to the blind; but he doesn't learn, sir; he tells me it's night when I know the sun shines."

"How can you say so, gran'father? I'm sure it's all the same as night now; I couldn't tell a bleak from a gudgeon by this light."

"Nor by any other light," said the old man, reproachfully; "when I was his age there wasn't a fish in the stream, or a fly over it, but I knew —ay, as well as I did my Bible; and there is much in the knowledge of the things that God makes to teach us God's power—not only His power, but His love: and I think more of the beauty of His works, now that I cannot see them, than ever I did when I had my blessed sight. But I should like to see the waters and the fish once more, and my little gran'child—the girl, I mean; I know this lad—a little rosy, curly-headed fat thing; it's his being so fat makes him so lazy."

The boy was as lean and as lank as a fishing-rod; he looked at us, and said with a smile—"Mother says I was as fat as Annie when I was a baby; gran'father calls mother a slim, pale girl, and she has *such* a red face!" This was an *aside*, but it recalled to us the exquisite poem of "The Blind Man's Bride."

The old sailor had such a touching habit of sitting with his head thrown back, and those sightless eyes up-looking to the heavens, and his fingers clasped round his rod,—it was quite a picture.

"My daughter does not tire of her old blind father," he resumed, after a pause, "nor indeed does her husband,—he is a good son to me : still I bless GOD and her MAJESTY I am no burden to them, except in the way of kindness—that is another blessing.  My daughter will not let me go near the river without the boy, so I promise her, and keep my word ; and the gentlemen who fish hereabout tell me of their sport, and I give them my advice, and sometimes they buy my nets.  And one will have me in the punt ; but I soon weary of that—I like best my liberty of the stream—I like to eat my dinner on the soft sweet grass, and to know that some of God's creatures, the wild winged birds of the air, will dine off the poor man's crumbs."

We made some observation as to his having a devotional spirit ; he answered that he ought to have : he had been shipwrecked once, and passed a night and part of a day on the deep floating on a spar.  He then learnt what it was to be alone with God, but he had NO FEAR ; he knew in Whose care he was.  This was said with a simplicity that was positively sublime.  " I have received," he said, while we walked with him towards his daughter's cottage, " I have received nothing but mercies and blessings all the days of my life ; yet I think I should have been happier if I could have looked on the blue waters and the bright fish to the last—I *think* I should—they are so pleasant !  And yet—I can't tell : I have such dreams about streams and fishes that I wake up as refreshed as if I had been ten hours angling.  Surely that in itself is a mercy, though I shall never, never in this world see fin of fish again !"

Half a mile or so from Park Place, and we arrive in sight of HENLEY BRIDGE, a graceful structure of five arches, erected in 1787, and which will be interesting to Art-lovers as containing two sculptured works— MASKS OF THE THAMES AND ISIS—from the chisel of the Hon. Mrs. Damer ;* they decorate the consoles of the central arch, exhibit talent

* Anne Seymour Damer was a lady of noble descent.  Her father, General Conway, was brother to the Marquis of Hertford ; her mother the only daughter of the fourth Duke of Argyll ; and she was cousin to Horace Walpole, who speaks enthusiastically of her graces of person and mind.  She was a real lover of her art—an art so seldom practised by ladies—and honestly earned a reputation her position in the great world might have given her with less labour, had she not desired the judgment of connoisseurs, as well as the praises of titled friends.  Her husband, the eldest son of the first Lord Milton, destroyed himself after he had been married nine years : he died in debt, and his widow sought

of no common order, and are interesting as examples of that genius
which adopted the most difficult of all the arts as the occupation and
enjoyment of rank and wealth.* This is not the only memory preserved
at Henley.  It was here that Shenstone wrote the familiar lines on an
inn :—

> " Whoe'er has travelled life's dull round,
> Where'er his stages may have been,
> May sigh to think he still has found
> The warmest welcome at an inn."

The in n—the Red Lion—is still there, but it has been long unoccupied ;
it gives, however, unequivocal proofs that it was abundant in comforts

MASKS OF THE THAMES AND ISIS.

during the days of its glory ; its large rooms are now unfurnished ; its
snug and " cozy " chambers are without light and warmth ; the stables
and outhouses, the lofts and hen-roosts, are all empty ; and those who
visit the house because of the associations it awakens, and contrast its
present loneliness with its former bustle and gaiety, may " sigh " that

consolation in renewed art-study, and travelled in Italy.  Her father, the general, resided at Park
Place—hence her contribution to the bridge.  Walpole left her Strawberry Hill for life.  She died in
1828, in the eightieth year of her age.

* That toward the source of the river represents the Isis—a female head, round which water-plants
are entwined; that on the other side is an aged male head, the Thames, crowned with bulrushes, and
from whose flowing beard little fish peep forth.  Both heads are very boldly executed, and have been
highly eulogised by Horace Walpole.

here a "welcome" is no longer to be found : his lament will not be lessened because in its successor he finds a grievous contrast in reference to all the good things of life of which an inn is proverbially productive. The town of Henley is happily situated : above and below the scenery is charming.   A fine old church adds to its interest ; and the bridge is one of the most beautiful of the many that span the noble river.*

Henley is in Oxfordshire ; but soon after leaving it we part from that county and enter Buckinghamshire—on the north side of the river, that

HENLEY-ON-THAMES.

is to say, for on its southern banks we are still in Berkshire, and continue so to be until we have passed Windsor.  As our boat rows us downward,

---

* The architect was a "Mr. Hayward :" he died before the work was even commenced, but his designs and plans were adopted.   His heart was evidently in his task, and the structure must be regarded as his monument.   He had, it is said, frequently expressed a wish that in the event of his death before its completion, he might be interred beneath the centre arch, but his desire was not responded to.   He lies, however, in the church close beside it, where there is a handsome tomb to his memory.   In this church, also, was interred the General Dumouriez famous in the early stages of the French Revolution : he died in the neighbourhood in 1823, at the age of eighty-four, having lived through the several eventful periods that intervened between his exile and the restoration.   In the churchyard was buried Richard Jennings, "the master-builder of St. Paul's."

we soon arrive in sight of FAWLEY COURT—a summer-house, situated on
a pretty island, attracts the eye as one of the graces of the Thames. It
is built after a Greek model. Close to this is the village of Remenham,
at the base of some high ground charmingly wooded. Fawley Court—
its Grecian summer-house, that is to say, on the small island—is famous

ISLAND, FAWLEY COURT.

in the history of the Thames as the starting-point of the Regatta, which
annually "glorifies" the river, and assembles here a host of gay and
happy lovers of water-sports. A few remarks on the racing-boats of the
Thames, and the "race," cannot here be out of place.

The most singular and the most peculiar of all the Thames boats, not
excepting even the "punt," is the racing-boat. This boat is of various
sizes, adapted either to a single rower, or to crews consisting of two,
four, sometimes six, and frequently eight persons: the eight-oared boats
being those which are employed in the more important races. The
boats themselves vary in form, being sometimes sharp at both stem and
stern, in which case they are denominated "wherries;" when they are
built flat at the stern, they are termed "cutters." Wherries are now
rarely built for more than two rowers; when there are more than two

B B

rowers, the boats are provided with accommodation for a steerer. In length these boats range from about twelve to nearly seventy feet, and they are always very narrow, being so constructed that they simply provide sitting room for their crews ; the oars are sustained by "rullocks," or "row-locks," which project considerably from either side, and thus afford leverage for the rowers. As would be expected, these fairy-like boats are built with the utmost care, the materials being usually the finest pine-wood, with fittings of mahogany. They are so exceedingly light that a man may carry one of the smaller ones on his shoulder with ease; their weight is sometimes no more than thirty-five pounds ; and their draught is very small, yet, when in progress, the boat is, fore and aft, on a level with the water ; where the rowers sit the gunwales have

RACING-BOAT.

a slight elevation to prevent the flow of water, which sometimes passes over the other parts of the boat, that are accordingly protected by a covering of light oilskin. The rowers' seats and the "stretchers," or boards for their feet to rest against, alone occupy the open space allotted to them, which is, in fact, simply a kind of trough. The rate at which an eight-oar boat progresses, if well pulled, is not less than twelve miles an hour. It is evidently a delicate operation to embark in one of these gossamer vessels, and to occupy it is always attended with some degree of danger, in consequence of the equilibrium of the boat being maintained entirely by the even balance of the oars. And yet accidents are of rare occurrence, while the light craft are taught to yield to the most ener- getic exertions of their manly crews, who exemplify, in high perfection, the practical application of the truly English adage, of "A long pull, a strong pull, and a pull all together." It is a nervous thing even to look upon the voyager in one of these boats; for our own parts, we would as readily trust ourselves on the back of a wild horse on an Indian prairie; and we marvel much that the cool self-possession of the "boating-men" themselves should so generally preserve them from casualties. But at Oxford, and on other parts of the river, all the men and boys, and many of the women, learn to swim; there is always a charm in peril—danger is ever a pleasant excitement; and so it happens that these boats are in far more frequent request than such as cannot upset.

The boat-race itself is indeed an animated and a brilliant spectacle: there the island spirit of England shows itself after a most characteristic fashion—the enthusiasm of those who are actually engaged in the struggle extending its influence to the spectators of every class who crowd the river-sides. At Oxford there are several races, which take place according to a prescribed order of arrangement during the spring and summer period of each academic year; and here almost every college has its representative afloat. There are few more striking sights than that afforded by the long line of dashing boats gallantly manned, covering the classic stream, and rushing over its waters between such a "run on the banks" as needs to be seen, and indeed to be shared in, to be adequately appreciated. The flash of the oars keeps time with the cheers of ardent and encouraging friends, who strive on land to emulate the speed of the swift skimmers of the waters; a victory achieved elicits still louder acclamations; and each race concludes amidst mingled congratulations, because of present success, and anticipations of future success in races yet to come. The number of the boats, and the comparative narrowness of the stream at Oxford, render it impossible for the competing crews to be arranged side by side; they consequently start and pull in a line a-head, the object of each crew being to *touch* with their own boat the boat before them in the line. Such a "bump" leads to a change of places in the case of these two boats; and thus the best boat's crew bump their way to the "head of the river," where, if they can, they may hold their honourable and honoured position.

The fine "reaches" of the Thames at Henley are yearly the scene of boat-races, open to all competitors, and which afford an opportunity for every variety of racing-boat to show its own capabilities and the powers of its rowers. In these races the two Universities of Oxford and Cambridge take a part, together with the "crack" boats of London, and with other worthy rivals from various parts of the country. The matches include races with eight, four, and two-oared boats; and there are also "sculling-matches," as those races are designated in which each boat is rowed by a single person. The incidents so familiar on the river-banks at Oxford, at Henley are repeated on a still more important scale—the very circumstances of the Henley races raising to the highest pitch the interest inseparable from them. The broad river here allows the rival boats in every race to be placed alongside of each other; and thus, with even bows, they spring forth upon a career which not unfrequently closes upon them still being side by side, the winner having perhaps half his boat's length in advance.

Still further down the stream the same light racing-boats may be seen in active exercise, and particularly at the matches of the Thames watermen, and at the grand annual contest between the picked eight-oared boats' crews of Oxford and Cambridge. This "University boat-race" was first pulled upwards of a quarter of a century back, at Henley, but now it is generally decided, like the watermen's races, in the neighbourhood of Putney. On these occasions the Thames swarms with boats of every size and kind, nor is a flotilla of river steamers wanting to complete the aquatic picture, and to contribute to the scene the smoky attribute of London. A clear course is, however, kept for the racing-boats, each distinguished by a tiny flag a few inches in length at the bow; and, happily, notwithstanding the crowded condition of the river, the animation of the races is rarely overcast by the sad reflections arising from any serious mischance.

Passing Culham Court, and underneath a range of wooded hills, we reach "Mile End," or Hambledon, lock. The adjacent country becomes exceedingly beautiful, varied by alternate mills, islands, meadows, and hills, with every now and then ornamental "forest trees" hanging over the stream, and giving pleasant shade to the current on its downward flow. Magpie Island is reached and passed; but those who have leisure may linger about this charming spot. The wood of Medmenham soon comes in sight; the ruined ABBEY is seen among the trees; and close beside it a pretty ferry, with the pleasant way-side inn of Mrs. Bitmead—a domicile well known to artists, her frequent guests, one of whom, who has since become "famous," painted a sign-board which hangs over the door, and is of so good a quality that it might grace the Exhibition of the Royal Academy. The abbey has been pictured a hundred times, and is a capital subject seen from any point of view; the river runs close beside it; there is a hill adjacent—Danes' Hill; dark woods and green meadows are at hand; gay boats and traffic barges are

MEDMENHAM ABBEY.

continually passing; the ferry is always picturesque; and the artist is constantly supplied "on the spot" with themes for pictures; especially he has before him the venerable ruin—"venerable," at least, in so far as the eye is concerned. Time has touched it leniently; some of its best "bits" are as they were a century ago, except that the lichens have given to them that rich clothing of grey and gold which the painter ever loves, and added to it here and there a green drapery of ivy.

The manor of Medmenham was, in the reign of King Stephen, given by its lord, Walter de Bolebec, to the Abbey of Cistercian Monks he had founded at Woburn, in Bedfordshire; and in 1204 the monks placed some of their society here, on this pleasant bank of the Thames; hence arose "a small monastery, being rather," as the writers of the order express themselves, "a daughter than a cell to Wooburn." In 1536, it was annexed to Bisham. At the dissolution, according to returns made by the commissioners, "the clere value of this religious house was twenty pounds six shillings; it had two monks, and both desyrin to go to houses of religion; servants none; woods none; debts none; its bells worth two pounds, one shilling, and eight pence; the value of its movable goods, one pound, three shillings, and eightpence; and the house wholly in ruine." It must have undergone considerable repair early in the six-teenth century, and probably very little of the original structure now

DOOR OF MEDMENHAM ABBEY.

exists, although relics of an-tiquity may be traced in many of its "remains." That portion which fronts the Thames is kept in pro-per repair, and a large room is used for the convenience of pleasure-parties. The whole of the back, however, is in a wretched state of dila-pidation, although inhabited by several families. The property belongs to the Scotts of Danesfield, a man-sion that crowns a neigh-bouring hill.

Medmenham derives noto-riety from events of more recent date than the occupa-tion of its two monks, without goods, and without debt. Here, about the middle of the last century, was established a society of men of wit and fashion, who assumed the title of Monks of St. Francis, and wore the habit of the Franciscan order. Although it is said the statements contained in a now forgotten but once popular novel—" Chrysal; or, the Adventures of a Guinea"—were exaggerated, the character which the " assumed " monks bore in the open world was sufficiently notorious to justify the worst suspicions of their acts in this comparative solitude. The principal members were Sir Francis Dashwood (afterwards Lord Le Despencer), the Earl of Sandwich, John Wilkes, Bubb Doddington, Churchill, and Paul Whitehead the poet. The motto,—" Fay ce que voudras,"—indicative of the principle on which the society was conducted, still remains over the doorway of the Abbey House. Tradition yet preserves some anecdotes illustrative of the habits of " the order," and there can be little doubt that this now lonely and quiet spot was the scene of orgies that were infamous.

The Thames now flows through one of the richest of its many rich valleys; and hence, until it arrives at Marlow, its windings are frequent and of long continuance,—the flatness of the view being relieved, looking back, by the wooded slopes of Culham, and the distant Chilterns, in Buckinghamshire.

The pretty and picturesque village of Hurley is now reached; it is in Berkshire; another village, that of Harleyford, occupying the opposite bank. Adjoining Hurley was Lady Place, formerly a priory for Benedictine monks, more recently a stately mansion, but now indicated only by aged garden-walls. The house was erected during the reign of Elizabeth, on the site of the ancient convent, and out of the debris of the buildings, by the then owner of the estate, Sir Richard Lovelace,— one of the brothers in arms of Sir Francis Drake. "He was a gentleman of metal," writes old Fuller, "who had the success to light on a large amount of the King of Spain's cloth of silver,—I mean, his West Indian fleet,—wherewith he and his posterity are warmer to this day." He was created Baron Lovelace, of Hurley, by Charles I.; but during the reign of his two successors, the house was the meeting-place of the several peers and leading commoners whose movements led, eventually, to the "calling in " of the Prince of Orange. "The meetings were held under cover of splendid hospitalities, by which the noble owner of the mansion is said to have exhausted his fortune." * The more secret and perilous consultations were, it is said, held in a vault underneath, originally the burial-place of the monastery. The house is described by Boydell, in 1794, as "a spacious edifice. The hall, which occupies a disproportionate part of it, is a noble room, with a light gallery round it. The saloon is wainscoted with English oak, which was sent over in panels to Italy to be painted, according to the family tradition, by Salvator Rosa. The views are undoubtedly Italian, and in the bold style of that great master." † The structure, having become much dilapidated, was altogether removed in the year 1837. Fortunately, Mr. Fairholt visited "the Place" about that period, and made sketches of the various objects of interest,—among others of the famous vault; and to his pen and pencil we are indebted for the following details.

Lady Place obtained its name from the monastery upon whose foundation it stood having been dedicated to "our Lady" the Virgin. The exterior had projecting wings and a porch, in accordance with the prevalent taste of the reign of Elizabeth, said to have been thus generally adopted in compliment to that sovereign, the ground-plan forming the initial of her name, thus—ⷨ. The inner arrangements were singularly inconvenient, except in the lower story, where they were much enriched with stucco ornament and painted landscapes; but the upper rooms were small, and the gutters of the roof ran through them, freely admitting both water and air. The vault below was reached by a trapdoor in the hall-floor, and was very solidly constructed, receiving its light from a grated window below the level of the garden. In one recess (that behind the figures in our cut) a square tablet was inserted,

---

* When the prince became converted into the monarch, as our King William III., he did not forget the service that Lord Lovelace had rendered him; he made him captain of the Band of Gentlemen Pensioners, and gave him other emoluments; but the taste for open-house keeping and display, engendered by his revolutionary meetings, never left him. He made great alterations at Lady Place, re-decorated the interior, and lived in an extravagant style; so that his possessions were sold, under a decree of Chancery, at his death, to pay the debts in which he became again involved.

† They were, more probably, the work of Antonio Tempesta, who designed in the same style, and was much employed in such decorations as these. The paintings had but little merit, and brought very small prices when the house was destroyed.

containing three inscriptions in as many compartments, giving the chief
facts connected with its history : first detailing its original foundation,
" at the time of the great Norman revolution, by which revolution the
whole state of England was changed ;" then, " that in this place, six
hundred years afterwards, the revolution of 1688 was begun, and it is
said that several consultations for calling in the Prince of Orange were
held in this recess, on which account this vault was visited by that
powerful prince after he had ascended the throne." The third inscrip-

THE VAULT AT LADY PLACE.

tion commemorated another royal visit in these words :—" Be it remembered that this place was visited by their majesties King George III.
and Queen Charlotte, on Monday, the 14th of November, 1785." The
visit of General Paoli, the celebrated commander of the Corsicans in
the revolution of that island, was also noted in May, 1790 ; as well as
the fact that, in digging below the floor, some bodies in Benedictine
habits had been found, the last denizens of the old monastery. As we
have said, there are now no remains of Lady Place, except the garden
walls, to indicate its " whereabouts."

Passing Temple Hall, the seat of the old and honourable family of

Williams, we arrive at BISHAM ABBEY, one of the most picturesque objects on the Thames, and also among the most venerable and interesting of all the ancient remains which time and use have consecrated.

The abbey and church are in admirable "keeping;" but each has its own peculiar features.    The abbey is now a modern residence, tasteful, and comfortably arranged, furnished, and decorated.    The mansion is old—of the 'Tudor period : it was built on the site of the

BISHAM ABBEY.

abbey—originally a preceptory of the Knights Templars, but subsequently a priory for canons of the order of St. Augustine, founded by William Montacute, Earl of Salisbury, in 1338.    His body was interred in the church, together with that of his son William.    Here also were laid the "mortal parts" of that Earl of Salisbury who died at the siege of Orleans, in 1428 ; Richard Neville, " the king-maker," killed at the battle of Barnet, in 1470 ; and Edward Plantagenet, son of the Duke of Clarence, beheaded in 1499 for attempting an escape from confinement.*

It is impossible to tread these grounds, sombre as they are,—for the

---

* The tombs of the Hoby family, of the times of Elizabeth and James I., are now the most remarkable monuments in the church.   The present mansion at Bisham was built about 1590, by the head of that family.

hues of dark and heavy trees are in solemn harmony with the ancient church, and the almost as venerable mansion,—without being impressed by a degree of awe amounting to sadness.   What a story might be told by those old walls, of the times when the Templars re-velled in their glory !

Immediately on leaving the shadows which the tall trees of Bisham throw on the water, the eye and mind are relieved by the graceful sus-pension bridge which spans the Thames at Marlow— Great Marlow.  It is a quiet town, and has the recom-mendation of being not very close to a railroad. Some thirty or forty years ago, however, it was as full of bustle and excitement as it is now of repose; for the Military College was here, and here some of the bravest and best of our soldiers were educated.  It was thus cir-

BISHAM CHURCH.

cumstanced, however, for no very long period—the establishment com-mencing in 1799, and removing to Sandhurst in 1812.

Marlow is the very paradise of the Thames angler : perhaps no part of the whole river, from its rise to its mouth, will afford him safer assurance of a day's sport; such sport, that is to say, as will content the unambitious lover of "the gentle craft ;" for if he covet to excel in its loftier achievements he must "go further a-field," and make acquaint-ance with streams more accommodating than that of the good and generous old " Father."

But the Thames angler loves the river hereabouts, not only because it seldom fails to fill his basket—here he obtains all the other enjoyments which our king of island rivers abundantly supplies.   Does he seek health and quiet?—He finds them here.   Does he love nature—the rural sounds as well as rural sights that give pure and true enjoyment?—They are here—everywhere.   Does he seek to call up, in fancy, the

THE INN AT MARLOW.

great of bygone ages—the worthies of his country, in palpit, in senate, or in arms—

>    —" The dead—
> Who rule our spirits from their urns?"—

Nowhere can he obtain so many associations with the heroic past.

Nor is it to be forgotten that among the other attractions of Marlow is one of the prettiest and pleasantest inns remaining in railway-ridden England; with a most kindly and accommodating landlady, who seems, by intuition—and certainly is from long practice—aware of all the ways and wants of brethren of the angle, who are her best, and, indeed, almost her only customers; for her "hostelry" is not in the town, but in a quiet nook close by the bridge on the Berkshire side of the river.

Fortunate will he be who is a dweller here; especially if Rosewell, one of the oldest and best of Thames fishermen, be his companion and guide to the several "pitches" where he is to look for his day's sport. He will rise with the lark, and all will be ready for him; the neat and clean punt is moored close beside that pretty little summer-house of trees and climbing flowers; the baits are in—gentles, and red worms, and graves, with soaked bread and clay for the manufacture of ground-bait; the rake will be there too, for at mid-day, probably, he will have a "try" for gudgeon, although his special victims are to be the roach and dace; and for these his "gentle-box" is full, the gentles being "well bred" from the liver of the ox; he has purchased them in London, no doubt; for he does not choose to incur the hazard that Rosewell's store may have been exhausted by some successful party of the day before.

He has had an early breakfast, and Mrs. Parslow has not neglected to draw an eel—a genuine Thames eel—of a pound weight, out of the tank pictured at the landing-place, and where she generally contrives to preserve a few for choice friends—true anglers, to whom alone they are given, and who alone should have them; or, it may be, he prefers the "new-laid egg" which yonder clucking hen has just contributed by way of welcome. He is off till dinner-time—or, what is more likely, if he be a genuine lover of the sport, his dinner is in the hamper that stands at the bow of the boat, for he may grow hungry just as the fish are biting most freely; and let us see the true angler who would leave a productive pitch for the best dinner that ever graced an alderman's table!

His rod is put together; it is just twelve feet in length, really tapering, but comparatively "stiff"—certainly so in the eyes of the trout fisher: it is made of bamboo, except the top, which is of hazel; his reel whistles full, and is in good order; a fine and new line of gut is fastened to his running line; the hook, very small—so small that it seems only made to suit a minnow, but is in reality large enough for a barbel of ten pounds

weight—is mounted upon horse-hair of sandy colour; the float, of elongated and shapely quill, is "a pretty thing to look at;" towards the end
of the line are some forty or fifty shot, small and distributed at intervals
—these sink the baited hook, for he is "bottom-fishing," and contrives
that the bait shall just pass half an inch or so above the gravel, and he
also wishes it to sink rapidly, so as to lose as little as may be of "the
swim." He is quite ready, and meanwhile Rosewell has chosen his first
pitch—there, in mid-stream; but by-and-by he will select ground
somewhere nearer the bank, or perhaps a position close to those weeds
that run a good way out into the current, or he may prefer a chance
under those aged pollards, whose roots run almost as far into, as their

FISHING PUNT.

branches do over, the river. The boat is moored; two poles, one at
either end, prevent its moving, and keep it steady; but you see how
cautiously this has been done—Rosewell knows the fish are there, and
that a clumsy push would be a warning to them to remove from dangerous quarters. Carefully, and with as little stir as possible, the plummet, secured to his hook by the bit of cork let into the lead, is sunk to
the bottom to sound the depth—it is ascertained to a nicety; a "half
hitch," effected by twisting the line round the top of the float, prevents
its slipping; two gentles are neatly placed on the hook, and the angler
begins his work. Rosewell soon collects the fish by throwing in a few
balls of ground-bait—bread, bran, and graves, and, it may be, coarse

gentles (always desirable), mixed with clay; the clay soon dissolves, and the fish come up at a "fin gallop" to learn the source of the supply, indicated by many floating particles.

Hah! a touch! they are gathering, and are growing bold; the float is carried under; strike! the smallest bend of the wrist is enough—force will break the hair, or pull the hook out of the mouth : it is well struck —you feel by the weight that "you have him;" it is a roach of half-a-pound—you know it is a roach, although you cannot see him—he makes no sudden spring, as he would do if a dace, or, still more, if a chub; there is no mistake about it now, for he comes sailing towards the boat, and you note the redness of the eyes and fins through the water. Do not hurry—patience is the angler's virtue—he is at your hand—draw in your line gently, and remove him from the hook to the well—that heavy-looking space which stands out near the boat's stern, through which the water runs by holes made in the sides; and to which you will, before the day is over, consign some ten, or, it may be, twenty dozen of his fellow-captives, who will swim about in happy ignorance that their destiny is to be transferred to that neat and graceful basket of white wicker-work, the form of which is as well known as the shape of a ship's anchor.

And such is Thames angling—a joy above all joys to those who love it, compared to which—

> " Other joys
> Are but toys!"

And although the "business" of the angler, thus pursued, may be, as it has ever been, a theme of sneer and sarcasm with those who throw a fly across the Tweed, and land a huge salmon, after an hour's labour to subdue him, the pleasure of him "who sits quietly in a summer evening on a bank a-fishing"—as that great and good man, Sir Harry Wotton, often did, and as so many other men, as great and good, have as often done—is not to be despised by those who have the power to ramble half the world over to seek enjoyment, and to find far less of it than is found by him who is content

> " To see his quill or cork down sink
> With eager bite of perch, or bleak, or dace."

A short distance below Marlow, a paper and corn-mill added to the lock completely block up the Thames, but there is a back-water in which the angler is pretty sure to find enjoyment. If he be a bottom-fisher, it is probable that Rosewell will take him half a mile lower down, and moor his boat at Quarry Point—a bay which is left undisturbed by river-traffic, and is shaded by the tall trees of Quarry Wood. This beautiful demesne is succeeded by that of Winter Hill, where the Thames becomes a broad sheet of water, and assumes the character of a small lake, from which there is no apparent outlet. On the Berkshire side there are

COOKHAM CHURCH.

many pleasant slopes crowned with villas, while on that of Buckingham-shire, the land is flat and marshy, but the distant hills give a valuable effect to the scenery—wooded here and there, and frequently varied by green fields and "arable land."

Shade-Oak Ferry is next reached, and here the river begins to assume a more busy and active character—barges, punts, boats, "canoes," and racing-boats are more often encountered; the shores are more populous than they have been hitherto, and we gradually lose that sense of solitude with which the grand old "Father" has so continually oppressed us higher up the stream. The woods of Hedsor—the seat of Lord Boston—companion us for a long way, and for some miles we keep in sight a remarkable structure which crowns the summit of a hill,—we learn that it is nothing more than a summer-house, placed there for the sake of the many views it commands; but it looks like the huge ghost of some mighty edifice which man has deserted. On the opposite bank— in Berkshire, that is to say—is COOKHAM, a pretty village, with a fine old church. A little lower down, and we row beside a lovely island of some acres in extent; it has been laid out in charming walks, with here and there seats for rest, and summer-houses,—every corner planted with fair flowers, shrubs, and cheerful evergreens. Another island—Formosa Island—somewhat further on, greets the voyager, and is also full of attractions.

We are now approaching that part of the Thames which supplies its most abundant beauties—of mingled wood and water, hill and valley, shrubby heights and richly cultivated fields. The river here closes in, or seems to do so; for although in reality wide, it is narrowed to the eye by the steep hills which rise from the banks on either side, clothed in varied foliage from the base to the summit. Those who accuse our great island river of insipidity, who, if they concede its claims to beauty, deny its pretensions to grandeur, will do well to visit the scenery between Hedsor and Maidenhead—to row beneath the thick woods of Taplow and Cliefden, and, looking up, they will have no difficulty in imagining themselves in one of the grandest and richest, in picturesque attractions, of our English lakes; indeed, they will require only the near and distant mountains to fancy themselves under the heights of Glena, in all-beautiful Killarney. Well may we rejoice to scan the charms of our glorious river, and ask the aid of Poetry and Art to give them fame and power. But the painter will fail here. He may select graceful nooks, and a thousand objects will, singly or in groups, present themselves as fitting subjects for his pencil; but he cannot convey to the eye and mind a just idea of the mingled grandeur and beauty of this delicious locality; while the poet will find only themes which have been, ever and everywhere, the chosen and the favoured of his order.

D D

Nature here has been liberally aided by successive lords, from that Duke of Buckingham by whom " Cliefden's proud alcove" was made

" The bower of wanton Shrewsbury and love,"

to that other duke—the Duke of Sutherland—who now happily owns it, and under whose superintending care, or rather that of his accomplished duchess, the mansion and grounds are among the loveliest, most graceful, and the most richly cultivated of the kingdom.*    If, however, those who row past these charming woods,—and note what has been

CLIEFDEN.

done by taste, in association with wealth, to render every part delightful,—ascend any of the many heights and examine the " prospect," near or distant, their enjoyment will be largely enhanced.    It is impos-

---

* " Cliefden House " was built by Charles Villiers, Duke of Buckingham,—that Villiers so familiar to all who read the records of pernicious follies and degenerating vices during the reign of Charles II.—

" In squandering wealth was his peculiar art."

The house has been twice destroyed by fire: that which now surmounts the hill was built a few years ago, for the Duke of Sutherland, by the architect Barry.

sible, indeed, to exaggerate the beauty and harmony of the foliage which
everywhere surrounds us,—

> " Beautiful in various dyes,
> The gloomy pine, the poplar blue,
> The yellow beech, the sable yew,
> The slender fir that taper grows,
> The sturdy oak with broad-spread boughs ;
> And beyond the purple grove,
> Haunt of Phyllis, Queen of Love ! "

But there are here hundreds of other trees which the poet could not
commemorate, for they were unknown to England in his time. All
climes and countries have contributed to the wealth of foliage at
Cliefden,—woods, lawns, and gardens are enriched by tributes from
every land to which enterprise has conducted British science, to gather
treasures converted from exotics into subjects naturalised and " at
home."*

Leaving this scene of mingled grandeur and beauty, to which the
Thames voyager will often look back, we pass through Boulters Lock,
and arrive at the bridge at Maidenhead. And here let us pause awhile,
—for we are in sight of "regal Windsor,"—and consider a few of
those "facts" which may augment the interest of the voyage, and
add to the enjoyment derived from acquaintance with the peculiarities of our great river. And first we ask the reader's attention
to the following notes, for which we are indebted to our friend
Professor Hunt.

The Thames flows over a certain set of geological formations, which
are known as the supercretaceous or tertiary strata ; these are a certain
order of deposits which are based upon the chalk.

The depth at which the chalk is found beneath the surface at a few
points around London, will give the best idea of the varying thickness of the tertiary formations on which our metropolitan city stands,

---

* It is worth noting that Thomson's masque of " Alfred " was first acted at Cliefden, and that, consequently, within those walls was first sung the national song of " Rule Britannia," composed by him
and set to music by Dr. Arne, on the occasion of its performance.

and through which the waters of the Thames have scooped out their
channel :—

|  | Feet. |
|---|---|
| At Hampstead Vale the chalk was reached at the depth of | 378 |
| At Camden Town | 230 |
| New Road, near Tottenham Court Road | 150 |
| Lambeth, at Hungerford Bridge | 250 |
| Church Street, Camberwell Grove | 105 |
| St. Luke's, Old Street | 160 |
| Fishmongers' Hall, Lower Thames Street | 237 |
| Near Surrey Canal, Kent Road | 34 |
| Manor Farm, in Lewisham | 20 |
| Rotherhithe | 46 |

Thus we learn that a series of chalk hills undulates between the valley
of the Thames, in a similar manner to those picturesque swellings and
depressions which mark the wood-crowned chalk hills of Reigate and of
Guildford.  Upon this bed of chalk, extending from Croydon on one
side to St. Alban's on the other, and from below Gravesend in the east
to Newbury in the west, we find a group of red mottled clays and
permeable sands, very variable in their composition and structure ; and
although they sometimes acquire a thickness of 130 feet, they frequently
thin out to a thickness of only 25 feet.

Above these sands and clays, having a very irregular boundary, we
find the *London clay*.  This formation, on the north side of the Thames,
extends to Southend, and may be traced along the coast to Aldborough.
On the south side of the Thames the London clay scarcely extends
eastward of the river Ravensbourne.  The towns of Croydon, Epsom,
Guildford, and Farnham are scarcely reached by this formation; but it
comes so near them, that they serve to mark the southern boundary.
On the north and north-west we find it skirting Hungerford, Reading,
Maidenhead, Uxbridge, Barnet, Thaxted, Ipswich, and Aldborough, the
city of London standing nearly in the centre of its greatest length.
This London clay in some places acquires a thickness of from 400 to
500 feet.

An upper group of permeable, loose, siliceous sands is known as the
*Bagshot sands*.  The nearest point to London reached by the *Bagshot
sands* is the hills of Highgate and Hampstead ; the main mass of them
extending from Esher on the east, to near Strathfieldsaye on the west,

and from near Guildford on the south, to Ascot and Virginia Water on the north, forming a well-known elevated tract, composed, in the greater part, of sandy heaths. Beside these, there are the superficial accumulations of gravel, clay, or brick-earth, which are usually classed as *drift*. These are dispersed with much irregularity over the face of the country, the London clay being covered by gravel at Clapham, Kensington, and Hyde Park, and by gravel and brick-earth at West Drayton.

If we follow the course of the river Thames from Aylesbury or from Oxford, we find it first flowing over the *Kimmeridge clay*, which consists, in great part, of a bituminous shale, sometimes forming an impure coal, several hundred feet in thickness. In this formation are found several extinct molluscous animals and Saurian remains. The river then cuts its way through the *lower green-sand*, again distinctly marked by the characteristics of its fossil remains. The *gault* is next traversed by it, and it passes the *upper green-sand* at Wallingford.

The gault consists of a dark blue marl, and is palæontologically characterized by the forms of *Cephalopoda* found within it. The upper green-sand has been regarded as the littoral deposit of that ocean in which our chalk rocks were formed. It derives its name from containing green particles of sand coloured by a chloritic mineral. These two formations have lately been rendered of great commercial importance, from the abundant excrementitious and other remains of fish, which are so rich in phosphate of lime, as to make the agriculturist eager to obtain these coprolites, &c., for fertilizing his soil.

Leaving Wallingford, the Thames passes through the chalk formations until it reaches Reading, whence it is found winding its way, still through chalk, to Henley and Beaconsfield, and round to Maidenhead: it then passes, for a short distance, through the sands and mottled clay of the lower tertiary strata, and, entering upon the London clay at Windsor, it makes that formation its bed, until, sweeping past the great metropolis, it again meets the lower tertiary sands at Deptford, a little below which the chalk once more appears; and, until the river empties itself into the ocean, it is found with sands and chalk alternating upon its banks.

A few words upon the London clay formation may not be without interest. It consists of a tenacious brown and bluish-grey clay, with layers of concretions called *Septaria*, which abound in some parts, and are collected for the manufacture of Roman cement. The principal fossils of the London clay are found at Highgate Hill, in the Island of Sheppey, and at Bognor, in Hampshire; from these localities 133 species of fossil shells have been obtained. The Island of Sheppey abounds with fossil fruits and seeds, which have been very carefully examined and described by Mr. Bowerbank. Thirteen fruits of palms have been discovered of the same type as the *Nipa*, now found only in the Molucca and Philippine Islands, and in Bengal. "These plants are allied," says Sir Charles Lyell, "to the cocoa-nut tribe on the one side, and on the other to the *Pandanus* or Screw pine. The fruits of other palms, besides those of the cocoa-nut tribe, are also met with in the clay of Sheppey; three species of the Custard apple (*Anona*), and fruits of the gourd and melon family in considerable abundance. Beyond these, fruits of various species of Acacia are in profusion—all implying the existence of a warm climate." Those remains of an ancient flora must not be supposed to have all grown on the Island of Sheppey; they were brought down by some large river—the parent of Father Thames—and were deposited upon the accumulated mud-banks of a large delta, as at the present day. We are informed by Dr. Hooker, that in the Delta of the Ganges are seen such numbers of the large nuts of the *Nipa fructicans*, that they obstruct the paddle-wheels of the steamboats.

Among the animal remains which have been discovered in the London clay, are the teeth and bones of crocodiles and turtles, and a sea-snake some thirteen feet long; strange animals allied to the hog, and a pachyderm, called *Coryphodon cocanus* by Owen, larger than any existing tapir.

"These"—we again quote Sir Charles Lyell—"animals seem to have inhabited the banks of a great river, which floated down the Sheppey fruits. They imply the existence of a mammiferous fauna, antecedent to the period when nummulites flourished in Europe and in Asia, and therefore before the Alps, Pyrenees, and other mountain chains, now forming the back-bones of great continents, were raised from the deep; nay, even before a part of the continent rocky masses, now entering into the central ridges of these chasms, had been deposited in the sea."

As the Thames flows below London it passes over the more recent accumulations of drift, in which the mammoth and the rhinoceros have been found; there have also been discovered, at Brentford, the bones of an hippopotamus; here lie mingled with those of aurochs—a short-horned ox—red deer, and a great cave tiger, or lion. At Grays, near Gravesend, exists the celebrated *elephant bed*, from which have been derived bones and teeth in immense quantities. From these facts we learn an instructive lesson of the earth's mutations; and that the bosom of that river which now bears upon it the wealth of the old and the new continents, to add to the luxury of the greatest city in the civilized world, once swept a mighty torrent through forests of palms, and bore the fruits which had fallen before the storm, in countless myriads, down to its wide-spread delta, there to be preserved as memorials of a mighty past. The hippopotamus laved in its waters, the rhinoceros and the elephant dwelt upon its banks. The country through which the Thames now rolls onward to the sea, was, ages ere yet man had existence, similar in most respects to the vast plains of Central Africa—the watershed of a wide swamp, rich in vegetation, excited by the influences of a tropical sun.

MAIDENHEAD is a small town, at some distance from the bridge—a structure of much elegance, built in 1772, from the designs of Sir Robert Taylor. The name is said to be a corruption of that which it bore so early as the reign of Edward III.—Maydenhithe, *hithe* being the Saxon word for haven or port: Camden, however, fancifully derives its title from the veneration paid there to the "head" of a Virgin, one of the "eleven thousand" whose bones may be now seen at Cologne! The view from the bridge, both above and below, is very beautiful: on the one side the trees rise from the river-bank to the wooded heights that surround Cliefden; while on the other the pretty islet, the Church of Bray, the bridge of the railroad, the near meadows and distant hills, attract the eye, and tempt the passenger to linger awhile in admiration.

In this district, indeed, are to be found all the several advantages
which the noble river so abundantly supplies : a channel of depth
sufficient for any required traffic, a populous and flourishing town close
at hand, pleasant cottages, comfortable inns, and villas, grand or graceful,
scattered at convenient intervals, by the bank-sides, on the slopes of
adjacent elevations, or crowning distant hills in the midst of " patrician
trees " and " plebeian underwood ;" while the heart-cheering turrets of
Windsor Castle occasionally come in sight, to add to the interest of the

MAIDENHEAD BRIDGE.

scenery the lessons and the pleasures of association.  The land is thus
fertile in themes, and the water is hardly less so : the barges, the punts,
the gay wherries, the racing-boats are everywhere ; and perhaps in no part
of the world are there to be obtained enjoyments so many or so full—at
once so quiet and so active—as are to be found in this part of the
Thames, where the venerable Father leads us to classic Eton and regal
Windsor.

The voyager will surely go ashore at Bray, not only to examine the
venerable church, but to speculate concerning that renowned vicar who
has obtained a larger share of immortality than any of his predecessors
or successors.  The vicar has indeed no tomb in his church to perpetuate

his memory, but his fame is preserved in song; and its application is not uncommon, even now-a-days, to those who find it convenient to change opinions.* BRAY CHURCH is a large and interesting structure, exhibiting

BRAY CHURCH.

that mixture of architectural features so frequently observable in buildings which have survived many ages of change. Inside are several old

---

* The vicar was named Symond Symonds. The authority for his history is Fuller, who says,—"The vivacious vicar thereof, living under King Henry VIII., King Edward VI., Queen Mary, and Queen Elizabeth, was first a Papist, then a Protestant, then a Papist, then a Protestant again. He had seen some martyrs burnt (two miles off) at Windsor, and found this fire too hot for his tender temper. This vicar being taxed by one for being a turncoat and an inconstant changeling—'Not so,' said he, 'for I always kept my principle, which is this—to live and die the Vicar of Bray.'"

The popular ballad is essentially incorrect in all its details, and, by changing the true period of the vicar's residence here, has represented him even worse than he was. It makes him commence his career in the time of Charles II., and continue a series of changes, religious and political, until the accession of George I. The song is, therefore, chiefly political, its concluding lines being the declaration—

"That whatsoever king shall reign,
    I'll be the Vicar of Bray!"

Ritson, who was such an industrious collector of our English popular songs and their music, has given the words and tune of this song in his "Select Collection of English Songs," 1783; but he was not able to say who was its author, although it was evidently written not more than sixty years before that period. It was most probably the production of one of the men of talent who visited Tonson at his house, close by Bray.

E E

monuments, the best being the brass of Sir John Foxley and his two
wives (of the early part of the fourteenth century); the figures occupying a sort of shrine, based on a column, which is again supported by a
*fox*, in allusion to their names.   Another fine brass to members of the
Norreys family is dated 1592; and there is a very interesting one to
Arthur Page, "of Water Okelye, in the parish of Braye," and Sesely his
wife, 1598, which shows that the name of Page was known in the
neighbourhood of Windsor when Shakspere chose it for one of the chief
characters of his immortal drama.   The tomb of Henry Partridge, of
the same era, is remarkable for an enumeration of the virtues of the
deceased, the chief place being given to the assertion that he

" Next to treason, hated debt." *

Soon after leaving Bray we step ashore at " MONKEY ISLAND :" the
fishing-lodge built here by the third Duke of Marlborough is now "a
house of entertainment;" and the grounds, although limited in extent,
are famous for "picnics" in summer seasons.   The room which gives a
name to the island is still preserved unimpaired; the monkeys continue,
on canvas, to do the work of men—to hunt, to shoot, and to fish : and no
doubt the "monkey-room," which is the *salon* of parties, is an attraction
profitable to the landlord, although he may not be successful in conveying
assurance, as he seeks to do, that these pictures are the works of Sir

---

* In this church is still preserved one of those chained books commonly placed in the sacred edifice

for general use in the days of the Reformation. The
custom began with the Scriptures, which were thus
chained to a desk for the consultation of the laity,
"free to all men." The Bray specimen belongs,
however, to a later period, the days of Elizabeth,
after the power of the Roman Catholic church had
gained a temporary supremacy in the days of her
sister Mary, who had, by her excess of severity,
given greater stability to the reformed faith. The
record of those who had suffered in the struggle
was published by John Fox, and his "Book of
Martyrs " became second only to the Bible in general interest.   It was placed with the sacred book for
general perusal in our churches, and the folio still
preserved at Bray is a tattered and well-worn copy
of the famed record of the struggles of the early disciples of the Protestant faith.

Joshua Reynolds.*  "Marlborough's Duke" must have expended large sums upon this "fancy," for the lodge is built of cut stone, and is evidently of a costly character; moreover, there is a detached building,

MONKEY ISLAND.

now used as a billiard-room, but in which, in the palmy days of the island, the guests probably had their banquets: it is a structure of much elegance, and no doubt was a charming retreat.

* In Westall's "Views on the Thames" the paintings are said to be the work of "a French artist named Clermont." Although clever in design, they are of no great merit in execution. One of the best of these groups we engrave,—it represents two of the animals awkwardly carrying home fish, the eels escaping from the basket. The most ludicrous scene occupies the centre of the ceiling, and is a burlesque on the triumph of Galatea; even the Cupid attending her is represented as a winged monkey with fluttering drapery, strewing flowers on the nymph, who, with her attendant tritons and sea-nymphs, are also represented as monkeys. The room is popular, and inviting to the numerous picnic parties by whom the place is visited throughout the summer season.

Of the many villas that intervene between Maidenhead and Windsor, the only one that requires especial notice is Down Place, once the residence of the famous bookseller, Jacob Tonson, the first of his fraternity who took an enlarged view of "the trade," and succeeded in achieving a celebrity and fortune previously unknown to it. "Genial Jacob," as he is termed by Pope, succeeded in gathering around him the chief talent of his day, and the famous "Kit-cat Club" was formed in his

DOWN PLACE.

house : it consisted of noblemen and gentlemen, with the Earl of Dorset at their head ; and under the plea of literary joviality they banded for a higher purpose—the defence of the House of Hanover. They took their name from one Christopher Catt, who originally supplied them with a simple dish—"mutton-pies," which always appeared upon their table. They had thirty-nine members, all distinguished for rank, learning, and wit, many holding important offices under government. Tonson acted as their secretary, and Sir Godfrey Kneller painted the portraits of the members, which were afterwards engraved and published.* Down Place is now a mansion of large size, to which many additions have from time to time been made. Our engraving is of the older part, where the wits and men of learning assembled under the protecting wing of the great bibliopole. A charming view of Maidenhead is obtained from any of the adjacent heights; while a still more attractive object is presented to the eye on the side opposite; for we

MAIDENHEAD.

are approaching "Regal Windsor." We have passed Surly Hall—now an inn, well known not only to the youths of Eton, but to all oarsmen of the river. Before we reach Windsor, however, we pass through Boveney Lock. There was a fishery here from a very early

---

* These portraits were long preserved at Down Place, and were all painted of one uniform size, which is still remembered, and the term used to designate a certain canvas, *kit-cat size*, measuring 28 or 29 inches by 36. The whole of this fine and interesting series of portraits are now in the possession of a descendant—W. R. Baker, Esq., of Bayfordbury: they are all in excellent condition, pure and clear; but the finest is certainly the portrait of Tonson himself, who is represented holding a folio copy of "Paradise Lost," of which he had the copyright, and by which he greatly added to his large fortune. His features exhibit a combination of shrewdness and inflexibility very characteristic of the man.

period; and it is recorded in the annals of Windsor that, in 1201, William, the son of Richard de Windsor, gave two marks to the king, in order that the pool and fishery in Boveney might be in the state it was wont to be during the reign of Henry II.  The men of this, and all other villages near Windsor, were accustomed to give toll at Windsor of all their merchandize.  When Eton College was building, Boveney and Maidenhead contributed their share of elm-tree wood for its con-

BOVENEY CHURCH.

struction.  The village is still but a small group of cottages, retaining very primitive features.  Let us step ashore for a brief while, to visit yon " wee " church, half hidden among lofty trees : it is the CHURCH OF BOVENEY, and is the last of its class we shall encounter; for, although we may meet some more aged and many more picturesque, there will be none along the banks of the great river that so thoroughly represent the homely and unadorned fanes where the simple villagers have been taught to worship. It is very small, and of the most primitive construction, consisting of four walls merely, the chancel end being railed off by wood-work. The font is large and simple in character, and there are traces of early mediæval work in the external walls; the pulpit is Elizabethan, but the open seats of oak may be much earlier; the roof is arched, but has originally been supported by open timber-work, —the cross-beams now alone remain.* We have engraved the interior as an example of one of our sacred edifices, where, through many ages, sate

"The rude forefathers of the hamlet."

After inspecting the interior, and wondering why so small a church was ever built, we returned to the churchyard, and stood for some little time beneath the shadow of a glorious old tree, whose boughs and foliage formed a protection against rain or sunshine. The old withered woman who had opened the church-door followed, and regretted the gentry should be disappointed, as there was "nothing to see." We differed from her, saying there was a great deal that interested us,— could anything be more picturesque or beautiful than the churchyard? She shook her head. "The churchyard was thick with graves, some with stones and some without, like any other place of the sort—a poor, melancholy place it was. She thought it so lonely and miserable, and yet sketchers were always making pictures of it; and she had seen a printed book once with a picture of it, and its history all done into print. She could not but think the gentry had very little to write about. Yes, there were stories about those who lay there—many stories. There was a story of two brothers—wicked men, she called them—who

---

* The key of the church is one of those massive pieces of metal-work constructed when strength was believed to have been the chief security in locks. As a curious specimen of a bygone fashion, we append a cut of it; such securities are now rare. It is unnecessary to add that in "old times" keys were frequently subjected to elaborate ornamentation, often of a costly character, and exhibiting considerable proficiency in art.

died, she could not well tell how; and as to the things cut upon tomb-stones, she set no count by such grand words—she knew her own know! People could get anything they liked cut on stones if they paid for it. There was a cold, proud man who lived at the Hall when she was a child—a bad, cruel man; his shadow would wither up the young grass, and the look of his eye was as bad as a curse. He died, as he had lived, full up of bitter riches: he was not buried in this churchyard —it was not grand enough for him—but in a fine new one, where so much was put on his tomb about his charity—he who would steal a half-penny out of a blind man's hat—about his justice, who would rob a foot off the highroad to add to his own field—about his being a *meek* Christian!" the woman laughed, scornfully; "meek! meek! the haughty reprobate! Well, a poor little lad, who had but too good reason to know the falsity of the whole, from first to last, wrote under it, 'It's all lies!' and though every one in the place said the lad was a true lad, and a brave lad, yet he lost his situation, and not one in the place dared give him food or shelter, so he left the neighbourhood, did the lad; but as sure as that sun is shining above us, so sure is there One who sifts the tares from the wheat—yes, indeed, the tares from the wheat. And I forget how it was, for I married out of the village, and just came back ten years ago, like a crow to the old nest,—only he grew rich, through honest labour; and his son is in the Hall now; and the great tombstone was cleared away, and nothing to be seen now but a broad slab, with never a word on it, over the bad man's dust and ashes."

She was a strange, weird-looking old creature, with odds and ends of information: like an artist who can paint a distance, but not a fore-ground, the past was with her light and bright enough, but the present was already her grave—she could tell us nothing of the present. She still leant against the old tree, and we were so soothed by the silence and tranquillity of the scene, that we lingered among the tombs, when suddenly we heard a quick, light step behind us, and before we could turn round to ascertain whence it came, a thin hand rested on our arm, and a pale face, the lips parted over white and glittering teeth, and the eyes, deep sunk and restless, were advanced so close to our own that we started back almost in terror. "Can you tell me the grave?" she inquired eagerly, but in a low voice: "oh! if you know it, do tell me! I know he is buried here—they all own *that*, but they will not tell me where; do tell me—I am sure you will—come, make haste!"

The lady was dressed in faded mourning, the crape was drawn and crumpled, and the widow's cap beneath her bonnet did not conceal a quantity of fair hair, which looked the fairer from being streaked with grey.

"What grave?" we inquired of the pale, panting little creature, who wrung her hands impatiently, "what grave?"

"Oh! you know—my husband's! Round and round, across, along— from the first tap of the *reveillé* to the last drum-roll at night, I seek his grave. I throw myself down and talk to the dead and buried, but they tell me to let them alone: and they say he is not here, but *I* know he is. We went out in the same ship and returned in the same ship, so we must be both here, you know. We went out in the same ship, and returned in the same ship," she repeated, mournfully, "and they buried him here. Oh! have pity—have pity, and help me to find his grave!" She hurried us on, pointing to each green mound we passed—"It is not that, nor that, nor that—no, no! do not look at the tombstones, there was no time to put one up—the enemy was too fast on us for that!" She cast herself on her knees beside a grave close to a bank, murmuring "Charles!" into the long grass, and holding up her finger to indicate that we should keep silence, expecting an answer.

At the instant a tall, venerable gentleman entered the lonely grave-yard—"Jane, my child—my darling," he said, tenderly, "here again! Come, my child, we can look for the grave to-morrow." The old man's eyes were filled with tears; but she did not heed him, murmuring amid the grass. "Forgive her," he said, "my poor child's mind wanders : her husband was killed at Inkerman, and she fancies he is buried where they were married!" It required some little force to raise her from the sward, and then, after a little struggle, he raised her in his arms, her head resting quietly on his shoulder—the large tree the next moment hid them from our sight.

BOVENEY LOCK is now reached, and, while the boat is passing through, we may look about us, and give consideration to some of those peculiarities which add interest and beauty to our noble river.

There are few objects which so essentially contribute to the attractions of the Thames as the swans, which are met at intervals in all parts of the river, but are encountered more frequently as we approach the villas

BOVENEY LOCK.

that ornament its slopes and banks. The bird is so well known that to describe it is unnecessary: few of the calmer waters of England are without this special grace and ornament: with the poets of all ages it has been a favoured theme :—

> " . . . . . The swan with arched neck
> Between her white wings mantling, proudly rows
> Her state with oary feet."

With this charming portrait "drawn from nature" by the poet Milton, we may associate that by the poet Wordsworth, when describing the

calm and solitary quiet of a scene he drew with so much delicious
fidelity :—

> " The swan on sweet St. Mary's lake
> Floats double—swan and shadow."

Happily, too, the swan is a very long-lived bird : Willoughby writes of
some who were reported to be three hundred years old, and though this
is probably an exaggeration, there are satisfactory proofs that many
"paddled" the same waters for more than a century. Few sights are
more pleasing than that of the royal bird, followed by her cygnets, either
among the rushes or into mid-stream of the Thames; to note the courage
which the parent displays in defence of its young ; to observe now and
then the mother taking her new-fledged offspring on her back, while
sailing proudly and majestically through a current more than ordinarily
rough and strong. We would almost as soon part with the trees which
border its banks as with the swans that grace the surface of our noble
river. The parent usually makes her nest in one of the aits or islands
where the tide rarely reaches it; this nest is composed of "reeds, rushes,
and other coarse herbage," but is seldom chosen with a view to shade,
and is usually found rather in exposed than retired spots, as if the beautiful bird was conscious of its right to protection, and knew it was under
the guardianship of special laws that secure its safety.*

The swans, which appear somewhat abundantly on the Thames
between Staines and Putney, are chiefly the property of the companies
of Dyers and Vintners of London; those about Windsor and Eton belong
to the Queen and the college, although the Vintners enjoy the right of
keeping them in this neighbourhood—beyond the jurisdiction of the city
of London. It was the custom, at the close of the last century, to send
six wherries as far as Marlow, manned with proper persons, to count and
mark the swans; it has of late years been made a festive journey by the

---

* Recently we visited the swannery of the Earl of Ilchester, at Abbotsbury, within a few miles of
Weymouth. The scene is a low series of swamps of salt water, which forms the land border of the
isthmus which is divided from the ocean by the singular pebble ridge that runs from Portland Island
for about eighteen miles inland. The number of swans here collected amounts, it is said, to seven
hundred : but they have been much more numerous. Walking in and out, for upwards of a mile,
through this morass, in which various channels are cut for ingress and egress to water, we continually
met the nests of the birds, then deserted : they were generally shaded by tall reeds and rushes.

citizens as far as Staines, and the voyage is termed "swan-hopping," a corruption of swan-*upping*, or *taking up* the young swans to mark them. Thus the orders for the game-keepers of the reign of Elizabeth show this clear use of the term, when they ordain "that the *upping* of all those swans, near or within the said branches of the Thames, may be all upped in one day." The swan was considered a royal bird, and was protected by laws of a peculiar kind, and it was the privilege granted to certain persons only that allowed them to be kept. In the reign of King Edward III., it was ordained that no person who did not possess a freehold of the clear value of five marks should be permitted to keep them. The right of marking was also subject to a fine of 6*s.* 8*d.* paid into the king's exchequer for each swan; and any person driving away swans in breeding time, or stealing their eggs, was liable to one year's imprisonment, and fined at the royal pleasure; and any person found carrying a swan-hook, by which the birds may be taken from the river, he not being an authorized swan-herd, or not being accompanied by two swan-herds, was liable to a fine of 13*s.* 4*d.* It is also ordained that every year the swans be examined and numbered on every river, and "that every owner that hath any swans shall pay every yeare, yearely, for every swan-marke, foure pence to the master of the same for his fee, and his dinner and supper free on the upping daies." A large number of similarly minute laws regulate the "Order for Swannes," which became the law for the protection of "the Royal Bird;" the grant, therefore, to the city companies was an especial compliment from the crown to the city—one of those concessions given at a period when the trade of England began to assume importance, and rival that of the Low Countries, when it became the wish of the crown to conciliate the wealthy traders, and accord to them various privileges once held by nobles only. The rule adopted for the marks was thus:—the bird, when young, was taken up in the presence of the king's swan-herd, and a mark was cut in the skin of the beak, the same that was upon the beak of the parent bird. These marks were entered in a book, and kept as a register of swans; any found without such mark were seized for the king, and marked with the royal mark. No new marks were permitted to interfere with the old ones; and all generally consisted of simple figures, and some few were heraldic. The following are examples :—

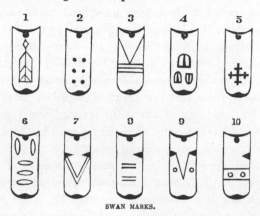

SWAN MARKS.

| | |
|---|---|
| 1. Eton College. | 6. Queen Victoria. |
| 2. Queen of Charles I. | 7. Vintners' Company (modern mark). |
| 3. Charles I. | 8. Dyers' Company (modern mark). |
| 4. Cambridge. | 9. Vintners' Company (ancient mark). |
| 5. Oxford. | 10. Dyers' Company (ancient mark). |

No. 6. is the royal swan-mark of Queen Victoria. This mark has been used through the reigns of George III., George IV., and William IV., to the present time. According to Mr. Yarrell (to whom we are mainly indebted for this information), the whole number of old and young swans belonging to her Majesty and the two Companies, at the swan voyage in August, 1841, was as follows :—

| | Old Swans. | Cygnets. | Total. |
|---|---|---|---|
| Her Majesty | 185 | 47 | 232 |
| The Vintners' Company | 79 | 21 | 100 |
| The Dyers' Company | 91 | 14 | 105 |
| | 355 | 82 | 437 |

Probably they have not since increased; but the numbers were formerly much greater; at one period the Vintners' Company alone possessed five hundred birds.* In the language of swan-herds, the male swan is called

* The marks are termed "nicks:" the Vintners' mark is two nicks; hence the well-known tavern sign, "the swan with two *necks*."

a Cob, the female a Pen ; the black tubercle at the base of the beak is called the berry.  Instances are given by Yarrell of singular instinct in cases of floods, when the birds have beforehand raised their nests two feet and a half above the level of the stream, to protect the eggs from inundations.  Mr. Jesse, in his " Gleanings of Natural History," observes that "each family of swans on the river has its own district, and if the limits of that district are encroached upon by other swans, a pursuit immediately takes place, and the intruders are driven away." Yarrell says, "their food consists of the softer part of water-plants, roots, aquatic insects, and occasionally small fish : a swan has been seen to eat a small roach ; they also eat grain and bread."

Having passed the lock, we are at once in the midst of " a bustle." We are ignorant that "the rule of the road" is not the law of the water, and run much risk, in our comparatively unwieldy barge, of upsetting one or more of the tiny cockleshells in which a youth is seated, rowing up the stream ; we cross rapidly over and give free passage—not without an audible reproach for our want of skill in Eton boat lore—to those

> " Who foremost now delight to cleave
> With pliant arms thy glassy wave."

The youths are on the banks, as well as on the water of old Father Thames :

> " A sprightly race,
> Disporting on thy margent green,
> The paths of pleasure trace."

Out of this " careless childhood" or heedless youth, must issue much of the after-renown of England—upon them mainly rest the hereafter of her fate.  The embryo statesman is here ; the philosopher in the bud ; the hero in the *eruca ;* the germ of that greatness, the high destiny of which is to preserve the honour and extend the glory of a kingdom upon which the sun never sets ; and as boy after boy passes— the father of the man—one can scarcely fail to murmur a hope, with a faith, in his career—

> " Hail to thee who shall be great hereafter ! "

In the lives of a very large portion of the foremost men of our country, it is an incident that they were "educated at Eton;" and to have been an "Eton boy" is the proud boast of many who have gathered laurels in peace and in war.

Eton is in Buckinghamshire, Windsor is in Berkshire. The river divides the counties—a very pretty bridge joining the towns. The College at Eton owes its birth to Henry VI.,—there

" Grateful Science still adores
Her Henry's holy shade,"—

the charter of incorporation bearing the date 1441. The buildings consist of two quadrangles, in one of which are the chapel and school, with

ETON COLLEGE.

the dormitory of the foundation-scholars; in the other are the library, provost's house, and lodgings of the fellows. The chapel is a handsome Gothic edifice, and is that which "tells" so well in all pictures of the place. A statue in bronze of the royal founder occupies the centre of one of the quadrangles. Few buildings are more happily situated;— "the meadows" adjoin it, the Thames rolls its refreshing waters immediately in front, while always in view are the towers of " regal Windsor," inciting to that loyalty which is ever the associate of virtue in the young.

The college, as originally founded by Henry VI., was, in accordance with the feelings of his age, charitable as well as scholastic ; * having also a number of priests to properly perform religious services in this " College Roiall of our Ladie of Eton," as it was first termed.  It then consisted of a provost, ten priests, six clerks, six choristers, twenty-five poor grammar scholars, with a master to instruct them, and twenty-five almsmen, who lived upon the foundation.  The king granted the lands of the dissolved monastery of Deerhurst, in Gloucestershire, to the college ; but this led to disputes with the powerful prelates of the Abbey of Tewkesbury, which lasted until the reign of Henry VII., when, by way of peaceful conclusion, an exchange was made with them for other lands.  Even during the progress of this suit, the lands originally granted were taken by Edward IV. to bestow on a more favoured college at Fotheringham, in Northamptonshire, founded by one of his ancestors.  When Henry VI. had decided on this establishment, he incorporated two small colleges, or hostels, at Cambridge, one of which he had founded two years before ; and thus King's College, Cambridge, originated, to which, as Lambarde remarks, " Eton annually sendeth forth her ripe fruit."  The college was especially exempted in the act of dissolution, and its revenues were then valued at £1101 15s. 7d.  It was by the command of King George III. that the scholars are termed " King's scholars."  They are eligible from the ages of eight to fifteen years, and are required by the statute to be " indigentes " (which they now never are), and skilled in reading, chanting, and grammar.  There was a curious old custom here known as the " Montem," which was discontinued only a few years since ;† the boys were dressed in various fancy costumes, and " begged " on the first Tuesday of Whitsun-week of all passers-by.  The money was termed " salt," and the gatherers

---

* " On the 30th of July, 1440, the king, preparatory to the settlement of the College, and probably at the suggestion of Bekynton, Bishop of Bath and Chancellor of Eton, visited Winchester, and examined the plan of Wykeham's foundation there." — TIGHE and DAVIS's *History of Windsor*. These authors say that it was " not only a place of gratuitous instruction and maintenance for indigent csholars, but also a plac ͛ of education for the children of wealthier families."

† It was discontinued in 1847, at the instigation of the Master of the College, who urged upon Her Majesty's Government various reasons for its abolition : the measure was, however, strongly opposed by many old Etonians.

"salt-bearers;" the proceeds were generally large, and were given to the senior boy to defray his expenses at Cambridge. Salt Hill, to which the scholars went in procession, is an artificial hill, or mound, about two miles from Eton. It is believed to be an ancient tumulus, probably used subsequently as a place of popular assembly. The ceremony was generally very gay, there being always among the spectators the relatives and friends of the aristocratic scholars who levied the "salt;" and who were little scrupulous in assailing the purses of their connexions, in their eagerness to make up the largest possible sum "for the honour of the college." The Royal Family more than once joined in the festivities of the day, particularly in 1793, when they all visited the college to see the procession start, and went afterwards to view the ceremonies there, and give their donations to the salt-bearers. The ceremony was triennial. The practice has been very properly discontinued; although rendered in some degree respectable by time, and certainly venerable by age, the usage was derogatory and humiliating. It is now only a matter of history, having passed away as one of the evidences of the "wisdom of our forefathers," which society has benefited by abrogating altogether: like many other matters of a bygone age, it was

"A custom more honoured in the breach than in the observance."

The mills at Eton are of great antiquity. In the "Annals of Windsor" we are told that in the time of the Conqueror there were two mills at Eton and a fishery. One of the mills at Eton and that at Clewer no doubt stood on the same spots where the "Tangier" and Clewer mills are now situated. Various causes tend to make a corn-mill one of the most permanent species of property. Wherever a mill is specified in Domesday Book, we generally find it still subsisting. Mills anciently belonged to the lords of the manor, and the tenants were permitted only to grind at the lord's mill. This circumstance sufficiently accounts, not only for the great number of mills noticed in the survey as objects of profit to the landholder, but for the large sums they are continually stated to yield. The fisheries at Eton and at Windsor also still exist on the same spots they occupied eight hundred years ago.

Collier, in his Map of Windsor, 1742, thus notes concerning Eton in his time :—"A wooden bridge over the river Thames joins Windsor to Eton, so called from its low situation among the waters ; for Eton is the same as Watertown, but, as they are running waters, and it is a gravelly soil, it is observed that no place is more healthy than this. It is well known for the college founded here by Henry VI., 1440,* and for the great number of the sons of noblemen and gentlemen that are sent to the school here for their education." The college at this time consisted of a provost, seven fellows, a master, usher, seventy scholars, and sixteen choristers.

The library is extensive, and contains some curious books ; its principal contributors were the Bishop of Chichester, Sir Thomas Reeve, Lord Chief Justice of the Common Pleas, and Dr. Richard Mead, whose collections included those of Mr. Richard Topham, of New Windsor.†

---

* Our engraving exhibits the seal of the college used in the reign of Edward IV. It is termed upon it "The Royal College of the Blessed Virgin Mary," and her assumption is depicted in the centre, above the arms of the sovereign. She is represented in royal robes, surrounded by glory, crowned and supported by angels from an aureole of clouds. There is much that is curious and instructive in the study of these old seals, irrespective of their interest as historic documents to the antiquary. Thus the conventional religious picture afforded by the present example, is so very characteristic of a certain era in the art of design, that a date is not necessary to determine its age by the eye accustomed to examine such relics. The regal dress in which the Virgin is wrapped, and the peculiar arrangement of the angelic host in the sky, are all indicative of a phase in the art of the mediæval era ; an art, however wanting in elegance, yet never without a certain earnestness and love of truth.

† The greatest rarity in the library is a copy of " Ralph Roister Doister," the earliest comedy in the English language. It was written by Nicholas Udall, before 1550, who was one of the masters of Eton school, and is noted by Tusser, the author of the " Five Hundred Pointes of Good Husbandrie," as his master when there, and as a very severe one to him and others.

We learn from the *Builder* that the Hall has been very recently restored, according to designs by Mr. Woodyer. " The roof is new, but simple in construction. Two large Gothic windows east and west replace those inserted by Wren. That at the west end over the dais has been filled with stained glass. In the upper part of the window the central light is occupied by a figure of the founder, King Henry VI., the smaller light being filled with armorial bearings and heraldic designs, and the six

WINDSOR CASTLE, occupying a hill to which there is an ascent from all sides, is seen from every part of the adjacent country, and the several distant heights; it is always a pleasant sight, not only as regards the scenery, but with reference to its many "happy and glorious" associations

ANCIENT WINDSOR CASTLE.

with the past, and its suggestions of hope and joy as the favourite dwelling of the Queen, the Prince Consort, and the royal family of England.*    Here, in its gardens, walks, or rides, they may be seen daily, during the period of their residence, protected by the loyalty that has become affection, and the duty that is a true pleasure.

The earliest engraved representation of Windsor Castle is that to be

---

lower lights are filled as follows:—1. Visit of King Henry VI. to Winchester, previous to the foundation of Eton College. 2. King Henry VI. purchasing the tenements which stood on the site of Eton College. 3. Henry VI. granting the charter to the college. 4. The appointment of the first provost. 5. Henry VII. when Duke of Richmond, a scholar at Eton. 6. Defence of the liberties of the college by Provost Westbury, under Edward IV. This window is the work of Mr. Hardman. The plain stone floor has been replaced by a pavement of Minton's encaustic tiles, containing various arms and badges connected with the college and founder. Behind the wall-panelling, where their existence was wholly unsuspected, were discovered three fire-places, the carving of that on the dais being as fresh as though just from the workman's chisel. There was also a small door discovered, communicating with the lodge, and is now again used by the provost. The screen (and gallery) at the east end, replacing Sir Christopher Wren's screen, contains the shields of the benefactors of the College."

* Until very recently there was no worthy History of Windsor—a singular deficiency in our literature. The want has, however, been at length supplied: two large volumes have been recently published, entitled, "Annals of Windsor; being a History of the Castle and Town, with some account of Eton and places adjacent. By Robert Richard Tighe, Esq., and James Edward Davis, Esq." They exhibit amazing research, and include every topic, important or trifling, desirable to illustrate the castle-palace. They contain many prints, plans, and maps, and may be considered as entirely exhausting the subject. From this work we have borrowed much, and gratefully acknowledge our debt to the accomplished and indefatigable authors.

found in Braun's "Civitatis Orbis Terrarum," 1594, which was drawn by a foreign artist—George Hoefnagle—for that work. We copy the portion that exhibits the walled forecourt, with the Chapel of St. George in the midst. The round tower beyond, as depicted in the same view, is very much beneath its present altitude : it was raised during the reno- vations by George IV. The walls here seen are the oldest remains of the fortifications. The towers which are so thickly set along them are of two characters—round and angular. The former are probably the remains of the castle as enlarged by Henry III. The portion inhabited

THE BELL TOWER.

by royalty beyond this consisted, in the reign of Elizabeth, of a conglo- merate of square and round towers, the work of successive ages of change, which adapted the fortress-home of the earlier kings to the more secured and refined life of the days of the "Lion Queen." The terrace is re- presented in this curious print as a simple embankment supported by wooden piles, with a row of rails to protect promenaders from a fall into the ditch below. The town at this time appears to have been a collec- tion of small cottages, and a shep- herd reposes with his sheep in the foreground of the view, while moun- ted courtiers pursue the deer in the park, accompanied by huntsmen who run on foot beside them. Such was the Windsor of the days of Shakspere. The present aspect of the castle is widely different ; but, during every change, there has been one striking feature preserved — the old BELL TOWER, which we here engrave. It formed one of the most ancient defences ; and is seen in the view engraved on the previous page ; it is now one of the most conspicuous points of the castle when viewed from the river, or seen in its full proportion as the visitor wends his way up the main street of the town to the principal entrance. This ancient erection was originally called Clure, or Clewer Tower, and subsequently Julius Cæsar's Tower. This western extremity of the castle, with its walls and towers, is the only portion of the building that has retained the original features of the edifice, as erected in the thirteenth century. Only a few years ago the walls were hidden by houses built close upon them, but they were all removed in 1851, the walls were again exposed, and the narrow, winding Thames Street widened and improved thereby. This north-western

CRYPT IN BELL TOWER.

tower has long been used as a belfry and clock-house,—probably from the time of Edward III., when it is certain there was a clock at Windsor, since in the last year of his reign the sum of £50 was expended upon a new bell for it; and there is reason to believe that the castle clock has always occupied the same situation.

The bell tower, anciently " the curfew tower," was in early times the prison of the castle; and in the crypt underneath, the cells are still perfect in which state prisoners were confined. On the stone walls are many initials and dates, several so far back as A.D. 1600, but none earlier, except such as are undoubtedly forgeries.  The accompanying engraving will convey an idea of this interesting interior,—in which, by the way, a subterranean passage has recently been discovered, said to lead under the Thames to Burnham Abbey, distant three miles, and supposed to have been constructed to facilitate the escape of the garrison at a period of anticipated peril.  Messrs. Tighe and Davis, speaking of this tower, remark that "the lower story has remained intact from its foundation. It consists of a chamber twenty-two feet in diameter, vaulted on plain

WINDSOR CASTLE.

massive stone ribs ; the walls twelve feet and a half thick, with arched recesses, terminating in loop-holes.  The whole is constructed with chalk, faced and arched with freestone, and is a perfect and most interesting specimen of the architecture of the period."

Camden conjectures, " plausibly enough," that Windsor derived its name from the winding shores of the adjacent river, being by the Saxons called " Wyndleshora:" in very ancient documents it is also so termed; and by Leland, Windelesore.  The earliest notice of " Wyndleshora " is to be found in the " deed of gift," by which the Confessor presented it to the monks of St. Peter, Westminster, he having a residence here. It did not, however, continue long in their possession, for the Conqueror, very soon after he subjugated England, "being enamoured of its situation, its convenience for the pleasures of the chase, the pureness of the air, and its vicinity to woods and waters," obtained it "in exchange," bestowing on the monastery Wakendune and Feringes, in Essex. He at once commenced building a castle on the pleasant site; and in the fourth year of his reign kept his court there, and held there a synod: for eight centuries and a half, therefore, Windsor has been the palace of the British sovereigns, and its history is in a great degree that of the kingdom over which they ruled.*

In the prodigious pile which now covers the hill, there can be little resemblance to the castle in which the first William received his proud Norman barons, and the humbled Saxon "thegns" he had subdued. It was not until King Henry I. had enlarged it "with many fair buildings," and kept his Whitsuntide there, in the year 1110, that it became famous as the royal residence. He was married to his second queen at Windsor, in 1122, and five years afterwards he held another "solemn feast" at the castle, when David, King of Scotland, and the English barons, swore fealty to the king's daughter, the Empress Maud, at which time Windsor was esteemed the second fortress of the kingdom. More than one parliament was held here in this reign; it was within its walls that John angrily awaited the meeting of his barons at Runnymede, they having refused to trust themselves by visiting the king in his stronghold, and the king merely leaving the fortress to append his signature to Magna

---

* The seal of the Corporation of Windsor is here engraved. It will be perceived that the castle forms the principal object. The inhabitants were first incorporated by Edward I., when Windsor was made the county town until 1314, when Edward II. transferred it to Reading. The genuine old name of the town, slightly Latinized into "Wyndlesorie," appears on this seal. The corporation consists of a high steward (H.R.H. the Prince Consort), recorder, mayor, six aldermen, &c. It was declared a free borough in 1276. The population, by the census of 1851, was about 9000. The borough sends two members to parliament. Its principal public structure, the hall and corn-market, was built by Sir Christopher Wren, in 1686.

Charta, and return sulkily to his fastness.  During the barons' wars the garrison was lost and won by both parties in turn.  The peaceful days of the first Edward note only the records of tournays and residence here.  His successor had several royal children born here; "Edward of Windsor" was his eldest, who afterwards figures so nobly in English history as Edward III.  It derived accessions of strength and beauty from many succeeding monarchs.  By the third Edward it was almost entirely rebuilt: the famous William of Wykeham being clerk to the works, "with ample powers, and a fee of one shilling a day whilst at Windsor, and two shillings when he went elsewhere on the duties of his office;" his clerk receiving three shillings weekly.  As evidence of the liberty the king's subjects then enjoyed, it may be stated that "three hundred and sixty workmen were *impressed* to be employed on the building, at the king's wages: some of whom having clandestinely left Windsor, and engaged in other employments to greater advantage, writs were issued prohibiting all persons from employing them on pain of forfeiting all their goods and chattels."  Good old times!

In the great civil war the castle was garrisoned for the parliament, and was unsuccessfully attacked by Prince Rupert in 1642.  Six years afterwards it became the prison of Charles I., who here "kept his sorrowful and last Christmas."

After the Restoration, the second Charles restored the castle from the state of dilapidation in which he found it.  But for its present aspect we are mainly indebted to his Majesty George IV., who, by aid of his architect, Jeffrey Wyatt, afterwards Sir Jeffrey Wyattville, and "assisted" by copious parliamentary grants, gave to the palace its high character; Art contributing largely to the advantages it received from Nature.  It is, however, to be regretted that these restorations were not postponed to recent times, when Gothic architecture is so much better understood; we may well imagine how infinitely more perfect the structure would have been if the successor of William of Wykeham had been Gilbert Scott, and not Sir Jeffrey Wyattville.  To describe Windsor Castle is foreign to our purpose; it would demand a volume instead of a page; and there are many guide-books that do so with sufficient accuracy. Visitors are admitted freely to examine all the more ordinary apartments;* and these are richly decorated by works of Art. The corridor contains a large collection of paintings by many of the old masters, mingled with several of our own time,—the portraits of Lawrence, and the commemorative pictures of Wilkie, Leslie, and Winterhalter. During a considerable portion of the year, Windsor Castle is the residence of the Sovereign. It is unnecessary to say that "the apartments" ordinarily called "private," but which are occasionally, and under certain restrictions, shown to visitors, are fitted up with a degree of graceful refinement unsurpassed in any mansion of the kingdom. They will not indeed vie in costliness of decoration, and extravagance of ornament, with many of the continental palaces; there is here no lavish expenditure, and but little of that "display" which excites more of wonder than admiration; but there is an elegant "fitness" in all things, appertaining more to comfort than to grandeur, and belonging less to the palace than "the home." But in furnishing and decoration, in the several chambers for state purposes, and in all they contain, there is amply sufficient to make the subject satisfied that the sovereign is worthily "lodged" when at Windsor, to rejoice that it is so, and fervently to pray that so it may continue to be through many generations yet to come.

Windsor Castle has been always described as the only royal residence in England; certainly, it is the only appanage of the crown that can be considered on a par with those regal dwellings in which other European sovereigns reside, or compared with some of the seats of our nobility scattered throughout the several shires. It is in truth a palace worthy of our monarchs, rising proudly on a steep which commands prospects innumerable on all sides. There is perhaps no single spot in our island from which can be obtained so grand an idea of the beauty and the wealth of England :

" And ye, that from the stately brow
Of Windsor's heights th' expanse below

* Tickets to view the state apartments may be obtained in London from Messrs. Colnaghi, Pall Mall East, and other publishers. But also, by a recent and very judicious arrangement, visitors may receive orders from J. Roberts, Esq., at the Lord Chamberlain's office, within the walls.

Of grove, of lawn, of mead survey,
Whose turf, whose shade, whose flowers among
Wanders the hoary Thames along
His silver-winding way."

But the value of Windsor is largely augmented by the associations that connect it with the past. Many of the illustrious names of ten centuries have their records here: here the Order of the Garter was instituted; Windsor Castle is the temple of the order; true heroes, many, have been numbered among the "poor knights," who have still their "convenient lodgings within the walls." *

St. George's Chapel is in the lower ward of the castle; it was begun by King Edward IV., the older chapel, founded by Henry I., having gone to decay, as well as that rebuilt by Edward III. The king, determined that his new building should equal any fabric then in existence, appointed the Bishop of Salisbury to superintend it: so costly and laborious was the work that it was not completed till the reign of Henry VIII., the roof of the choir being the last thing done, in the year 1508. Sir Reginald Bray, the prime-minister to Henry VII., succeeded the Bishop of Salisbury as clerk of the works, and he was a liberal contributor to its completion; his cognizance occurs on several parts of the building. Some remains of the older chapel of Henry III. are still, however, believed to exist on the north side of the dean's cloisters, and at the east end of the chapel, behind the altar, where one of the doors is covered with old wrought iron-work of much beauty.

The chapel is the mausoleum of many kings. The earliest buried here was the unfortunate Henry VI.; but his tomb has been long since

---

* This establishment was formed by Edward III. They were originally called "*Milites Pauperes*," subsequently "Alms, or poor knights of Windsor," but are now distinguished only as "military knights of Windsor." Their number is thirteen of the royal foundation, and five of the foundation of Sir Peter Le Maire, in the reign of James I. There is also an establishment (founded by the will of Mr. James Travers), but not within the walls, for seven naval officers. By one of the early regulations it was declared that "the knights should be elected from gentlemen brought to necessity through adverse fortune, and such as had passed their lives in the service of their prince." This wholesome rule has been seldom adhered to until of late years. During the sovereignty of Queen Victoria no claims have been regarded except those of merit and service. It is a gratifying sight, and one of which all Englishmen may be rightly proud, to see these gentlemen thus comfortably provided for in their honoured age.

destroyed, and the royal arms, under a simple arch, marks the spot where it once stood. In the north aisle is the tomb of Edward IV.; it consists of a simple slab, over which is erected an open screen, highly enriched with Gothic tabernacle-work in iron, which has been gilt. In the year 1789 the vault below was opened, and the skeleton of the king discovered in a plain leaden coffin. In a vault beneath the choir King Henry VIII. lies buried; he has no monument, but one was in course of erection by him when he died, which he directed to be made more stately than the tombs of any of his predecessors. They were all despoiled and destroyed in the great civil war. One of his queens, Jane Seymour, is also buried at Windsor, and so was King Charles I.*

St. George's Hall was built by Edward III. as a banqueting-room for the Knights of the Garter, when they met to celebrate the festival of their patron annually at Windsor. The old seal of the warden and college of the chapel of St. George, at Windsor, is curious, as depicting the king kneeling to the patron saint of England. It has that minutiæ of detail which gives so much interest to these early works. At this time the festival was celebrated with tournay and processional display; many noble foreigners were invited to be present, and the

EDWARD III. AND ST. GEORGE.

utmost splendour of feudal pomp was lavished on the ceremony. For more than two centuries feasts of this kind were annually held at Windsor. The new statutes of the order, made by Henry VIII., pre-

---

* The tomb-house now used as a royal burial vault was originally designed by Wolsey for himself. it was fitted as a chapel by James II., and, after his abdication, allowed to decay, until George III., in the year 1800, gave orders that it should undergo a thorough repair, in order to be used as a place of interment for himself and family—a purpose to which it has been since dedicated.

cluded the necessity of holding the great feast here ; and in the reign of Elizabeth it was arranged to be held wherever the court happened to be. So showy were these displays, that knights-companions were allowed to bring fifty followers ; and admission to the order has always been considered one of the highest honours an English sovereign can bestow. Their number (exclusive of foreign princes) is limited to twenty-five. The stalls of the sovereign and the knights-companions of the Garter are situated in the choir of St. George's Chapel. Each stall is enriched with carving, and behind is the armorial bearings of each knight, and above the silken banner emblazoned with his arms. The royal stall is on the right of the entrance, and is distinguished by a larger banner of velvet, mantled with silk.

Of the Order of the Garter, Selden says :—" It exceeds in majesty, honour, and fame, all chivalrous orders in the world," and has " precedence of antiquity before the eldest rank of honour of that kind anywhere established." Of course a chivalric institution of the middle ages, so entirely adapted to the knight-errantry then practised, has lost much of its meaning and use in modern times ; it is now simply a distinction ; but it is the noblest the sovereign of these realms can bestow, and among the brotherhood are enrolled the names of sovereigns of other kingdoms, who willingly admit the honour accorded by such companionship. The origin of the order is still involved in doubt. The recent historians of Windsor, whose work we have several times quoted, tell us, " the annals of the institution, the chroniclers of the time, and the public records, do not afford the slightest information on the subject; and although some writers on the order have treated with contempt the romantic incident to which its extraordinary symbol has been ascribed, they have neither succeeded in showing its absurdity, nor suggested a more probable theory. The popular account is, that during a festival at court, a lady happened to drop her garter, which was taken up by King Edward ; who, observing a significant smile among the bystanders, exclaimed with some displeasure, ' Honi soit qui mal y pense '—' Shame to him who thinks ill of it.' In the spirit of gallantry which belonged no less to the age than to his own disposition, conformably to the custom of wearing a lady's favour, and perhaps to prevent any further impertinence, the king is said to have placed the garter round his own knee." *

But greatest among all the many attractions of Windsor Castle are, perhaps, those which are presented to the visitor by the views he obtains from the terraces, or any of the adjacent heights, and especially from the battlements of "the Round Tower,"—

> " Of hills and dales, and woods, and lawns, and spires,
> And glittering towns, and silver streams."

He stands in the centre of a panorama of unequalled beauty, and he is, as he ought to be, proud of his country. Look where he will, some object of deep and exciting interest meets his eye. Immediately beneath him, and seeming as if part of the grand demesne, is Eton, with its many associations of the present and the past, and fertile in hopes of the future. Here Wellington learned his first lessons in war; here, in his boyhood, the victory of Waterloo was fought and won; here William Pitt, and here also his great father, were the embryo pilots who steered "the ship" through the storm; here Bolingbroke, Camden, Walpole, Fielding, Boyle, Fox, Porson, Canning, and a host of other immortal men laid the foundations of that renown which became the glory of their country. Farther on is Slough, where, in a comparatively humble dwelling, the Herschels held commune with the stars.† Yet a little farther is the churchyard in which Gray lies,—that of "Stoke Pogis,"—beneath the tomb he erected to his mother and his aunt; it is the square tomb seen in our cut, and is without his name upon it, but a plain tablet on the wall records that "opposite this stone, in the same tomb upon which he has so feelingly recorded his grief at the loss of a beloved parent," his remains were deposited, August

---

* Such was the opinion of one of our soundest historical antiquaries, the late Sir Nicholas Harris Nicolas, who first expressed it in his History of the Order of the Garter, and afterwards in his communication on the early history of the order, "Archæologia," vol. xxiii. He thinks the anecdote "perfectly in character with the manners and feelings of the time, and the circumstance is very likely to have occurred." It should be noted that this writer had no tendency to "romance," and but expressed the conviction of a mind devoted to dry research; but his conviction was essentially based on probabilities.

† The famous telescope of Dr. Herschel is still preserved in the garden of the house in which he lived, and may be seen without much difficulty by persons desirous of rendering homage to the memory of the great astronomer.

1771.   The churchyard is well worthy of a pilgrimage—it is a pleasant
field walk of about two miles from Slough, and retains many features
alluded to in the famous "Elegy."   Still nearer Windsor is the ivy-
covered tower of Upton, which is very ancient, and bears traces of
Norman workmanship.   It is believed by many to have been the one the

STOKE POGIS CHURCH.

poet had in mind, if not in eye, while writing.   It certainly accords better
than that at Stoke Pogis with his description—it is, and has been for
centuries, "ivy-mantled."   Upton was one of his early haunts; the
gloomy character of the church and neighbourhood in twilight must
have been well suited to the thoughts of the poet in this his most
popular work.   In the distance are the hills and woods that shadow the
cottage in which Milton wrote; the mansion in which Edmund Waller
and Edmund Burke lived and died; and the little graveyard of "the
Friends," where William Penn is at rest.

Iver, Langley, Bulstrode, Dropmore, Burnham, and Dorney—places honoured in history and cherished in letters—will be pointed out to those who examine the rich landscape in this direction. Looking eastward and southward, other historic sites, and other examples of beautiful scenery, come within his ken. On a level with the eye is a range of hills —St. Leonard's Hill, Highstanding Hill, Priest's Hill, and Cooper's Hill; while further eastward are St. Anne's Hill, and St. George's Hill. At St. Leonard's Hill dwelt "for a season" the Earl of Chatham, "the

THE IVY-MANTLED TOWER.

great father of a greater son;" there, too, is Binfield, where Pope "lisped in numbers,"—

"First in these fields he tried the sylvan strain ;"

under the trees of Windsor Forest, in his boyhood, he conned his lessons, accompanied by his tutor, an old French Roman Catholic priest. Cooper's Hill overlooks Runnymede, commemorated in the beautiful verse of Denham—

"Here his first lays majestic Denham sung ;"

while St. Anne's Hill looks down on the town of Chertsey, where dwelt in calm retirement, after seasons of exciting labour and thought, Charles James Fox, and where

"The last accents flow'd from Cowley's tongue."

Gazing up "the Long Walk,"—that noble tree-avenue of three miles, —the visitor sees the statue of George IV., a colossal work, standing on a rock, and placed on a mound; from this point we obtain a peep into the ancient glades, and contemplate those venerable sovereigns of the forest, who wore their green leaves in glory when the Conqueror was at Hastings.

To enumerate half the places seen from Windsor Castle, and which time, circumstance, and some heroic or grateful memory have rendered famous, would occupy pages of our tour. We may not forget, however, that the sight is often cheered and gratified while wandering over the view from "Windsor's heights" by those well-managed and productive "farms," which, under the personal care of the Prince Consort, are examples and lessons to the English gentleman.

But to the present age, and the existing generation, the castle at Windsor is suggestive of holier and happier feelings than those we derive from the past. The most superb of our palaces is accepted as a model for the home of the humblest, as of the highest, British subject; the lowliest in position, as well as the loftiest in rank, deriving their best example from those graces and virtues which are adornments of the proudest mansion of the realm. And not alone is this "home" pre-eminent for domestic happiness: the personal character of the Sovereign, and that of her illustrious Consort, influence every class and order of society; they are the patrons of all improvements for the good of their country; all its charities are helped and forwarded by them; under their just and considerate rule, at a time when every state in Europe was in peril, there was no disaffection at home: loyalty has become the easiest of English duties; those who teach the present generation the old and venerated lesson, "Fear God and honour the Queen," have to contend against no prejudice, to reason down no opposing principle, to overcome no conscientious scruples that rational liberty is abridged by earnest and devoted homage to the crown. It is the universal heart of her kingdom which utters the "common" prayer—"that God will with favour behold our most gracious sovereign lady Queen Victoria; endow her plenteously with heavenly gifts; grant her in health and wealth long to live, and strengthen her that she may vanquish and overcome all her enemies."

The "Little Park," so called because of its immediate contiguity to the castle, and to distinguish it from the "Great Park," is described as

HERNE'S OAK : THE EARLIER.

about four miles in circumference; it derives interest, in addition to its intrinsic beauty, as the scene of those revels which Shakspere has described in his "Merry Wives of Windsor." *   And here was the famous tree—"Herne's Oak"—round which "the hunter"—

"Some time a keeper here in Windsor Forest"—

* The Little Park was enclosed some years ago, during the present reign, and the meadow below the slope was given in exchange to the people of Windsor, who now play at cricket there, and use it for fêtes and other amusements.

was doomed to walk " all the winter time." The veritable tree was cut down by an unfortunate mistake at the close of the past century. Ireland, in his picturesque views of the Thames, published in 1792, describes it as then standing, and gives an engraving of it, which we copy.

There are, however, many in Windsor who believe that *this* tree was not *the* tree, but that a venerable ruin which still exists, and to preserve

HERNE'S OAK: THE LATER.

which every possible care has been taken, is actually that to which the " immortal poet " made reference in the drama of which the scene is laid in this neighbourhood. Among the most strenuous advocates for this view of the case is Mr. Jesse, whose works exhibit so much of pure fancy in combination with observation, thought, and genuine love of Nature ; and there can be no doubt that the venerable father of the forest, whose cause Mr. Jesse eloquently adopts, was aged when Falstaff was pricked by the fairies under the branches of some denizen of the forest " thereabouts :"*

> " Under its boughs, all mossed with age,
> And high top bald with grey antiquity."

This tree is of a picturesque character, it is venerable and interesting, and the reader will be pleased to examine its likeness, as an example of the antique features of the sylvan scenery of Windsor.†

---

* An inscription has been placed on this tree from Shakspere, as if to identify it with that to which the poet alludes. Messrs. Tighe and Davis, in their great book on Windsor, have again entered into the entire question as to the fate of the old tree; they have come to the conclusion that the genuine tree has been destroyed, and that the present one is one of the old trees in an avenue once known as Queen Elizabeth's Walk. It is a tree of no remarkable size, and was alive in 1796, when the real tree was cut down.

† The question as to the identity of this tree with that named by Shakspere was anxiously inquired into by Mr. Knight in his edition of the immortal poet's works, and he places beyond doubt the fact of its destruction. West, the president of the Royal Academy, used to relate that King George III. "had directed all the trees in the park to be numbered, and upon the representation of the bailiff that certain trees encumbered the ground, directions were given to fell those trees, and that Herne's Oak was among the number." Mr. Nicholson, the landscape painter, some time after this made further inquiries on the point, and requested Lady Ely to ask the king himself, and he confirmed the story, saying, " that when he was a young man it was represented to him that there were several old oaks in the park which had become unsightly objects, and that it would be desirable to take them down. He gave immediate directions that such trees should be removed; but he was afterwards sorry he had given such an order inadvertently, because he found that, among the rest, the remains of Herne's Oak had been destroyed." If any doubt remains, it will certainly be removed by the fact that about the period the following lines appeared in a newspaper (the *Whitehall Evening Post*). Mr. Thomas Wright, F.S.A., has courteously forwarded them to us, as copied by him out of an old volume of " cuttings " collected by his father.

" ODE,

" UPON HERNE'S OAK BEING CUT DOWN, IN THE SPRING OF 1796.

---

> ' There is an old tale goes, that Herne the hunter,
> Some time a keeper here in Windsor Forest,
> Doth all the winter time, at still midnight,
> Walk round about an oak,' &c.
> SHAKSPERE's *Merry Wives of Windsor.*

" Within this dell, for many an age,
Herne's Oak uprear'd its antique head ;—
Oh ! most unhallow'd was the rage
Which tore it from its native bed.

The storm that stript the forest bare
Would yet refrain this tree to wrong ;
And Time himself appear'd to spare
A fragment he had known so long.

'Twas mark'd with popular regard,
When famed Elizabeth was queen ;
And Shakspere, England's matchless bard,
Made it the subject of a scene.

So honour'd when in verdure drest,
To me the wither'd trunk was dear ;
As, when the warrior is at rest,
His trophied armour men revere.

That nightly Herne walk'd round this oak,
The superstitious eld received ;

And what they of his outrage spoke
The rising age in fear believed.

The hunter, in his morning range,
Would not the tree with lightness view :
To him Herne's legend, passing strange,
In spite of scoffers still seem'd true.

Oh ! where were all the fairy crew
Who revels kept in days remote,
That round the oak no spell they drew,
Before the axe its fibres smote ?

Could wishes but ensure the power,
The tree again its head should rear,
Shrubs fence it with a fadeless bower,
And these inscriptive lines appear :

' Here, as wild Avon's poet stray'd '—
Hold !—let me check this feeble strain—
The spot by Shakspere sacred made,
A verse like mine would but profane."

From the parks at Windsor we are naturally led to some consideration of Windsor Forest: there is nothing of its class in the kingdom more entirely beautiful,—in a word, it is worthy of the magnificent castle to which it is attached. Although now of comparatively limited extent, it was "anciently" among the largest forests of the kingdom.* "It comprised a part of Buckinghamshire, as well as a considerable district of Surrey, and ranged over the whole of the south-eastern part of Berkshire, as far as Hungerford." In Surrey it included Chertsey, and its

WICKLIFF'S OAK.

eastern boundary is said to be marked by an aged oak-tree, still standing, at Addlestone, and under the boughs of which tradition states that Wickliff preached. The reader will, no doubt, be gratified if we submit to him a picture of this tree also.

Let us vary our more matter-of-fact details by the introduction of one of those sketches which, though of little importance in themselves, like the lights in a picture, may give strength and value to a subject.

---

* One of the most beautiful spots in Windsor Forest is "the Heronry;" the birds are still numerous there. It lies in the vicinity of the red brick tower at the western extremity of the park. The neighbouring scenery strongly calls to mind the sylvan descriptions in "As You Like It." It is probable that Shakspere derived many of his ideas of forest scenery from Windsor Forest.

Many years have passed since we believed we knew every house, cottage, lodge, and tree in the picturesque neighbourhood of Old Windsor; indeed once, when in very ill health, we spent three months at a keeper's lodge; his wife had been the favourite servant of an old friend, and we were especially recommended to her care because of the air, and quiet, and new milk, and fresh eggs, and the quantity of game (no imputation on the good keeper's honesty). It was then we learned all the green paths and brown roads, and dales and dells, of this charming locality; spending hours, day after day, in the forest, with no other companions than a sure-footed pony and the keeper's only child—a particularly shy, mild, blue-eyed, blushing sort of girl, who looked fifteen, but was quite twenty; who used to cry over "Paul and Virginia" at least once a week, and knew by heart every word of "Turn, gentle hermit of the dale," and "Margaret's Ghost;" who loved moonlight, believed in fortune-tellers, and confessed that whenever she tossed a cup she found a true-lover's knot in the bottom. It was, therefore, evident that the girl had a lover somewhere; but as we had never seen him, we asked no questions. We had taken several excursions together, and we fancied we had made considerable progress in all kinds of forestry: could tell the different sorts of birds'-nests at a glance; could find a hare's form, and could track a rabbit; could tell how the wind blew, and where the deer lay; and knew many lonely roads and winding paths where that enemy of tranquillity, "the public," had never been.

One evening, returning from a delicious ramble, our fair guide turned into a cover so close that we almost laid down on the pony's neck to avoid contact with boughs and brambles; and when that peril was past, we found ourselves on a long strip of upland which stretched away for a considerable distance. This narrow elevation, had it been near the castle, or any other dwelling, would have formed a terrace, sloping as it did on each side into the wildest underwood, running on boldly and unsheltered, save at its abrupt termination, where, in far back times, two trees had been planted, designed perhaps to form what their interlacing boughs really had formed—a natural arch. Through this there was a bird's-eye peep at the Thames: there lay, like a vast mirror, the calm, silent river, lending its magic light to the landscape, touched here and there by the rose-coloured and saffron tints of the setting sun; indeed, the sun had set, but the tender farewell colours still lingered on the clouds, and were reflected by the faithful river. The scene was so unexpected, and so fascinating, that we drew up with an exclamation of delight, much to the pony's contentment, who immediately began to crop the grass. After a sufficient pause, so rapidly were the tints fading that, as we rode slowly along the ridge towards the trees, the river, in the deepening twilight, assumed a very soft, grey, lake-like effect—it was the perfection of repose. We asked our fair guide (whose bustling, thrifty mother had given her the out-of-the-way name of Rizpah) if this elevation was supposed to be natural or artificial, and she informed us that some said it was thrown up in old times in a single night, so that one of the ancient queens could sit there on her palfrey to see a battle. This was not satisfactory, but our guide had no more to tell. Rizpah, however, deficient as she was in historic information touching the pathway, became quite eloquent in its praise; she thought it the prettiest spot in park or forest—the river shone so bright between the trees. Did we not observe how beautifully the ferns waved at either side?—they were so large: and in the little valley beyond the trees, just down the slope, there were so many orchids; and at the other side of the wood-cutter's hut (yes, that distant brown ridge was a wood-cutter's hut) there were such lovely beds of iris, and such reeds! Should she go and gather some? the pony could not well go along in the hollow—the felled timber lay here, and there, and everywhere; but she could run over them—it was so pleasant to spring from one log to another! But the blackbird was whistling his evening hymn, the bees and butterflies had folded themselves up for the night, and the "whang" of the cockchafer, and peculiar cry of the owl—not the "hoot-tu-who!" but the waking cry, a struggle in his throat, trying his voice, as it were, before he commences his fearful shout—warned us that the night would fall before we arrived at the lodge if we tarried longer; and so we told Rizpah very decidedly—for she always tried to have her own way—that we would come another time—the dew was falling, and we dared not linger.

The girl looked disappointed, and we turned our pony (nothing loth) homeward; suddenly a clear sharp cry—the nearest attempt a woman makes at a shout—broke upon our ear, and in less than a minute it was answered. We looked for Rizpah, and saw her running towards us from beneath the long shadows of the arched trees.

"What cry was that?"

"It was I," replied the panting Rizpah, as she laid her hand on the pony's neck, and seemed intent on picking her steps, though the path was broad and clear, a rich carpet of short grass and moss; "it was I; and did you not hear the echo?"

"Echo!" we repeated; "we heard an answering shout, but no echo."

"It is a curious echo," persisted Rizpah; "we have many curious sounds in these parks and forests."

Now we had been fully convinced that Rizpah was practising upon our credulity, and were half amused and half provoked at the coolness and self-possession of the shy, innocent-looking forest girl, but we simply repeated, "Very curious indeed; was the echo there when the queen sate on her palfrey to see the battle of the Thames?"

Rizpah replied, with her usual mixture of coolness and innocence, "She did not know."

Rizpah's mother was a stout, rosy dame, simple-minded and straight-forward—bright, cheerful, good-natured, and somewhat noisy; but though her voice was loud, it was not unmusical or inharmonious, and there was a tenderness in its tone when she spoke to the sick or the old, or the little children who sometimes found their way to her door, that was quite pleasant to hear. Her husband was like all other "keepers"—a tall, broad-shouldered man; we never saw him out of his dun-coloured leather leggins, or without his gun, and hardly ever heard his voice. She patted and petted him and her daughter, and patronized them in an easy, good-natured way, as if they were both little ones. She extended this care-taking to ourselves; and thus saved us all trouble in our domestic arrangements, while evidently increasing her own happiness. A great portion of that happiness depended on her being considered a "clever woman;" she was proud of that, proud of being clever and clear-sighted.

On our return, we were reproved for being out so late, and Rizpah war rather sharply questioned as to the cause. We had just commenced telling the good dame about the echo, when Rizpah, who was preparing tea, poured, as if accidentally, a little of the boiling water out of the teakettle on her mother's favourite cat—a cat, by the way, who was chained every evening at six o'clock to the fender, to prevent its poaching. The scolding and commiseration which followed interrupted the story.

The cottage was a perfect bower of ivy, and clematis, and roses, and woodbine : along the south wall each climber seemed to flourish over its own particular territory, but at the gable end, where our rooms were situated, all mingled together; while the eaves were tenanted by birds, which even the cat did not seem inclined to disturb.

"If you please," said Rizpah, while removing the tea-tray, "there is no use in telling mother about the echo ; she never believes in it, or in anything—not even in Herne the Hunter, or the fairy bridges at full moon over the Thames. Father and I never tell her anything of that sort."

"But she could test the echo."

"It's too far for mother to walk, and the pony would not be able to carry her ; so, if you please, it's better to say nothing about it. She would begin to fancy things."

"What things, Rizpah ?"

"Oh, I don't know," replied the girl, blushing ; "mother has a very active mind : I would rather you said nothing about it." And she raised her soft liquid blue eyes to ours with such an appealing look, that we said quietly, "Very well," and commenced reading.

In about an hour we heard a soft, low whistle, a little to the right; it was repeated twice. We opened our door, and passing along a passage, entered the kitchen ; there stood Rizpah, looking decidedly sulky, with extended hands, holding a very thick skein of worsted, which her mother was slowly winding, talking all the time in an unmistakeable lecturing voice.

"I fear," I said, "there are poachers about; I have heard a whistle repeated three times."

"It's only the wind in the woodbine," said Rizpah, quickly; and while she spoke the clock struck nine.

"It's too early for poachers," said the dame, "and the moon is at full; they know better than to be about at this hour, or at full moon."

"It was *not* the wind in the woodbine, Rizpah," we replied, "nor in the ivy either—surely we must know the whistle of a man from the whistle of the wind : besides, there is not sufficient air afloat to move the petal of a rose."

At that moment an ill-favoured, snub-nosed, rough-coated, faithful, ugly dog—one of those miracles of canine sagacity and bad temper to be depended on only in moments of difficulty and danger—stood suddenly up on his hind legs, and placing his stubbed, vulgar paws on the ledge of the window, pricked his ears, bared his teeth (Rizpah used to call it laughing), whined, and wagged a nothing of a stump, which courtesy might designate a tail, most vigorously.

"Down, Dicken! down, sir!" exclaimed Rizpah, stamping her foot.

"Oh! oh!" said the dame, throwing her ball on the floor, "is *that* the wind in the woodbine? Soh! There's but one human creature beside your father and us two that Dicken laughs at!" The dame threw up the window, and there was a rustling among the branches; but Rizpah held the struggling Dicken in her arms.

"It's either father or the white owl in the ivy," faltered Rizpah, still restraining the dog.

"Father, or the white owl in the ivy!" repeated the dame, in her loudest and most contemptuous tone; "why, you jade, you know father's always a-bed and asleep, on moonlight nights, until eleven. The owl in the ivy, indeed! why he was found dead this morning." In a moment she had seized one of the guns, which always lay in a corner of the kitchen, and presented it at the darkness. Rizpah fell on her knees screaming, and Dicken sprang out of the window.

"What's to do here?" inquired the keeper's gruff, determined voice

K K

from the outside, and we saw him dimly under the shadow of the projecting roof; "put down the gun, mother, and open the door; it's quite
time to put a stop to this hide-and-seek foolery."

Rizpah, trembling and blushing, rose from her knees: it was not so
dark but she saw that her father had taken a prisoner. "Oh, mother!
mother!" she exclaimed, "father knew he was come back—and oh!
mother! mother!"

And "Ah, Rizpah! Rizpah! was *that* the echo from the Thames? Is
that great six-foot-one young man the 'wind in the woodbine?' Is the
individual you call 'Paul' the 'owl in the ivy?' Sly, sly, quiet little
blushing Rizpah! for shame!"

The next morning it was the dame who looked sulky, and instead of
patting and petting Rizpah, it was Rizpah who petted and patted the
dame. There might have been "family reasons," which did not concern
us, but it was evident that the usually self-contained gamekeeper had
determined Paul should marry Rizpah, and that Rizpah offered no opposition. The dame was either tired out or won over—perhaps a little of
both; at all events, we lost our forest guide, but not before we knew the
forest well.

Leaving the bridge that connects Windsor with Eton,—the Castle to
the right, in Berkshire, and the College to the left, in Buckinghamshire,—
we pass a long and narrow and prettily wooded ait, Romney Island, so
well known to Etonians, and dear also to brethren of the angle,—for
here good old Izaak passed many pleasant days of spring and summer
with his beloved friends, Cotton, Donne, and that great and excellent
man, Sir Henry Wotton, appointed by James I. Provost of Eton, "as
the fittest place to nourish holy thoughts, and afford rest to his body and
mind," after his busy life as an ambassador. We may fancy the four
high and pure souls luxuriating under the shadows of refreshing trees,
their simple enjoyments augmented by rare converse concerning Nature
and her works: kindly, and loving, and gentle hearts; all in their decline
(for Sir Henry was sixty when he took orders and office there), yet fresh
and green, and *young* in age; each illustrating that passage which he
who was "chiefest" among them so sweetly and so truly wrote:—

" This man is free from servile bands,
Of hope to rise or fear to fall ;
Lord of himself, though not of lands—
And having nothing, yet hath all."

We soon pass through WINDSOR LOCK, still lonely and retired, although so much of business and bustle is close at hand.*

WINDSOR LOCK.

Under the railway bridge of the Great Western we then row, between another ait—" Blackpott's "—and " the Home Park," until we arrive at VICTORIA BRIDGE, a new and exceedingly graceful structure, which connects Windsor with the pretty and picturesque village of Datchet. The bridge, which has its companion a mile or so lower down the stream—the Albert Bridge—was built in 1851, from the design of Thomas Page, Esq., civil engineer, the acting engineer of the Thames

---

* For the sketch we engrave we are indebted to Commander King, the gallant son of one of " the military knights," who, by the gracious kindness of his sovereign, " reposes " here in happy tranquillity, after a long life of honourable and active labour.] [Captain King is well known to, and highly respected by, all artists and lovers of art. He was for many years a regular contributor to the walls of the Royal Academy ; and his copies of Claude are among the best that have been made from the pictures of that great master.

Tunnel, and the engineer for Westminster Bridge. "Datchet mead" is the name given to the lowland on the banks of the Thames between the river and the Little Park. It is the scene of Falstaff's adventure in the buck-basket, and "the muddy ditch close by the Thames' side" existed until the time of Anne, when it was converted into a covered drain, and known as Hoghole. The embankment raised to form the approach to this new bridge destroyed the last vestige of this hole, together with the small

VICTORIA BRIDGE.

brick arch over it. The scenery about this bridge is very charming—quiet lawns, rich woods, and the noble castle, meeting the eye on all sides. Passing other pleasant places, and some graceful islets, which give their charms to the river scenery, we arrive at Old Windsor.

Old Windsor—as the village is still called, although Windsor proper has gradually lost its prefix of "New," by which it is distinguished in all earlier documents, and by which it is indeed even now "officially" described—was formerly a place "of consequence." At the Conquest it contained a hundred houses, "twenty-two of which were exempt from taxes—out of the rest there went thirty shillings." It was a manor belonging to the Saxon kings, and they are conjectured to have had a palace here from a very early period. A few serfs and swineherds dwelt in straggling huts near the old palace or manor-house of the Saxon kings at Old Windsor, tending their swine in the woods, which, stretching southwards and westwards, formed the outskirts of the Royal Forest of Windsor. It is certain that Edward the Confessor some time kept his court here, and it was that sovereign who presented the manor to the Abbot of Westminster, to increase the wealth of the monastery he had there founded. The site of the palace at Old Windsor is not known with certainty. A farm-house, which until recently stood west of the church and near the river, surrounded by a moat, probably marked the site. Scarcely raised above the level of the Thames, which flows close to it and supplied the moat with water, the palace had no natural defence, and was used rather as a convenient spot for hunting and hawking than as a place of strength.* When the Conqueror was firmly fixed upon the throne, he obtained the land from the monastery in exchange, and commenced building the Castle of Windsor on the elevation in the vicinity so peculiarly adapted for the site of a castle, according to the established rule of these defences. But the palace at Old Windsor was not deserted by royalty until long after the Castle was built. The probability is, that this castle was a simple military defence, and had no conveniency for residence until Henry I. completed, in 1110, additional buildings, and royally opened his home at Whitsuntide; after which we hear little of Old Windsor, except that the manor passed into a variety of hands, by whom it was held from the king by the service of finding a man with lance and dart to attend the royal army. Since the fourteenth century it has been held on lease under the crown.

Perhaps there are not so many dwellings in Old Windsor now as there were when the Norman took possession of England : and naturally and rationally preferring the height to the dell—to overlook the Thames rather than submit to its occasional inundations—commenced the fortress that has endured for eight centuries and a half, without having encountered any of those "battles, sieges, fortunes," to which so many other "strong places" have succumbed. Yet in Old Windsor there is nothing old ; we search in vain for any indications of antiquity ; there is no "bit of ruin" to carry association back. A new road from Windsor leads

---

* Tighe and Davis's "Annals of Windsor."

partly through the Long Walk, beside the model farm of his Royal
Highness the Prince Consort, and a turn to the left conducts to the
venerable church.   It is a by-road, rarely trodden except by those who
worship; a group of noble trees, and some yews of great age, completely

OLD WINDSOR CHURCH.

surround and almost hide the sacred edifice.   It is not, however, of very
early date, and is rather picturesque than beautiful.

In the churchyard was buried that unhappy lady—fair and frail—
who, as an actress and an author, obtained some share of notoriety at the
close of the past century, and who was celebrated by the name of
" Perdita," from her clever impersonation of that character in Shakspere's
" Winter's Tale."   A tomb covers her remains, but it is overgrown with
nettles : there have been none, for half a century and more, to care for
the last resting-place of unhappy " Mary Robinson."   An unpretending
gravestone, near at hand, honours the memory of another who is there
buried, one who was neither more nor less than a simple shepherd.

A sensation, difficult to describe, oppressed us when, after a lapse of
many years, we found ourselves in the ever green churchyard of Old

Windsor; we felt a loneliness that was not tranquillity—an undefined longing it was for perpetual repose: all around us was so still that even the song of the robin, and the footfall of the little wren upon the crisped leaves, disturbed our musing. It was a bright, glowing autumn day: there was no wind, no breeze, not enough to send another brown leaf from the oak—hardly any air to breathe: a very bright day for England, for the soft vapours, so thin and gauze-like, which here and there veiled the azure firmament, could hardly be called "clouds"—a cloudless autumn day: yet no shine of sun could penetrate the matted branches of the grand outspread yews. It flooded them with light; their luscious berries were of more than coral brightness. It was wonderful to stand off at a little distance from these resolute, unyielding trees, presenting the same outline, the same tone of colour, to one century after another, and note how their uppermost platforms—tier after tier of firm-set boughs—rejoiced in that great sunlight, while beneath reposed the dark ground, carpeted by accumulated spines of countless years. "Old Windsor!" fallen from its ancient state, and but a suburb to the glorious pile beyond it! So "old" it is, that every vestige of its antiquity has mouldered into dust—the sacred dust that cherishes the roots of grand old trees, and yields nourishment to the very grass whereon we tread!

There was a change: the fitful autumn had called up a dark, heavy sweep of clouds, so suddenly, that we knew not whence they came: yet there they were, hanging like a mighty pall across the hemisphere, obscuring the full-faced glory of mid-day, and casting a grey, filmy hue over all the landscape. But we were compensated for the loss of light by the variety of shadows that passed over the church and trees, and we sat on a tombstone to watch their progress. All the tombs in this quiet field of graves have a green-grey tone of colour, caused, perhaps, by age or damp, or a mingling of both; they are in wonderful harmony. Upon some of them are time-honoured names; some are railed in, but the iron has lost its hard and exclusive character—it is either enwreathed by ivy or overgrown by moss. You would rather not believe that those who desired to preserve those particular graves were cold, *defiant* people, who wished to protect what belonged to them from the contamination of vulgar dust and ashes, but loving, tender folk, who "honoured their dead" with fervour in simplicity. How we cling to the desire of being remembered *here*, as if we doubted how we should be recognised here-after! yet how few are the bright names that endure even ten years after their owners have removed into the narrow house—how few of the many swept away by the surges of "TIME" obtain an immortality derived from Heaven!

"It be a goin' to rain," said an old labourer, who had wheeled a barrow, heavily laden with autumn prunings, up the broad gravel walk, close to where we sate : until he spoke we were unconscious of his presence. We looked up, not knowing whether the words were addressed to us or muttered to himself. Although he had that neglected look we too often observe in aged peasants,—as if circumstance ignored the poet's notion of "a brave peasantry, their country's *pride*,"—his wrinkled skin was fair, and the red tint of the winter apple was on his cheek; there was unextinguished fire in his light blue eye; the face and form were alike Saxon. In his youth the old man must have been conspicuous for strength and beauty. He had withdrawn his hands from the barrow, and wiped his furrowed brow with the remnant of a spotted handker-chief. "It be a goin' to rain," he repeated, in answer to our look of inquiry, "though the clouds are drifting towards the castle, and may break over there : but there's no telling at this time o' year—they're here one minute, and gone the next. There's not much in the church-yard to please you ; only, maybe, like the rest of the gentry, you want to see what we used to call the tomb of the Fair Shepherdess. Lor! when that tomb was put up first, what numbers came to see it! but there's nothing changes its object so much as curiosity—what people think so much of to-day they don't care about to-morrow. I've seen such loads of lords and gentlemen gazing at that tomb—but not so many ladies. She was a play-actor once, and they called her the Fair Perdita, which is shepherdess, you understand, the fair shepherdess—but to see how one may go from bad to worse! They say a king's love fell upon her like a mildew, and, for all her beauty, withered her up; and then she died, poor thing,—bad enough off too. And her daughter,—she has

been to see her mother's tomb often, as I know well, for I have been on
the spot, and opened the gate to her : and she'd bow and smile like a
real lady : but always—and I minded it well—always she came either
at early morning or in the gloom before night. She'd hang over the
railing, even in winter, like a wreath of snow : it always seemed as
though she loved, yet was ashamed of her ; and she died just eighteen
years after her mother. She could not have been more than five years
old when the poor foolish mother died. I can tell over the inscription to
you—I learnt it all by heart years and years ago, to repeat to the poor
who could not read, and the rich who could not see ; but, lor !" he added
in a somewhat peevish tone, " everybody reads and sees now.—
' Mrs. Mary Robinson,'—that's the Perdita,—' Mrs. Mary Robinson,
author of poems, and other literary works : died on the 26th of December, 1800, at Englefield Cottage, in Surrey, aged 43 years.' And then
the daughter—not married, you understand—' Maria Elizabeth Robinson, daughter of Mary Robinson, of literary fame, who died at Englefield
Cottage, January the 4th, 1818, in the 23rd year of her age.'—Two
young deaths, and that's the end on't. Why, you'll hardly believe it,
*now*, when the gentry come and ask which is ' Perdita's' tomb, and I tell
'em, maybe they'll hardly damp their shoes to look at it, and ask each
other what poems 'twas she wrote, and no one knows—not one can tell !
But, some fifty years ago, I've seen some, and from the Castle, too, who
would tell them all over plain enough."

We sought to divert the old man's attention from a painful theme by
remarking that there was another tomb in the churchyard of such natural
and simple interest that we should be glad to know if " Thomas Pope,"
whose grave was close to the church-door, had been one of his
friends.

The expression of his face changed in a moment : we felt at once that
we had fallen in his esteem. " Tom Pope," he said, in an indignant
tone, " was only a common shepherd—just as *he* himself was ; only a day
labourer—nothing more than that ! Those who put up the stone needn't
have faced it right by the church-door, in the very eyes of the congregation : for his part, he didn't know what the gentry could see in such a

headstone, to stand gazing at it, as they often did, on the Sabbath—
exalting one poor man above another."

We told him we thought he ought to feel proud of such a distinction
for one of his own class, and that we honoured the memory of the *real*
shepherd far more highly than that of the make-believe shepherdess:
the one had left an unsullied name, and an example worthy of imitation;
the other—poor, fluttering butterfly!—no woman could look on *her*

AT OLD WINDSOR.

grave without a blush and a tear.  Could he repeat the epitaph on
Thomas Pope?

"Ah, ah, ah!"—what a cackling, bitter laugh it was! so contemptuous—"No—ah, ah! the gentry who liked might read *that* for
themselves.  He had nothing to say against Tom Pope!—Tom never
had a coat on his back in all his life; nothing but a smock-frock,—and,

ah, ah! to put a tomb over *him!* 'Faithful and honest,'—why, to be
sure, many as 'faithful' were left under smooth grass: to think of *his*
being exalted on a tombstone!"

We were so foolish as to persist—though the old man had resumed
his barrow—in the attempt to reason him out of his nature,—a nature
by no means peculiar to a Berkshire labourer. "Surely he ought to feel
proud of a distinction conferred upon one of his own people."

Alas, alas! Tom Pope was none of *his* people: *his* father died at
ninety-two—no one put a tomb over *him.* He himself would be eighty
come Easter; and full sure he was no one would put a tomb over *him.*
It was evident he considered the record of Thomas Pope's virtues an
insult. He found no fault with the homage rendered to the gaudy
imitation; the mock shepherdess had his sympathy,—she did not belong
to his race: the real shepherd had his contempt. "Why should he have
a tomb, *when no one would put a tomb over him?*" The old peasant
wheeled away his load without further parley.

This is the touching inscription on the headstone to the memory of a
*real* shepherd, conferring distinction and honour on the churchyard of
Old Windsor—

THOMAS POPE,
SHEPHERD,
WHO DIED JULY THE 20TH, 1832,
AGED 96 YEARS.
CHEERFULLY LABORIOUS TO AN ADVANCED AGE,
HE WAS MUCH ESTEEMED BY ALL CLASSES OF HIS NEIGHBOURS,
SOME OF WHOM HAVE PAID THIS TRIBUTE OF RESPECT TO THE MEMORY
OF A FAITHFUL, INDUSTRIOUS, AND CONTENTED
PEASANT.

ALSO,
PHŒBE, WIFE OF THE ABOVE,
WHO DIED MARCH 2ND, 1843,
AGED 90 YEARS.

A passage through the churchyard leads to the Thames, and just at
the corner is a quaint old house, which the artist thought it worth his
while to copy, less for the mansion, however, than for the scenery about it.

A mile or so from Old Windsor, and we enter the county of Surrey,
on the right bank—Buckinghamshire remaining with us some way

further on its left; the two great metropolitan counties then continuing on either side until, east of London, they meet the shires of Essex and Kent.   The first object that arrests the eye of the tourist is the spire of the church at Egham; but his attention is soon directed to an object of even greater interest—COOPER's HILL.   The hill is indebted for much of its fame to the poem of "majestic Denham;" it has other, and earlier, claims to distinction: although little more than "a steep," its slopes are

VIEW FROM COOPER'S HILL.

gradual and ever green: it is beautifully planted—perhaps was always so—in parts; and is now crowned by charming villas, lawns, and gardens: it was, however, altogether a poetical fancy which thus pictured it—

> " his shoulders and his sides
> A shady mantle clothes; his curled brows
> Frown on the gentle stream, which calmly flows;
> While winds and storms his lofty forehead beat—
> The common fate of all that's high and great."

Denham, although born in Dublin, where his father was some time Chief Baron of the Exchequer, was "native" to this neighbourhood: here his ancestors lived and were buried.   At Egham Church there are several monuments to their memory: his own dust reposes in Westminster Abbey. If he bestowed celebrity on Cooper's Hill, he derived hence the greater portion of his fame: the poem was published at Oxford in 1643, during the war between the King and the Parliament; its popularity was rapid, and has endured to our own time. Dryden described it as "the exact standard of good writing;" and "Denham's strength" was lauded by Pope.

But Cooper's Hill has an advantage greater even than that it derives from the poem—

> "The eye, descending from the hill, surveys
> Where Thames among the wanton valleys strays;"

for at its foot is immortal Runnymede, and midway in its stream is the little island on which, it is said, John, the king, yielded to the barons, who there dictated to the tyrant terms that asserted and secured the liberties of their country. Runnymede is still a plain level field, unbroken by either house or barn, or wall or hedge. We know not if by any tenure it has the right to be ever green; but we have always seen it during many years as a fair pasture—upon which to-day, as seven centuries ago, an army might assemble.

The small ait or island—MAGNA CHARTA ISLAND—is situate midway between Runnymede and Ankerwyke—now a modern mansion of the Harcourts, but once a nunnery, founded by Sir Gilbert de Montfichet and his son, in the reign of Henry II. Even the walls are all gone; but some ancient trees remain, under one of which tradition states the eighth Henry met and wooed the beautiful and unfortunate Anna Boleyn.

It is a mooted point whether the barons held the island, or the king selected it as the place where the eventful meeting was to take place. In Tighe and Davis's "Annals of Windsor," the name of Runnymede, which the field then bore, and still retains, is said to be derived from *Rún* and *mede*, signifying in Anglo-Saxon, the Council Meadow. It is probable, therefore, that Edward the Confessor occasionally held his *witan* or council there during his residence at Old Windsor, and that the barons chose the ait as well on account of its previous association with those very rights they met to assert, as because it was a convenient distance from Windsor, sufficiently near for the king, but far enough removed to prevent any treacherous surprise by his forces. The early historians, indeed, expressly assert that the spot was chosen by the barons, the king, according to some, having suggested Windsor as the

MAGNA CHARTA ISLAND.

place of meeting. According to local tradition, the conference took place and the charter was signed on a little island in the river near Ankerwyke, and opposite the meadow, and now called Magna Charta Island. The Charter bears date June 15, 1215. It is certain that

John "took refuge in Windsor Castle in 1215, as a place of security against the growing power of the barons;" nor did he quit the protection its walls afforded him until after the signing of Magna Charta. The result of this great political gathering is one of the events in the world's history. Hence, as Hume but coldly writes, " very important liberties and privileges were either granted or secured to every order of men in the kingdom : to the clergy, to the barons, and to the people."

Magna Charta may be considered as a general condensation of the laws for the proper guidance of the kingdom, and the liberty of its subjects, which had descended from the time of Edward the Confessor, and had been confirmed by other kings, particularly the Conqueror. The severe forest laws, and other obnoxious introductions of Norman usage, were always distasteful to Englishmen ; and on the accession of Henry I. the celebrated Charter of liberties abolished many vexatious enactments, and placed the right of the subject on a clearer basis. Stephen and Henry II. both confirmed these laws ; but the troublesome days which succeeded supplied excuses for their infringement, and the gradual encroachment of the crown on the general privileges of the subject, induced the barons and people to demand from John a clear and full declaration of their rights, to be solemnly confirmed for ever.

There has long been preserved in our British Museum an ancient Charter which purports to be that which John signed at Runnymede. It is part of the manuscript treasures so industriously collected by Sir Robert Cotton ; there is a somewhat curious history of its discovery by Sir Robert at his tailor's, just when he was about to cut it into strips for measures. The story is related by Paul Colomies, who long resided in England ; but the indefatigable historian of Magna Charta, Mr. Richard Thomson, inclines to doubt the truth of the anecdote, and prints a letter from Sir Edward Dering at Dover Castle, in 1630, to Sir Robert Cotton, in which he states that he possesses the document, and is about to send it to him. This famous parchment was much injured by the fire that took place at Westminster in 1731, and destroyed the building containing the Cottonian Library ; it is greatly shrivelled and mutilated, and the seal reduced to a shapeless mass.  Mr. Thomson is of opinion, that though this famous copy "has been considered of inferior authority to some others brought forward by the Record Commission, on account of its deficiency in certain words and sentences, which are added for insertion beneath the instrument, yet the same circumstance may very probably be a proof of its superior antiquity, as having been the first which was actually drawn into form and sealed at Runnymede; the original whence all the most perfect copies were taken.*  It was fortunately engraved in facsimile by Pine, before the fire had injured it; and one of the most important clauses is given in our woodcut; it is that which provides for the free and immediate dispensation of justice to all, in the words:—"No freeman shall be seized or imprisoned, or dispossessed, or outlawed, or in any way destroyed; nor will we condemn

A CLAUSE OF MAGNA CHARTA.

him, nor will we commit him to prison, excepting by the legal judgment of his peers, or by the laws of the land."†  By this important clause the liberty and property of the subject were preserved until after open trial.

There is another fair copy of this document in the Cotton Library.

---

* The Charter purports to be given " under our hand at Runingmede, between Windsor and Staines." The signature of the king was in all probability " his mark," as was usual with the uneducated nobles of his era.  It is a curious fact that no sign-manual of a British sovereign is known to exist before that of King Richard II.  The usual sign-manual was a rude cross placed before the name written by some " learned clerk."

† The original abbreviated Latin would read in full thus:—" Nullus liber homo capiatur, vel imprisonetur, aut dissaisiatur, aut utlagetur, aut exuletur, aut aliquo modo destruatur, nec super eam ibimus, nec super eam mittimus, nisi per legale judicium parium suorum, vel per legem terræ."

The Record Commissioners, however, seem to attach most importance to that preserved in Lincoln Cathedral, which is supposed to be the one sent by Hugh, then Bishop of Lincoln, to be placed among the archives there. This is very carefully written, and contains all the words and sentences noted for insertion in the body of that preserved in the British Museum. There is another among the archives of Salisbury Cathedral, which is thought to be the one entrusted to Herbert Poore, the Bishop, or William Longespée, the Earl of Salisbury, for preservation there, in accordance with the old custom of placing copies of such important documents in the great clerical depositories. These are the only ancient examples of this great grant; but there are many early entries of it in old legal collections, reciting the whole of its clauses, and verifying their accuracy. These were confirmed by other English sovereigns ; and the Great Charter was thus the foundation of English liberty.

It is to be regretted that no monument marks the spot, at Runny-mede, where the rights and liberties of the people of England were maintained and secured, although several attempts have been made to raise one here. The very name, however, is a memory imperishable : the ait and meadow are places of pilgrimage to all who boast the Anglo-Saxon blood; and few are they who cross the Atlantic to visit Father-land without offering homage to their great ancestors in this meadow of eternal fame—repeating, with raised and hearty voice, the lines of the poet :—

> " This is the place
> Where England's ancient barons, clad in arms,
> And stern with conquest, from their tyrant king
> (Then render'd tame) did challenge and secure
> The Charter of thy freedom. Pass not on
> Till thou hast bless'd their memory, and paid
> Those thanks which God appointed the reward
> Of public virtue."

In the island which forms so charming a feature in the landscape, the Harcourts have built a small Gothic cottage—an altar-house, so to call it. It contains a large rough stone, which tradition, or fancy, describes as that on which the parchment rested when the king and the barons affixed their signatures to " the Charter." It has the following inscrip-tion : " Be it remembered that on this island, in June, 1215, King John of England signed the Magna Charta; and in the year 1834, this building was erected in commemoration of that great event by George Simon Harcourt, Esq., Lord of the Manor, and then High Sheriff of the County."

COTTAGE ON MAGNA CHARTA ISLAND.

A little below Ankerwyke, the Coln, which divides the counties of Buckingham and Middlesex, joins the Thames. The river rises near the small market town of Chesham, Bucks, and passing by Cherreys, waters the town of Rickmansworth, Herts, reaches Uxbridge, flows by the once famous village of Iver, refreshes the villages of Drayton and Harmondsworth, and, gathering strength, "goeth," to borrow from old Leland, "through goodly meadows to Colnbrook, and so to the Thames."

There is little to interest the voyager after he leaves this interesting neighbourhood, gradually losing sight of Cooper's Hill, until he approaches Staines; we have leisure, therefore, once again to admire the rich foliage of the river—that which ornaments its surface or decorates its banks. We direct the reader's attention to some of the objects that here gratify and instruct.

A pretty little weed that decks the still recesses of the river is the amphibious Persicaria (*Polygonum amphibium*), a plant that seems to thrive equally well on land or water; in the former situation being one of the most troublesome of weeds to the river-side farmer, but when it takes to the water forming one of its greatest ornaments; the green and red shaded leaves floating on the surface, above which rise the

PERSICARIA.   a.

bright pink flower-spikes in groups, that wave and dance with every ripple of the water, are always pleasant and cheerful.

In no place do we remember to have met with that most elegant of plants, the Forget-me-not (*Myosotis palustris*), in such beauty and luxuriance as in some of the fresh grassy nooks that we every now and then come upon in the course of our voyage. This is the *true* Forget-me-not, the *Virgiss-mein-nicht* of the Germans, with whom originated, if we mistake not, the romantic knight and lady story to which it owes its name— a name that is often given erroneously to other commoner and less beautiful species with small blue flowers. The glossy green foliage and thick waxen flowers of the true flower sufficiently distinguish it from others, independent of the scientific distinctions. In all European countries, but more especially

FORGET-ME-NOT.

in this country, the Forget-me-not has been a favoured theme of the poets. There is hardly one of them who has not made it a subject upon which to build some sweet theory of remembered friendship or love. It is attractive, not alone for its own peculiar grace and delicacy, but because it is found everywhere in England; there is no flower more "common," yet there are few more beautiful and none more suggestive.

The tall, rosy-flowered plant that makes such a show among the river-side herbage, is the Large-flowered Willow Herb (*Epilobium hirsutum*), called by the country folks "Codlings and Cream," from a

supposed resemblance to those luxuries in the smell of the young foliage of this herb. As cattle are fond of eating it, it has been recommended for cultivation as fodder in wet places where other useful plants will not grow, and where the willow herb flourishes luxuriantly.

This is one of those conspicuous plants for form and colour that tell with such charming effect when introduced in the foreground of river pictures, in company with the dock-reeds, loose-strife, meadow-sweet, the yellow flag, and other water-nymphs so dear to the landscape-painter of the school of nature.

LARGE-FLOWERED WILLOW HERB.

Happily that school is increasing in numbers and in strength : happily, too, there is a growing disposition to avoid those evils which arise from a willingness to copy deformities rather than to seek and find beauty in combination with truth. We cannot too frequently impress on the artist the exceeding value of the charming and graceful " bits" he will continually encounter on the banks of the Thames.

While revelling among historic sites, and enjoying the rare banquet of foliage, of which Father Thames is so profusely lavish " hereabouts," we may not, however, forget that we have yet much to say of the fish that abound in his waters. The Carp and Tench are of his produce, although they are not found in quantities sufficient to tempt the angler, and do not often come to his bait. We describe them nevertheless, for they belong to our river. The common Carp (*Cyprinus carpio*) inhabits most of the ponds, lakes, and rivers of England, always preferring

muddy to clear bottoms; it is very tenacious of life, and grows to an
enormous size, sometimes weighing between fifteen and twenty pounds.
The mouth is small, and has "no apparent teeth;" the body is covered
with large scales; the general colour is a golden-olive brown, "head
darkest;" the fins dark brown; the belly a yellowish white.    In the
"Boke of St. Albans," by Dame Juliana Berners, printed by Wynkyn de
Worde in 1496, the carp is mentioned as a "deyntous fisshe;" and in
the privy purse expenses of Henry VIII., in 1582, various entries are
made of rewards to persons for bringing "carpes to the king."    It is,
however, not a native, although the period of its introduction to England

CARP.

is not ascertained.    The Prussian carp is much smaller than the common
carp.    The carp with which we are most familiar is the "golden carp;"
of late years it has become, so to speak, domesticated, and adds essentially
to our home enjoyments in vases and drawing-room tanks, where it is
usually associated with minnows and other "small fry" of the river
being kept in health by water plants, which grow freely in comparative
confinement.    The date of the first introduction of "gold and silver fish"
into England is "differently stated by authors," as 1611, 1691, and 1728.
Yarrell does not attempt to fix the period.    There is no doubt that they
were first imported from China.    In Portugal, and, indeed, elsewhere,
they are completely naturalised, inhabiting many of the streams and
rivers; it is probable they will be so ere long in England, for they breed

freely in many of our ponds, and seem to require no especial care, either
in winter or summer. "The extreme elegance of the form of the golden
carp, the splendour of their scaly covering, the ease and agility of their
movements, and the facility with which they are kept alive in small
vessels, place them among the most pleasing and desirable of our pets."
They become remarkably tame, frequently taking food from the hand,
and appearing to distinguish clearly between an acquaintance and a
stranger.

The Tench (*Tinca vulgaris*) differs essentially in character from the
carp, although its habits are similar, frequenting the same localities, and
delighting in muddy bottoms; its origin is also foreign; and it is
exceedingly tenacious of life. The scales of the tench are small; the

TENCH.

head is rather large and "blunt;" the general colour of the body
is a greenish-olive gold, "lightest along the whole line of the under
surface; the fins darker brown;" it grows sometimes to a large size,
not unfrequently weighing from five to seven pounds. The angler
finds it very difficult to make prey of this fish; they are usually shy, and
"take to the mud" when alarmed; occasionally they bite freely. We
have ourselves taken out of a pond five or six dozen in a day, each of the
average weight of three pounds; finding on that occasion a small pellet

of new bread the most effective bait. Yarrell, however, states that "the best bait for them is the dark red meadow worm," and that the time when they are most readily taken is "early morning." They are not numerous in the Thames, and are there never fished for expressly, although every now and then one will make acquaintance with an angler's hook. The Thames, however, as we have often said, has other fish besides the carp and tench to tempt the brethren of the gentle craft.

We are now approaching the ancient town of Staines;—its bridge and its church-steeple are in sight; but before we reach them there is an object standing on one of the aits that claims our especial attention. We must step ashore to examine it, for it is THE BOUNDARY STONE of the

THE BOUNDARY STONE.

City of London; and here its jurisdiction ends—or did end, we should rather say, for by a recent enactment all its rights and privileges, as regard the river Thames, were transferred to "a Commission."

The conservancy of the river Thames was vested in the Lord Mayor and Corporation of the City of London by long prescription, confirmed by various charters and acts of parliament. Apart from the Courts of

Conservancy, which were held by the Lord Mayor in person, attended by the Recorder and other officers, with much state, most of the administrative duties of Conservator of the Thames have long been performed by a committee of the corporation, known as the "Navigation and Port of London Committee," consisting of twelve Aldermen and twenty-nine Common Councilmen. Their jurisdiction extended from Staines, in Middlesex, to Yantlet, in Kent. Their duties were to prevent encroachments on the bed and soil of the river, or anything being done on its banks to impede navigation ; to regulate the moorings of vessels in the port, deepen the channel, erect and maintain public stairs, keep in repair the locks, weirs, and towing paths, regulate the fisheries, and seize unlawful nets, &c. In the performance of these duties they were aided by four harbour-masters, an engineer, water-bailiff, and other officials appointed by the corporation.

The revenue arose principally from two sources, viz. the tonnage dues on ships frequenting the port, and the tolls paid by vessels passing through the locks, or using the landing-piers. The corporation also received, not as conservators of the river, but as owners of its bed and soil, rents for wharfs, piers, and landing-places, which they granted licences to erect. The produce of the tonnage dues was about £18,000 per annum—a sum more than sufficient to cover the expenses charged upon them, as the corporation were in possession of a surplus of about £90,000 ; but as the application of these dues was, by act of parliament, strictly limited to the river below London Bridge, no benefit could be derived from the possession of such surplus to the upper portion of the river, where the amount received from tolls was small, and, in consequence of the great competition of the railways with the carrying trade of the river, had latterly become so much diminished as to fall far short of the annual expense.

Notwithstanding the difficulty in which the corporation were placed, with a surplus below bridge, which they were unable to appropriate, and a deficiency above bridge, which they had no means of making good but by pledging their corporate estates—they have shown no hesitation in the performance of the duty cast upon them. Meanwhile circumstances had arisen to prevent that efficient management of the Thames which it has ever been the constant object of the corporation to secure. A claim was set up by the crown to the *bed and soil* of the river. The right to the conservancy of the Thames had been contested in the time of Queen Elizabeth, by the then Lord High Admiral, and decided in favour of the city; but the right to the bed and soil of the sea-shore, and of navigable rivers, between high and low-water mark, is comparatively a recent claim on the part of the crown. A bill was filed against the corporation to enforce this claim, and requiring them to show their title; and after protracted proceedings, extending over a period of thirteen years, a compromise was effected. The city, with a view to the interests of the public, consented to acknowledge the title of the crown to the bed and soil of the river, and the crown consented to grant a title to the corporation, stipulating, at the same time, that a scheme, suggested by Government for the future management of the river, should be adopted and embodied in an act of parliament, which act has recently come into operation.

The Thames Conservancy Act, 1857, placed the authority over the river Thames—within the limits of the ancient jurisdiction of the city—in a board consisting of twelve persons, viz. the Lord Mayor for the time being, two Aldermen, and four Common Councilmen, elected by the Court of Common Council, the Deputy-master of the Trinity House, two persons chosen by the Admiralty, one by the Board of Trade, and one by the Trinity House. The members are severally to remain in office for five years, unless otherwise removed, and are eligible for re-election. The revenue arising from the tonnage dues below bridge, and the tolls and other receipts above bridge, together, form one. fund for the management and improvement of the navigation of the river; and of the receipts arising from embankments, or other appropriation of the bed and soil, one-third is paid to the crown, and the remaining two-thirds added to the general fund above mentioned.

Thus was almost regal authority, enjoyed for ages by the citizens of London, and exercised by their chief magistrate and corporation in a spirit of munificent liberality that did honour to their administration, quietly supplanted and absorbed by the greater power of the crown. Our hope is, that public interest may not suffer by the change. Those who have visited the Thames *above* "the city stone" cannot fail to lament that the whole of the river has not been under their jurisdiction: between Staines and London all matters have been admirably and liberally managed; from Staines upwards they have been shamefully neglected. There are numerous "Boards of Conservancy" from Cricklade downwards, not one of which seems to have the least idea of cleansing the river, repairing its banks, or facilitating its navigation and traffic. If we are to judge of other "reforms" which the corporation of the metropolis is doomed to undergo by this reformation of the conservancy of the Thames, we fear we may not anticipate a change that will be advantageous.

It is to be hoped that the "improving" spirit of the age will not proceed so far as to remove this ancient boundary mark; but that the inscription it still retains—"God preserve the City of London"—will be uttered as a fervent prayer by generations yet to come: for, of a truth, upon the prosperity of the metropolis of England depends the welfare of the kingdom.

Staines—or, as it is written in old records, Stanes—is on the Middlesex side of the river,—a busy and populous town, with a venerable and picturesque church. A handsome bridge connects it with the county of Surrey, from whence there are direct roads to Windsor, Egham, and Chertsey. This bridge was erected in 1832, George Rennie being the engineer. It was opened in state by their Majesties King William IV. and Queen Adelaide. "The bridge consists principally of three extremely flat, segmental arches of granite, the middle arch being of seventy-four feet span, and the lateral ones sixty-six feet each: there are also two adjoining semicircular arches, each ten feet in the span, for towing-paths. Besides these, there are six brick arches of twenty feet in the span, two on the Surrey side and four in Middlesex, to admit the water to flow off during land-floods." Our engraving is taken from "above bridge," and underneath one of the arches is seen the comfortable little inn, "The Swan," well known to all brethren of the craft, and especially those who frequent "Staines Deep," * where, during the autumn months, abundance of large roach will usually reward the pleasant toil of the punt-fisher.

Staines was the site of one of the earliest bridges in England. The Roman road to the west crossed the Thames here, and the Roman

STAINES BRIDGE.

station at this place is called in the Itinerary of Antoninus, *Pontes,* so that even then there was a bridge across the river. The Roman bridges in England seem to have been most commonly wooden, supported on

---

* "Deeps" are portions of the river staked and otherwise protected, in order to prevent the use of nets, and so to facilitate the sport of the angler, for whose especial benefit they are formed. Usually old boats are sunk in these deeps : the fish collect about them, and cannot be removed by any "coarse" process. The deeps between Staines and Richmond have all been formed at the expense of the Corporation of London : to them, therefore, Thames anglers have long been, and will long be, largely indebted. To the angler, at all events, the transfer of power from the Lord Mayor to the Commission is a subject of regret; and he is a recreant brother, who, obtaining a day's sport in any of the "deeps," will fail to repeat the prayer of the boundary stone—"God preserve the City of London."

stone piers. Perhaps the remains of the latter may have given the place its name.

The river proceeds hence between low banks, which are frequently inundated during winter, until we reach the lock at "Penty-Hook"— Penton-Hook—an artificial passage by which boats are enabled to avoid a "long round" of a mile or so. But he who voyages for pleasure will find this ancient passage very desirable : it is generally an entire solitude ; water-birds revel here ; butterflies are always numerous ; the Thames trout is seldom absent from its tiny breaks and waterfalls ; and the Abbey river is one of its tributaries, suggestive of memories when the monks of Chertsey had here their productive fisheries, which kept their ponds and preserves continually full. This retired and tranquil branch of our dear river is in high favour with the angler ; and perhaps there is no single nook of the Thames, from its rise to its fall, where he can receive so large a recompence of quiet pleasure. Does he " scrape " for gudgeon ?—here he will find a dozen " pitches," each of which yields enough for a day. Will he try his skill among the roach and dace, baiting with a single gentle a " No. 12 " hook mounted on a single hair, and a somewhat heavy float—for the stream hereabouts is deep and rapid ?—he is either a poor craftsman, or will be singularly unfortunate, if he do not basket his ten dozen before he issues from the bend into the main current. Does he covet the " big " chub ?—let him throw his mimic grub under any one of those overhanging willows, and the chances are he will hook one of more than three pounds' weight. But, especially—is he a barbel fisher, and has the luck to have Galloway aiding and assisting his sport ?—he is sure to catch more than he will like to carry home, if he has to walk from the bank to the railway. Galloway, who lives close to Chertsey—or, as he will tell you, "Chersy" —bridge, is one of the best fishermen on the Thames, and if any day in his company be not a good day, the fault will not be his ; for he knows not only every pitch, but every stone of the river between his own immediate locality and a few miles above it and below it. He is not only an experienced and intelligent, but a most obliging and "painstaking " guide and counsellor, and seems always to consider that ample

sport is ever a part of his contract,—so, as we have said, if the evening
bring disappointment, the cause has been beyond his control.  But if a
neophyte visit the Thames in search of sport, whose line is strong
enough, and hook big enough, to snare and land a Severn salmon,—if
his shot are swan-shot, and his float a pretty toy, and his rod bends like
a reed in a storm, or is as stiff and straight as a "popilar tree"—what
then can Galloway do ?—what but shrug his shoulders, gently hint that
the water is too clear or too thick for sport, and grumble "under breath"
a wish that such brutal tackle were in "Norroway."  And to this heavy
affliction he is often doomed ; while the "angler" seeks the train with a
light load, and growls his discontent against the liberality of the bountiful Father, who has only refused reward to a bungler in the art.

Let the true angler, who knows his art and loves it, spend a day with
Galloway at Penty-Hook, and we assure him of a day's enjoyment such
as he will rarely find elsewhere, or in other company ; for Galloway is
full of anecdote such as the fisherman likes to hear and tell.  The barbel

THE BARBEL.

loves quiet; in this locality he always finds it, and Galloway knows his
haunts and his habits well.

The Barbel (*Barbus vulgaris*) is said to be so called from the barbs
or wattles attached to its mouth.  It feeds on slugs, worms, and small

fish, and is therefore always found at the bottom. It is a poor fish " for the table," and no mode of " dressing" that we have ever heard of can make it tolerable as a dish ; yet large quantities are sold in the London markets, principally (why we could never ascertain) to the Jews. In the Thames, and also in other rivers, they grow to a large size, sometimes weighing as much as fifteen or sixteen pounds ; and when they are " on the feed," which is usually during the autumn months, when the weed begins to rot, it is no uncommon thing for the angler to catch upwards of a hundredweight in the course of a day. We have ourselves achieved this feat several times ; and once, under Teddington Weir, killed two fish, each of which weighed ten pounds and a half : for confirmation of this fact we refer any sceptic to James Kemp—one of the Kemps of Teddington, to whom we shall make reference in due course.

The usual practice is to fish for barbel with " the ledger ;" it is, however, " a custom more honoured in the breach than the observance,"— for it gives the angler nothing to do except to watch the running out of his reel, and to " haul in," as if a stone were fastened to his line. By this mode, a large piece of lead is attached to the line within about two feet from the hook ; the hook being baited with a large lob-worm, it is then thrown in, and the barbel " runs away" with it, literally hooking himself, for the weight acts as a check. This is, however, coarse and clumsy fishing, for a fish worth little or nothing when it is caught. Far otherwise is it when the barbel is hooked with a very small hook, mounted on fine gut, or it may be the single hair of roach tackle : then the strong fellow gives ample " play," and probably half an hour will necessarily pass before the landing-net is in requisition, and he is safely deposited in the well of the punt—especially when the water is deep and the current strong.

To us, our days of barbel fishing are pleasant and very healthful memories—the truest luxuries of an active and busy life ; and although we have killed trout in the rivers and lochs of Ireland and of Scotland, and salmon under the beautiful fall of Doonas, on the mighty Shannon, we recur with greater pleasure to those hours of repose and relaxation we have passed at Penty-Hook, when winding up and letting out a line, to the end of which was attached a stout and strong barbel of some seven pounds—our assured property from the moment the hook entered his leathern mouth.

From Penty-Hook there is nothing to interest the voyager until he reaches the pretty FERRY AT LALEHAM. He may, if he pleases, step ashore at the clean and neat ferry-house here pictured, and either dine on the bank, or in one of the small rooms, to which access is readily obtained. In any case, he will do well to look about him. The steeple of a church adds its eloquent grace to a pleasing although flat landscape : it is the church at Lalcham. On the opposite side is the square tower

LALEHAM FERRY.

of Chertsey Church. Cattle are feeding on the luxuriant grass in Chertsey Mead, or cooling themselves in the shallow stream ; the ferry-boat is conveying foot passengers only, for the river here is not deep, and a mounted traveller may cross it, swimming merely the small " bit " that forms the channel of the barges. Rising just above him is St. Anne's Hill—so long the happy and quiet home of Charles James Fox, and now the property of his descendant, Lord Holland. Looking eastward, he has in view the wooded rise of Woburn, and farther on that of Oatlands. Immediately beside the banks, however, there is nothing to claim attention until he arrives at Chertsey Lock, right under which, apparently (for there is here a fall of some magnitude), is CHERTSEY BRIDGE.

Let us step ashore, and, having refreshed ourselves at "The Chequers,"—the inn pictured in our print,—walk a mile or so to visit Chertsey town.

We are arriving at Chertsey, in the evening, after a pleasant day at Penty-Hook : it is eight o'clock ; we hear the chimes of the curfew, heard very rarely in England now-a-days, but in the quiet little town, of

CHERTSEY BRIDGE.

small traffic and no manufacture, the ancient custom is still maintained, the curfew tolling so many times to denote the day of the month—once for the first, and thirty times for the thirtieth.*   We pass the church,

---

* The ringing of the curfew is one of the oldest of English customs.   Though popularly believed to have been introduced by William the Conqueror, it was more probably an ancient usage as a precaution against fire, in remote days of defective local rule, when houses were chiefly built of wood, and fires were frequent.   The curfew, or *couvre-feu*, itself was a metal case, which closed over the wood ashes and extinguished them.   Eight o'clock was the hour at which all persons were enjoined to put out fires and lights and retire to bed.   On the continent the custom was general.

part ancient, and part new : if we enter it, it will be to see a beautiful bas-relief by Flaxman of the raising of Jairus's daughter. It is behind the church—between it and the river—we shall find the remains of once and long-famous CHERTSEY ABBEY. These remains consist of a few stone walls, the graveyard, now a rich garden, and the fish-ponds, which even to-day hold water, by which cattle of the adjacent farm are refreshed. The abbey was founded A. D. 666, and held almost imperial rule over

REMAINS OF CHERTSEY ABBEY.

numerous villages, extending its "paternal sway" into Middlesex, and even so far as London, where its mitred abbot had a "fair lodging." It was of the Benedictine order, its foundation being almost coeval with the conversion of the Saxons by Erchenwald, first abbot of Chertsey, and afterwards Bishop of London. Gradually it grew to be one of the wealthiest and most powerful abbeys of the kingdom, fostered and endowed by nearly every English monarch, from the Conqueror down,

until the eighth Henry dissolved it, and gave its rich possessions to the
Abbey of Bisham, which, having enjoyed them for a time, relinquished
them in turn to various "civilians and laymen." Chertsey Abbey
received the remains of the pious but unhappy Henry VI.,—

> " Poor key-cold figure of a holy king,
>    Pale ashes of the house of Lancaster, "—

subsequently interred at Windsor. Its glory extended far and near;
its jurisdiction in Surrey was almost unlimited; its wealth was prodigious; its abbot ranked with princes—and ruled them. It is now
difficult to trace its site; of the enormous and very beautiful pile, scarcely
one stone remains upon another. Those who delve the adjacent ground
rarely do so without disinterring long-buried bones : indications of its
ancient glories now and then present themselves—broken capitals, stone
coffins, encaustic tiles, and fragments of painted glass ; but Chertsey
Abbey is little more than an historic memory. Our engraving exhibits
all of it that yet remains.

THE GOLDEN GROVE.

If the visitor has time, he will stroll through the town to visit
St. Anne's Hill, and do pilgrimage to the home, and lawns, and gardens,
and quaint summer-houses, and lonely walks so closely associated with

the memory of Charles James Fox. On his way he will pass " THE
GOLDEN GROVE," where lives one to whom many owe a debt for large
enjoyment and much instruction—Sir George Smart. Directly fronting
his plain and simple house is the famous oak-tree, which no doubt the
monks planted near to one of their out-dwellings, which still bears the
name of Monk's Grove. Let him pause awhile at the gate of wrought-
iron, at the entrance to the dwelling of Charles James Fox, and walk to

GATEWAY TO FOX'S HOUSE.

the summit of the hill, from which, on a clear day, he may obtain a view
of St. Paul's,—although distant twenty miles and more. The view is
indeed glorious and beautiful from this charming height—Windsor on
the one side, London on the other. A slight descent leads him into a
close and thick wood, at the bottom of which is a picturesque " bit "—

St. Anne's Well, a relic of the chapel that once existed here, and was probably erected when the abbey was founded, twelve centuries ago.

ST. ANNE'S WELL.

We return to Chertsey, and passing up its main street, stand before a quaint old building, where a good and benevolent clergyman now resides—the Rev. John Clark, the son of the long distinguished Chamberlain of London : the house is the Porch House, in which the poet Cowley lived, and where he died on the 28th July, 1667. He was interred in Westminster Abbey ; his body having been conveyed in a funeral barge upon the waters of the Thames he loved so well—

> " What tears the river shed,
> When the sad pomp along his banks was led ! "

A throng of nobles followed him to his grave ; and the worthless king

he had served, and by whom he had been deserted, is reported to have
said that he had not left a better man behind him in England. Although

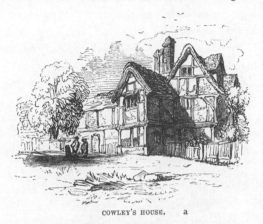

COWLEY'S HOUSE. a

"the Porch"—from whence it received its name, "the Porch House"
—was long ago removed, Cowley's house retains much of its original

COWLEY'S SEAT.

character. The room in which he died is still intact, and a group of
trees—COWLEY'S SEAT—flourish in vigorous age.

We may not extend our visit, although a drive through the pretty village of Addlestone—joining the railroad there—would be a worthy finish to a long summer's day of pleasure.*   We return to Chertsey Bridge, and resume our voyage downward, admiring, as we pass, the pleasant woods and wooded heights of Woburn, and welcoming another of the river's many tributaries—the Wey, which joins the Thames a mile or so below the bridge at Chertsey.   The Wey rises in Hampshire, about a mile from Alton—"famous for ale."   It passes through Farnham, Godalming, Guildford, Woking, Byfleet, and Weybridge, where it is joined by a small streamlet—the Bourne, and also by the Basingstoke Canal.   The junction of the three streams is so picturesque that we

THE WEY BRIDGE.

supply an engraving of the scene.   Following their course to the Thames margin, let us now glance at Chertsey Mead, which, it is said, produces the best hay in England; and where, during a large part of the year, there is right of commonage, of which the neighbour-

* The whole of this district has been fully described by Mrs. S. C. Hall, in "Pilgrimages to English Shrines;" and the reader who desires to know more concerning it is referred to that volume.   We have introduced two of the prints by which it is illustrated, in order to make more clear our details concerning St. Anne's Hill, and the residence of Charles James Fox.

ing farmers avail themselves to fatten cows that supply London with
pure milk.

The Wey enters the Thames at a mill in the curve of the stream, but
the ordinary course for boats is to the lock at Shepperton.  The woody
grounds of Oatlands now begin to rise on the right, and a short distance
to the left is SHEPPERTON CHURCH and village.  Close to the river are
the house and grounds of W. S. Lindsay, Esq., M.P.  Some fine trees

SHEPPERTON CHURCH.

hang over his boat-house.  These grounds are, perhaps, the most beautiful to be met with all along the river-banks : those who have taste as
well as riches have always the power to give to others a large share of
the luxuries they themselves obtain from wealth.  The distance to
Shepperton by water from Chertsey Bridge is about four miles ; but the
direct way by land is not more than a mile and a quarter.  Another
turn of the river brings us to Lower Halliford.  The river is now free
of any striking feature until we approach the long bridge at Walton :
the village is half a mile inland, and hidden from view.  At a sharp turn
of the river before we reach the bridge is COWAY STAKES.  Our sketch
is taken from the bridge, looking back toward Weybridge Church, its
tall spire and the high land of Oatlands Park being the chief features of

the view. The small arch in the foreground is a waterway. Between this point and the two dark trees of the middle distance, still lie under the Thames all that remain of the stakes which, tradition says, are those that impeded Cæsar. When the water is low and clear, some of the fragments, it is said, may still be seen imbedded in the clay; others have been taken from the river, black with age, but still sound.

Cæsar has left a circumstantial account of his battle here with the British tribes. It occurred B.C. 64, on his second visit to our island,

COWAY STAKES.

when, satisfied of the insincerity of submission of the natives to Roman rule, he resolved to penetrate farther than he had hitherto done, and quell opponents under the command of Cassivellaunus. He narrates the sort of guerilla warfare the Britons carried on against his forces, by continually harassing them in small parties, "so that one squadron relieved another," he says, "and our men, who had been contending against those who were exhausted, suddenly found themselves engaged with a fresh body who had taken their place." He accordingly determined to come to a general engagement, and invade the territory of Cassivellaunus. He describes leading his army towards the Thames to ford the river, which he says could only be passed on foot in one place, and that with difficulty. He had gained intelligence from prisoners and deserters that his passage was here to be disputed: when he arrived at the river, he perceived a large force on the opposite bank drawn up to oppose him; "the bank moreover was planted with sharp stakes, and others of the same kind were fixed in the bed of the river, beneath the water." But nothing could restrain the impetuosity of his legionaries, who dashed into the river, and drove off the Britons.

The venerable Bede notes that these stakes "are seen to this day, about the thickness of a man's thigh, stuck immovable, being driven hard into the bottom of the river;" and Camden, in his "Britannia," says of Oatlands, "It is a proper house of the king's, and offreth itself to be seene within a park; neer unto which Cæsar passed over Thames." He then narrates the event, concluding by saying, "In this thing I cannot be deceived, considering that the river here is scarce six foot deep. The place at this day of these stakes is called Coway Stakes; and Cæsar maketh the borders of Cassivellaunus, where he setteth down his passage over the river, to be about fourscore Italian miles from the sea which beateth upon the east coast of Kent, where he landed, and at the very same distance is this passage of ours."

In the time of Cæsar there can be no doubt that the whole of the low land about here was a swamp, and the Britons secured themselves in the rude earthworks they had constructed in the woody land which overlooked the river. There are intrenchments of this sort on St. George's Hill, at Weybridge, and also on St. Anne's Hill, Chertsey. There are traces of others at Wimbledon, proving that this range of elevations was made use of for defence. We have mentioned the old hill camp which formed one of the defences of the Cotswold Hills; and here we may properly devote a brief space to a consideration of the early inhabitants of the banks of the Thames.

When Cæsar visited Britain, the old Celtic population was considerably intermixed with the Belgæ, who had taken possession of the richest parts of South Britain, and kept up a close alliance with the Gaulish traders, to whom the people of the Kentish coast greatly assimilated. Strabo slightly describes the personal appearance of the old Britons, in their long dark garments fastened round the waist, and long hair and beards. Herodotus and Pliny speak of their puncturing and staining their bodies with the juice of herbs, as a mark of noble descent. Cæsar notes that they were "clad with skins; all the Britons stain themselves with woad, which gives a blue colour, and imparts a ferocious aspect in battle; they have long flowing hair, and do not shave the upper lip." *

The river Thames has preserved, as if in a museum, some relics of its ancient masters. Our engraving exhibits a group of antiquities found in the stream, and upon its banks. Of these the early British shield of bronze, with its great central boss, and double row of smaller ones, was dredged up from the river between Little Wittenham and Dorchester, a neighbourhood that formed the site of several hostile engagements.†
The leaf-shaped bronze sword was found also in the river near Vauxhall, and is remarkable for its similarity to the early Greek weapons found at

ANTIQUITIES FROM THE THAMES.

Pompeii. The other antiquities of the group belong to the Saxon period, and the banks of the Thames are rich in such memorials.

The other objects depicted were discovered in tumuli on the high land at Long Wittenham, in Oxfordshire. The umbo, or boss, at the right corner of the group, was originally fixed on the large wooden shield adopted by the Saxons. At Dorchester, many remarkable antiquities have been found; among the rest a large brooch, richly ornamented.

---

* Of the various native tribes noted by Ptolemy, the Dobuni occupied Gloucestershire and Oxfordshire; the Belgæ, Wiltshire and Hampshire; the Attrebates, Berkshire; and the Trinobantes, the greater part of Middlesex and Essex. Kent was held by the Cantii, a large and influential tribe which, as early as the time of Cæsar, was subdivided among four ruling chieftains.

† At the junction of the rivers here, still remain the intrenchments of the early Britons.

The more ordinary decorations for the person generally found in Saxon tumuli are exhibited in our second group, consisting of brooches and hair-pins found at Fairford and Long Wittenham. Three varieties of the former have been selected; they are all of bronze, the central one being of the most ordinary form. That to the left is cup-shaped, the surface decorated with raised ornament, which has been strongly gilt. That to the right is formed of white metal, decorated with incised ornament, and washed with silver; a pin behind assisted in securing them to the dress. The hair-pins crossed at the back of the central brooch are

SAXON PERSONAL ORNAMENTS.

also of bronze, having pendent rings attached to the upper part of each, one being slightly ornamented. With them were found finger-rings, consisting of a flat coil of bronze, beads of clay in variegated colours, and a variety of smaller articles for personal decoration, showing some considerable amount of refinement in the wearers. The inhabitants of Middlesex and Kent appear, however, to have been always in advance of the Saxons of the inland counties, which may be ascribed to their connection with the continental traders, and their superior wealth. The contents of their tumuli indicate a higher refinement, and a different taste in decoration. Antiquaries are now beginning to classify the Saxon tribes in England with much certainty, by the data afforded by these relics from their last resting-places.

Such were the people—progenitors of a race destined to establish the name and customs of Anglo-Saxons over the whole world. In thus tracing them to their source, we find much that is worthy of study in their life on the banks of the Thames " in the old time before us." Scattered among their graves are instructive illustrations of their history not to be found in the pages of the chronicler, but worthy of note; and in our descent of the stream we shall yet have to note the relics of their brethren, which also testify to their history as clearly as do the more enduring monuments of stone to the histories of classic nations.

Before we pass under the bridge at Walton, we are called upon to leave the boat, and walk a brief distance to visit the village and the church : both are full of interest. In the village is the house of the President Bradshaw; at Ashley Park, not far distant, the Protector is

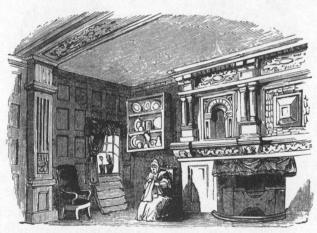

INTERIOR OF BRADSHAW'S HOUSE.

said to have some time resided; at Hersham, in the vicinity, lived William Lilly, the astrologer,—

" A cunning man, hyght Sidrophel,
That deals in Destiny's dark counsels,
And sage opinions of the moon sells,"—

and his remains lie in WALTON CHURCH. On St. George's Hill is an ancient encampment of considerable size, which, although of date anterior to the Romans, was, as we have intimated, probably occupied by Cæsar when preparing for his struggle with the Britons, under Cassivellaunus ; and it may be safely conjectured that his legions passed from this height into the valley to cross the Thames at Coway Stakes—" ea celeritate atque impetu." From the summit of this hill is obtained one of the most striking and magnificent views to be found anywhere in England, extending not only over Middlesex and Surrey, but into Buckinghamshire, Hertfordshire, Essex, Kent, and even Sussex.

Bradshaw's house is now in a dilapidated state, inhabited by poor persons, but it retains several indications of its ancient grandeur ; a chimney-piece is shown in the appended engraving ; it is one of the remaining ornaments of a wainscoted chamber, in which, probably, " the regicides" often sate in council ; there is a village tradition that here the signatures were affixed to the death-warrant of the king.

WALTON CHURCH.

We must enter the church, and—having examined a gorgeously-sculptured tomb, of much artistic value, from the chisel of Roubiliac, to the

memory of Viscount Shannon—"the fair black marble stone" that records
the name of "the astrologer"—the white tablet that marks the grave of
Henry Skene, the tourist—the singular monument to John Selwyn,
whose heroic achievement of killing a stag after having leaped upon his
back, in the presence of Queen Elizabeth, is commemorated in "a brass,"
now let into the wall—Chantrey's beautiful statue of a mourner leaning
on a sarcophagus, to the memory of "Christopher D'Oyley"—we may
criticise an object no less interesting as a record of the olden time—it is

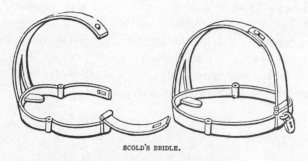

SCOLD'S BRIDLE.

"the scold's bridle," one of the few "examples" yet remaining in
England.   It bears the date 1633, and the following inscription,—

> "Chester presents Walton with a bridle,
>   To curb women's tongues when they are idle,"—

and was presented to the parish by the person whose name it bears,
because he had lost an estate "through the instrumentality of a gos-
sipping, lying woman."   Its construction and mode of fastening are
shown in the engraving; when locked, a flat piece of iron enters
the mouth, and effectually keeps down the "unruly member." The
venerable church, has, therefore, several objects of interest,—we can
name but few of them; yet we may not forget that in the adjacent
graveyard was interred, some eighteen or twenty years ago, one

> "Who blazed,
>   The comet of a season,"

an eloquent writer, a brilliant wit, a man of large knowledge and extensive learning; his grave is without a mark; we had a difficulty in finding

the secluded spot in which he lies : yet there are many who remember "William Maginn," perhaps with more of admiration than respect, and who will grieve that no stone distinguishes the place in which he rests "after life's fever."

We again make our way to the Thames, and join our boat, passing under the long and narrow bridge here pictured, from a sketch by W. E. Bates. "It is, in fact, a sort of double bridge, a second set of arches being carried over a low tract of ground, south of the principal bridge which crosses the river. From this bridge there is a pleasant

WALTON BRIDGE.

view of the Thames, above and below, Coway Stakes being immediately beneath us, and the new "villa-planted" demesne of "Oatlands" rising gracefully from its banks.* We must pause awhile in

* Oatlands is now "a village" of handsome houses, many of them with charming gardens and grounds. A large hotel has been recently erected, and is, we understand, exceedingly well conducted and made comfortable to visitors: the vicinity yields in attraction to none; it is distant fifteen miles by railway (the South-Western) from London. The palace at Oatlands, in which dwelt Henry VIII., Queen Elizabeth, the Consort of James I., the Queen of Charles I., and the Queen of Charles II., has long since disappeared; its site being occupied by a modern mansion, which became the property of the Duke of York, was at his death purchased by Mr. Ball Hughes, known as "the Golden Ball," and, having passed through "various hands," has been divided into "building lots." The

" the deep " immediately under it, for it is famous fishing ground ; and here, perhaps more than in any other part of the Thames, the angler finds the bream abundant.

The Bream (*Abramis brama*) inhabits most of the lakes and rivers of England, but appears to be found in the Thames only in special localities : often as we have fished in the glorious river, we have never yet caught one except in that part of it which we are now describing. The bream is often killed in large numbers, and frequently of weight between two and four pounds ; sometimes much heavier. It is, however, a poor fish—a degree worse than the barbel, as food ; although

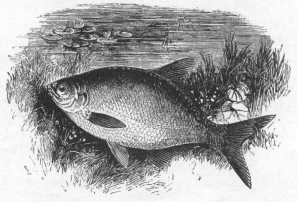

THE BREAM.

Izaak quotes, in reference to it, a French proverb, to the effect that " he who hath bream in his pond is able to bid his friend welcome ;"

---

famous grotto still remains : it was constructed at great cost for the Duke of Newcastle, by three persons—a father and two sons—who were employed in the work during several years. It consists of five chambers, the sides and roofs of which are encrusted with spars, ores, shells, and crystals. In a little dell adjacent are several stones, numbering, perhaps, sixty or seventy : they are the gravestones of pet dogs,—the pets of Her Royal Highness the Duchess of York,—and many of them have appropriate inscriptions. The Duchess died at Oatlands, in 1820, and was interred at Weybridge Church, where a monument was erected to her memory, with a beautifully sculptured figure by Chantrey. That old church has been taken down, and a new and very graceful structure built a few yards from its site. Chantrey's monument has been re-erected in the new church ; but the vault, originally in the transept, is now in the churchyard. The tall spire of Weybridge Church is seen from all parts of the adjacent country.

and Chaucer considers it worthy of note, as among the preparations for a feast :—

> " Full many a fair partrich hadde he in mewe,
> And many a bream and many a luce i ɔ stewe."

The fish is flat and broad ; the tail being long and " deeply forked." The colour is yellowish white.*

Passing between low lands for the distance of about two miles, we arrive at SUNBURY †—a pretty village on the Middlesex side. There is

SUNBURY.

a weir of considerable length, and lower down a lock : the lock has been recently constructed on " scientific principles "—the waters being raised and lowered by machinery, but the effect of the " improvement " is to embarrass and delay the voyager.‡

---

* There is a good and experienced, as well as a very civil and ever-ready fisherman here,—J. ROGERSON,—whose cottage adjoins the bridge, and whose punts are moored at the adjacent bank. Besides the bream which abound in this locality, there is a good barbel pitch close at hand, and the roach and dace are plentiful enough to give assurance of a day's sport. The inns at Walton are " comfortable " for anglers.

† " In ancient records this place is called Sunnabyri, Sunneberie, Suneberie, &c. Sunnabyri is composed of two Saxon words—*sunna*, the sun, and *byri*, a town—and may be supposed to denote a place exposed to the sun, or with a southern aspect."—*Lysons.*

‡ " About a mile below Sunbury Lock there is a turn on the left bank, or a back-water meeting the

Flat and uninteresting are the meadows that stretch away from the Surrey bank of the Thames, as we voyage below Sunbury. Tall osiers, for the most part, shut out all distant views from the water. The villages of West and East Moulsey succeed in their turn. Between the former village and the river lies the low open tract, or common, known as Moulsey Hurst, and memorable chiefly in the annals of pugilistic encounters and horse-racing. East Moulsey has very rapidly increased during the last few years. Fine trees have disappeared, and rows of genuine suburban residences have sprung up in their places. A new church of an agreeable aspect has been added to the group, near the Hurst; and opposite to the Palace of Hampton Court, the terminus of the railway, and a cluster of hotels have established themselves. The old church of East Moulsey is small, and belongs altogether to a period in which Moulsey itself was simply a country village, and had not yet risen to the dignity of a metropolitan railway station.

Situated on the Middlesex side of the Thames, the village of Hampton rises from the river's edge, and its long series of villas, with their orderly looking trees and well-kept gardens, with here and there a fishing cottage peering from beneath thick masses of overhanging foliage, skirt the stream. At the entrance into Hampton from Sunbury there are several good houses, that stand back at some little distance from the Thames; and in front of them the water-towers and other buildings of the London and Hampton works, for the supply of the metropolis with water, have been recently erected. An attempt has been made to impart an architectural character to these edifices, but they present a very questionable appearance after all. The passage across the water from Moulsey Hurst is effected by means of a truly primitive ferry-boat. Immediately adjoining the landing-place stands Hampton Church, occupying a commanding position on rising ground. To the edifice, however, unhappily may be assigned a "bad pre-eminence," as

being among the very worst examples of the church-building of thirty
years since. At that period the old church was pulled down, and the
present wretched affair was erected at great cost. The village extends
for some distance from the river towards the north; and at about a mile
from the church in that direction it has very recently expanded into a
second village, which bears the name of New Hampton. From the New
Hampton road Bushy Park extends to Kingston and Teddington, and
for the space of half a mile it reaches almost to the river's side, below

GARRICK'S VILLA.

the Hampton Villas. Of these residences the most striking is "GARRICK'S
VILLA," once the property and the favourite residence of the great master
of histrionic art. The garden, like its neighbours, abuts upon the river;
but the house stands beyond the road, and, consequently, it is separated
from the water-side part of its grounds: a communication, however,
suggested by Dr. Johnson, exists in the form of a very picturesque
short tunnel under the road. Here, beneath a weeping willow that
droops gracefully into the water, stands "the Grecian rotunda, with
an Ionic portico" (it is really a little octagonal water-side summer-

house), which in Garrick's time gave shelter to Roubiliac's statue of
Shakspere, that has since been promoted to the Hall of the British
Museum.*

The river bends slightly towards the south as it flows eastward, before
it changes its course below Hampton Court for a northerly direction.
More than one small island divides the stream at Hampton, and many
are the fishing-rods that may be here seen patiently extended over the
beautiful forget-me-nots, and other flowering plants which are grouped
with the thick rushes and bending willows. As we advance, we
approach a second series of water-side residences,—the murmuring
sound of the "overshot," or weir, of the lock, becomes more distinct,—
and our boat enters and passes through "Moulsey Lock," the last but
one on the Thames. The present lock has been newly built within the
last four years. Hampton has the questionable fame of possessing
the ugliest and the most inconvenient bridge on the Thames, although a toll
is still demanded from passengers. It is of wood, and was built in 1778,
"by a builder at Weybridge." Close to it, in Surrey, is the terminus
of the South-Western Railway; and near it is a neat little country inn,
"the Castle," with small but comfortable rooms overlooking the river.
We float under this bridge, and in another minute we have landed close
to the principal entrance to the Palace of Hampton Court. From the
bridge itself, the view both up and down the stream exhibits English
scenery in its highest perfection. But we hasten on to the Palace,
passing a row of shops, hotels, and dwelling-houses. "Hampton Green"
opens out before us, stretching away to our left, where it is bounded by
a small cavalry barrack. In front of us are more houses, and immediately beyond them appear the noble hawthorns and horse-chestnuts of

---

* The " Temple of Shakspere," as Garrick called this building, was constructed expressly for
Roubiliac's statue, a commission from the actor to the artist, who did his utmost to produce a good
work—to his own loss ; for Garrick, with his usual tact at driving a bargain, gave little more than
would pay for the model and the marble. The artist was also subjected to the meddlesome taste of the
actor, whose vanity was unbounded, and who threw himself into the affected posture of poetic inspira-
tion, which he insisted the statue should exhibit. When the work was finished, the sculptor executed a
new head, as Garrick demurred at a faint vein of colour in the marble. The only portrait of Roubiliac
we possess represents him working enthusiastically on this statue, which he certainly desired to make
his *chef-d'œuvre*. It passed to the British Museum, by Garrick's desire, on the death of his widow.

Bushy Park. This "Green," in the olden time, was the tilting-ground; it is now the scene of much holiday merry-making during summer months. The palace stables stand between the Green and the river. Here also are a few tolerable houses, of which more than one promises the best of "entertainment," "provided at the shortest notice," for visitors of all classes and of all tastes.

The "Toy," so long the recognised chief of the Hampton Court hotels, has ceased to exist in its former capacity, the building having been altered to form a group of private residences. A rapid "decline" preceded this "fall" of the "Toy." * In the days of Dutch William, who spent much time at Hampton Court, many were the rump-steak dinners given by the monarch himself at the "Toy" to his courtiers; and on these occasions, dense, without doubt, were the clouds of tobacco-smoke that enveloped both the guests and their royal host. The present "Toy," however, is an excellent hotel.

The palace itself is shut off from the Green by a long and massive wall of dark-red bricks, having in front of it a broad walk, now deeply shadowed with noble elms and chestnuts, leading from the river to Bushy Park. This was a favourite promenade with Mary, the consort of William III.; and here, also, the Low Country maids of honour and other ladies, who in those days graced with their presence the English court, might continually be seen. Hence the place obtained the popular name of the "*Frau* Walk," which has since degenerated into the "*Frog* Walk," by which it is now known.

At the entrance to the palace precincts, on either side, a lion and a unicorn discharge their patriotic duty of "supporting" the royal arms. We enter. On our right are some porter's-lodge-looking buildings, with a single good red-brick house—a family residence. On the opposite side, stretching away towards Wolsey's noble gateway-tower, is a long range of cavalry barracks, with their guard-house, stables, canteen, and

---

* Much speculation has arisen with reference to the singular title—the "Toy." It may, however, be derived from the *tois* or *toils*—movable fences of net-work that were used as barriers in many of the games, once played daily on the adjoining green—the tilting-ground, or (as it is styled in a survey of the year 1653) the toying-place of the Tudors and Stuarts.

other accessories. Our barracks are generally successful specimens of the art of unsightly and inconvenient building; and here, where something better might have been expected, this unworthy art has achieved its climax. The associations of "Royal Hampton's pile," however, which throng thickly upon our minds, are not interwoven with deeds of chivalrous valour or of military renown,—except, indeed, such as are inseparable from the present purposes to which the palace is so happily

ENTRANCE TO HAMPTON COURT.

applied. "The o'er-great cardinal" and his unscrupulous master rise before us; then come visions of the unfortunate Charles, of phlegmatic William, of decorous "Anne," and of the first George with his broken English. Rich, indeed, is the palace of Hampton Court in materials for a domestic history of almost unparalleled interest. We can but glance at the more salient points in the sketch for such a history.

In the time of Henry III. the manor of Hampton ("Hamntone" it is written in the Domesday Survey) was held by the Knights Hospitallers of St. John of Jerusalem, and from them Wolsey obtained a lease for the purpose of building on the site of the old manor-house his stately palace. The works were commenced about the year 1515, and they were urged on with such rapidity that the cardinal shortly after made Hampton his residence, or, as Skelton would have it, he held his "court" there. The splendours of Hampton Court when in the hands of Wolsey speedily produced that dangerous " envy " which in 1526 induced him to present his palace with all its sumptuous furniture to the king. Henry VIII. accepted the gift without hesitation ; and, in return, graciously "licensed the lord cardinal to lie in his royal manor at Richmond at his pleasure ;" also permitting him occasionally to occupy Hampton Court itself. In 1527, Montmorency, the French ambassador, was received at Hampton Court in such a style that the Frenchmen did "not only wonder at it here, but also make a glorious report of it in their own country."

The great hall was built by Henry VIII., after the palace had come into his possession, and he added other buildings to the pile, "till it became more like a small city than a house." With his characteristic selfishness, he also afforested the country around, converting a wide tract of the adjoining lands into a chace, which he stocked with deer. Henry spent much of his time at Hampton Court. There Edward VI. was born, and there Jane Seymour died. With Edward himself Hampton Court was a favourite residence, and so it continued to be during several succeeding reigns. James I. held there the "conference" of 1604. Many of both his happier and his most anxious days were spent there by Charles I.* In 1656 Cromwell purchased it, and made it his principal abode. It was in equal favour with Charles II. after the Restoration ; James II. resided there less habitually ; William III. and Anne may be said to have made it their home. The first and second Georges followed in the steps of their predecessors in so far as Hampton Court is

---

* It was from Hampton Court that Charles I. fled to the Isle of Wight, on the night of November 11, 1647, and so brought to a climax the long rupture between himself and the parliament. The night was dark and stormy ; the king was attended only by one servant, Lord Ashburnham, and Sir John Berkeley. They went towards Oatlands, and so through the wood there, the king acting as guide. In one of the letters he left behind him he says, " I confess that I am loath to be made a close prisoner under pretence of securing my life." This journey was the last act of freedom of the unfortunate king.

concerned. But since their time a change has come upon what Lord Hervey (Pope's "Lord Fanny") was pleased to call the "unchanging circle of Hampton Court." The state apartments and the hall are thrown open freely to the public daily, with the exception of Fridays only; and the rest of the palace is arranged to form a series of residences for families who may be considered to have claims upon their Sovereign and their country. Her Majesty the Queen is known to feel a warm interest in Hampton Court, and the appointments to the residences in the palace are made expressly by the royal command. Recent circumstances have greatly enhanced the interest which attaches to this royal house, thus converted into a palace of the people. In place of persons of high rank but narrow means, Hampton Court has now become, for the most part, the residence of the widows and orphan families of officers who have fallen in the Sikh war, and in the Crimea; and we may feel assured that many of those families who mourn the lost heroes of the fierce struggle in India—our Havelocks and Neills—will here find honourable and honoured homes.

The palace originally consisted of five principal quadrangular courts, but of these three only now remain. To these, however, must be added a variety of offices, and many ranges of subordinate buildings. The first and second courts are for the most part remains of the original palace, with the exception of very questionable classic additions in the second court and the great hall of Henry VIII. The third court is the work of Sir Christopher Wren, and is a dull and heavy affair. The hall has lately undergone a complete restoration, which has been thoroughly well done: the grand open timber roof, the finely-proportioned windows with their brilliant new heraldic glazing by Willement, the showy array of banners, the groups of armour, and the quaint and still bright-hued tapestry, all combine to realize the most romantic vision of a palatial hall. Adjoining the hall is a truly appropriate withdrawing room.

To the state apartments we ascend by the "king's staircase," at an angle of the second court. A series of wretched allegories cover the walls and ceilings of this staircase; they are the work of

Verrio.* We first enter the "guard-chamber," where there are some curious weapons of by-gone days. Here commences the miscellaneous collection of pictures, some originals, others copies, many curious and valuable, and more equally uninteresting and worthless, which cover the walls of the long range of noble rooms. There are a few relics of the state furniture also here, and a considerable quantity of fine china. The Cartoons demand a far more detailed notice than our space will admit; we content ourselves, therefore, with a few brief words of ardent admiration, and a strong expression of hope that these most precious of our national "Art-treasures" may be removed from the sombre gallery to which they are now consigned, in order to take their rightful place in a worthy "National Gallery" in London.

Among the more remarkable pictures are some historical works of great interest, by Holbein and others; a group of the "Charles the Second Beauties," by Lely, and a companion group of portraits by Kneller of the ladies of the court of William III.; various other portraits; two fine Giorgiones; Andrea Montagna's really grand "Triumph of Julius Cæsar," and the Cartoons. Two very remarkable pictures by Mabuse, which were sent to the Manchester Exhibition, were *returned* from thence to Holyrood instead of to Hampton Court; they were long supposed to be portraits of the Scottish James who fell at Flodden, and of his English Queen Margaret, the sister of Henry VIII.; but the researches of Mr. David Laing, since they have been removed to Scotland, seem to prove satisfactorily that the portraits are those of King James III. and Margaret of Denmark, and that they were painted about 1484, for the Church of the Holy Trinity, Edinburgh.†

From many of the windows there are charming views of the gardens and the park. With these views we now hasten to form a more intimate

---

* Verrio was one of the most famed of a school of artists, who, in accordance with a taste generated at the court of Louis XIV., covered the walls and ceilings of English mansions with enormous allegorical pictures. He has been immortalized by Pope in the lines descriptive of "Timon Villa:"—

" On painted ceilings you devoutly stare,
Where sprawl the saints of Verrio and Laguerre."

† An excellent "companion" to "Hampton Court" was compiled a few years ago by Henry Cole, Esq., C.B.: no doubt it has been since revised. It is sufficiently elaborate to answer all purposes of the visitor.

acquaintance. We descend by a different staircase, and passing along the colonnades of the "fountain court," we enter the gardens. They are admirably kept, and their formality is both characteristic and pleasing. There is a fountain in a circular basin opposite to the centre of Wren's façade; and here are a brilliant throng of such gold and silver fish as might have satisfied Wolsey himself with their size and their lustrous hues. The gardens extend from the river to Bushy Park. In front of the palace, and also reaching to the Thames as it sweeps onward to Kingston, lies the "Home Park," with its splendid trees, noble deer, formal sheet of water, and the picturesque lodge of the ranger. A noble terrace-walk passes in front of the palace, and on reaching the river it is continued at right angles to its former course, and parallel with the stream; here, between the terrace and the "Home Park," are some fine

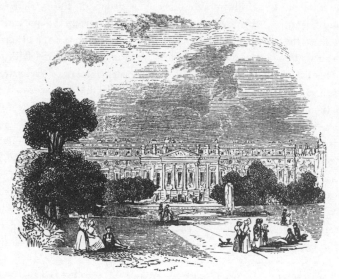

HAMPTON COURT: GARDEN FRONT.

specimens of wrought-iron work, that will repay a careful study. Returning towards the palace, we observe the bell that summons the attendant gardener who has the charge of the "private garden." To this garden the public are admitted, but they are expected here to pay a small gratuity.

The garden is well worthy a visit. It affords some fine views of the palace, and it also contains the famed "vine," which fills its ample hothouse, and displays such a collection of clusters as it is probable never elsewhere hung upon a single tree.* We return to the open gardens, and walk past the palace. Leaving behind us a newly-built tower, we enter the "wilderness," a thickly-planted space to the north of the main edifice, where some of the finest trees in England are grouped together.† At the extremity of this wilderness is the "MAZE." ‡ We need no guide

THE MAZE.

to lead us to the entrance that tempts all visitors to explore the intricacies within; for more than one of the pleasure-seekers of the day is there before us, and their laughter is by no means kept within the hedges of the maze, though it does not transgress beyond the bounds of moderation. And this remark leads us to observe that the great boon of free public access to Hampton Court Palace and Gardens is thoroughly appreciated by the public. Rarely, indeed, is an individual to be seen who needs to be reminded that he is acting with impropriety. Thousands and tens of thousands of persons of all classes avail themselves of the opportunity so liberally afforded them of enjoying this beautiful place;

* This vine produces the grape called the Black Hamburgh; it spreads over a surface of 110 feet, and in some seasons has yielded more than 2500 bunches of grapes.

† This wilderness was planted by King William III., with a view to hide the irregularities of the north side of the palace, where the old domestic offices were situated.

‡ This is a curious relic of the ancient taste in gardening, and was planted in the reign of William III. It consists of narrow walks between tall clipped bushes, which wind intricately to the open space in the centre. There is only one way by which it may be reached, and any deviation leads to a stoppage and a necessity for retracing the path.

and yet the few police who are on duty find their office almost a sinecure. This is as it should be.

The reader will permit us to vary these comparatively dry details of facts by introducing a sketch of one of those "characters" so frequently encountered on or about the river.

During our later visits to Hampton Court, we have felt disappointment that we did not meet at the old landing a man who had long been associated with our memories of the neighbourhood. He was known by the *sobriquet* of "Fresh-Water Jack." We missed the blithe rosy face, the bright eyes, the broad joyous smile of the young Irishman, who was accustomed to assure us he knew of our approaching visit to "the Coort" by a "drame" he had. He was lame; and we remember once endeavouring to obtain for him a situation where he might earn his "crust" on dry land, believing he might lose altogether the use of his limbs from being so continually in and about the water; but Jack said he couldn't bear the thought of quitting the beautiful "ould river," that he knew, and that knew him : besides, so many would miss him,—his friends—God bless them !—who called to see him and the "Coort" any-way *once* a-year. "A fresh-water Jack," he would say, "is all as one as a king—he never dies." So there 'd be another in his place before he 'd been a mile away from Hampton : and sure some of his own beautiful ladies and gentlemen might be murdered by them thieving "jacks," "and the sin o' that would be on his soul to the end of his days, and may be afther." No; as long as he had one leg to stand on, and two hands to help, he 'd keep his ground in the "wather."

Poor Jack ! when he declared his tongue was loosely hung he said but the truth ; he told us, on the first day of our acquaintance, all he had, or rather all he chose, to tell—for Irishmen, however voluble, have their reserves. He professed great love and admiration for the Thames ; but it was evident that, no matter what his worldly interests might be, his heart was in a perpetual state of transit between Cork and Kerry. He had plenty of information about the river, and was an excellent fisherman "when not on duty;" knew where to get gudgeons, and where the barbel lay, and would keep a keen eye and a steady hand to his work;

but say a word of "the Lee" or "the Shannon"—just name Killarney—down would go the rod, the pole might float where it pleased, in an ecstasy he would pitch all the ground-bait over at once, and, with sparkling eyes and fluent tongue—if he had not done so previously—inform you that "in troth" *he* was an Irishman himself, and what was bether still, a County Cork man—and what was twice as good as that, a boy from Clonakilty! "Sure, then, I'll never turn the back of my hand on ould Ireland. People says to me, 'Why do you say you're Irish, Jack, when you have such beautiful English on the top of yer tongue?' but I'd scorn to be an imposture. No, if Ireland hadn't a rag to her back, or a string to her harp, every blade of her grass would be dearer to Jack O'Conner than all the timber on the Thames,—and that's a bould word, for well I know the forests it floats all over the world, and I've nothin' to say aginst them; but for all that, I'd rather this minute have a blade of the grass that grows on my mother's grave than the whole of 'em."

We remember inquiring, if Jack loved his country so tenderly, why he had left it. Jack twisted his shoulders and said, "The rason?" Why, betwixt the famine and the sickness, there was nothing left for him to love but the bare sod; but he added, "Even with all the sickness and the hunger, I'd have stuck to that sod if it wasn't for the hurt I got in mee knee (saving yer presence); but if boys with the use of their four bones couldn't get more than the wet potatoe and the sup of wather, how could such a *bocher** as meeself get through?—and all mee people either dead or gone to the Far West! If I had the luck to take the pledge, and keep it, it's not *here* I'd be, anyway. I got my wound through being *overtaken†* during the full of the May moon, at the corner, as you turn from *the Lake* to go up to the blessed Church of Aghadoe. I thought I wasn't quite right in meeself, and I knew my neighbours—the GOOD PEOPLE‡—from the skirl of the pipes coming through the air, just like the song of a bird through the leaves of a forest; and I felt the drowsiness coming over me,—'Keep up, John

---

* Lame man.      † Tipsy.      ‡ Fairies.

Conner,' I says, 'and don't be taking the breadth of the road instead of the length of it; but go on.' Well, I tried hard, but I couldn't foot a straight line; and I heerd them coming closer and closer; and I had sense enough to be ashamed of meeself one minute, and glad the next, because the only girl I cared for wasn't there to see. 'And it's a purty pass I'm come to,' I says, 'when I don't wish *you*—darlint of my heart! —to be near me!' and yet I wasn't so overtaken intirely but I knew where I was; and I saw the leaves dancing in circles on the road, and the dust wheeling, and every now and agin a buz in my ear, and I tuk off my hat, not to be wantin' in manners, as they passed, though I wished meeself far enough away; and then of a suddent I minded there was a slip of a rowan-tree growing over the gripe of the ditch, and I knew if I could catch a hoult of one of its dawshy boughs, or even get under its shade, I'd be as safe as if I was in the holy cardinal's hall up there, and his holiness himself *to the fore ;* \* so here goes, I says, and I made a spring, thinking to clear the gripe—for in them times I was free and firm of foot as the finest deer on Glena; but as ill luck would have it, mee head was light, and mee feet heavy wid the brogues,—for it was a holiday, so I had 'em on,—and into the gripe I went: if there was wather in it, I'd have been drownded like a blind puppy, but as it was, I lay like a turtle, and the moon looking mee full in the face like a Christian. I roared and cried; but sure I knew no one could hear me that would give me a taste of help; and I wanted to think of mee prayers, and if I could have got at one, I'd ha' been safe enough; but I was bothered between the goin' and the comin' of the good people's pipes, and the song *she* had sung for me, and me only, not two hours gone,—the song warbled round mee heart, and the pipes, as I said, bothered mee ears, and I knew by the prayers keepin' their distance that there was somethin' goin' to happen beyant the common ; and sure enough, it wasn't long 'till they gathered round me, like a swarm of bees round a Maybush, first peepin' and pryin' at me, as if I was a grate curosity, and not one of 'em the length of mee hand, and titterin' and

* Present.

sniggerin', all as one as the young girls of flesh and blood are so fond of doing when they set their comeithers on some unfortunate boy without sense, or, indeed, with sense—for one sort is just as 'asy made nothin' of as the other. Then they made a ball-room of mee chest, footin' and patterin' over me; and the young ones made a horse of mee nose, and the king and queen had high tay on mee forehead, and a game of hide-and-seek through mee hair. I knew that as long as the good people liked to divart themselves that way, I should say nothin' against it, though if I could have thought of a prayer, they'd have had it; so I lay as still as a dead lamb until one, all over in a shine of silver, cried out they must have some shooting, and then there was a grate scrimigin' and racing, and trying their bows and arras; and they set to pulling the hair out of mee head for bow-strings, and I bearing it all like a Christian, and yet couldn't think of a Christian prayer! Oh! my grief! Well, though they war little, the high heels of their dawshy shoes ran like iron into mee flesh, and I desired to ax them to go 'asy, particular those on mee nose, who kickt it crooked, and left it so—as your honor may see, if you pay me the compliment to look straight in mee face." And certainly Jack's nose leaned considerably more to one side than to the other—this gave him a quaint, roguish expression. He continued, "Well, I dun know how it was, but I begun to think of mee poor mother; and though she wasn't a prayer, she was the next thing to it,— she taught me all she knew that way, as well as every other way; and surely, the more I thought of her, the lighter grew the little iron heels, and somehow, the dawshy craythurs themselves seemed as if the light shone through them; but still they kep' on at their new play, shootin' their little arras, which sparkled for all the world like stivers of diamonds, so bright and swift—made out of dew and moonlight, and the webs that glitter on the hedges of a summer morning—so that I was fairly bothered watching them, now thinkin' this and now thinkin' that; and my mother seemed a grate ould picture in the thick of it. At last I spied up at the sky, and sure enough I thought I saw the first strake of day, like an angel's smile in the heavens, and with that I said asy to myself, 'Oh, Holy Mary!' That done it—and me too!—Skirl—whirl—wish—e!—

all round me. But one, a little spiteful devil, with a hooked nose, and a red feather in his cap, came out of the mob, and taking his stand on the top of a bouchlawn, draws his bow, and looking at me as a judge looks at a prisoner, 'Take that, John O'Conner,' he says, 'for findin' fault with the heels of mee boots, that war made before the Flood,' he says, 'and are better than new now!' and with that he lets fly at me, and the arra hot me in the knee. I thought the life would lave me that very minute; but life is tough, and hearts are tougher. I sat up, and sure enough when I did, the heavens were all in a glow o' pink like a bride's blushes, and an innocent rabbit was staring me full in the face. I might have taken a priest's word for it, and believed it nothin' but a drame, only for the lameness and the arra, which I drew out with this hand (*that's so honoured as to hand ye safe ashore,* mee noble lady): and mee poor mother kep it for a corker* for many a day to fasten her shawl. One Sunday she forgot a warnin' she had, and took it to Mass, and she never saw it afther."

Poor Jack! his place, to our fancy, can never be efficiently filled. We inquired for him, and, to our astonishment, heard that, fascinated by the blandishments of a recruiting sergeant, he had exchanged the Thames for the " Connaught Rangers."

" But his knee—his lameness!" we exclaimed.

" Please, my lady," said the new " Jack," " his knee was bosh, and his lameness bosh. He made a good thing of it here—all blarney: he got shillings where I get pence. He was born with a silver spoon in his mouth."

" How? has any one heard of him lately ?"

" Oh yes; he was in the Crimea, and distinguished himself, they said : led a something, which I don't believe—all bosh !—lost a leg and an arm (I should not wonder if they grew again, like the lobster's)—was made a sergeant, and got a pension, and a lot of medals at his button-hole, and a Queen's handkerchief in his pocket. Pity he doesn't come back to his old place—he should have it cheap."

---

* A *corker*—strong pin.

What a grumbling water-rat! We were more than proud of our old acquaintance; but we hoped he had not fooled us so entirely, and are more than willing to believe his lameness *was* real, and that time had removed the impediment to preferment.

From the "Maze," at Hampton Court, we cross over the Kingston Road into Bushy Park, passing through a cluster of hotels, lodging-houses, and private residences. Famous are the horse-chestnuts and thorn-trees of Bushy, but fame has done them no more than justice. The thorns are supposed to have given its name to the park. The fern here is picturesque, and the deer abound on every side. Some of them are very tame; so much so, that they will even eat from the hands of visitors who, in the summer season, assemble for a sylvan repast beneath the trees. There is a public drive across the park to Teddington, and more than one foot-path promises a delightful walk to the pedestrian. Opposite the principal entrance, in the great avenue, is the "Diana" fountain, which stands in the midst of a large circular piece of water, and exercises its vocation after a very agreeable manner. The lodge and the stables of Bushy are separate buildings, and though rather extensive, they do not claim any special notice,—except, indeed, to state that the former was the favourite residence of William IV. and good Queen Adelaide.

Bushy Park must be regarded as forming an integral part of the royal domain of Hampton Court. Having traversed its pathways, and rested in the shade of its trees, we retrace our steps to the palace, and returning through its courts to the river where our boat awaits us, we set forth on our voyage downward. The first object that attracts our notice is the junction of the "silent Mole" with the waters of the Thames. This tributary, itself produced by the union of a numerous series of small streams and brooks, some of which rise in Sussex, and others in Surrey, assumes the importance of a river near Reigate, in the latter county, from whence its course lies in a north-westerly direction. Winding amidst the lovely scenery of central Surrey, the Mole flows on past Dorking, Leatherhead, and Cobham; and then, taking its leave of bold hills and rich woods and ancestral mansions, it hastens through

the flat region of the Moulseys towards the Thames.  Much has been
written, both in poetry and prose, upon the Mole, and many are the
landscapes that other artists besides Witherington have painted near
its tranquil waters.  As late as the times of the lordly builder of
Hampton Court, known as the "Emlay," this river has both changed its
name and acquired its celebrity, from the singular circumstances that
attend its career in the neighbourhood of Box Hill and Norbury Park.
Here the bed of the stream is composed of a very porous earth, in
which, at some little depth below the surface, many cavernous hollows
are supposed to have been formed.  In ordinary seasons the supply of
water is sufficient, as well to fill these hidden recesses as to maintain
the stream itself at its ordinary level; not so, however, in any time of
drought; then the stream fails, and for some distance the channel is
dry, with the exception of here and there a standing pool.  Near the
bridge at Thorncroft the ground again becomes solid, and here accordingly the exhausted river rises in a strong spring, and resumes its

WOLSEY'S TOWER.

original condition.  As will be readily supposed, this singular interruption to the course of the Mole gave rise, at early periods, to a variety
of marvellous legends.  Old Camden does not fail to give his version of
the wonder, and, according to him, the Mole at Box Hill absolutely

leaves the surface of the earth for a while in order to traverse a dark
and subterraneous channel, arched out for its reception, and for some
hidden purpose, by the great engineer, Nature. We may add, that at
Wey-pool, in the "porous" region, the river has hollowed out a basin
about thirty feet in diameter, in which the curious process of its absorp-
tion may be observed.

On the banks of the Mole there is yet a remnant of Wolsey's palace,
"his palace of Esher-Place," to which he retired after "losing the favour"
of King Henry, who had despoiled him of all his possessions, leaving
him nothing—compelling him to beg from the monks at Leicester
Abbey even

> " A little earth for charity ! "

William Wainfleet, who held the see of Winchester from 1447 to
1486, built a stately mansion of red brick on the borders of the Mole,
and it became the episcopal residence. It was repaired and partially
rebuilt by " the o'er-great cardinal;" and of this erection the gatehouse
yet remains, a striking object on the banks of the pleasant river.

Milton speaks of the

> " Sullen Mole that runneth underneath ;"

Pope of the

> " Sullen Mole that hides his diving flocd ;"

And Drayton pictures the Thames hastening to soft dalliance with
the Mole,—when he is reproved by his parents, Thame and Isis, who
desire him, in preference, to mate with the Medway—

> " But Thames would hardly on : oft turning back, to show
> From his much-loved Mole how loth he was to go."

Having passed the confluence of the Mole with the Thames, our boat
sweeps by the palace gardens, and we glide swiftly along between the
Home Park and the pretty village of Thames Ditton. Once again we
find ourselves amidst a flotilla of punts, and great is the amount of
serious fishing we observe to be going on. On our right some small
willow-bearing islands attract notice, and we learn that these are
spots famous in the history of Thames picnic parties—so famous,

indeed, that during the summer season they vie with Bushy Park itself
as scenes of much happy and harmless enjoyment of this description.
We pass the islands, and land on the Surrey bank of the river, with the
view of improving our acquaintance with Ditton. In the Domesday
Book it is stated that "Wadard holds of the Bishop (of Bayeux) *Ditone*,
in the hundred of Kingstone ;" and it included the rich manors of
Cleygate and Weston—the former belonging to the abbots of Westminster, the latter to the nuns of Barking. The church is "of remote
origin, but has been greatly altered at different times, and enlarged by

THE SWAN AT DITTON.

additional erections." It contains some remarkable tombs and brasses,
most of them of a late period. Our print exhibits the long-famous inn,
" THE SWAN ;" and the stately mansion—" Boyle Farm "—the residence of Lord St. Leonards. " The Swan " is, as we have said,
" famous," but only in the records of the angler. Time out of mind,
Thames Ditton has been in favour with the punt-fisher, not alone
because sport was always abundant there,—its pretty aits, close beds of

rushes, and overhanging osiers being nurseries of fish,—but because the river is especially charming "hereabouts," and there are many associations connected with the fair scenery that greatly augment its interest to those who enjoy the recreation of the "contemplative man." All anglers, therefore, are familiar with the pleasures to be found in this quiet and attractive nook of the Thames. Our own memory recalls to us a day we cannot soon forget : it was passed in a punt with Theodore Hook—a lover of the gentle art, as many have been to whom "society" and the gaieties of life were necessities. Hook was in strong health at that time—it was in the year 1834; the fountain of his wit was in full and uninterrupted flow; it is not difficult to imagine, therefore, the stores of incident and humour that were opened up between the first cast of the plummet into the stream and the winding up of the reel when the declining light gave notice that refreshment was provided at "the Swan." *

* On that occasion Mr. Hook produced some lines, which we believe are little known, and were not published with his name ; we therefore reprint them from the *New Monthly Magazine* (then edited by Mr. S. C. Hall) for July, 1834, in which they were printed. They were *composed* in the punt, and afterwards written down. It is needless to refer to Mr. Hook's wonderful facility in improvising verse.

" When sultry suns and dusty streets
    Proclaim town's *winter* season,
And rural scenes and cool retreats
    Sound something like high treason—
I steal away to shades serene,
    Which yet no bard has hit on,
And change the bustling, heartless scene
    For quietude and DITTON.

" Here lawyers, free from legal toils,
    And peers, released from duty,
Enjoy at once kind Nature's smiles,
    And eke the smiles of beauty:
Beauty with talent brightly grace l,
    Whose name must not be written,
The idol of the fane, is placed
    Within the shades of DITTON.

" Let lofty mansions great men keep—
    I have no wish to rob 'em—
Not courtly Claremont, Esher's steep,
    Nor Squire Combe's at Cobham.
Sir Hobhouse has a mansion rare,
    A large red house, at Whitton,
But Cam with Thames I can't compare,
    Nor Whitton class with DITTON.

" I'd rather live, like General Moore,
    In one of the pavilions
Which stand upon the other shore,
    Than be the king of millions;

For though no subjects might arise
    To exercise my wit on,
From morn till night I'd feast my eyes
    By gazing at sweet DITTON.

" The mighty queen whom Cydnus bore,
    In gold and purple floated,
But happier I, when near this shore,
    Although more humbly boated.
Give *me* a punt, a rod, a line,
    A snug arm-chair to sit on,
Some well-iced punch, and weather fine,
    And let me fish at DITTON.

" The ' Swan,' snug inn, good fare affords
    As table e'er was put on,
And worthier quite of loftier boards
    Its poultry, fish, and mutton:
And while sound wine mine host supplies,
    With beer of Meux or Tritton,
Mine hostess, with her bright blue eyes,
    Invites to stay at DITTON.

" Here, in a placid waking dream,
    I'm free from worldly troubles,
Calm as the rippling silver stream
    That in the sunshine bubbles ;
And when sweet Eden's blissful bowers
    Some abler bard has writ on,
Despairing to transcend *his* powers,
    I'll *ditto* say for DITTON."

As a fishing station, Ditton has lost some of its ancient fame; and the inn had fallen also from its "high estate." Latterly, however, it has been considerably "brushed up;" the landlord and landlady seem very attentive to their guests; the rooms are remarkably clean and neatly furnished, and anglers may again enjoy there the quiet comfort which ought to succeed a day of pleasant toil. Moreover, there are several good and experienced fishermen at Ditton; and punts, as well as row-boats, may be generally obtained.

Esher is about two miles from Thames Ditton; but those who voyage the Thames will surely pay a visit to this village, charming for its scenery, and deeply interesting from its associations. It was anciently named *Aissele* (so in Domesday), *Aissela*, and *Ashal*. In this neighbourhood is Claremont, so sadly connected with the brief history of the Princess Charlotte, who died here on the 6th November, 1817. It is now the property of his Majesty the King of the Belgians. Here too resided the unhappy Lord Clive, of whom parliament pronounced that he rendered "great and important service to his country." The house is plain, but the grounds are exceedingly beautiful, and are kept with much care. In the church at Esher are interred Anna Maria Porter and her mother, who resided many years in a small cottage in the village.*

At Thames Ditton, too, William and Mary Howitt lived in one of

---

* So far back as the year 1825 we visited the accomplished sisters, Jane and Anna Maria Porter, at their pretty cottage; and we have given a record of this visit in the "Pilgrimages to English Shrines," from which we borrow the appended engraving. A tomb was erected by her daughters over the remains of Mrs. Porter: it gives the dates of her birth and death, and contains this memorable passage—

"RESPECT HER GRAVE, FOR SHE MINISTERED TO THE POOR;"

it is in the churchyard; a cypress flourishes at the head of the grave. Not long after the death of her mother, Anna Maria was laid by her side. The last time we saw Jane Porter—it was at Bristol, a few months before her death, in 1850—her parting words to us were these, "Whenever you are at Esher, do visit my mother's grave."

While at Esher the sisters were in the wane of life, but having good health, and still occasionally writing; enjoying honourable repose: having obtained a large amount of fame, and being in easy and comfortable circumstances. Anna Maria, although the youngest, died first, Jane surviving her sister several years. They must have left a mass of interesting correspondence; and their lives afforded materials for an interesting biography. It is to be regretted that no use has been made of either since their deaths. They published novels when talent in women was comparatively rare, and they obtained an amount of fame perhaps beyond their deserts: yet their many books still hold a prominent place in public favour. They were undoubtedly, however, the precursors of "Waverley;" and Sir Walter Scott followed in the steps of these eminent and excellent ladies.

the many pretty and graceful "home-dwellings" that abound in this vicinity.

There is little to attract the voyager between Ditton and Kingston. The banks of the river are on both sides low, generally bordered with rushes, with occasional aits, on which grow the "sallys" which supply so many of the basket-makers of London. We have therefore leisure

THE COTTAGE OF JANE AND ANNA MARIA PORTER.

here to consider some of the wild flowers of the water, of which we shall soon lose sight, for we are approaching the "roads," from which they have been driven by the "higher state of cultivation."

The neighbourhood from Staines to Twickenham is rich in aquatic vegetation, both as regards the number of species and the prodigal luxuriance of their growth : in one small still pool, a few yards in extent, intercepted from the stream by a narrow strip of beach, we found in flower at one time specimens of the noble White and the Yellow Water-lilies, the beautiful Fringed Villarsia, or Yellow Buckbean, the delicate Frogbit, the Arrow-head in fine blossom, the Purple and the Yellow Loosestrife; and on the bank the fine bold foliage of the Water-dock, Wild Teasel, Reeds, and many of the minor or less remarkable species that create the wealth of a river Flora. It was delightful to the eye and mind of the poet, painter, botanist, or the simple lover of nature. Several of these plants we have already pictured as they have occurred in the course of our tour; we may here describe two or three not hitherto noticed.

The Yellow Water-lily (*Nuphar lutea*), which is so constantly found in company with its fairer sister, the White Lily,—though indeed it

cannot rival the latter in size and beauty,—produces by its contrast of colour a charming effect. These two together stud the river with silver and gold, giving an almost tropical luxuriance to the still nooks which are their favourite haunts, and where they develop

YELLOW WATER-LILY.

themselves in full glory. The structure of the yellow lily is extremely curious on a close examination, which shows a very complicated and ornamental arrangement of the interior parts round a central object, the seed-vessel, which in shape bears a resemblance to a flagon or bottle; and this circumstance, in conjunction with the flower emitting a decidedly spirituous odour, has given rise to its having received, in the provinces, the Bacchanalian cognomen of "Brandy-bottle."

There is another yellow flower that, at a little distance, bears a close resemblance to the last, but, on a nearer inspection, is found to be very distinct; this is the *Villarsia nymphoides*, or Yellow Buckbean, gene-rally spoken of by botanists as a great rarity: it may probably be so in most localities, for we have never met with it excepting in the Thames from Windsor downwards, where in some parts we found it growing in rich profusion. The leaves are very like those of the Water-lily in shape and texture, though smaller; and they float in a similar way on the surface of the water, above which rise the bright yellow blossoms, of a graceful contour; the petals being edged with a delicately-cut fringe, which gives to the flower a peculiar elegance. This is one of the numerous

YELLOW BUCKBEAN. a

native "aquatics" that are worthy of cultivation by every possessor of an ornamental water; or it might be easily grown within the limits of an in-door tank or aquarium, the culture being extremely easy.

What a striking appearance the Wild Teasel (*Dipsacus sylvestris*) makes, rear-ing its erect form above the humbler herbage, and crowned with those curious bristling heads which, in the early part of the year, are clothed with diminutive lilac flowers, and later in the season form the receptacle of the seeds. This handsome plant is interesting also as being closely allied to the Fuller's Teasel, so largely employed in the preparation of woollen cloths,—if, indeed, the two plants are not, as some botanists suppose,

WILD TEASEL.

varieties of the same species modified by cultivation and difference of soil, which in one develops the delicate hooks to which the Fuller's

T T

Teasel owes its efficacy, and for which no artificial substitute has yet been found.  The heads of the latter plant are fixed on to the circumference of a large broad wheel, which is set in motion, and the cloth is held against them till the action of the crooked awns has sufficiently raised the nap.  The Teasel is of commercial importance, and is cultivated in fields as a regular crop in the West of England, and also in some parts of Essex, but especially in Yorkshire—that county having of late years taken the lead in the manufacture of woollen cloths.

Among the insect tribes, too, we meet with a variety of interesting objects, the water-side vegetation being a favourite haunt of numerous

CREEN TORTOISE-BEETLE.

species, who there find abundance of food and shelter: many have presented themselves to our notice during our rambles, but want of space has prevented our figuring or describing more than a very small proportion of them.  Here, on a burdock leaf, its usual habitation, we found that curious and pretty little insect, the Green Tortoise-beetle (*Cassida equestris*).  In appearance it really very much resembles a miniature tortoise, the upper part of the body being expanded into a shield which conceals the feet and head.  But it is in the grub state that its habits are most singular, the tail being provided with a forked appendage, upon which the creature heaps a mass of extraneous matter, so that it carries about with it an artificial canopy that answers the purpose of defence and concealment.

These pauses in voyaging the Thames are always full of interest; instructive also, no matter what may be the object for which we " step ashore."

As we approach Kingston, we pass the new buildings of the company which supplies the Surrey side of London with water.  The edifices themselves are by no means picturesque; nevertheless, as objects that cannot fail to attract the eye of all voyagers, we have thought it well to engrave them. The locality in which they are placed is called "SEETHING WELLS;" and they are "The Chelsea and Lambeth Water-works."*

For the following detailed analysis of the Thames water, at Kingston,

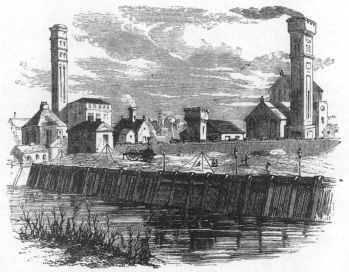

WATER-WORKS: SEETHING WELLS.

we are indebted to the kindness of Mr. Henry Witt, F.C.S., Assistant Chemist to the Government School of Mines :—

|  | Grains in the Imperial Gallon. |
|---|---|
| Sulphate of Lime | 4·506 |
| Carbonate of Lime | 9·616 |
| Carbonate of Magnesia | 0·970 |
| Chloride of Sodium (common salt) | 1·661 |
| Chloride of Potassium | trace |
| Carbonate of Soda | 1·950 |
| Organic matter | 1·631 |
| Suspended Clay | 3·603 |
| Carbonate of Ammonia | 0.0034 |
| Total | 23·9404 |

---

* "The hot spring at Seething Wells was once thought an almost infallible remedy in certain cases of ophthalmia."

But the composition of the water varies at different seasons of the year. The following represents the average composition at Kingston, as deduced from a large number of analyses, made by Mr. Witt, throughout the year 1856 :—

| | Grains in the Gallon. | | |
|---|---|---|---|
| | Maximum. | Minimum. | Mean. |
| Total impurity | 28·148 | 18·37 | 23·488 |
| Suspended matter | 4·41 | 1·17 | 3·054 |
| Organic matter | 1·63 | 0·55 | 1·050 |
| Dissolved Salt | 22·108 | 16·65 | 19·404 |
| Common Salt | 3·87 | 2·065 | 2·633 |
| Lime | 10·91 | 6·487 | 7·884 |

These analyses show how excellent in quality is the water now supplied to London from Kingston, or rather Thames Ditton, by the Chelsea and Lambeth Water Companies.

The shallow wells of London cannot but be condemned as drinking waters, on account of their almost invariable contamination with sewage ; the deep wells which sink into the chalk are inconveniently hard ; but the Thames water at Kingston is sufficiently free from organic matter to be perfectly wholesome as a beverage, and sufficiently soft not to give rise to serious inconvenience on that account.

The water is pumped into large subsiding reservoirs ; whence, after remaining about six hours, it passes on to the filters. These are large beds of sand, gravel, &c., through which the water passes at the rate of about 6¼ gallons per square foot per hour.

The filters are composed of the following strata in a descending order :—

| No. | | Feet. | Inches. |
|---|---|---|---|
| 1. Fine sand | | 2 | 6 |
| 2. Coarser ditto | | 1 | 0 |
| 3. Shells | | 0 | 6 |
| 4. Fine gravel | | 0 | 3 |
| 5. Coarse gravel | | 3 | 3 |

After complete filtration, the purified water is pumped up to a covered reservoir on Putney Heath, whence it descends by gravitation to London, passing over the river in two iron tubes, supported by a new bridge, recently erected for the purpose between Putney and Fulham.

The two new subsiding reservoirs comprise an area of three acres, and are each capable of containing ten million gallons of water. The two filter-beds adjoining comprise an area of two acres, and are each capable of filtering ten million gallons in twenty-four hours. The two high level covered reservoirs on Putney Heath are two and a half acres in extent, and hold twenty feet deep of water. They command a service of 170 feet above Trinity high-water. The aggregate nominal engine power employed in pumping is 700 horses. The average quantity of water pumped daily is about 6,900,000 gallons.

Kingston is among the oldest of English towns; and is said to have been "the metropolis of the Anglo-Saxon kings." It is difficult to say what is meant by "metropolis of the Anglo-Saxon kings." The metropolis of the kings of Wessex, to whom Kingston belonged, is always understood to have been Winchester. But the kings would not necessarily be crowned there, as that ceremony might take place anywhere within the boundaries of their kingdom. Kingston seems, however, to have been a famous place when the Romans found and conquered the Britons in this locality. Some writers have advanced arguments for believing that the "ford" which Cæsar crossed was here, and not at Walton; and indications of barrows, fosses, and ramparts of Roman origin, are to be found in many places in the neighbourhood. It is more than probable that a bridge was here constructed by the Romans. The Saxons followed in due course, and here they had many contests with their enemies the Danes; but A.D. 838, Egbert convened at Kingston an assembly of ecclesiastics and nobles in council,* and here, undoubtedly, some of the Saxon kings were crowned: "The townisch men," says Leland, "have certen knowledge that a few kinges were crounid there afore the Conqueste." Its first charter was from King John, and many succeeding sovereigns accorded to it various grants and immunities. During the war between Charles I. and the Parliament, Kingston was the scene of several "fights," being always on the side of the king. The town is now populous and flourishing, although without manufactures of any kind. Since the establishment of

---

* "This record, in which the town is called 'Kyningestun, famosa illa locus,' destroys the supposition that it did not receive that appellation till the reign of King Athelstan, and proves that it was a royal residence, or at least a royal demesne, as early as the union of the Saxon heptarchy."—*Lysons.*

a railway, villa residences have largely increased in the neighbourhood ;
and the two suburbs, Surbiton and Norbiton, are pretty and densely-
crowded villages of good houses.   The church has suffered much from
mutilation and restoration ; it is a spacious structure, and was erected
about the middle of the fourteenth century, on the site of an earlier
edifice.   Amongst the monuments is a fine brass, to a civilian and his
wife, of the year 1437.*   Of existing antiquities there are but few :
county historians, however, point out the sites of the ancient Saxon

THE KING'S STONE.

palace, "the castle," the Jews' quarter, and the Roman town, Tamesa ;
and the game of "foot-ball," it is said, is still practised by the inhabitants

---

* It is to the memory of Robert Skerne, of Kingston, and Joan, his wife ; she was the daughter of
the celebrated Alice Pierce or Perrers, mistress to Edward III., and afterwards wife to Sir William
de Wyndesore.   This brass abounds with beautiful details of costume, and records the day and year of
Robert's death :—

"May he in heaven rejoice who lived on earth sincere,
    Who died upon the fourth of April, in the year
    Of Christ, one thousand twenty score and thirty-seven."

on Shrove Tuesday, in commemoration of one of the feats of their ancestors, by whom the head of a king-assassin was "kicked" about the Saxon town. But perhaps the most interesting object now to be found in Kingston is "THE KING'S STONE." It had long remained neglected, though not unknown, among disregarded heaps of debris in "the new courtyard," when it occurred to some zealous and intelligent antiquaries that so venerable a relic of remote ages was entitled to some show of respect. It was consequently removed from its degraded position, planted in the centre of the town, and enclosed by a "suitable" iron railing. It is now, therefore, duly and properly honoured, as may be seen by the engraving.*

KINGSTON BRIDGE.

KINGSTON BRIDGE, to which we now conduct the tourist, is a convenient and graceful structure, erected from the design of M. Lapidge,

* The stone formerly used to stand near the church-door, and was from time immemorial regarded as that upon which the Saxon Kings of Wessex were inaugurated according to the old Teutonic custom —a custom long prevalent in Germany and the northern nations, and still adopted in the coronation of the sovereigns of England; the old sacred stone of Scone, on which the Scottish kings were crowned, was brought from thence by Edward I., in 1296, and placed beneath the English chair where it still remains. Kingston is expressly mentioned, in a charter of King Edred, A.D. 946, as the royal town where consecration is accustomed to be performed. Speed records the coronation of nine sove-

and opened, in 1828, by the Earl of Liverpool, then High Steward of the borough. It took the place of an ancient wooden bridge, the successor, it is said, of one which the Saxons built to replace that which the Romans had constructed.

And so we leave Kingston, looking back upon the pleasant and prosperous town, pursuing our course downward between low banks, with here and there a mansion of note, but meeting nothing for comment until we approach Teddington; its "lock" being the last—or, more properly, the *first*—lock on the Thames.

Before we visit Teddington, however, we ask the reader's permission to introduce one of those sketches with which we seek to vary our descriptive details.

When Gilbert Golding, who was considered at that time as "smart a lad" as ever dipped oar in the waters of the Thames, married Fanny Meadows, every one said he had caught a Tartar; that is, every one who did not incline to the other belief—that a Tartar had caught him! At all events, they were married in the church of Teddington: Gilbert a tall, lithe, graceful youth of twenty-one; Fanny a short, strong, thick-armed woman of thirty. Gilbert, fresh and fair, looked younger than he was: Fanny, dark and sallow, seemed older. Gilbert had a soft, low voice, that went whispering amongst the reeds and water-plants like the

---

reigns here : the first was Athelstan, by Aldhelm, Archbishop of Canterbury, A.D. 924, followed by his brothers Edmund and Edred ; then came Edgar, Edward the Martyr, his brother Ethelred II., and Edmund II., in A.D. 1016. Two intervening kings, Edward the Elder, and Edwy, are stated by the same author to have been also crowned here, but this is more conjectural than strictly historic. Some writers have deduced the name of the town from the stone, thus—King's-stone ; but the proper deriva-

tion is clearly obtained from its *name*, which means simply " a *manor* belonging to the king." The kings had manors scattered all over the country, many of which still bear the name of Kingston, which does not necessarily imply a town. In fact, *manor* is perhaps the best translation of the word *tun.*

Athelstan, the first of the Saxon kings crowned at Kingston, was the first of the race who placed on their coins the title of King of all England. The various kingdoms of the heptarchy had by this time been consolidated, but he never actually possessed the whole kingdom. We engrave two specimens of his silver pennies, on one of which he is styled " Athelstan Rex Saxorum," and on the other, " Athelstan Rex totius Britanniæ." Both inscriptions are in an abbreviated form.

breath of a south wind: Fanny's voice was keen and sharp as a north-wester. Gilbert was a "beau" in his way; his braces, embroidered after a criss-cross, quaint fashion, in scarlet worsted, were bright on his striped shirt: he was very particular, poor fellow, as to the width of the stripes. The broad black riband round his throat was tied in a jaunty bow; and on Sundays he had always a sprig of myrtle, a rose, a car-nation, or some pretty cottage flower, in the button-hole of his smart blue jacket.

Fanny was anything but a "belle:" her plain straw cottage bonnet was tied firmly on her head, tight down at the sides, by a broad, thick, blue riband, that had been dyed at least three times, and would "come out in black" as good as new in winter. During the week she dressed in cotton, of some dark obscure pattern, chiefly of a chocolate hue; and her broad, strong feet, and stout ankles, were cased in blue stockings and hob-nailed shoes. On Sundays she went faithfully and reverently to church in a miraculously thick silk, which, according to the tradition of Thames Ditton, had been given to her mother, who was lady's-maid to a grand old Lady Thornbury—who never would have hooks put in her wardrobe, because her dresses could stand by themselves.

Fanny's Sunday bonnet differed little from that worn during the week; but it was tied down with a broad white riband, and there was a peculiar bow at the side—the position of the bow had not varied the eighth of an inch for ten years.

Gilbert was considered the handsomest lad in Teddington: the best that could be said of Fanny was, that she was always clean and respectable. Why were they married? Gilbert had neither family nor friends; but he had one ambition—he wanted to scull his own wherry. Fanny told him she had saved as much money as would purchase two. They were married.

Fanny never wanted to be thought of, or what is called "petted," by her handsome husband; but, she took care of him and of his earnings, and, in process of time, of his three boys. All her sharpness would not have made Gilbert careful, so she managed to be care-taker to the whole family, and her petty acts of wilfulness seldom roused his easy nature

U U

even to remonstrate : if he was suddenly called upon to act, by some contradiction, or little feminine rebellion, he soon gave in, lounging off to his boat, and returning with a bright smile, all for the sake of "peace and quietness." She was as particular as he could be as to the breadth of his stripes and the trimness of his dress, and cultivated the flowers he loved best. She ministered with the unconsciousness of strong love to all his little weaknesses, and so had her way in important matters. Many of the pretty girls of Teddington—aye, and in the sleepy, but well-to-do town of Kingston—did not hesitate to say that the handsome boatman was thrown away on an ugly old wife : older than he she was to a certainty; but Gilbert Golding was evidently happy and prosperous under the trial : and her desire to please her husband, whom she loved with the strength and determination of her perhaps coarse, but fervent nature, was so great, that at his request she altered the bow of her bonnet, and permitted him to choose her a new dress!

How the girls of Teddington did stare and flout! but Fanny went steadily to church with her little lads, stiff and sturdy as ever, apparently unconscious of her finery : still, it must be confessed, it was impossible not to wish that Fanny had been Gilbert, and Gilbert Fanny. Both Gilbert and his wife were in much favour at "The Anglers," and the landlord never failed to recommend the handsome waterman and his boat to what he called "nice customers." Fanny considered his boat her fourth child : she cherished, and dried, and re-covered the cushions, and had a summer and a winter set. There was no boat could vie with Gilbert's : she bought striped awnings, and contrived quite a picturesque and pretty canopy, that kept off rain or sunshine. She always "helped" her husband to paint the "Forget-me-not," as the boat was modestly called; and Fanny's help in this, as well as in other matters, consisted in "doing it all herself." Her voice was sometimes raised beyond its usual pitch ; but, on the whole, as Fanny's duties multiplied, so did her temper and manners soften.

One light evening in June, Gilbert wafted to "The Anglers" the gentleman he had been rowing about all day, moored his boat, eat his supper, kissed his boys and his wife, told her he would wash the boat himself, and prepare her for the next day. He only stopped in his little garden to gather a carnation, and proceeded to the boat, which he unmoored, and sculled into the shadow of one of the distant aits.

The evening closed in, the moon rose; it was a soft, balmy evening, a delicious evening,—not a ripple on the water. Gilbert did not return to supper. No one at "The Anglers" had seen him since he disappeared behind the ait; most likely he had been called by some one who wanted a moonlight row—nothing more likely. Fanny prided herself, amongst other strong-minded notions, on never being anxious or uneasy about anything—" It would all come right; and if it did not, what odds?"

However, when "the neighbours" were asleep, and the moon was gone down, and the church clock " gone one," Fanny might have been seen peering through the half-darkness, rustling among the boats, and after unmooring one, rowing from ait to ait—down one channel, up another, frighting the water-fowl, and calling, in a suppressed voice— even there ashamed of her anxiety—" Gilbert!—husband!—Gilbert!"

No one heard her shriek of terror when, right across a creek, she discovered the " Forget-me-not" alone, unmoved by breeze or ripple! In a moment she sprang on board. Where were the oars?—one lying across the seats, another floated within reach of her hand.

" Gilbert!—husband!—Gilbert!" She was unanswered, unechoed, in the stillness of the lonely night.

She hastened to the village, and shouted loudly and strongly from house to house, that they were to get up and seek and find, for that Gilbert's boat was drifting beside the bank—but where was Gilbert Golding? They must wake up and find her husband. And so they all did—that is, they arose and sought; and during the remnant of that night, and all the following day, they dragged the Thames, and hunted, and took counsel together, and dragged the waters in every creek and willowy bay for him they did not find.

Fanny looked for neither sympathy nor kindness—she rather repelled both; yet seemed endowed with almost supernatural strength, and worked as seldom woman was known to work before. She kept the boat in repair, and twice each year repainted with her own hand her husband's name upon it. She would not sell it, but let it out, and always saw to its mooring and cleaning. As her boys grew up, she steadily refused to let them take to the water: she said "their father would not like it." All her words and deeds proved that she did not, or would not, consider him dead; and during moonlight nights, no one was surprised to hear Fanny unmoor a boat and paddle it beside the banks, and among the reeds and willows—now in, now out of the moonshine—always returning to her widowed bed before dawn of day.

There were no three finer lads in Surrey than the three Goldings—good, steady boys, constant and attentive at school, and afterwards constant and attentive to their work. We came upon those three lads quite unexpectedly one sultry summer afternoon: we were sauntering through

SHEEP WASHING.

a friend's grounds (you may see the top of the house above the trees) along a pathway which led to an unprotected foot-bridge that crossed a small arm of the Thames, half pool, half rivulet, sometimes more than half empty—at times like a water-garden, at others a little mimic sea.

We knew by the rapid tinkling of the sheep-bells, and the bleating from a pen which skirted the pathway, that something particular was going forward among the sheep.  Upon the bank stood Edward Golding, in vigorous yet kind contention with a strong-minded young ram, that objected to being washed ; while William, the second lad, waist high in the water, stretched out his arms to receive the obstinate animal, and the youngest was occupied with a little lamb, which soon ran bleating and dripping to its mother.  The lads enjoyed the work, and the worthy farmer assured us he would rather have the Golding lads to help at his sheep-washing than any three men in the parish, for " Ye see," he said, "they are both strong and tender."  Fanny must have been proud of her boys, but she did not say so.  She toiled on, thought and worked, silent and reserved even to her own children ; and though considerably "aged," still passed more than one sleepless night during each full moon rowing amongst the sedges between the aits—up one channel, down another.  Poor Fanny !

The very night of the sheep-washing the lads took their homeward way, singing one of the Christmas carols in joyful tune.  As they drew near home their voices fell, for though their humble cottage home abounded in comforts, and they knew their tea would be ready, the cake baked, and their shoes and stockings warm on the hearth, still there was always something about their mother that forbade merriment : they could tell her all their little troubles, and she would give them good advice, and something like sympathy in her own hard fashion ; but she had neither ears nor smiles for their joys.  They saw the door was open— their mother met them on the threshold—a strange awe crept over them, and they stood round the little table without speaking, looking from one to the other.  The cake was cut, and two persons had evidently been sitting there.  Fanny pointed this out to them, but did not speak.

" What is —— ? "  The inquiry was arrested by their mother's impatient, almost imperious gesture.  Silently she glided towards her little bed-room.  The check curtains of the bed were drawn : she seized the arm of her eldest son, and croaked, rather than whispered—

" I knew he would come back, alive or dead—I knew he would come back : he is now between the living and the dead. Remember, he is not to be questioned why he went, or where he has been : he is my husband—your father, boys. He is come home—home—six years gone— eight years gone—but he is home ! Hush ! Let us pray, and thank God ! "

Silently they knelt down—silently they prayed—silently the incense of thanksgiving rose and passed to Heaven. Nor did they see their father until morning ; and then, instead of Fanny, a grey-headed, weather-beaten man unmoored the " Forget-me-not."

When his wife was not present, his neighbours did not hesitate to question him as to the cause of his disappearance, and where he had been.

" He wanted to see the world," he said, " and had done so ; and was not a little glad to get home again."

And that was all !

It is a popular fallacy to derive the name of Teddington from Tide-end town, from an idea that the first lock on the river being here, here the " tide " may be supposed to " end." In old records it is called Todington and Totyngton.* The manor is supposed to have been given to Westminster Abbey by Sebert, the first Christian king of the East Saxons. The church is of common-place character. We have engraved it, nevertheless, for it contains several remarkable and interesting memorials,—among others a monument to " Peg Woffington," †— and also because it is so familiar a friend to " brethren of the angle," who have long regarded the Deep under the weir at Teddington as among the pleasantest of all their river memories. These memories are in truth very pleasant, for although it has " fallen from its high estate,"

---

* " There can be no other objection to this etymology than that the place is called Totyngton in all records for several centuries after the name first occurs."—*Lysons.*

† The tomb of " Mrs. Margaret Woffington, Spinster," as she is termed upon it, is a plain oval medallion. She died, aged 39, in the year 1760, and had achieved great popularity as an actress, particularly for the impersonation of male characters of the foppish type ; her most celebrated part being that of Sir Harry Wildair, in Farquhar's play of " The Constant Couple." She was seized with the indisposition which proved fatal to her when speaking an epilogue at Covent Garden Theatre.

and is by no means as productive of sport as it used to be, there is still plenty to be had in several "pitches," where abound all the various denizens of the populous river; while enjoyment is ever enhanced by associations with the past, which are suggested at every spot of ground beside which the punt is pushed or moored.

The fishermen here are "the KEMPS:" they have followed that vocation from father to son for more than a century and a half; and although

TEDDINGTON CHURCH.

some of them have been occasionally in bad repute as preferring the occupation of the poacher to that of the angler, others of the family have made and established good names, which they continue to preserve "to this day." The best of them is James Kemp, whose cottage stands in a small row by the water side, while the senior of the race keeps the neat and clean "Angler's Inn," through which there is a passage to the boats. James is the oldest of our river allies; we fished with him when his strength was insufficient to moor a punt, and for more than twenty years he was our companion on that "glorious first of June," to which the angler looks forward with intense anxiety, for on that day the Thames is open to labourers with the rod and line.*

The Lamprey (*Petromyzon marinus*) and the Lampern (*Petromyzon fluviatilis*) are both obtained at Teddington : the former occasionally, the latter periodically during winter in large quantities. "These fishes are, in reference to their skeleton, and in some other respects, the lowest on the scale of organization among vertebrated animals ;" they are cartilaginous, and live by suction, their mouth being so formed as to

LAMPREY AND LAMPERN.

induce a very powerful contact with the object to which they are attached, whether to stones, to prevent their being swept away by currents, or to the prey to which they adhere, "their small, numerous,

---

* Teddington Lock is now a new lock, the venerable and picturesque having given way before the march of "improvement." It is, as we have stated, the first lock on the Thames. It may interest the reader here to enumerate the several locks between Oxford and Teddington :

| | | | | |
|---|---|---|---|---|
| Iffley. | Wallingford. | Shiplake. | Boulter's. | Chertsey. |
| Sandford. | Cleeve. | Marsh. | Bray. | Shepperton. |
| Abingdon. | Goring. | Hambledon. | Boveney. | Sunbury. |
| Culham. | Whitchurch. | Hurley. | Windsor. | Moulsey. |
| Clifton. | Maple Durham. | Temple. | Old Windsor. | Teddington. |
| Days. | Caversham. | Marlow. | Bell Weir. | |
| Benson. | Sonning. | Cookham. | Penton Hook. | |

For this list, as well as for some other valuable information, we are indebted to "The Oarsman's Guide," a little book, so small as to fit the waistcoat-pocket, but which no voyager of the Thames should be without.

rasp-like teeth eating away the soft parts down to the bone." The lampern is rarely eaten, but the fishery at Teddington furnishes a large supply to Holland, where they are used as bait for cod and turbot. "Formerly the Thames alone supplied from one million to twelve hundred thousand annually to the Dutch;" but of late years the fish have become comparatively scarce. They are caught in eel-baskets, and are remarkably tenacious of life. When attached to any object, the water obtains access and egress by seven small apertures on each side of the neck; hence its popular name of "seven eyes." They are of a dusky colour, not unlike the eel, which they resemble in other particulars.*

Those who visit Teddington will do well to walk up the village and examine some ancient houses, with some of which enduring memories are associated; especially they will ascend a small hillock to visit STRAWBERRY HILL. Of late years it has undergone many alterations; we have preferred to picture it in its zenith, when in the full enjoyment of its fame—such as that fame was.

Strawberry Hill, the favourite residence of Horace Walpole, was built by him in 1747; but he was long afterwards employed in enlarging and improving it, as his collections of *vertu* increased. It was originally a small cottage built by a nobleman's coachman for a lodging-house, and tenanted by a toy-woman, named Chevenix: so Walpole, in one of his letters, declares his house to be "a little plaything house I got out of Mrs. Chevenix's shop." The style of architecture he adopted was the florid Gothic, and to him the merit is certainly due of directing attention again to its merits. However questionable we might now consider the taste that constructed a fire-place after the fashion of the tomb of Aylmer de Valence, in Westminster Abbey, it must be remembered that the true principles of mediæval architecture had to be resuscitated; and that this study of original authorities was a step in the right direction,

---

* The generic character is thus given by Yarrell:—"Body smooth, elongated, cylindrical, like that of an eel; the head rounded; the mouth circular, armed with hard, tooth-like processes, the lip forming a continuous circle round the mouth; seven apertures on each side of the neck, leading to seven bronchial cells; no pectoral or ventral fins; the skin towards the tail extending in a fold from the body both above and below."

X X

and infinitely better than the pseudo-Gothic of greater architects than
Walpole. He succeeded in imparting a very picturesque character to
his mansion, and it soon became a " show-house," so that its owner was
besieged with visitors, and looked upon a wet day as his only chance of
peaceably possessing it. In it he wrote his famous " Castle of Otranto,"
and his more famous Letters; and in the grounds he established a
printing-press, amusing himself by producing therefrom luxurious
editions of his own works and those of his friends. The mansion was

STRAWBERRY HILL.

very slightly built, being little more than lath and plaster; Walpole
himself declared " he had outlived three sets of battlements:" and on
the occasion of the great sale here, a temporary building was erected
in the garden, as the long gallery in which it was originally intended to
be held, was believed to be too fragile to be filled with people. The
extensive character of the collection he left may be gathered from the
fact of twenty-four days being devoted to selling it. The lots averaged

one hundred and fifty per day, consisting of books, prints, coins, and medals; paintings, and drawings of all ages and styles; and a vast collection which may be classed under the general name of "curiosities," embracing arms and armour, Roman pottery, Raffaelle-ware, porcelain of Dresden and Sèvres, furniture of an ancient and curious kind, antique rings, snuff-boxes, and historic relics of much general interest—comprising, in fact, the combined results of a taste that seldom is found in one individual—partaking of the educated scholar, the curious book-worm, the lover of Art, the antiquary, and the collector of "nic-nacs;" for the house contained a variety that might suit the taste of all such persons. Walpole, at his death, bequeathed it to the Hon. Mrs. Damer, the lady sculptor, whose works on Henley Bridge we have already engraved. To her he left also the sum of £2000 for keeping it in repair; the reversion of the house to pass on her death to the Countess Dowager of Waldegrave: but Mrs. Damer gave it up to the latter lady before her own death. Walpole had managed, by entails and jointures, to secure his collections from being scattered through several generations; but, all legal obstacles being removed, the renowned George Robins "distributed" them in April and May, 1842. The greatest interest was excited, as the collection comprised very rare things, which had been comparatively unknown for the previous half century, and large prices were realized for the various lots. The present Countess of Waldegrave is, however, anxiously replacing in the old house such articles as she can recover; and though it will be hopeless to expect to restore a tithe of its original contents, every item regained will add to the general interest of the whole.

POPE'S VILLA is the next remarkable residence after Strawberry Hill is passed, from which it is distant but a very short walk. Pope died before Horace Walpole had completed his purchase; but the house then remained in the condition in which the former had left it. Our cut is copied from an engraving exhibiting it as in Pope's era. He purchased this house in 1715, and removed to it with his parents from Binfield. The high road from Twickenham to Teddington passed in front of the house, and the small piece of ground at the back, toward the Thames, was all the garden Pope could command without crossing the road, where the large garden was situated; he accordingly formed a tunnel beneath the road, and, decorating it with spars, it became "the grotto," so celebrated by his friends, and so ably described by himself, and immortalized by the verse he wrote for it. He had little care for money, and as he made more than he wanted for necessity, he spent it in continually improving his house and garden. Speaking of this once to Spence, he said, "I never save anything, unless I meet with such a

POPE'S VILLA.

pressing case as is an absolute demand upon me; then I retrench fifty pounds or so from my own expenses. As, for instance, had such a thing happened this year, then I would not have built my two summer-houses." His half-sister, Mrs. Racket, once said to the same person, "It is most certain that nobody ever loved money so little as my brother." He died at Twickenham in 1744, and was buried in the church, with his father and mother. After his death the house was sold to Sir William Stanhope, who added new wings to it, enlarged the gardens, and formed a second subterranean passage. His daughter marrying the Right Hon. Welbore Ellis (afterwards Lord Mendip), the estate passed into his hands, and he guarded with jealous care every relic of Pope. At his death Sir John Brisco succeeded to the ownership; and when he died it was unfortunately purchased by the Baroness Howe, in 1807, who at once ordered it to be destroyed, and erected a new mansion at the distance of a hundred yards from the site.

Pope's taste in improving his house and gardens certainly induced a dissemination of taste in general by other imitations, and he led the way to modern ornamental gardening. His favourite work was his grotto, which he constantly amused himself by adorning, and was equally fond of descanting upon in very glowing terms to all his friends. Warburton says that " the improvement of this grotto was the amusement of Pope's declining years." He has left an interesting description of it in a letter to his friend Blount, written in 1725. He says—" It contains a spring of clearest water, which falls in a perpetual rill, that echoes through the cavern night and day. From the river Thames you see through my arch up a walk in the wilderness to a kind of open temple, wholly composed of shells in the rustic manner ; and from that distance, under the temple, you look down through a sloping arcade of trees, and see the sails on the river passing suddenly and vanishing as through a perspective glass. When you shut the door of this grotto, it becomes on the instant, from a luminous room, a camera-obscura, on the wall of which all the objects on the river, hills, woods, and boats, are forming a moving picture in their visible radiations. And when you have a mind to light it up, it affords you a very different scene. It is finished with shells, interspersed with pieces of looking-glass in angular forms; and in the ceiling is a star of the same materials, at which when a lamp of orbicular figure, of thin alabaster, is hung in the middle, a thousand pointed rays glitter and are reflected over the place. There are connected to this grotto, by a narrower passage, two porches,—one towards the river, of smooth stones, full of light, and open; the other towards the garden, shadowed with trees, and rough with shells, flints, and iron ores. The bottom is paved with simple pebble, as is also the adjoining walk up the wilderness to the temple, in the natural taste, agreeing not ill with the little dripping murmur and the aquatic idea of the whole place." The porch and entrance to the grotto is seen in our engraving. Pope never tired over improving it, and composed the following inscription to be placed in it:—

> " Thou who shalt step where Thames' translucent wave
> Shines a broad mirror through the shadowy cave,—
> Where lingering drops from mineral roofs distil,
> And pointed crystals break the sparkling rill—
> Unpolished gems no ray in pride bestow,
> And latent metals innocently glow,—
> Approach: Great Nature studiously behold,
> And eye the mine, without a wish for gold!
> Approach: but awful! Lo! th' Ægerian grot,
> Where, nobly pensive, St. John sat and thought;
> Where British sighs from dying Wyndham stole,
> And the bright flame was shot thro' Marchmont's soul!
> Let such, such only, tread this sacred floor,
> Who dare to love their country, and be poor."

Villas, many of them very fanciful in construction, now line the Middlesex bank of the river—few, however, being on the Surrey side—until we reach the populous village of Twickenham.

In the days of Pope and Walpole, Twickenham seemed likely to realize the prediction of the latter, "that it would become as celebrated as Baiæ or Tivoli." It was the fashion to construct residences on the Thames banks, and to make the village a retiring place for the celebrities of London. Hudson, the painter, and the early instructor of Sir Joshua Reynolds, erected a dwelling near Pope's Villa, and in close contiguity to one built by Scott, "the English Canaletti," as he was termed, and the friend of Hogarth. Sir Godfrey Kneller—"Kneller, by heaven, and not a master, taught"—also retired to Twickenham to spend the latter years of his life.* On a stone inserted in the church wall, noting a grant of space, to increase the limits of the churchyard, by the Duke of Somerset, in 1713, Sir Godfrey is named as one of the churchwardens. †

---

* He resided at Whitton, a hamlet of the parish. He built a substantial brick mansion there: the hall and staircase were painted by Laguerre, under his superintendence, but it is said to exhibit some of Sir Godfrey's own handiwork.

† He also officiated as a justice of peace for the county, and several amusing anecdotes are given of his adjudications in what he considered equity; in some instances quite opposed to the letter of the

The parish church is situated upon the edge of the river, but it is almost hidden from view by a large island, sacred to picnic parties, and known as Eel-pie Island, from the popular refreshment provided there. It is of considerable length, and has a house for the entertainment of water-parties, the whole of this " ait " being devoted to their service and

TWICKENHAM CHURCH.

use. A narrow arm of the Thames divides it from the village of Twickenham, and nearly opposite the middle of the island stands the church, in front of which is the old vicarage with its gardens. The church tower is an old stone fabric, apparently of the time of Henry VII. The body of the church was rebuilt in 1715: it had fallen to the ground on the night of the 9th of April, 1713, owing to neglect. It is

law. Thus, on one occasion, a soldier was brought before him for stealing a joint of meat, but having pleaded that it was the butcher's fault for putting such a temptation in his way, Sir Godfrey took his view of the case, and discharged the man, giving the astonished butcher a severe reprimand! Pope has alluded to the decision in his lines—

" I think Sir Godfrey should decide the suit,
Who sent the thief (that stole the cash) away,
And punished him that put it in his way."

chiefly remarkable as the mausoleum of Pope and his family. They are buried in a vault in front of the communion rails. Pope erected to the memory of his parents a tablet in the east wall of the north gallery;

POPE'S MONUMENT.

and upon the north wall a monument was erected to the poet himself, by Bishop Warburton.*   It is of pyramidal form, of dark grey marble,

---

* It is the one nearest the spectator in our engraving. The monument, at the extremity, to which the female figure points, is that which the poet placed to the memory of his parents. Beneath Pope's monument are the lines—

"POETA LOQUITUR,

"FOR ONE WHO WOULD NOT BE BURIED IN WESTMINSTER ABBEY.

"Heroes and kings, your distance keep,
    In peace let one poor poet sleep;
Who never flattered folks like you:
    Let Horace blush, and Virgil too."

Pope expressly directed, in his will, that he should be buried " near his dear parents," and that he should be " carried to the grave by six of the poorest men of the parish, to each of whom I order a suit of grey coarse cloth as mourning."

with a medallion of the poet, as if suspended upon it, above which is a
laurel wreath. On the outer wall of the church, on the same side, is
the tablet Pope placed to the memory of Mary Beach, "in gratitude to
a faithful old servant," who had been his nurse and constantly attended
him for thirty-eight years. Near it is another tablet to the memory
of Mrs. Clive—the "Kitty Clive" of Garrick's era ; it bears a long
rhyming inscription, commencing—

> " Clive's blameless life this tablet shall proclaim,
> Her moral virtues and her well-earned fame."

After making a competency by her exertions as a comic actress, she
retired to Twickenham, and resided at a house on the site of Marble
Hill Cottage. Mrs. Pritchard, the great tragic actress, on whom

TWICKENHAM AIT.

Garrick principally depended in his great plays, also lived at Raymons
Castle, close by.

On the right bank of the river, the long line of Petersham Meadows
terminates at the grounds of Ham House, which is almost hidden in a
mass of noble trees which surround the house and grounds with their
umbrageous foliage. This noble old mansion was built in 1610 (as appears
by a date over the principal entrance) by Sir Thomas Vavasor, who was
appointed, with Sir Francis Bacon, one of the judges of the Marshal's
Court in the year ensuing. It was sold to the Earl of Dysart in the
reign of James I., "whose widow, Katherine, on the 22nd of May,
1561, surrendered it to the use of Sir Lionel Tollemache, and Elizabeth
his wife, her daughter, who, in the year following, surrendered it to the

use of Sir Lionel's will." * This daughter, by her second marriage, became Duchess of Lauderdale, and was remarkable for the political power she possessed, being one of the busiest women of a busy age. Burnet describes her as "a woman of great beauty, but of far greater parts. She had a wonderful quickness of apprehension, and an amazing vivacity in conversation. She had studied not only divinity and history, but mathematics, and philosophy. She was violent in everything she set

HAM HOUSE.

about; a violent friend, but a much more violent enemy." After the Restoration she became the chief politician; "she took upon her to determine everything; she sold all places; and was wanting in no methods that could bring her money, which she lavished out in a most profuse vanity." The small dull chamber in which she is traditionally reported to have received the king and courtiers, is still preserved intact; and her favourite chair still remains there, with her reading-desk and walking-cane beside it. The interior of the mansion is an excellent

---

* Manning and Bray's " History of Surrey."

specimen of the noble houses of that era; the ceilings are painted by Verrio, and the ornaments and furniture display the massive magnificence of decoration then in fashion; the bellows and brushes in some of the apartments are encased in silver ornament, and the several drawing-rooms contain valuable and interesting relics in profusion; few mansions in England are more crowded with pictures and objects of *vertu* than this. The long gallery is hung with portraits of the principal statesmen of the courts of the Stuarts.*

On the left bank a pleasant field-path leads to Richmond, over fertile meadows, studded with noble mansions. The first of importance after passing the ait is Orleans House, a noble mansion of red brick with white quoins. Here resided the Princess of Denmark, afterwards Queen Anne. The young prince, her son, used to amuse himself by exercising a troop of boy soldiers on the ait we have spoken of. Caroline,

ORLEANS HOUSE.

Queen of George II., was once entertained here by the then proprietor of the mansion, who on that occasion built the octagon room, which forms

---

* In a small room adjacent, the famous opposition ministry to Clarendon, known as the "Cabal" (from the initials of the names of the five noblemen who formed it), was wont to meet. It is still called "The Cabal Chamber." A full description of this interesting house, with many illustrations, may be found in "The Baronial Halls" (vol. ii.), edited by S. C. Hall, F.S.A.

so conspicuous a feature in the view. It bears the name of Orleans House, from having been rented by the Duke of Orleans at the commencement of the present century; and here Louis Philippe, afterwards King of the French, passed some of the happiest years of a life of unusual adventure. In the course of the changed fortunes that awaited the family of that sovereign after his abdication of the throne of France, the house has again become the home of one of his sons. Next is Marble Hill; it was designed, and the building superintended, by Henry, Earl of Pembroke, the estate having been purchased, and the house erected, by King George II., for the Countess of Suffolk.

A very pleasant walk from Ham leads to the pretty and retired village of Petersham, on the high road between Richmond and Kingston. It was famous in times long gone by, but is now chiefly remarkable for the well-known establishment of Dr. Ellis—Sudbrook Park—renowned for its "water-cure," by which many have obtained happiness with health. We believe there is no place of the kind throughout the kingdom better conducted; the principle, adopted with so much success, is no doubt greatly aided by the pure air, the tranquillity of umbrageous walks, the close vicinity to Richmond Park, and that relief from thought and labour which best ministers to disease, either of body or mind.

Petersham is very closely associated with our earliest and pleasantest memories of the Thames: many years have passed since we occupied a small cottage in that quiet village; and with it not a few of our happiest associations are connected. We ask leave of our readers, therefore, to introduce to them one of these "memories;" desiring to make them acquainted with a character who cannot yet have been entirely forgotten in that quiet and comparatively unaltered neighbourhood.

Peter Petersham—we knew him a long time ago in the pretty village of Petersham; his name was Peter, and so we always called him Peter Petersham, or Petersham Peter—it did not matter which. He was then a stalwart green-eyed man—indeed we fancied he had a green-toned skin—and his hair looked more like a tangle of green water-plants than human hair—it was so damp and clinging. We seldom strolled without meeting him in the lane that led from the corner of our cottage garden to the noble avenues and quaint imaginings of Ham House, where old Lady Dysart then resided, and used to drive out of those stately gates (which seemed intended to send forth only stately carriages with six portly horses—the carriages containing only big wigs and high heads) in a tiny carriage drawn by a pony, who seemed to think his life depended on his swiftness. A wonderful old lady she was—nearly ninety—quite blind, highly rouged, and wearing a round black hat, and a cloth something, that seemed an ancient riding-habit. It was pleasant to see the "turn-out" bowling along the avenue. As we have said, we seldom reached the superb trees without encountering Petersham Peter, looking as if he were the river god, who kept his cold guard in the midst of the stately "pleasaunce"—all walled in so grim and green— and had been suddenly seized with a desire for roving, to ascertain if the world was going on as it did in the days of old Lady Lauderdale. Peter was very erect, and looked as if his figure were draped for effect; his garments hung loosely about him, and he carried a dangling fishing-net on a pole, with several eel-baskets and indescribable things he used for Thames fishing, or poaching, or anything "handy." Sometimes you came upon him stretched at his full length upon a bank sloping to the Thames; however sleepy or heavy he might look, be sure he was watching a kingfisher, or noting if any particular "jack," or miraculous eel, made their water-home in his immediate neighbourhood. Sometimes while rowing round an "ait," or crossing to Twickenham, Peter was seen rising from among the reeds or rushes, or leaning in one of his most picturesque attitudes by the hollow trunk of an aged willow. Sometimes you met him in Richmond Park, and he knew every dell and tree, and could tell you where the "liveliest snakes," and greenest lizards, and best flies for fly-fishing, were to be found. He called bottom fishing "mud-grubbing," and always said that whoever was fond of catching fish in an unnatural, "unlegitimate" way, deserved hanging. What Peter's unnatural and unlegitimate way of catching fish was is more than we believe was known : he had his own ideas on the subject, and very quaint and original they doubtless were ; but our own opinion was, that Peter caught fish, or aught else, when and how he could, without reference to any standard of right or wrong. We have said that a long pole, with a landing-net dangling from one end, rested on his shoulder; he also carried no end of rods, and lines, and traps for moles or beetles—queer implements only comprehended by himself. He was a good practical entomologist, though he made rare mistakes with the scientific names, which he always attempted; and whenever he had a rare specimen to show, he would suddenly drop all his paraphernalia on the grass, and beckoning to you in a peculiarly mysterious manner, exclaim,—" Ah! ah! now for a sight; he be a wonder! I never did see—there he be! I got un!—in *vulgaris* a genu-ine mole cricket, but proper *Grigollot taltapa vulgares*. Ah! ah! ah! Let un alone, miss—you do be always wanting to touch un; you'll get bitten some time. You'd pull a snake by the tail, you would; or a toa-ad out on his hole—never did see sich a young lady. 'Taint fem-enine to have no fear. Young ladies as I know come down from Lon'on for a day's pleasure; they go hootin' and screamin' and faintin', they do, at their own shadder—pretty little innocent dears they be. But, loak! they got no sense—no, not a bit o' sense; fear'd o' frogs—don't know a frog from a toa-ad; fear'd o' earwigs, scream into next week at a spider, and doan't know an eel from a sarpint—that's edication! They cum to me, and they say, 'Mister—what's your name?' An' I say, 'Peter.' An' they say, 'I want a nightingale, Mr. Peter.' An' I say, 'Do 'ee?' An' they say, 'Yes; I want a nightingale to take to town this evening; and you must engage it to live and to sing—only it mustn't sing too loud; and it must be quite tame, and eat out on my hand.' Them's the sort o' knowledge they have!—t'expect the bird that's born to freedom and fresh air, that the hand o' man was never intended to rest on, to be tame, and to be sure to live, like one of them dirty sparras! I knew a chap once—he was a rare one—well, he sold one of them wise young uns a sparra for a nightingale; he pulled some feathers out of it to make it look slim. The innocent look of the young un when she said,—'Oh, it's a brown bird!'

" ' Yes, miss,' he says.

" ' I wish you would make it sing just a little now for me to hear it.'

" ' I can't, miss—it's a nightingale, not a dayingale.'

" ' Ye'r sure it's a nightingale?'

" ' Honour bright as the Thames in sunshine.' "

" Then," we exclaimed with one voice, " Peter, it was *you* who sold the young lady a sparrow as a nightingale ; for you always, when you tell a great story, or commit a great fraud, say, ' Honour bright as the Thames!' "

" Do I, miss ? Well, maybe it was me—maybe I was taken in meeself—maybe I didn't find the differ until it was sold," and Peter laughed. " Ah! ah! the fun was, one of the company said it was as like a sparra as one pea is like another ; how I did laugh to myself, for she grew quite offended like, and insisted that this was a light brown bird, but that a sparra was next to *black*. She had Lonnon sparras in her eye, pretty dear !"

Petersham Peter would cheat you whenever and wherever he could ; he had a supreme contempt for all who were not as conversant with country concerns as himself; and, if possible, he entertained a still greater contempt for those who did not render due homage to the river Thames. Peter did not deny that there were other rivers in the world, but he was indifferent, quite indifferent about them ; they might be longer, and broader, and deeper—but they were not the Thames !

" Lookee," Peter would say, when, from a mere love of mischief, we drew depreciating comparisons between the Thames and other rivers—we mean, when we depreciated the Thames—" lookee, it's all very well to say there be finer rivers, and I say, Show un, and they never do show un ; so why should I believe un ?"

" You wont go and see them, Peter?"

" Why should I ? Ain't I well here ? Can't I see every cloud that passes in that clear water, without the trouble of lookin' up ? Doesn't the Lord Mayor, and the kings of all the nations of the yearth, stand on Richmon' Hill—the band playin' and the barges goin'—and bless the 'lmighty Father for their eyesight to show un sich a river ? Likely they'd come *here* to look at un, if she wasn't the finest upon yearth ; the birds o' y'air sing sweeter upon her banks than they do in Windsor forest—it's a fact. An' as to fish ! match me Thames eels in Europe, that's all. Doesn't the king of the French send for 'em ? Finer rivers, is there ? I say, Show un. The Thames is my fayther and mother too ; I never knowed any other—I don't own any other. Wasn't I found in a clump o' withies, a roaring agin' a March wind ? And Mathey Prongs, the ould angler, didn't he first think I was a fish, and threw his rod at me over the bed o' yellow water-lilies, and when the hook struck me, I stopt roarin', and laughed. Ah ! ah ! So he knew I was a Briton, and worth the rareing, and brought me home rowled up in his landin' net. And didn't the dame—Dame Prongs—(my mammy I calls her)—didn't she feed me up on roach, and dace, and gudgeons, and eels ? And when was I, from the time I could go alone, a day out of the waters o' the Thames ? It wouldn't drown me, or gi'e me cold ; it was mother's milk to me. Didn't I play with the cygnets until the swans thought me of their own brood ? The water-coot wouldn't leave her eggs while I counted them ; and though I'm not a reg'lar anything—not boatman or fisherman—I makes a good livin' at times out on its waters, at times out on its banks. Sure I've a right to speak o' my own Thames ! There isn't a rower, a punter, or a barger from Oxford to Kew that doesn't give me good morra or good night by land or water."

Years came and went—they are ever coming and going—all of mingled sunshine and shadows ; the sunshine very bright—the shadows, thank Him who orders both, seldom deepening into gloom. Sometimes we spent our summers abroad, sometimes among our own islands, amid its hills and valleys, its palaces and cottages, enjoying its rivers and its lakes—enjoying, and not unfrequently agreeing with Peter, that there *might* be finer rivers than the Thames—only "show un."

The few persons we knew at Petersham had quitted it, or added to the mounds in its churchyard. We seldom went to Richmond without inquiring about Peter ; but we never heard of him ; he was nowhere seen ; his haunts knew him no more : his name even seemed forgotten.

Lately we have been mightily taken with aquaria ; there is great fascination in our mimic lakes, whether of fresh or salt water, in their glass enclosures. We like to see our fish sporting amid forests of valisneria, and the zoophytes clinging literally to their native rocks. One of our practical friends, whose vivarium is our admiration (perhaps our admiration is mingled with a little envy), in a most generous and disinterested manner offered to send us his wise man—not of the woods, but of the rivers—a most wonderful old man, who knew every water-plant, every insect, every fish and creeping thing to be found near, or in, the waters of the Thames. It was very generous thus to open to us the floodgate of his own knowledge; we could not help sighing when we thought of poor Petersham Peter—what a treasure he would be to us now—what plants, and water insects, and fish we should have! And then we might "out-Herod Herod;" we might introduce *our* wise man to our friend, and between the two wise men we should rival Mr. Mitchell and his acres of vivaria in the Zoological Gardens. But Peter must have long ago GONE HOME; he was an old man thirty years back.

Our friend's wise man came: at a distance he looked like a doubled-up fishing-rod, with its loose case hanging about it. He was stooping over a very dirty, rusty tin can. We could not at first see his face—when we did, it was so tangled and matted over with grizzled hair, that, except for the rapid movement of his very restless but human eyes, it might have been the face of an enlarged Skye terrier—it was literally all hair. We asked what he had brought, and the contents of the can, whose names, as he poured them out, would have formed *addenda* to Yarrell's "British Fishes;" many of them were new to us, perhaps it was from the manner in which the old fisherman pronounced their names. He was certainly *very* old—the veins and muscles of his hands were lined and netted under the horny skin like fret-work—surely warm, gushing, life-sustaining blood could not creep, much less flow, through these ossified veins! He had by a restless movement of his head thrown back his hair from a high, narrow forehead, and there the skin seemed literally pleated—furrow after furrow of bronzed skin—fold upon fold. He would have been more interesting, though probably less picturesque,

if he had been something cleaner; but *that* was hardly to be expected.
Still he was a picture Rembrandt would have copied; had he been
dressed for effect, the effect probably would not have been so good,—
there was marvellous relief to the blue jacket and loose trowsers in the
deep red waistcoat, and bright (dirty bright) folds of what looked like an
Indian scarf wound round his throat, one end tossed over his shoulder,
the other descending below his waist; the wonderful folds and shadows
of his hair and beard,—the strange markings, such iron-pen markings,
on his brow and hands,—his wrists rugged and gnarled as the "crouch
oak" at Addlestone, that has numbered five hundred years,—his back
bowed,—his marvellous leanness, and the deep booming of his voice,
echoing as if from an empty cask suddenly inspired by vitality,—his
eyes, too, blinked and glittered when he stooped over the large can, we
saw their reflection in the water like twin balls of fire. He was a strange
old man—so strange and unlike any creature we had ever seen, that
while he bent and bowed over his can, drawing up first one, and then
another little sparkling floundering fish out of the water, we gave no
heed to his words, but simply looked at him; at last, dropping one of
those abominable loaches—they are always making believe to die, yet
they never do die, and are so greedy—well, dropping a panting loach
into the can, he exclaimed—"What 'ill un buy? will un buy nothing?
—there's no more suitable fish for vivarrummis to be had,—all as tame
as silky lambs,—cum when ye whistle, wag their tails, eat out of un
hands. Bless 'ee, I've got lizards would follee un over the house like
dogs, and won't drink Lunnon water—there! I'm tellin' no lie, HONOUR
BRIGHT AS THE THAMES IN 'SHINE!"

"And you," we said, "you are Petersham Peter!"

The old man drew himself up as erect as he could, and looking
strangely about, exclaimed in a low, husky voice, "Who said that? say
un agin."

"You are Petersham Peter!"

He advanced slowly towards us, shading his bewildered eyes with his
hand, peering awfully into our face, examining us feature by feature.
At first his eyes gleamed brightly, then they became dark and dull, and

heaving a heavy sigh, he turned away—" I doant know 'ee, I never saw un before."

" Yes, Peter, you did,—years ago, when we were young,"—and we recalled such little incidents as had made impression on our own minds.

" Ah ! ah ! mole-crickets, and nightingales, an' pleasant meadows— sweet hay—cygnets. Ah ! and the ould little grand lady in her flying carriage, she went to dust sooner than Peter. Ah ! You never know'd harm of ould Peter, did ye ? *Did ye ?*" he repeated almost fiercely.

" No, Peter—never !"

" I wouldn't ha' wronged the noble river of a can of water ! I loved it,—you know I loved it ! My own river ! I always said when they talked of finer rivers, ' Show un,' but they never did, though they sent me to seek un, away—away over the sea. It was no great harm I done, to send an old man out of his country ; they thought I'd never live to cum back, but I did, ye see : but I 'm not Petersham Peter now. I 've never been that side o' Lunnon since "—he paused, and then smoothing his hair down he made a sort of bow, assuming a low, querulous tone, " I 'm a very old man, lady, and no clear in y'n brain, or y'n eye ; I 'm broken all-the-gather. I keeps Greenwich way, and gets me little live stock out of rain-full streams and green-jacketed pools, I does,"—he looked round stealthily, and added, "*they* doan't know me Greenwich way—*they never did.* Some night I 'll try to watch for moonshine, and just ha' one look over the hill, before I die, at the gay river. Only when I cum agin, don't call me *that* name. Maybe, if ye did, some one, unawares, might ask for my ticket o' leave, and, hush ! *I got none ;* but I 'm not worth sendin' out o' the country agin. I 'm not clear y'n brain, or y'n eye !" He paused, shook his head, and while mechanically dipping up his fish in the miniature landing-net, he soliloquized, glancing dreamily at us—" It cum so stunnin', yet so sweet it cum over me—so queer, ' Petersham Peter,'—just like a boat hail from tother world ! I wish I knew rightly who you be ! You can't be she ; she was slim as rod osier, and wonderful fond of letting all my fish go out of the well o' the boat right into the river. Ah ! ah ! Turn all the eels out of the pots, if she could, and wouldn't spit an emperor of Morocco—

*vulgaris.* Ah, dear! I forget it. She was as bright a young un as the Thames in sunshine! No, no! why, you'd make two o' she! an' yet, how be it? Petersham Peter!"

Perhaps in England there is no single view so beautiful as that obtained from the summit of RICHMOND HILL; nay, it is scarcely too much to say there is nothing more charming in the world. Such is the opinion of many foreigners who have beheld the landscape attractions of

VIEW FROM RICHMOND HILL.

all lands, and such is surely that of those who, having travelled long and far, return to their own country with a confirmed conviction that Englishmen find nowhere any scenery so delicious as that they possess "at home." No doubt there is much that is wider, and broader, and grander—more magnificent and more comprehensive—which voyagers elsewhere may enjoy, but none within the same limits so gifted with surpassing loveliness. The scene from Richmond Hill has, therefore, been at all times a fertile theme of the poet and the painter, although neither art nor language can render it sufficient justice.

"Heavens! what a goodly prospect spreads around
Of hills and dales, and woods and lawns, and spires,
And glittering towns, and gilded streams!"

Such was the exclamation of one of the many poets who have offered homage to "the Hill;" we may quote another :—

"Where Thames along the daisied meads
His wave in lucid mazes leads—
Silent, slow, serenely flowing,
Wealth on either side bestowing."

But, in fact, there are few whom the Muse has not stirred into life, when gazing from either of the adjacent heights upon a scene so entirely beautiful—at once so gentle and so grand, so graceful and so rich.

RICHMOND HILL.

As we approach Richmond from Twickenham, and pass a slight projection at Ham, we come in sight of "the Hill." From the river the rise appears very slight : on the summit are several good and "tall" houses, the most conspicuous of which is the far-famed "Star and

Garter" inn; and here all visitors will linger, entering either its prettily arranged grounds or its stately chambers for refreshment, and gazing from one of its windows over the thick and apparently dense foliage that seems to cover the whole valley underneath, through which the all-glorious father meanders " silent, slow," the source of that green fertility which makes the landscape "beautiful exceedingly." * "The eye, descending from the hill," marks the tortuous course of the river, above and below, glances among "the palace homes of England," and watches the gay boats, of " all sorts and sizes," that float upon the surface, issue from tiny creeks, or continue moored beside lawn-slopes: gaze where we will, there is ever something to stir the heart, and justify that love and pride of country which rivals or foes attribute to Englishmen as a vice!

The distant views from any of the heights are as fair and beautiful as those immediately around and underneath. Looking over Richmond Park we behold stately Windsor; further off, the hills of Buckinghamshire—the historic Chilterns; and nearer, those over Runnymede and Chertsey. Turning eastward, we look on many of the steeps that, rising above the Lower Thames, fling their shadows on the sails of a hundred nations, thronging that part of the great highway of the world which lies between the Nore and London Bridge. Surely the tourist may exclaim, and justly,—

> "Earth hath not anything to show more fair,"

challenging the wide world to produce a scene which so happily combines the grand and the beautiful—

> " In wondrous perspective displayed,
> A landscape more august than happiest skill
> Of pencil ever clothed with light and shade :
> An intermingled pomp of vale and hill,
> City and naval stream, suburban grove,
> And stately forest where the wild deer rove ;
> Nor wanted lurking hamlet, dusky towns,
> And scattered rural farms of aspect bright."

---

* So close are the trees, and so little can be seen of the intervening meadows and gardens, that a story is told of an American from the Far West, whose eye, having been accustomed to endless and trackless forests, saw the beauty as a blemish, and declared it to be *his* opinion that " the valley wanted clearing."

A gate on the summit of the hill leads into Richmond Park. The public enjoy a right of entrance, and it is pleasant to know that the right is rarely or never abused. The park was first enclosed by Charles I., but there were certain neighbouring owners who " could not be prevailed upon to alienate their property upon any terms." His majesty, however, seems to have convinced those "village Hampdens;" notwithstanding that the affair "made a great clamour, and the outcry was that he was about to take away his subjects' estates at his own pleasure." Jerome, Earl of Portland, was made the first ranger, in the year 1638. In 1649 the park was given "to the City of London, and to their successors for ever." At the Restoration it found its way back to the Crown, of which it is now a mere appanage of comparatively little value, although her Majesty has sought to make it practically useful by presenting some of its residences to men who are, or have been, benefactors of their country.

At that end of the park where a gate leads to Mortlake, and near a cottage in which resides one of the most estimable gentlemen of the age—Professor Owen—there still lives and flourishes a tree that has been famous for many ages: it is the SHREW-ASH. It is interesting to note how little odds and ends of superstitions are rooted, like wild primroses, in out of the way wilds—the nooks and corners of our intellectual country. It is so difficult to define where faith ends, and superstition begins, that sometimes we lose sight of irrationality, in sympathy with the sentiment that is blended with the superstition. The shrew-ash is only a few yards beyond the pond which almost skirts the Professor's lawn—where herds of dappled deer come fearlessly from the high ground of the park to drink at early morning, and again while the sky is yet glowing with the tints of the setting sun. This venerable and celebrated tree stands on rising ground.

White, in his "Natural History of Selbourne," describes a "shrew-ash" as "an ash whose twigs or branches, when gently applied to the limbs of cattle, will immediately relieve the pains which a beast suffers from the running of a shrew-mouse over the part affected,—for it is supposed that a shrew-mouse is of so baneful and deleterious a nature that wherever it creeps over a beast, be it horse, cow, or sheep, the suffering animal is afflicted with cruel anguish, and threatened with the loss of the use of the limb. Against this evil, to which they were continually liable, our provident forefathers always kept a shrew-ash at hand, which, when once medicated, would maintain its virtues for ever. A shrew-ash was made potent thus : into the body of the tree a deep hole

THE SHREW-ASH.

was bored with an auger, and a poor devoted shrew-mouse was thrust in alive, and plugged in, no doubt with several quaint incantations long since forgotten. As the ceremonies necessary for such a consecration are no longer understood, all succession is at an end." The shrew-ash in Richmond Park is, therefore, amongst the few legacies of the kind bequeathed to their country by the wisdom of our ancestors. We once knew a queer, spiteful, old Kentish gardener, who suggested, in open defiance of legendary lore, that it would be far wiser to bury a shrew *wife under* an ash, than stop up a poor innocent shrew-mouse in it. He laughed to scorn all superstitions; and many of his old neighbours believed he would live and die a "cast away," he was so fond of holding everything connected with "good old times" in utter contempt.

Our readers will perceive that across the hollow of the tree near the top there is a little bar of wood: the legend runs that were this bar removed every night, it would be replaced in the same spot every morning! How? Who can tell how? The legend calls the fact "established," and so we are bound to believe it. The superstition now is, that if a child, afflicted with what the people in the neighbourhood call "decline," or whooping-cough, or any infantine disease, is passed nine times up the hollow of that tree, and over the bar, while the sun is rising, it will recover. If the charm fail to produce the desired effect, the old women believe the sun was too far up, or not up enough, or the "verse" (for we have been told there is a spoken charm) not properly repeated. If the child recovers, of course the fame of the tree is whispered about,—for the oldest crone would hardly dilate on such a subject in her usual voice at mid-day. There is an Irish saying that "every whisper has four wings," and thus the tale spreads. There is a sort of shrew-mother to every shrew-ash—the veriest ancient in the parish; withered and bent, with lean arms and long fingers, that clutch her staff, her picturesque scarlet cloak giving that life to the landscape of which painters never tire. She acts as guide and teacher to any young mother who has an afflicted child—and faith in the charm; and the two may be seen in the grey light of morning—the little creeping crone, and the tall girl enveloped in a cloak or large shawl, beneath whose folds is cherished her precious burthen. She follows through the long dewy grass, and heeds nor deer nor cattle; but she fears the chill air will make her darling worse, though she dare not say so, for she must not anger the aged crone even if she handle the child roughly, as she thrusts it up and passes it over, under and over, until the accomplishment of the mystic nine. The child wails, of course, but that is not heeded by the sybil: it is speedily pressed to the warm bosom of its mother, and they

creep away stealthily, half ashamed or afraid to be seen by their neighbours.

The shrew-ash in Richmond Park is still used and still firmly believed
in, the superstition having by no means entirely lost its force.   The
friend who communicates this fact to us has more than once seen at
daybreak a young mother, with her sick babe, resorting to the ash for
cure, and eagerly watching under its withered branches the first streak
of sunlight in the east.*

We must descend the hill and enter the ancient village—the now
populous town of Richmond.   We cannot long delay, although it is full
of associations, any one of which might demand a chapter instead of a
line.   It is, however, essential that we visit the church, and then stroll
to the green, in order that we may stand on the site of the ancient
palace, " to which the former kings of this land, being wearie of the citie,
used customarily to resorte, as to a place of pleasure, and serving highly
for recreation."

At Richmond resided Nicholas Brady, and here he translated and
versified the Psalms.   Here lived, and in the church is buried, James
Thomson :†   here he

" Sung the seasons and their change ;"

and many memories of him are preserved in the house where he resided,
" in unaffected cheerfulness, and general, though simple elegance."
There are few who walk through the fair town, or row along the waters

---

* Superstitions regarding trees have been rife in every age and country, and may be referred to the
"sacred groves" of the ancient idolaters, or the custom of consecrating trees to particular divinities,
tinctured with the prevailing superstition of the more modern nations of the north, and tinged with a
darker belief in mysticism.   Hence the witch-hazel is believed to be as efficacious as the horse-shoe in
preventing the incursions of a witch for evil purposes, if a branch be fastened over a door.   But for
charms in disease, no tree has been so much used as the ash, which, in addition to the power it is supposed to possess, as narrated above, was also believed to cure other diseases.   If the wound made in the
tree was bound with packthread, the child recovered as the tree recovered ; but the life of the patient
depended so entirely on that of the tree, that if it was wilfully destroyed the disease returned and terminated in death.

† Thomson lived in a small cottage in Kew Lane.   It has been enlarged and altered since his time.
There was no monument to his memory in the church, until the Earl of Buchan placed, in 1792, a brass
plate in the north aisle to denote the spot where he was buried, June 29, 1748, " for the satisfaction of
his admirers," as the inscription states, " unwilling that so good a man and sweet a poet should be
without a memorial."

that lave its banks, who will not recall the graceful tribute of a brother poet—

> " Remembrance oft shall haunt this shore,
>   When Thames in summer wreaths is drest,
>   And oft suspend the dashing oar,
>   To bid thy gentle spirit rest ! "

RICHMOND CHURCH has few old features, and the most remarkable monuments are on the exterior.   At the south-west angle is a marble

RICHMOND CHURCH.

tablet, executed by E. W. Wyon, to the memory of Barbara Hofland, authoress of "The Son of a Genius," &c.   She was born at Sheffield, in 1770, and died at Richmond, November 9, 1844.   "She endeavoured," says the inscription, "with Christian humility, to recommend, by her valuable example, the lessons inculcated in her writings."   We knew her long and well, and to know her was a privilege.   After a life of

active and useful labour, and the calm and patient endurance of many
trials, she rests amid the scenery she loved so well, and near the places
she cherished most in her warm and tender heart. The world owes her
much; she was one of its best teachers. Her works will endure longer
even than the monument that records her name, for they are the experience of her own naturally devout mind, her generous sympathies, and
her womanly wisdom. Here, in later times, died and was buried the
great actor, Edmund Kean. To his memory a simple monument has
been erected by his accomplished son,* who, inheriting much of the
father's genius, has avoided the "perilous pleasures" that led to death
at the comparatively early age of forty-eight. There is no gentleman
more thoroughly respected, or more entirely entitled to respect, than the
younger Kean. If the stage owed a large debt to the acting of the
father, it has contracted a larger to the son, for his judicious and liberal
"management," and especially for having made its "means and appli-
ances" sources of instruction as well as of delight. Many other great
men and women have left their names as perpetual memories in this
neighbourhood: it is full of associations, and these, added to the charms
of beautiful scenery, must ever keep for Richmond a fame unsurpassed
by that of any other locality in the kingdom.

On Richmond Green is all that now remains of the OLD PALACE OF
SHEEN,† consisting of a stone gateway, and a smaller postern gate beside
it. Above the large gate is sculptured the arms of England, supported
by the dragon and greyhound, indicating its erection in the time of
Henry VII. Beside it may be traced a few portions of the old brickwork of the palatial buildings, with the characteristic reticulated pattern

* It consists of a medallion portrait, surrounded by drapery, and was erected in 1839. Kean
died in the house adjoining Richmond Theatre, in May, 1833. This theatre was built under the
superintendence of Garrick, and was frequently patronized by George III., when living at Kew. Many
great actors have played there. It was here the accomplished actress and excellent lady, Helen Faucit,
made her *debût*.

† "It is well known that this place received its present name by royal command in the reign of
Henry VII., who was Earl of Richmond in Yorkshire. In Domesday it is not mentioned: a record of
nearly the same antiquity calls it Syenes; the name was afterwards spelt Schenes, Schene, and Sheen.
Some writers, founding their conjectures upon the latter word, which signifies bright or splendid, have
supposed it to be expressive of the magnificence of the ancient palace."—*Lysons*.

which gave diversity to the walls. It is believed to have been the entrance to the wardrobe court.*

REMAINS OF RICHMOND PALACE.

The ancient name of Richmond was Sheen, signifying *beautiful* (from the German word, which still bears the meaning) ; it was considered as part of the Manor of Kingston, in the Domesday Survey, when it was crown property. Edward III. died in the mansion of Shene, at which time it was a pleasant retirement for the English sovereigns. Henry V. rebuilt the palace, with "curious and costly workmanship," which was destroyed by fire in 1498. Henry VII. immediately gave orders for the rebuilding of the palace, and ordained that it should be named *Rich-*

---

* The arms over the great gate, though much decayed, are still clearly to be distinguished as those of King Henry VII., who was Earl of Richmond before he conquered his opponent, Richard III., on Bosworth Field. The supporters of the royal arms of Henry are unlike those of any other English monarch : the shield is supported by the red dragon of the House of Cadwallader, the last king of the Britons, from whom Henry claimed his descent, and the white greyhound of the House of York, as represented in our cut. Henry VIII. retained the dragon, but adopted the lion of England, instead of the greyhound, for his other supporter.

*mond*, after his own title, before he had achieved the sovereignty of England on Bosworth field.   King Henry VII., and his son, Henry VIII., took much pleasure in the palace here, and frequently held tournaments and festivals at Richmond.   Henry VII. died in the palace; Katherine, the first queen of the eighth Harry, was confined here of a son; and the Emperor Charles V. lodged here on his visit to England in 1552.   The manor was afterwards granted to Anne of Cleves, on her voluntary divorce from Henry VIII.; and Queen Mary and her husband, Philip of Spain, frequently resided in the palace, which was also a favourite with her successor, Elizabeth, who entertained the King of Sweden within its walls, when he visited England to make her a proposal of marriage.   She died here on March 24, 1603.   The sons of James I., Henry and Charles, both held the manor; and here the latter laid the foundations of his important Art-collections.   In 1627 the manor was settled on his queen, Henrietta Maria.   After the execution of Charles, the parliament sold the manor.   Hollar has published a view of it as it appeared in the reign of Charles I.   It was a picturesque edifice, abounding with towers and pinnacles.   On the Restoration the king restored it to the queen-mother; and it was leased to Sir Edward Villiers.   It was much dilapidated, and was soon afterwards pulled down.

The many attractions of Richmond, and its proximity to the metropolis—from which it is distant eight miles—have always made the neighbourhood a favourite of the high-born and the wealthy.   A long list might be given of "great people" who have had their dwellings on the hill or on the river banks.   Buccleuch Lodge is among the most conspicuous and the most beautiful as we reach its slope, just after passing the bridge, voyaging westward.

There yet remain some of the fish of the Thames to which attention should be directed; and as we are approaching that part of the river where the sport of the angler terminates, we may describe two, although neither of them is found in abundance so low down.   Richmond, however, has been always in favour with professors of the rod and line, and it is rarely we pass the banks of Buccleuch Lodge without encoun-

tering half a dozen punts; for during autumn the roach is numerous
here, and of small barbel there is usually a plenty.

The Chub is a shy fish, and although sometimes taken with the worm
or gentle when bottom-fishing, it is more frequently caught on the surface with a mimic fly or cockchafer; and then under overhanging trees,
where skill is requisite. They often grow to a large size in our river:
we have more than once hooked a fish weighing five pounds. In its
general aspect the chub resembles the dace, but is somewhat more taper;
it is of little value as food, the flesh being poor and "waterish;" never-

THE CHUB.

theless, old Izaak gives an elaborate recipe for "dressing him"—for
drying up his "fluid watery humour"—and for giving him such a sauce
as may "recompense the labour."

The Pope, or "ruffe," is found in great abundance in many parts of
the river; it bites greedily, and it is a common practice to take ladies to
a "pope pitch," inasmuch as there is sure to be plenty of sport, the
pope biting like the perch, and with a certainty of being hooked by a
very small effort of skill. It resembles the perch, too, in other particulars, the fins being sharp and somewhat perilous to delicate fingers.
It is small in size, seldom exceeding in length five or six inches.
An idea prevails that the pope is a fish between the perch and

gudgeon, but there is no foundation for it, other than its general likeness to the one, and its habitat being the gravelly bottoms frequented
by the other.

We cannot part from this branch of our subject—the pleasure supplied to anglers by the all-bountiful river—without a word or two of

THE POPE.

comment on "the Thames Angling Preservation Society"—a society
by which much has been done to preserve the river from illegal nets,
and to punish the poacher. Its formal meetings are held once a year
at Richmond—in July. Its report is published annually: the excellent
secretary, Henry Farnell, Esq., is indefatigable in his efforts to advance
its purposes; every angler is bound to support a society which does so
much to enable him to enjoy a day's ample sport in any of "the deeps,"
which it materially aids to preserve and to "furnish."

We resume our voyage, setting out from RICHMOND BRIDGE—which
we engrave from a photograph taken by Dr. Farre—first turning with
pleasure to the pretty and well-known ait, and looking back every
now and then for a charming view of the town and the surrounding
scenery.

As, however, we shall not again have occasion to step on shore and
examine the treasures of the river Flora, we may delay the reader

awhile in order to present to him another bouquet of the wild flowers that grow so luxuriantly, and at the same time submit to his scrutiny

RICHMOND BRIDGE.   a

a few of the insects concerning which his curiosity will be continually excited as he rows or wanders along its banks.

On the leaves of the Willow-herb we found a grotesque-looking creature, which at first sight appeared to be staring malignantly at us from his perch; but, on a nearer examination, those sinister eyes (as we thought them) proved to be mere painted resemblances of these organs; and, to carry out the illusion, the "spots" are situated on an enlarged portion of the body, representing a head, from which proceeds

CATERPILLAR OF THE HAWK-MOTH.

an apparent proboscis somewhat like an elephant's trunk, whence the

3 B

creature has been named the Elephant Hawk-moth (*Chœrocampa Elpenor*), of which this is the caterpillar state. It is of a dusky colour, and on the sides are several of the curious eye-like spots; but when seen from the front, with only the two larger spots visible, the appearance is somewhat startling. The true head and eyes are comparatively minute, and are situated at the end of the proboscis-like portion of

THE ELEPHANT HAWK-MOTH.    a

the body. The moth into which the "creature" is eventually transformed, presents a decided contrast to the weird aspect of its caterpillar form in its earlier state of existence, being a soft, elegant fly, beautifully painted with rose-colour and olive-brown : it may be frequently met

with in the same situations as its caterpillar, either flying rapidly in the twilight, or at morning reposing inactive in some shaded and retired spot. It is, therefore, both curious and interesting.

There is a very charming little moth, called by collectors the China-mark Moth, constantly met with in moist, reedy places, and, of course, found abundantly by the banks of the Thames. This pretty species has white wings, elegantly marked with brown and grey. Its caterpillar

CHINA-MARK MOTH.

makes itself a curious habitation by cutting out portions of a leaf, and then attaching them together into a kind of portable tent, which accompanies the little animal in all its wanderings.

The botany of the river-side, as we have intimated, becomes far more scanty as we approach the more populous districts lying on either side, almost uninterruptedly until we reach London : and we cannot without

regret take leave of the fair Flora that has afforded us such unfailing pleasure and interest, from the very cradle of the infant stream in Gloucestershire, through its whole course down to our present position, whence, for a time, objects of more immediately human interest must occupy our attention. We may notice one more favourite, which we have hitherto omitted to mention, but which forms a very striking and beautiful feature in most of the flowery groups that ornament the old locks, and conduce so much to their picturesque effect. We allude to the Meadow Crane's-bill (*Geranium pratense*), a plant with elegantly cut foliage, and clusters of large bright purple flowers.

MEADOW CRANE'S-BILL.

The Reed (*Arundo phragmites*) must be familiar to every voyager on the Thames, whose banks are almost constantly edged with deep beds of this common though graceful plant. The presence of these reed-beds is a powerful aid in the picturesque effect of the "bits" for which this river is so famous : witness the good service they render in the foreground of pictures by Boddington, and other painters, to whom the Thames scenery is so dear; though, after all, in the best-painted picture we must still lose the peculiar charm of the reed—its graceful motion, as it rocks and waves its feathery crest in the wind. But besides playing its ornamental part so well, the reed is not without some pretensions to the useful, both in its natural position, where it serves to protect embankments and dykes for preventing the encroachment of the water, and also, when cut, for thatching, and various purposes of building and gardening. Moreover, the flower-heads will dye wool green, and the roots are said to be useful as a medicine in bilious complaints ; but for the accuracy of this crowning recommenda-

THE REED.

tion we cannot vouch from our own experience, for the tourist amid these charming scenes will have little need of a remedy " against the bile,"—and so we contented ourselves with admiring the " effect" of our friends, the reeds, *in situ*. We have more than once directed the attention of the ornamental designer to the lessons he may receive from Nature on the banks of the river Thames.

Passing under the railway bridge, which crosses the Thames at the eastern boundary of Kew Gardens, we have them on our right hand for more than two miles. The left bank affords more diversity, and to that we direct special attention. The first object which attracts the eye is a palatial building, now appropriated to the Female Naval Orphan Asylum. It was commenced by Lord Kilmurry as a residence, but has been greatly enlarged, and is now devoted to a high purpose—as one of those noble institutions which do honour to England, rendering memorable over the world the words, " Supported by Voluntary Contributions." About half a mile brings us to Isleworth Church, with its ancient ivy-covered tower. The body of the church is of red brick, and was constructed in 1705. It contains a few of the monumental brasses which were in the older edifice ; one of them represents a knight in armour of the fifteenth century ; but the most curious is affixed withinside the Duke of Northumberland's pew, and is here copied ; it preserves the figure of one of the last of the English nuns, being to the memory of " Margaret Dely, a syster professed in Syon, who decessed the VII of October,

Anno, 1561,"—during the short while the nunnery was restored to the Roman Catholic service in the reign of Queen Mary. The village of Isleworth is chiefly devoted to garden-ground, and the growth of vegetables for London markets. Though never occupying a position in history, Isleworth is noted in our most ancient surveys. Simon de Montfort encamped here with the refractory barons, in 1263 ; and Fairfax fixed his head-quarters here in 1647. It is a straggling, unpicturesque village, offering no inducements to delay the tourist.

Sion House, which occupies the site of the ancient religious foundation, is close beside the church ; it was originally granted to a convent of Bridgetine nuns, by Henry V., in the year 1414 : they seem to have led a quiet life of much prosperity ; upon its dissolution, in the reign of Henry VIII., the revenue of the Convent of Sion was valued at the very large sum of £1731 8s. 4½d. per annum. The king retained the desecrated buildings, and here imprisoned his unfortunate queen, Katherine Howard, while arranging her judicial murder. The body of the same king rested here on the road to his mausoleum at Windsor. Edward VI., in the first year of his reign, gave the building and site to the Protector Seymour, Duke of Somerset. On his attainder it was granted to the Duke of Northumberland, in whose family it has since remained, except during the short period when it reverted to the Crown during the reign of Mary—the forfeiture being occasioned by the ambition of the duke, whose son married the Lady Jane Grey : it was in Sion House she accepted the crown, having been conducted thence as queen to the Tower of London, so soon afterwards to die on a scaffold within its walls.

Queen Mary was induced to restore the nunnery at Sion, and endow it with the manor and demesnes of Isleworth. It was dissolved by Elizabeth, who, however, retained the lands until 1604, when they were again given to the Dukes of Northumberland. The present house was constructed soon afterwards, and has some rich interior details. The exterior is singularly plain, a mere quadrangle of heavy stonework. It contains some fine pictures. One of the prettiest and pleasantest *points* on the river is the graceful PAVILION we have here introduced.

WATER PAVILION AT SION HOUSE.

Brentford commences at the end of the walls of the park at Sion; but the greater part of the town is happily hidden by a long island thickly covered with trees. It is one of the most unpicturesque towns on the river, abounding in gas-works, factories, and distilleries; its streets presenting an appearance of dirt and neglect, heightened by alleys, the abodes of squalid poverty. A large part of the population are employed in the extensive market-gardens in the neighbourhood. The town takes its name from the small river Brent, which here flows into the Thames, rising in the adjoining county of Hertford, and pursuing a tortuous course through the centre of Middlesex. It is a small stream, but its junction with the Thames at an important locality led to the foundation, in very early times, of a village here, the establishment of a large nunnery on the opposite side of the ford materially aiding its growth.

And so we arrive in sight of Kew Bridge; but before we row under it, we must step ashore to visit some of the attractions of this ancient and renowned village.

Kew—"the situation of which near the water-side might induce one to seek for its etymology from the word key or quay"—has been variously written at various times "Kayhough, Kayhoo, Keyhowe, Keye, Kayo, and Kewe." Lysons, half a century back, describes its greenhouse as famous, being 140 feet in length; and Darwin, about the same period, pictured its garden as "a crowning glory"—

> "So sits enthroned, in vegetable pride,
> Imperial Kew, by Thames's glittering side."

The historian and the poet, could they rise from their graves, would see with wonder and delight the greenhouse and the garden of to-day, filled with the floral beauties of a hundred lands,—miles of walks among flowers under glass.

Inasmuch as there is an admirable and cheap guide-book for the use of visitors, compiled by the accomplished Curator, Sir William Hooker, we are relieved from the necessity of details descriptive of these beautiful gardens and conservatories: it will suffice to say that, although still the property of the Crown, and in charge of the Board of Works, the public are freely admitted every day, under a few needful restrictions; that the privilege is enjoyed by very large numbers *daily*; and that the result fully bears out the belief, that where advantages are given to "the people," they are neither lost nor abused by carelessness or cupidity. Cases of impropriety are rare, while it is certain that health, instruction, and gratification, have been largely derived from the means thus generously placed at the disposal of all.

Between Richmond and Kew there is no bridge; there are, however,

three ferries, one of which we have introduced as a very picturesque " bit."
It is that which leads to Isleworth, and is called the RAILS-HEAD FERRY,
a name it obtained before the introduction of those iron ways which now

RAILS-HEAD FERRY.

conduct tourists from London to the far-famed " Hill," and thence to
" regal Windsor."

Although we do not delay the voyager by describing the gardens, we
ask him to visit the ancient and venerable PALACE, famous during

" Good King George's reign,"

and interesting now, although it is lonely and without inhabitant—
standing as a striking and somewhat gloomy monument to record the
liberality of the sovereign and his successors, who gave the adjacent
grounds to the people.   It was once the property of Sir Hugh Portman,
" the rich gentleman who was knighted by Queen Elizabeth at Kew,"

and was built during the reign of James I., although it retains very little of the style of architecture of that period, being of red brick, but exceedingly plain and without ornament.    In 1781 it was purchased by George III.; his queen, Charlotte, died there, and during many years it was the favourite suburban residence of the royal family.

KEW PALACE.

Under the superintendence of her Majesty, the grounds were " ornamented with various picturesque objects and temples, designed by Sir William Chambers, among which is one called the Pagoda, in imitation of a Chinese building, 49 feet in diameter at the base, and 163 feet in height."   No doubt this was a marvel at the time of its erection; it is still a conspicuous object from all adjacent parts, and the temples are attractions judiciously distributed.

It is more than delightful to escape in summer from the turmoil of the hot, dusty, London world, to the peculiar serenity and surpassing beauty of Kew; the gardens are so full of interest, so varied, so suggestive, and so instructive, that a much larger space than we can devote to the subject would fail to convey an idea of the treasures they contain ; we are willing, therefore, to let fancy go back to the time of Queen Charlotte, whose love of nature laid the foundation of that which now yields —sometimes to many thousands in a day—so much of health, pleasure, and information.  The square red "palace"—which her Majesty loved sufficiently well to select as a residence, above all others, after the death of her beloved husband—seems lonely and silent in the midst of that fragrant paradise, where trees are bursting into bloom, and birds are pouring forth the rejoicings that specially belong to the "sweet month of May;" but there is no difficulty in peopling it with "the great" of the past, and seeing, by the light of history, the beautiful and brilliant family that once held court

"Beside the Thames at Kew."

In those days the "gardens" were, like the palace, the exclusive property of the Crown : but when the latter ceased to be a "royal residence," our good and ever-considerate Queen, desiring to enlarge the circle commenced by Queen Charlotte, devoted the whole of the estate to the fruits of botanical research ; and it was finally determined that the public should be admitted daily.  Thus the "gardens at Kew" may be ranked amongst the great teachers, as well as the healthful luxuries, of the people.

It is delightful to see how truly this privilege is enjoyed by the various classes who visit Kew : the humble but well-dressed artizan and his family are generally "taken" with the beauty of the grounds and the marvels of the "House of Palms ;" brilliant ladies, whose dresses rival the flowers in variety of tone and colour, linger in the "houses," or enjoy the charming promenades under shadows of lofty trees ; the botanical student pores over the "specimens," both in the beds and in the houses—too often, while alive to what is rare or curious, forgetting the *beauty* of the "wonderful works of the Creator."  Long after the mere pleasure-seeker has returned to London by the rail or the river, you may observe two classes of persons lingering in Kew Gardens—the mere botanical student, and the artist, sketching for popular botanical publications, that add so much to the interest and the information of our drawing-rooms. Foreigners are especially delighted with Kew Gardens; the vegetation, the absolute *green*—so vigorous and fresh with us, is never so bright on the Continent as it is in England; and however rare and wonderful the collections are in foreign lands, there is usually a slovenliness in their display which no English gardener could endure: our lawns excite the especial admiration of strangers, who are lavish of praise of our "good order" and "arrangement." To thoroughly appreciate "Kew Gardens" they should be repeatedly visited; the changing seasons vary the character of their loveliness: there is always something fresh to admire, something new to learn; and though the "new museum" is so totally devoid of architectural excellence as to be a blot where it might have been a beauty, yet its contents are of the greatest value and interest, and such as lead from the threshold of science by paths which the research and learning of great botanists render comparatively smooth and easy.

"Kew Green" is one of the most "quaint" and peculiar "bits" of scenery within ten miles of the metropolis. The church may be taken as the principal feature,—a clean, bright, stately English church, neither new nor old. This "green" is irregularly "flanked" by houses of all heights and qualities; some trellised, some bare and stately, others hid away in the bright foliage which climbs their walls; some standing boldly forward, others receding modestly behind trees.

The church stands on the west side of the green. Its graveyard contains the graves of several remarkable men, among whom may be named Gainsborough and Zoffany. Gainsborough was never a resident here: he resided for many years at Schomburg House, Pall Mall; it was at his own request that he was buried at Kew, beside the grave of his old friend, Kirby, author of a once celebrated work on Perspective; but Zoffany lived in the little hamlet called Strand-on-the-Green, which adjoins the bridge on the Middlesex side of the river.

Gainsborough's tombstone is the central slab in the foreground of our engraving. He had desired that his name only should be cut upon the stone; it is, therefore, simply inscribed, "Thomas Gainsborough, Esq, died August 2nd, 1788, aged 61 years." A similarly brief inscription records the death of his wife ten years afterwards. There is enough of the " country churchyard " yet remaining at Kew to make it a fitting resting-place for such a painter : one who has left us some of our most charming pictures of natural scenery. It is no unpleasant spot, for trees

GAINSBOROUGH'S TOMB.

shadow it, and a free air is around. It is a more agreeable pilgrimage to the grave of Gainsborough than to the place of greater honour— the crypt of St. Paul's—where so many of his brethren lie. In a few years, however, Kew may be part of London ; for buildings are rising rapidly between the sequestered village and the outskirts of the metropolis.

The Bridge at Kew is a comparatively modern structure. Looking eastward a pleasant ait fortunately takes away from Kew and its river walks the view of " Brentford's tedious town." Hence, in Middlesex, there is little to claim attention until we approach Chiswick ; while, on the Surrey side, we pass along by the side of osier beds, with nothing worthy of notice until Mortlake is reached. " The name of this place has been generally supposed to be derived from *mortuus lacus*, or the

dead lake ;" in Domesday it is called " Mortlage." Cromwell House, one
of its attractions, has been recently pulled down.    It is erroneously
described as a residence of the Protector ; but Mr. Lemon, of the State
Paper Office, informs us that in the collection there are several letters
dated thence by the Lord Henry Cromwell, of the reign of Henry VIII.
Dr. Dee, the famous astrologer, lived at Mortlake, in a house near the
water-side, a little westward from the church ; and here Queen Elizabeth
came to visit him, and see his famous glass, into which he conjured
spirits for magical purposes.    He had attended Elizabeth before on

KEW BRIDGE.

frivolous errands of superstition, particularly when a wax image with a
pin stuck in it was found in Lincoln's Inn Fields, and the queen and
council were in great alarm lest it boded evil to her life.    When the
queen came to Mortlake in March, 1575, she did not enter Dee's house ;
" Her Majesty," he tells us, " being taken down from her horse by the
Earl of Leicester, master of the horse, at the church wall of Mortlake,
did see some of the properties of that glass, to her Majesty's great con-

tentment and delight." *     Upon the ground where Dee's laboratory
stood were afterwards erected the tapestry works of Sir F. Crane; they
were established in 1619; and to this circumstance we are probably indebted for the possession of the famous cartoons of Raphael, purchased
as copies for the artizan.     Leading from Mortlake are byways to Rich-

MORTLAKE CHURCH.

mond and to Kew, through low and ill-drained grounds, principally
market gardens.     Here and there, however, we meet some stately

* He records the incident in his very curious diary.  The queen, who believed in his powers of
judicial astrology, was desirous of seeing for herself the spirits he conjured in his magic crystal.  She
came from the palace, at Richmond, to Dr. Dee's house, but the funeral of the astrologer's wife had
only been performed two hours before, which was the reason that her majesty would not enter the house.
Aubrey tells us that Dee was buried in this church "in the chancel, a little toward the south side."

manor-house, seated in solitary and aristocratic grandeur amid groups of ancient and wide-spreading cedars.

MORTLAKE CHURCH is in part a very ancient edifice, dating so far back as 1348, although the earliest date on the building is 1543.* The outward door of the belfry is, however, said to be the only remaining part of the original structure. It is full of interesting monuments. Mortlake is a long street of houses, with gardens to the Thames. Its chief feature from the river is a large brewery; but it has a few picturesque remains of old gardens, occasionally preserving an old "bit" of the scenery, which may serve to show its peculiar character—a mingling

OLD SUMMER-HOUSE AT MORTLAKE.

of the antique with the grotesque—relics of old grandeur in combination with squalid poverty—picturesque only in pictures.

That portion of Barnes which is called the Terrace immediately succeeds Mortlake; it is a pretty and pleasant row of houses, chiefly let as lodgings, the place being much in favour during the summer months.

* This date is on a stone over the belfry door, inscribed " Vivat R. H. 8."

The village lies further back from the river—a straggling village, with a cluster of houses surrounding a pond. Some parts of the church are said to be as old as the time of Richard I.* The old "house"—Barne-Elms—in which Queen Elizabeth visited Sir Francis Walsingham, where lived Sir Henry Wyat, and where some time resided the poet Cowley, is one of the famous points of the district.

Until we arrive at Putney, there is nothing to detain the tourist after he leaves Barnes, unless he desire a peep at several "cozy" houses, called the Castelnau Villas ; we must, therefore, conduct him into Middlesex, and ask him to land at Chiswick, proceeding thence to the hamlet of Hammersmith.

There are few localities in the vicinity of London so interesting as the pretty and pleasant village of Chiswick. Its principal attraction is the charming and very beautifully decorated mansion of the Duke of Devonshire, with its delicious grounds and gardens. "The house was designed and erected by Richard Boyle, Earl of Burlington, whose skill in architecture has been proved by his works, and whose encouragement of his favourite science greatly promoted the progress of that taste which has since produced so many fine architectural examples in this country." The model which the architect generally followed is that of the Villa Capra, near Vicenza, the designer of which was the famous Palladio. It is magnificently furnished, and contains a collection of rare and valuable pictures. Here Charles Fox died, on the 13th September, 1806 ; and here George Canning "put on immortality," on the 8th of August, 1827.

---

* Mrs. Ann Baynard was buried here on the 10th June, 1697. We read in Lysons that "she was so fond of the study of divinity that she learned Greek to read St. Chrysostom in the original ; besides which she had numberless other accomplishments, on which, as she possessed them in common with many young ladies both of that and of the present age, I shall not enlarge." There is not now the least trace of her monument, which was at the east end of the churchyard. The inscription is copied from Aubrey :—

> " Here lies that happy maiden who often said
> That no man is happy until he is dead ;
> That the business of life is but playing the fool,
> Which hath no relation to saving the soul ;
> For of all the transactions that 's under the sun,
> Is doing of nothing—if that be not done,
> All wisdom and knowledge doth lie in this one.

The interest of Chiswick House is, however, surpassed by the church and churchyard of the village. In the former the architect, Kent, the associate of Lord Burlington in the adornment of the house and grounds, reposes in the vault of his patron; and here there is a fitting monument to Charles Whittingham, the printer, whose skill and taste gave to the Chiswick press a fame that "went over the world." The graveyard contains the ashes of many persons of note: the imperious Duchess of Cleveland here mingles with common clay; here "repose the remains" of Cromwell's daughter, Mary; here Holland, the actor, Garrick's friend, exchanged his motley for a winding-sheet; here Lord Macartney, the pioneer to China, rests from his labours; here calmly sleeps a man of marvellous genius, the exile Ugo Foscolo; here lies the painter Loutherbourg; and here, still speaking from his sculptured tomb, reposes the great artist, William Hogarth. The monument was erected by a subscription among his friends, and the epitaph was written by Garrick :—

> " Farewell! great painter of mankind,
>     Who reach'd the noblest point of art;
> Whose pictured morals charm the mind,
>     And through the eye correct the heart.
> If genius fire thee, reader, stay;
> If nature touch thee, drop a tear;
> If neither move thee, turn away,
>     For Hogarth's honour'd dust lies here."

At Chiswick Hogarth lived, died, and was buried; and his house—in which his predecessor was Sir James Thornhill, and his successor the excellent and accomplished clergyman, Cary, the translator of Dante—still stands, as a place of pilgrimage; it was his home, who, "while he faithfully followed Nature through all her varieties, and exposed with inimitable skill the infinite follies and vices of the world, was in himself an example of many virtues." *

The house at Chiswick was that in which Sir James Thornhill resided at the time of his daughter's elopement with Hogarth. It is gloomy, with high walls; long walls of brick bound the way to it from the main

---

* Vide " Pilgrimages to English Shrines: the Tomb of Hogarth." By Mrs. S. C. Hall. Also " Tombs of English Artists: Hogarth," by F. W. Fairholt, *Art Journal*, April, 1858, from which we b rrow our illustration and description.

street of the village. In the days of Anne it was far from the metropolis, but now it is as much a London suburb as Islington was then. Large as the house appears, it is really somewhat small, for it is all frontage, and only one room deep, without any back windows. The garden is not larger than such a house would require, and the small stable at its further extremity has over it a room Hogarth used as a studio. Against the garden wall are two narrow upright slabs of stone, commemorating

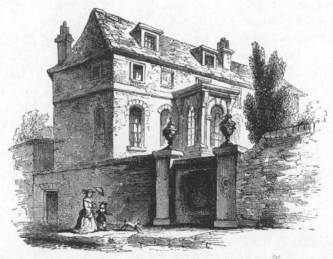

HOGARTH'S HOUSE.

the graves of his dog and bird. The words upon the former—"Life to the last enjoyed, here Pompey lies"—are a satirical paraphrase on the epitaph to Churchill, the satirist, in Dover Church, with whom he had passed some years of friendship, but who had bitterly attacked Hogarth at the close of his career; not, however, without provocation on the part of the latter.

In Chiswick churchyard the painter reposes, and he is not the only artist buried there. Loutherbourg rests under a most heavy and ambitious monument; a slab against the wall near it records the name of James Fittler, the engraver; and William Sharpe, another of our best

English engravers, was buried, by his desire, near Hogarth.   The tomb
of the latter artist is a not ungraceful structure, exhibiting on one side
a *basso-relievo* indicative of his art; an inscription on the east side
notes the death of Hogarth, in October, 1764, at the age of sixty-seven,
and his wife in November, 1789, at the age of eighty.   His sister's
death is recorded on the south side, in August, 1771, at the age of
seventy; and that of Mary Lewis, his niece, who acted as saleswoman
at his house in Leicester Square, and who died in 1808, at the age of

HOGARTH'S TOMB.

eighty-eight.   The other face of the monument has an inscription to his
mother-in-law, the widow of Sir James Thornhill, who was first buried
in this grave in 1757.   This monument had fallen into much decay, and
had become the theme of public comment; but it has been admirably
restored, and on a small piece of granite at its base is inscribed,—
" Rebuilt by William Hogarth, of Aberdeen, in 1856."   All honour to
his northern namesake's liberality and taste !

We might linger long, and with advantage, in this the most inte-

resting of the many graveyards of England, in which repose the ashes of
the great; but we must resume our voyage, glancing at "the Water-
works," one of the metropolitan supplies of "pure water," and landing
at the graceful suspension bridge which crosses the Thames and conducts
to Hammersmith.*

The name of Hammersmith is not found in any record prior to the
reign of Elizabeth, yet it is now a populous suburb of the metropolis;

HAMMERSMITH BRIDGE.

for, although distant some five miles from Hyde Park Corner, there is
scarcely any interruption to the line of streets that leads to it through
Knightsbridge and Kensington. Its pretty and picturesque church
dates no further back than the reign of Charles I. It was built at the
cost of Sir Nicholas Crispe, merchant of London, a loyal adherent of the

---

* The bridge was constructed in 1828, from the designs and under the superintendence of William
Tierney Clarke. He afterwards erected one similar at Prague, in Bohemia.

monarchy during the contest between the Crown and the Parliament. His history is touchingly told in an inscription placed under an effigy of Charles I., at the base of which is a pedestal surmounted by an urn.

" Within this urn is entombed the heart of Sir Nicholas Crispe, Knight and Baronet, a loyal sharer in the sufferings of his late and present Majesty. He first settled the trade of gold from Guinea, and there built the castle of Cormantine. Died the 26th July, 1665, aged 67 years."

In the churchyard are many monuments with foreign names, servants in the household of the Margravine of Anspach, who once inhabited

HAMMERSMITH CHURCH.

Brandenburgh House—a house which became famous as the residence of Queen Caroline, the wife of George IV. It was razed to the ground very soon after her death.

We resume our voyage, and passing between banks on which are several graceful villas, although generally the land is low and cannot be healthy, we come in sight of the ugly structure—ungainly piles of decaying wood—which, crossing the Thames, unites the villages of Putney and Fulham. Both these villages are famous in history, and we must delay the tourist while we visit them. Let us land at Putney, first noticing that group of houses, in the centre of which is one that is familiar to all the "oarsmen" of the river, the well-known "STAR AND GARTER," the head-quarters of several aquatic clubs. The illustration has been sketched to include one of the most conspicuous, though not the most picturesque, objects in this part of our course—the Club-house of

THE STAR AND GARTER, PUTNEY BRIDGE.

the London Rowing Club, the largest association of amateurs that has ever existed on the Thames in connection with this healthful recreation. It has been recently erected at considerable cost; and if the popularity of the club continues to increase as it has done during the last two years, it will, we imagine, soon be found too small for the accommodation of its members.

We take this opportunity of introducing to our readers drawings and descriptions of the principal varieties of boats used upon the Thames, so that—with such as we have already noticed—we may furnish a perfect idea of "the craft" of all kinds which float over its surface. We owe to the courtesy of Messrs. Searle, of Lambeth, the very eminent boat-builders, the privilege of making our sketches in their yard at Stangate, while every facility in the way of accurate description was afforded to us by them.

The Thames watermen have long been celebrated for their superior style of rowing; in all their matches with foreign competitors they have invariably been successful; and, indeed, until the last few years, no other English watermen stood the smallest chance when contending against them. It was only after repeated unsuccessful contests that the Tyne watermen proved victorious, and this result was only obtained after acquiring the Thames style of rowing. Latterly, the Manchester and Liverpool watermen have greatly improved; but the Thames men may still be considered the best in the world.

The boat which is universally used by the above-bridge watermen is known as the Thames WHERRY. The peculiarities of this boat are, its

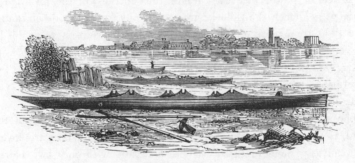

THE THAMES WHERRY.

shallowness (which is compensated for by its spreading in the centre), and its sharpness at the head and stern—the head, or bow, tapering gradually from the rullocks (row-locks), and from the keel, until it ends in a sharp point, which is cased in iron; the stern also tapers off, but ends with a stern-post, rising perpendicularly from the keel, to which a rudder can be attached at pleasure.

The boat represented is what is technically termed a *ran-dan* wherry —that is to say, it has three sets of rullocks, so that three persons can row at the same time in it (but this is not compulsory, as the watermen generally row single-handed): when this is the case, the men fore and aft each row an oar, and the one in the centre rows a pair of sculls—on him also devolves the task of steering the boat.

The waterman's wherry is built heavy enough to bear the weight of six or eight passengers besides the rower, but as this kind of boat is particularly adapted for speed, much lighter ones of the same construction have been built for amateur pleasure-boats, and for rowing purposes.

These light racing wherries are all *outrigged*,—but as this term may not be understood by the general reader, we will here give a short description of an outrigged boat. In order to gain great speed, boats have latterly been built very long and very narrow, thereby offering less resistance to the water; but, as the boats were built more narrow, the oars and sculls had to be shortened in proportion, and in consequence a great deal of power was lost, through the shortness of the leverage; to obviate this defect, the rullocks are carried out from the side of the boat by a light framework of iron, by this means the rowers are enabled to use very long oars or sculls, whilst the boat is built as narrow as possible. Outriggers were first brought into general notice by the Claspers (Tyne watermen), who rowed at the Thames Regatta about twelve years back.

The outrigged wherries are very subject, from the lightness of their build, to ship the water, to obviate which the head and stern are covered with canvas. Some of these wherries are built with only two pairs of rullocks; these· are used either for two pairs of sculls or a pair of oars.

The lightest kind of wherry is generally called a *sculler*, or *wager-boat;* they are chiefly used for matches, and require great skill and dexterity on the part of the rower, as the slightest thing upsets them—the lightest only weigh thirty-five pounds; to the racing boats we have more directly referred in our notices of Oxford.

The SKIFF is another kind of boat much used on the Thames; it greatly differs from the wherry in form, being sh orter and wider, and the gunwale rising higher from the water: it is much better adapted for rough water, and is consequently in general use among the below-bridge watermen.   This boat is also used for sailing.   There is a boat now in great vogue on the Thames, called a Gig, which differs very slightly from the skiff, the chief distinction being that the gunwale

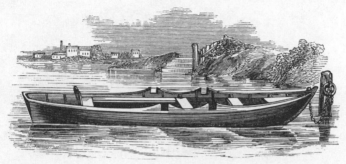

THE SKIFF.   a

of the gig is perfectly straight from stem to stern, whilst that of the skiff rises at both ends ; the bow of the latter boat also slopes gradually up from the keel, whilst that of the gig rises very abruptly.

THE SHALLOP.

The SHALLOP is a boat built on the same principle as the skiff, but of a much larger size, and with an awning to cover the sitters : this awning is sometimes supported by a light iron framework, and some-times it is formed of wood.

The chief peculiarity of the FUNNY is its having a *head* and *stern*

3 F

exactly alike; it is a shorter boat than a wherry, and more easily managed, which makes it valuable to amateurs.

THE FUNNY. a

CUTTERS is the generic term used on the Thames for long oared boats, built for four, six, or eight rowers; they are outrigged, and

EIGHT-OARED CUTTER.

covered at the head and stern with canvas: the eight-oared boats are seventy feet long.

"Putney," according to Lysons, "is in Domesday called Putelei; in subsequent records it is spelt Puttenheth, or Pottenheth." The village leads up-hill, through a street of good villa houses, to Wimbledon and Roehampton. It has an old church, and is famous as the birthplace of three remarkable men: West, Bishop of Ely, the son of a baker here; Thomas Cromwell, Earl of Essex, whose father was a blacksmith in the town; and Gibbon, the historian.

The tourist will derive greater interest, however, from a visit to the Middlesex side of the river, and that interest will continue almost unbroken until he reaches London : along its Surrey banks are to be seen only objects that blot the landscape, however much they may add to the solid wealth of the country; for, excepting a group of very ugly and cheerless, though costly domiciles, that have replaced as many quaint old dwellings of a by-gone time, and which skirt the river immediately after leaving Putney, there is but a succession of factories and small cottage houses, which serve to shelter labourers and artizans; unwholesome-looking swamps divide the space with yards, and quays, and waggon-sheds, auxiliaries to manufactories of gin, soap, starch, silk, paper, candles, beer, and vitriol—the first named and the last being no doubt mutually dependant for aid and assistance. Such is the only picture to be contemplated all the way; it includes long, straggling Wandsworth, and longer and still more straggling Battersea, both with modern and ugly churches, that of Battersea being especially odious, inasmuch as it is thrust forward almost into the current, and it is impossible to avoid looking at an object, in producing which the architect seems to have studied how far it was in his power to render it repugnant : we, therefore, pass rapidly over the Surrey side of the Thames between the bridges at Putney and Battersea.

We breathe more freely as we cross the bridge and enter the village of Fulham ; resting awhile, it may be, at the venerable and still comfortable inn, which was there "beyond the time of legal memory," to enjoy a chat, perhaps, with Phelps, the veteran waterman, who still plies his "trim-built wherry," and is even to-day a good specimen of what his class were long ago, before the application of steam and the omnibus deprived them of their employers, and made mockeries of the privileges of—"jolly young watermen." Voyaging down stream, however, there are a few houses upon the banks which may not be passed without a word of comment. The first is Craven Cottage, once the residence of Walsh Porter, and in later times of Sir Bulwer Lytton ; we recall the days we have passed there with more than mere pleasure. The Bishop's Palace succeeds—from which one good man has recently been removed to a vault in the neighbouring church, to be succeeded by another who has already made the country his grateful debtor. The house that has "a gothic look" is Prior's Bank : we know not who dwells there now, but not many years ago it was the residence of "a pair of friends," who made it renowned, not alone for genuine and liberal hospitality, but for refined elegance, and as a new birth-place of the graces, the whims, the amusements, and the "teachings" of that "olden time" of which the mansion externally and internally professed to be a copy. The place is hallowed in the memories of many men of letters, of art, and of wit, who

FULHAM CHURCH, AND PRIOR'S BANK.

had, and gave, enjoyment there : Prior's Bank will find a place in the biographies of not a few "celebrities" of the nineteenth century. In a little group of small cottage houses close beside, lived Theodore Hook during the greater part of his life ; a history of this small dwelling might fill a volume ; it has been removed to make way for a hideous bridge (uglier, if possible, than its neighbour), by which a water-company carries supplies to London ; while the Yorick of so many "tables" sleeps among a crowd of right reverend prelates, in a retired nook of the churchyard close at hand. The church and churchyard will largely repay a visit ; in the latter repose the ashes of forty bishops, so at least says the cicerone of the place; but the series may begin with Irkenwald, that bishop under "Sigibert, king of the West Saxons, and Conrad, king of the Mercians," to whom Fulham—then called Fullenhanne or Fullen-holme, which signifies *volucrum domus*, "the habitacle of birdes or the place of fowles"—was originally given. Be they forty, more or less, however, among these pillars of the English church are men of whom the British nation will be for ever proud; men of learning, virtue, and piety; honour to their memories; he must be of a cold heart and of a dead imagination who can stand unmoved in this small area of tombs, where sleep in death Sherlock and Lowth, and many others, "whose works live after them," and to whose graves tens of thousands yet to come will bow in grateful homage.

Between Fulham and Chelsea, to which we now hasten, passing by several graceful villas, we arrive at "Cremorne," a popular place of

BATTERSEA BRIDGE.

amusement that has taken the place of old Vauxhall. But an object of far higher interest soon greets the voyager; it is the hospital in which

the old and worn soldiers who have served their country repose after
their toils. We have first, however, to row under BATTERSEA BRIDGE.
Like that of Putney, it is coarse, unseemly, and inconvenient in
character, all its defects being brought into strong relief by the beautiful
structure which now crosses the river a little lower down.

We must step ashore at Chelsea; for this locality is fertile of useful
suggestions and interesting associations.

Lyndsay House is seen on the left, and its old history is full of
interest, enhanced by the records of later residents. Here the painter,
Martin, lived and worked; and near it the great artist, Turner, died—
ungracefully, to say the least. But associations multiply as we pass

CHELSEA CHURCH.

London-ward. A narrow lane, such as we still see sometimes at port
towns, leads to the venerable church. The monument to the memory of
Sir Hans Sloane occupies the east corner of the churchyard. The
church and many neighbouring localities derive interest from associations
with the history of that great and good statesman, Sir Thomas More.
At his house, in Chelsea, the eighth Harry frequently visited his
"beloved Chancellor,"—"a house neither mean nor subject to envy,
yet magnificent and commodious enough," with gardens " wonderfully

charming," with "green meadows and woody eminences all around." *
Here the Abbot of Westminster took him into custody for refusing to
"take the king as head of his church;" and for denying the king's
supremacy, he was beheaded on Tower Hill. He had anticipated his
death, and had caused his tomb to be made in the church at Chelsea.

SIR THOMAS MORE'S HOUSE.

Whether his body was interred there is doubtful; but the place is full
of memories of him of whom it was quaintly said—

> " When MORE some time had chancellor been,
>     No MORE suits did remain;
> The same shall never MORE be seen,
>     Till MORE be there again."

A few yards farther—leaving to the right the pretty pier at which
steam-boats ply every ten minutes, and where a few of the old watermen still linger—we reach that famous row of "good houses" known as
CHEYNE WALK,† a pleasant promenade, and one of the most memorable
"bits" that skirt the river-side.

---

* The house stood some distance from the river, at the back of Lyndsay House, on ground now
occupied by the Moravian burial-ground. The gardens reached to the Thames, and from their water-
gate More stepped into the barge that carried him to the Tower.

† Our view of Cheyne Walk is taken from the centre, looking towards London. The first house on
the left, with the old sign-board in front of it, is " Don Saltero's Coffee-house," a place much renowned

A few steps onward, if we are foot passengers, " a row " of a hundred yards if we are voyagers—passing on the left the old " Physic Garden," bequeathed, in the year 1673, by Charles Cheyne, Esq., Lord of the Manor of Chelsea, to the company of Apothecaries for a term of years,

CHEYNE WALK.

and afterwards purchased and presented to them by Sir Hans Sloane— and we reach the long-renowned HOSPITAL OF CHELSEA. We picture the side view, as it is seen on ascending or descending the river. Assuredly there are few who cross the Thames to visit either the railway station at Battersea, or Battersea Park, who will not have their attention directed to this deeply interesting monument of an age which is unhap-

in the days of Queen Anne, and celebrated by Steele in his *Tatler*. Himself and other wits of the day patronised its proprietor, James Salter, whom they christened " Don Saltero." He had been servant to Sir Hans Sloane, and opened this house in 1695 with a collection of curiosities, the refuse of Sir Hans' collection, calling his house " the Museum Coffee-house." It was greatly added to by continued gifts, and this " eminent barber and antiquary," as Steele styles him, became famous for his " curiosities." The walls were covered with glass cases, stuffed alligators hung from the ceiling, and a " catalogue of the rarities to be seen " published, " price two-pence." It is a singular specimen of what were popular curiosities a century ago : " A piece of Solomon's Temple ," " Job's tears which grew on a tree, wherewith they make anodyne necklaces," " a giant's tooth," " a young frog in a tobacco-stopper," and " a flea-trap," are among the " curiosities ;" with which, however, were mixed really curious things. Pennant mentions having been taken there when a boy, and that his father saw there Richard Cromwell (son of the Protector), " a little and very neat old man, with a most placid countenance."

pily suggestive less of pride than of humiliation, but of which this home
for battle-tried and weather-beaten soldiers is one of the redeeming
points; where for two centuries the brave men who receive grateful
proofs of a nation's gratitude tell

"How fields were won."

Of Chelsea Hospital the front view is the most striking; for, though
it does not possess any very remarkable architectural feature, it has a

CHELSEA HOSPITAL: SIDE-VIEW.

certain "nobility of look," and all its associations are of great interest.
The foundation of the hospital—or, as its inmates prefer to call it, "the
college"—is known to have been one of the few good deeds of the
voluptuary, Charles II.—being an exception to the rule as regarded the
sovereign

"Who never said a foolish thing,
And never did a wise one."

There is a tradition, but it is without proof, that "the merry monarch"
was influenced to this merciful act by his mistress, Nell Gwynne. Be it
as it may, it was a fortunate circumstance for the country. Many a

3 F

battle has been won for these kingdoms by the knowledge that the maimed soldier can never be a deserted beggar—by the certainty that honourable scars will be healed by other ointment than that of mere pity—by the assurance that shelter and comfort are prepared for the wounded or aged, of whom a nation becomes the guardian and protector. In this " Palace Hospital " are contained—so that all visitors as well as inmates may continually see them—various trophies taken at victories gained by British soldiers over those of France : it is a proud as well as a numerous collection.

"It has often been remarked by foreigners," says Faulkner, in his account of Chelsea, "that the charitable foundations of England were

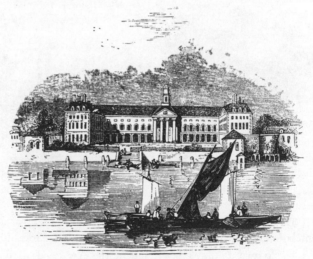

CHELSEA HOSPITAL : FRONT VIEW.

more fitted, by their grandeur and extent, for the residence of kings ; while her palaces, by their external appearance, seemed better calculated for the reception of the needy and unfortunate. But surely they could not have paid a nation greater honour ; and when we survey the noble fabrics at Chelsea and at Greenwich, we cannot but feel proud that we live in a country which constantly affords an asylum to the helpless

wanderer—which relieves the wants of the needy and allays the sufferings of the sick to an extent, and with a liberality, unknown throughout
the rest of Europe."

This edifice stands upon the site of a college founded by King
James I. for the study of polemical divinity. It was originally projected by Dr. Matthew Sutcliffe, Dean of Exeter, in the early part of
that king's reign. James laid the first stone in May, 1609, and in the
same month of the succeeding year granted a charter of incorporation,
in which the number of members was limited to nineteen, and a provost,
and the institution was to be named " King James's College." Sutcliffe
liberally gave toward the foundation all he could, and he was empowered
by an act of Parliament to receive any aid in the way of bequest or
contribution, but so little came that " scarce an eighth part was erected,
as only one side of the first quadrangle was ever completed, and this
range of building, according to Fuller, cost above three thousand
pounds." After Sutcliffe's death, in 1629, it languished, and was finally
broken up in the troubles of the Great Civil War. In the year 1669,
Charles gave the ground and buildings to the Royal Society. They
endeavoured for some time to let the premises advantageously, but
failing in their attempts, they sold them again to Sir Stephen Fox, Lord
Commissioner of the Treasury, for the king's use, for the sum of £1300.

On the 12th of March, 1682, Charles II., attended by his principal
courtiers, laid the first stone of the present Hospital buildings, and Sir
Christopher Wren was the architect. Evelyn notes that in the following
month—" I was desired by Sir Stephen Fox and Sir Christopher Wren
to accompany them to Lambeth, with the plot and design of the college
to be built at Chelsey, to have the Archbishop's approbation." This
was obtained ; and Archbishop Sancroft gave £1000 toward the building, Sir Stephen Fox promising " that he would settle £5000 per annum
on it, and build to the value of £20,000." Tobias Rustat, yeoman of
the robes to the king, also contributed £1000, and presented the bronze
statue of Charles II. which still adorns the quadrangle. The entire
building was not completed till 1690, and the total cost is said to have
been £150,000. It accommodates about 400 inmates. The colonnade

and portico toward the river afford an agreeably sheltered walk for the old men in bad weather, and communicates between the two wings. The hall is spacious, and in it is a large allegorical picture of Charles II. on horseback, by Verrio, whose ceiling-painting at Hampton Court we have already noted.  The chapel has an altar-piece by Sebastian Ricci, painted when he visited this country in the reign of Anne; it represents the Resurrection of our Saviour.

Battersea Park has been laid out only within the last two or three years; it is therefore in its infancy—the shrubs are miniatures; but to the next generation it will be one of the chief adornments of the metro-politan suburbs.  From it we look upon the old wooden bridge, and the Dutch-looking church and village of Chelsea.  Beyond the hospital is the NEW BRIDGE, constructed by Thomas Page, Esq.  It is a toll bridge;

THE NEW BRIDGE AT CHELSEA.

and it has been pleasantly said that " Government gave a park to the people, and placed a toll-bar at the gate to keep them out of it."  The bridge is the most beautiful of the many that cross the Thames between its source and its fall into the sea; and its value is much enhanced by the charmingly constructed station that stands in a dell almost at its foot—"the West End Crystal Palace Station," that communicates also with Brighton and the southern counties of England.

Close to the gardens of Chelsea College, on the London side, stood the once-famed RANELAGH.* The line of trees which parts the college garden from the small garden appropriated to the veterans who are here domiciled after their warlike labours, was once a part of the "walks" of Ranelagh; and a few years ago the remains of the lamp-irons which lit it were still upon some of the tree stems. This most aristocratic place of amusement was opened in 1742. The great feature of the spot was

RANELAGH.

an enormous Rotunda, a hundred and eighty-five feet in diameter, in which concerts took place, and which is the conspicuous object in our view, copied from a print published in 1743. Royalty and nobility patronised the place largely. During its fashionable career Ranelagh and its pleasures are frequently referred to by the writers of the era,

* It obtained its name from being erected on the site of the mansion of Richard, Earl of Ranelagh, who was Paymaster-General of the forces, and one of the Commissioners of Chelsea Hospital, during the reign of Charles II., and obtained from the Crown a grant of the land. He died in 1712, and in 1733 the house and grounds were sold in lots.

but none have left better accounts than the amusing letter-writer, Horace Walpole: in a letter to Sir Horace Mann, dated May 26, 1742, he says :—" Two nights ago Ranelagh Gardens were opened at Chelsea ; the prince, princess, duke, much nobility, and much mob besides, were there.   There is a vast amphitheatre, finely gilt, painted, and illumi- nated, into which everybody that loves eating, drinking, staring, or crowding, is admitted for twelve pence.   The building and disposition of the gardens cost nineteen thousand pounds.   Twice a week there are to be *ridottos* at guinea tickets, for which they are to have a supper and music."   For a time it drew all company away from Vauxhall, which until then was unrivalled.   In 1748, Walpole notes that its attractions had not decreased : " Ranelagh is so crowded, that going there t' other night in a string of coaches, we had to stop six-and-thirty minutes."   But its reign was brief,—half a century saw it terminate ; fashion soon changed ; Ranelagh was found at last to be " dull"—the public got tired of merely parading round the orchestra.in the great hall, and listening to music. Bloomfield has described the effect on himself :—

> " To Ranelagh once in my life
> By good-natured force I was driven ;
> The nations had ceased their long strife,
> And peace beam'd her radiance from heaven !
> What wonders were here to be found,
> That a clown might enjoy or disdain !
> First, we traced the gay circle all round,
> Ay—*and then we went round it again !* "

The diameter of the interior of the Rotunda was one hundred and fifty feet.   Round the walls were forty seven boxes for refresh- ments, with doors at the back leading to the gardens ; they were lit by bell lamps, and divided from each other by piers covered with looking-glass.   Twenty-three chandeliers hung from the ceiling.   An arcade and gallery projected from the lowest story of the building outside ; the entrances were by four Doric porticoes.   When the attrac- tion of concerts failed, masquerades were substituted ; but patronage diminished, and in 1805 it was taken down.   The new road from Sloane Street to the Suspension Bridge passes over a part of the grounds.   In the immediate neighbourhood was the " Old Chelsea" porcelain works, concerning which very little is known, but which produced efforts of art that may vie with the best issues of Dresden and Sèvres.

The whole of the district hence to Westminster, and from the river inland to Pimlico was formerly a most lonely and dangerous locality, and so continued until the commencement of the present century. The Five Fields and Tothill Fields, which comprehended nearly the whole space, were desert spots, crossed here and there with footpaths and raised causeways, flanked by ditches, which divided a few wretched gardens, containing some half-dozen ruined sheds scattered over the ground, inhabited by the very worst classes of the London community, and where it was not safe for strangers to travel. Hollar has preserved its features in his "view of the pest-houses" in Tothill Fields, in 1665; London is seen in the distance, as if on the confines of a desert. These pest-houses were set apart in this dismal and secluded locality for the cure of such unfortunates as were afflicted; and the churchwardens' accounts furnish us with notes of monies paid for their support. Now this spot is thickly covered with houses, streets, and squares; and aristocratic Belgravia occupies the once worthless marsh-land of old Chelsea.

The opposite bank of the river was sacred to the market-gardener until a very recent period. The first great change was effected by the South-Western Railway, which fixed its opening station originally at Nine Elms, where an extensive "goods station" still remains. Between this spot and Vauxhall Bridge, thirty years ago, was a place of general recreation, known as Cumberland Gardens: it consisted of an open space toward the Thames, laid out in grass-plats, and surrounded by open boxes and tables for refreshments, after the style of old-fashioned suburban tea-gardens. The ground is now occupied by a distillery. The bridge which crosses the Thames at Vauxhall is of cast iron, and was begun by Rennie, and finished by Walker. It was opened for traffic in 1816. The trees seen above the houses at the foot of the Surrey side of the bridge are those of Vauxhall Gardens, which have been of late years only opened at long intervals: they were once the glory of English pleasure-gardens, frequented by the highest in the land, from the gay days of Charles II. to those of "the Regency;" and were

celebrated in musical history for talent of the highest kind here introduced to the public. In the old orchestra, whose towering summit
may be seen from the Thames, the greatest musical celebrities have
sung. Handel, Dr. Arne, and Hook superintended its concerts, and
Hogarth decorated its walls with paintings. It obtained its name from a
very old mansion which once stood near it.* This old manor-house of
FAWKES HALL, as it existed in the reign of Charles I., is shown in our
engraving; at that time it was described as a "fair dwelling-house,

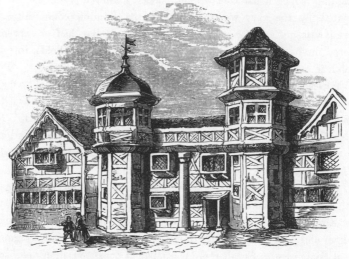

FAWKES-HALL.

strongly built, of three stories high, and a pier staircase breaking out
from it, nineteen feet square." This staircase occupied one of the towers,
in accordance with the ancient plan, and the house was a curious specimen of the old timber houses of the gentry in the sixteenth century.
It appears to have obtained its name from Foukes de Brent, who married

---

* It has supplied a name to similar places abroad, where "Wauxhall" indicates generally a garden
illuminated for promenades and singing. Its old title is given by Pepys in his Diary, who describes
how he went "by water to Fox Hall, and then walked into Spring Garden." Over the gate of the old
house at Vauxhall, erected for his own residence by Jonathan Tyers, the proprietor at the early part
of the last century, the old name, "Spring Garden," may still be seen.

the heiress of the manor, the Countess of Albemarle, sister to Baldwin, Archbishop of Canterbury; and it was granted, by the name of the manor of Foukeshall, by Edward II. to his favourite, Hugh le Despencer. In 1615, the records of the Duchy of Cornwall prove the premises now known as Vauxhall Gardens to have been the leasehold property of Jane Vaux, widow of John Vaux, citizen and vintner of London, and a benefactor to the parish of Lambeth. It has always remained, with the manor of Kennington, as the property of the Crown, and belongs to the Prince of Wales as part of his Duchy of Cornwall.

Evelyn and Pepys note, in their instructive and amusing diaries, many of their visits to this favourite resort of the Londoners. The reason of its popularity may be gathered by Pepys's description of his own inducements to go there. He found there in May, 1667, " a great deal of company, and the weather and garde s pleasant: and it is very pleasant and cheap going thither, for a man 1. ᐧ go to spend what he will or nothing, all as one. But to hear the nightingale, and the birds, and here fiddles, and there a harp, and here a Jew's trump, and here laughing, and there fine people walking, is mighty diverting." Evelyn styles it, "a pretty contrived plantation." Addison has left us in the *Spectator* a good description of the garden in May, 1712, when it had lost nothing of its rural beauty. His visit is supposed to be in company with the immortal Sir Roger de Coverley, as he " had promised to go with him on the water to Spring Garden in case it proved a good evening." He details the boat journey from the Temple Stairs, and continues: " We were now arrived at Spring Garden, which is exquisitely pleasant at this time of the year. When I considered the fragrancy of the walks and bowers, with the choirs of birds that sang upon the trees, and the loose tribe of people that walked under their shade, I could not but look upon the place as a kind of Mahometan paradise. Sir Roger told me it put him in mind of a little coppice by his house in the country, which his chaplain used to call an aviary of nightingales." The nightingales disappeared as the suburbs of London increased; and it is said that after the gardens came into the possession of Jonathan Tyers, and the birds got thinner, men were hidden among the trees to imitate the

3 G

note of the popular favourites.  Tyers obtained his lease in 1730; and he introduced music, illuminations, and amusements of various kinds; occasionally adding to the attractions by employing such artists as Hogarth and Hayman to decorate his saloons with pictures, and Roubiliac with statuary.*  In 1740, the price of admission was one shilling; season tickets at two guineas admitted two persons on each night; "no persons in livery to walk in the gardens."  At this time it was usual to go in boats from London; but in 1750, on the opening of Westminster Bridge, Mr. Tyers purchased and pulled down a number of old houses opposite Lambeth Church, which gave an opportunity for making a coach road to the gardens, and "on the first night of the entertainments

THE LUFF-BARGE.

beginning, so great was the novelty of visiting that delightful spot in a carriage, that the coaches reached from the gardens to beyond Lambeth

* The famous statue of Handel, the work which first brought this great sculptor into public notice, was executed for the Gardens.  After passing through many hands, it was purchased about five years ago by the Sacred Harmonic Society, and is now in their rooms at Exeter Hall.

Church, which is near a mile." *   Tyers died in 1767, and was so much
attached to the gardens that he caused himself to be carried round them
but a few hours before his death ; after which event they were conducted
by his sons till 1785.   In fact, no public place of amusement has such
abundant "memories" associated with its career as Vauxhall, and none are
of such ancient standing, connecting the era of Charles II. with our own.

Dropping quietly down the stream, we often encounter the LUFF-BARGE.
It is a smaller class of barge than the square barge of the Thames,
being sharp forward, and altogether more like an ordinary vessel.   Perhaps this accounts for the name of clipper-barge, which it sometimes
receives.   Luff-barges are rigged with a sprit and foresail, without a
mizen, and generally carry goods where larger vessels are unable to go :
their trade is mostly confined to London and the upper part of the river.

On the Middlesex bank of the river, at a short distance from the
bridge, we may note one of those steam-boat piers which have been such
conspicuous objects in our journey from Wandsworth to London, and
which the traffic in cheap boats has rendered necessary for the thousands
of passengers who have again taken "the silent highway of the Thames"
for their road.   Twenty years ago this enormous traffic did not exist,
and in the early part of the last century, fishermen threw their nets in
the river here, not without hope of a salmon.   Now, the water is in a
constant state of turmoil and mud, rendering the necessity for occasional
visits, at different spots, of the BALLAST-DREDGER †—a heavy-looking but
picturesque boat, that clears the stream by a rotary series of iron

---

* Nicholl's "History of Lambeth."

† Curious things are occasionally " fished up " from the Thames by these machines.  The Seal of
Edward I. for the port of London was found in 1810, and has been engraved in " Hone's Every-Day
Book," vol. ii.  We engrave two bronze swords found in the Thames, near Vauxhall.  They are the

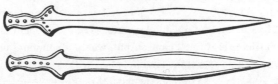

primitive weapons of the ancient Britons; and, as others precisely similar are found in Roman settlements, they were probably brought by ancient traders in exchange for British tin.

buckets, which dig into the soil, fill themselves, and, passing up an incline, empty into a boat beside them the deposit of gravel and mud.

The MILLBANK PRISON, once termed the Penitentiary, which is seen in the background of our view of the pier, is the only great prison on the Thames bank. Its ground-plan is very peculiar, and in all maps of London looks like an ornamental star : a series of wings radiate from a centre, where the governor's house is placed, which thus commands

BALLAST-DREDGER.

the whole establishment. It originated with Jeremy Bentham, and is chiefly used for hardened offenders, or criminals condemned to transportation or the hulks. The site was purchased of the Marquis of Salisbury for £12,000, in 1799. The soil is a deep peat, and the foundations had to be laid on a solid concrete. It lies low, and is unhealthy. The only entrance is at the Thames front, where a commodious esplanade is formed, and there is a stone landing-place with stairs. It is calculated that from 4000 to 5000 prisoners pass through it yearly. It contains more than 1500 cells, and was constructed at a cost of nearly half a million of money. It is now in much disfavour, owing to its situation, and is greatly dreaded by offenders; it may be said to be the most terrible of London prisons. The steamboat pier is one of a series erected on the Thames banks, between Wandsworth and Greenwich, for the use of the boats plying "above bridge" or "below,"—"*the*" bridge being London Bridge, once the only one which spanned the river. These piers float between solid frameworks of timber, which break the force of the tide, and support lamps. The landing-stage is commodious,

MILLBANK PRISON AND STEAM-BOAT PIER.

with open seats for voyagers, protected by an awning. A flight of steps leads from the centre to the shore; and the whole is constructed to adapt itself to the rise and fall of the river at the ebb and flow of the tide.

Lambeth is on the opposite bank, and consists, as we see it from the river, of boat-builders' houses, lightermen's sheds, gas-works, manufacturers of cement and glue, potteries for stoneware,* drain-pipes, &c., and whitening-makers, whose wooden-framed open warehouses, with their thousands of "pennorths" drying in the air for the use of the London housemaids, are conspicuous objects in the uninviting scene.

---

* "The Vauxhall Pottery, established two centuries since by two Dutchmen, for the manufacture of old Delft ware, is probably the origin of all our modern potteries."—*Curiosities of London.* By J. Timbs, F.S.A.

LAMBETH PALACE and CHURCH now come in view; they are among the most interesting old buildings on the banks of the river. The church was rebuilt in 1852, and is a beautiful example of modern restoration. Before that time it was in a most neglected and unsightly state,—now it

LAMBETH PALACE.

is a model of neatness, and the memorial windows are very beautiful :* one is dedicated to the late Archbishop Howley, whose benevolent career was especially deserving this recognition.

Close beside it is the old brick gate-house of the palace, for more than six centuries the residence of the Archbishops of Canterbury. It was built by Archbishop Morton at the close of the fifteenth century. It consists of two square towers connected by an embattled recessed centre; the whole built of red brick, with stone quoins, the bricks

---

* In the churchyard, which is also beautifully kept, is the tomb of John Tradescant, who, at his house in the fields beyond, formed the first important museum in this country, in the reign of Charles II. It passed, at his death, to Elias Ashmole (who is also buried here), and now forms part of the Ashmolean Museum at Oxford.

arranged in an ornamental manner by the introduction of coloured glaze, forming a large chequered pattern over the surface, a fashion first introduced in the reign of Henry VII., when these towers were erected.   There is a spacious arched gateway and postern in the central recess. *  In these towers is the Record Room, filled with ancient archives connected with the See of Canterbury.   There is also a small prison here, walled with stone, and fitted with three strong rings of iron for the security of prisoners, one of whom — Richard Grafton — has recorded his name upon the walls.   On the water-side, the gate-house is connected by a long brick wall with the Lollards' Tower.   Above this wall may be seen the noble old hall (now converted into a library) built by Archbishop Juxon in the reign of Charles II.   It is constructed of dark red brick, dressed with stone, and having a series of bold buttresses.   The lantern which sur-mounts the centre of the roof is crowned by a vane, upon which is exhibited the arms of the See of Canterbury, impaled with those of Archbishop Juxon, and crowned with the mitre of the See.   This noble hall has been injured in its effect by its conversion into a library, the bookcases crowding the walls, and projecting too far forward.   It was first adapted to this use in 1830.   The library contains many valuable manuscripts and early printed books.   It is 93 feet in length, and 50 feet in height.   The Lollards' Tower is faced with stone towards the river, and still bears on that side the arms of Archbishop Chichely, by whom it was built in 1435; beneath them is an ornamented niche, where a figure of St. Thomas-à-Becket was once placed.   The prison is in the small adjoining tower, only to be entered by a steep staircase leading from the larger one.   It is seen to the extreme left of our view,—a narrow irregularly shaped room, fastened by an oaken door, formed of three layers of wood strongly riveted, and studded with great nails, the door case being of arched stone.   The room is about eight feet in

---

* " At this gate the *dole* immemorially given to the poor by the Archbishop of Canterbury is con-stantly distributed.   It consists of fifteen quartern loaves, nine stone of beef, and five shillings' worth of halfpence, divided into three equal portions, and distributed every Sunday, Tuesday, and Thursday among thirty poor parishioners of Lambeth, the beef being made into broth and served in pitchers."— TIMBS' *Curiosities of London.*

height, nearly fifteen in length, and eleven feet wide; lighted by two deeply-recessed narrow windows. The walls and ceiling are thickly covered with wood.\* A few names and inscriptions have been cut in

THE LOLLARDS' PRISON.

this wood by unhappy prisoners once confined here. The rings which chained them still remain. These lonely walls speak loudly of the nature of the good old times, when "dissent" led quickly to "death."†

We cannot here dwell on the interesting associations this venerable palace conjures up in the mind, nor attempt to record the varied impressions that arise from a visit within its ancient walls. For the artist it abounds with antique "bits:" one of its most picturesque rooms, the "GUARD CHAMBER," we engrave. It is mentioned by that name as early as 1424, and in it Archbishop Laud held his state on the day of his

---

\* A modern author has imagined that this was for the "comfort" of the prisoners; such an idea did not exist in the old times. It was intended to deaden all sound of the voice, either in talking or under the influence of torture, and is upon "the approved model" of the horrible dungeons of Germany and Italy, which were similarly constructed.

† Though popularly known as "The Lollards'" Tower, it cannot be proved with certainty that Wickliffe's followers were imprisoned here; but the great Reformer was examined in the old chapel of this palace, and it is more than probable that some of his sect were here confined. The inscriptions above-named seem to belong to the era of Henry VIII.

consecration. The roof is singularly elegant, with oaken ribs richly carved; it was admirably restored in 1832, having been previously hidden by a flat ceiling of plaster. The palace was restored throughout by Archbishop Howley between the years 1828 and 1848. This munificent prelate devoted a large sum to this necessary work of renovation and improvement; he rebuilt the whole of the residential portion in the

GUARD CHAMBER, LAMBETH PALACE.

Tudor style of architecture, at a cost of upwards of £60,000. The garden still preserves a park-like appearance, bounded by large trees. The gardens and grounds cover eighteen acres; but they are now surrounded by houses and factories that deface their beauty and destroy their salubrity.

From Lambeth to the opposite bank is one of the oldest ferries on the river, leading to "the Horseferry Road," which obtains that name from this ancient river-way. Successions of coal and corn wharves now

line the banks* until we reach the HOUSES OF PARLIAMENT. This magnificent pile starts up like a glorious giant from the hovels near it.  Its

HOUSES OF PARLIAMENT.

history is too well known to require lengthened notice here.  Designed
and erected by Sir Charles Barry, the buildings cover nearly eight acres

---

* When Vauxhall Bridge is passed, the terribly dirty state of the Thames becomes apparent; the
picture that follows is scarcely overdrawn :—

"The enormous traffic of London, its increased dirt, and even its increased and statutory habits of
cleanliness, its sewage, coal-smoke and coal-gas, tiers of barges, and steamboat piers, have done their
work; but not so the Corporation of London, ancient conservators of the *status quo* of a river, noble in
spite of its debasement; not so the Crown, or, worse than all, the population of London, and we may
say, the nation itself.  The lunging surf of the river steamers stirs from its oozy bed, in the rear of
some friendly obstruction, the sleepy sediment of the tainted Thames.  A ceaseless passage of steam-
craft ploughs through the sludgy compromise between the animal, the vegetable, and the mineral
kingdoms.  Feeble rays from a clouded sun glimmer through the murky atmosphere, and play with tarnished glister over the dingy flood.  Fishes, wiser in their generation than ourselves, have forsaken in
disgust a medium which in these latitudes has long since ceased to be a definite element; poisoned
by impurities to which their simple natures are utterly averse, and scared by circumstances over
which they feel they have no earthly control.  Odours that speak aloud stalk over the face of
the so-called 'waters.'  The Avernus of the Fleet Ditch finds articulate echo in the Cocytus of the
great Effra Sewer; and as we watch the tiny drainlet that dribbles down the shore at dead low-
water, we see how it is that 'every little helps' to corrupt the stream below, and adds a fiercer zest
to that satanic *Julienne* whose reek is for ever rising on the wings of Azrael, and foreshadows the
terrors of a new and a warmer world!"—*The Oarsman's Guide.*

of ground. The river front is 940 feet in length ; and there are more
than 500 apartments in the entire pile, exclusive of official residences,
state apartments, and the "Houses" of the senate of England. The
eastern or river front has a noble terrace 700 feet in length, and 33 feet
in width, lighted at night by a series of lamps on the parapet. It communicates with the retiring rooms used by the members of Parliament,
and is an agreeable promenade in summer evenings. The entire face of
the building is richly decorated with heraldic sculpture, displaying the
coat-armour of the English sovereigns from the earliest period, with

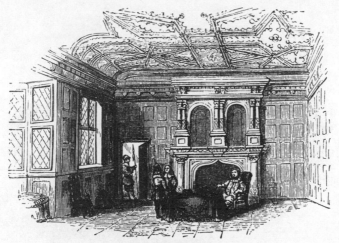

THE STAR-CHAMBER.

badges and inscriptions. At each end of the terrace are projecting
wings, with high towers, surmounted by gilded pinnacles and elaborate
sculptured ornament, being the most picturesque features of the entire
design. The vast Victoria Tower, seen to the left of our view, which
forms the royal entrance from New Palace Yard, is 340 feet in height,
and 80 feet square. The clock-tower, at the other extremity of the
building, is an imposing erection, second only to this gigantic tower,
but more highly enriched by ornament and gilding. The bell within
it weighs eight tons, and the clock-face is twice the size of that at

St. Paul's. Before the great fire of October 14, 1834, the river-frontage exhibited a strange mixture of old brick and stone buildings, with the stone front of the ancient "Chapel of St. Stephen" in the midst. The Speaker's house and garden were here; and close to the bridge was the old "STAR CHAMBER," rendered memorable by the state prosecutions of Charles I. From this official department issued the numerous levies, forced loans, and royal prosecutions which led to the great civil wars. The building was taken down in 1836. Our engraving is copied from a

OLD WESTMINSTER HALL.

drawing made before its demolition. It received its name from the stars painted on its ornamental ceiling.

The old Hall of Westminster now forms the vestibule to the Houses of Lords and Commons, and the Law Courts. This noble building was added to the old Royal Palace of the English kings, which once stood on this spot, by William Rufus, and was enlarged, altered, and adapted to its present form at the close of the fourteenth century, by Richard II. The roof, formed of Irish oak, and richly carved, is one of the most remarkable pieces of ancient carpentry at present existing. During the progress of reparations made in 1835, portions of the older Norman details of the building were discovered. The north porch, seen in our view, is believed to have been erected under the superintendence of William of Wykeham; we now, however, only look upon his design, for the entire front, having greatly decayed, was renovated in 1822. It was happily uninjured by the great fire which destroyed the surrounding buildings. Our engraving exhibits this front and the Law Courts as they were seen at the commencement of the present century, and is copied from a painting lent to us by the excellent Lord Chief Baron. The buildings to the left were the first removed, together with the Star Chamber. At that time the Law Courts retained (at the angle nearest the Abbey) some of the brickwork of the sixteenth century.

Westminster Bridge, the work of Labelye, a Swiss, was the second erected over the Thames, London having but one bridge until the year 1750, when this was opened. It was built on caissons, and the foundations are bad ; the stone is also decayed, and the bridge is now ruinous. At the present time workmen are employed night and day on the construction of a new bridge of iron, with stone piers, which is being executed by the admirable engineer, Mr. Page, who erected that at Chelsea.

Wordsworth's fine sonnet, "composed on Westminster Bridge, September 3, 1803," should not be omitted here. It is a noble picture of London at early morning : —

> " Earth hath not anything to show more fair ;
> Dull would he be of soul who could pass by
> A sight so touching in its majesty !
> This city now doth like a garment wear
> The beauty of the morning ; silent, bare,
> Ships, towers, domes, theatres, and temples lie
> Open unto the fields and to the sky,
> All bright and glittering in the smokeless air.
> Never did sun more beautifully steep
> In his first splendour, valley, rock, or hill !
> Ne'er saw I, never felt, a calm so deep !
> The river glideth at his own sweet will ;
> Dear God ! the very houses seem asleep,
> And all that mighty heart is lying still ! "

Richmond Terrace, and the houses in "the privy garden," known as

Whitehall Gardens (in one of which Sir Robert Peel died), occupy the site, as they partly preserve the name, of the royal gardens and palace which once covered the spot; the latter was destroyed by a fire January, 1698, through the carelessness of a Dutch washerwoman, one of William III.'s servants.  It was an inconvenient series of old buildings, all of it that now remains being Inigo Jones's famous banqueting-hall, the only portion ever executed of the great architect's grand design for its entire renovation.  Views of the street and river fronts may be seen in Brayley and Britton's "Londiniana," vol. ii.; and these authors say— "Had the building been completed according to Inigo Jones's design, it would have comprised four pavilions of similar character to the present banqueting-house, and we cannot but lament that an edifice conceived in a style of so much grandeur, and so truly worthy of becoming the abode of a British sovereign, should from any cause have been suffered to remain incomplete."  The "cause" was irresistible,—financial difficulties, and the Great Civil War in England, effectually stopped its progress.  The banqueting-room is now converted into a chapel.  The ceiling is decorated with an apotheosis of James I., painted by Rubens while on a visit to the court of Charles I. in the character of ambassador : he was paid £3000 for his work, and was knighted at Whitehall, February 21, 1630.  The painting was "repaired" by Kent in the time of George II., and again by Cipriani at the latter part of the last century ; Pennant says the latter artist had £2000 " for his trouble ;" it is to be regretted that either artist was "troubled" on this score, for their labours have overlaid and obliterated the work of the great Fleming.  Rubens' masterly sketch for the central compartment of the roof is preserved in our National Gallery.  It was purchased in 1842 for £200.

The palace of Whitehall, with its gardens and surrounding buildings, as it appeared in the reign of Charles II., when seen from the Thames, is given in our engraving, from an ancient drawing in Wilkinson's "Londina Illustrata."  The statue of James II. does not appear at the back of the banqueting-house, thus enabling us to fix the date of the original sketch.  The privy garden to the left of this, now covered with aristocratic residences, was then a garden, laid out with parterres and fountains, reaching from the Thames to Parliament Street. The old Horse-Guards is seen beyond, and the peculiar nature of this *bird's-eye* view enables us to see a portion of St. James's Park beyond, and the canal in its centre edged with trees. At the upper corner of the extreme left of the view a portion of the old brick building of the Treasury, and the turrets of the famous gateway, designed by Holbein,

OLD WHITEHALL.

may be perceived,—they are the relics of "York Place," the famed residence of Cardinal Wolsey, and the palace which belonged to the see of York by bequest from Bishop Walter Gray, who died 1255. Wolsey added greatly to the grandeur of the building, and lived full royally within its walls. Cavendish, his gentleman-usher, has preserved a glowing account of the state, banquetings, and masques which enlivened it during his palmy days. His household amounted to five hundred persons, exclusive of retainers, and he selected them from among "the tallest that he could get in all this realm." Skelton, in his severe satire on Wolsey, furnished a dangerous parallel between the stateliness of the cardinal and that of the sovereign :—

> " The Kynges Courte
> Should have the excellence ;
> But Hampton Courte
> Hath the pre-emynence,
> And York Place
> With my Lorde's Grace
> To whose magnifycence
> Is all the confluence."

Here Wolsey banqueted the king, nobles, and ambassadors, and here the monarch first met Anne Bullen, and afterwards " privily married her in his closet at Whitehall." Wolsey's property had ceased therein at the beginning of 1630, when the king took all his possessions and changed the name of the building. Shakspere has immortalized some of the scenes here enacted, recording this change of masters in the speech of one of his characters, who exclaims—

> " Sir, you
> Must no more call it York Place, that is past ;
> For since the Cardinal fell, that title's lost :
> 'Tis now the king's, and called *Whitehall*."

Along the banks of the Thames, in the olden time, was a series of noble residences extending from Whitehall to the Temple. The first of these was SUFFOLK HOUSE, which occupied the site of the present Northumberland House, and was erected on the site of the dissolved hospital of St. Mary Rouncival, by Henry Howard, Earl of Northampton, in the reign of James I. He died there in 1614, and it then became the property of the Earl of Suffolk, and was called Suffolk House, when it was sketched by Hollar in the early part of the reign of Charles I. This sketch is preserved in the Pepysian Library, and is copied in our cut; it was a large quadrangular mansion, inclosing a courtyard, its lofty towers rising proudly on each side. The domestic offices were detached from the main building, and reached to the water-side ; the space between, shaded by tall trees, was laid out in walks and gardens. A gate in the centre and a flight of steps led to the Thames—an essential convenience, when every nobleman kept his barge and liveried watermen, and the river was a great highway.

The daughter of this Duke of Suffolk marrying the Earl of North-umberland, the house passed into his possession, and received the name of Northumberland House.   Many alterations have been made in it, but it is still the most interesting aristocratic residence in London, retaining its old garden, separated from the Thames only by the wharves in Scot-land Yard, above which wave the tree-tops, shutting out all surrounding houses from the quiet garden, and giving an air of almost pastoral

SUFFOLK HOUSE.

repose to the back of the noble mansion, whose roof, crowned by the lion crest of the duke, can be distinguished from the river.   It is the last of the old palatial residences of the nobility left to grace its banks.

We next reach Hungerford Market*—with its picturesque suspension-bridge for foot passengers, completed in 1845, under the direction of Mr. I. K. Brunel—and notice the group of hay-boats, with their bril-liantly painted hulls, and brightly-coloured sails, unloading at the wharf

---

* The market takes its name from Sir Edward Hungerford, who, in the reign of Charles II., had a house on this site, which he converted into a market.

beside it. They bring their cargoes of hay often from a long distance, and may be seen encountering the roughest weather. A number of them always come up every tide to Hungerford Bridge, where their freight is principally landed.

Continuing our course toward the City from Hungerford Bridge, let us briefly describe the olden glories of the Thames banks, when the space between the river and the Strand was occupied by the palaces of the

HAY-BOAT.

nobility. Close beside the bridge, on the site of the present Buckingham Street, stood YORK HOUSE, which we engrave from Hollar's view. It was anciently the town residence of the bishops of Norwich, and obtained its name from the exchange made with the archbishops of York, who adopted it as their palace in London, until Archbishop Mathew, in the reign of James I., exchanged it with the Crown for several manors. It was afterwards granted to the Lord Keeper, Sir Nicholas Bacon, who died here in 1597. His son, afterwards the famous Lord Chancellor Bacon, was born here in 1560. He was so strongly attached to the place of his birth that when the Duke of Lennox proposed that he should sell it, or exchange it, he replied, " York House is the house where my father died, and where I first breathed, and there will I breathe my last breath, if it so please God and the king." *  In the reign of Charles I. it became the residence of his favourite, George Villiers, Duke of Buckingham.  It was bestowed on

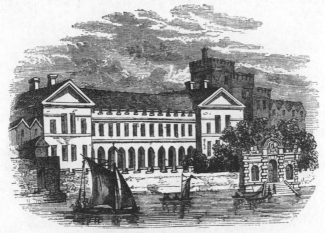

YORK HOUSE.

Fairfax, the parliamentary general, in the Great Civil War; and his daughter, marrying the second Duke of Buckingham, re-conveyed the property to the descendant of its earlier owner, who resided here after the Restoration; but his dissipated habits led to a necessity for its sale. It was then pulled down, and various streets were built on the site; they preserve his worthless name in the titles, " George Street, Villiers Street, Duke Street, Of Alley, and Buckingham Street."  The house

* Aubrey has preserved an anecdote of Bacon, which incidentally shows the purity of the Thames in his day :—" His Lordship being in Yorke House garden, looking on fishers as they were throwing their net, asked them what they would take for their draught.  They answered, so much.  His Lordship would offer them no more but so much.  They drew up their net, and in it were only two or three little fishes.  His Lordship then told them it had been better for them to have taken his offer.  They replied, they hoped to have had a better draught; but, said his Lordship, ' Hope is a good breakfast, but an ill supper.' "

was a noble building, remarkable for the sumptuous character of its internal fittings, as well as for the fine antiques the duke had purchased from Rubens. It was chiefly used by him for state occasions. Bassompierre, during his embassy to England in 1626, visited it, and describes it as "extremely fine," and the most richly fitted up of any he ever saw. The stairs which led to the river were surmounted by Inigo Jones's celebrated water-gate, still standing at the end of Buckingham Street,

DURHAM HOUSE.

one of the most interesting and beautiful relics of ancient architecture in the metropolis. The garden joined that of Durham House.

DURHAM HOUSE, which stood on the site of the present Durham Yard, and occupied that portion of ground now covered by the Adelphi,* possessed very great historic interest, and preserved some antique features when Hollar drew the sketch (about the year 1640) from

---

* The Adelphi was built by the brothers Adam, and named from the Greek word αδελφοι (brothers), in compliment to them, because of the difficulties they had surmounted in erecting the important structure on what was bad and unprofitable ground—a muddy deposit from the Thames. It is constructed on vast arches, celebrated as the "night residence" of houseless and abandoned persons, the "Pariahs" of London life. The centre house of the terrace, No. 5, was occupied by Garrick, who died in it, January 20, 1779, and there "lay in state" previous to his interment at Westminster. His widow also resided there, dying in the same room as her husband, in 1822.

which our engraving is copied. The strong walls of stone, the pointed arches, and the fortress-like towers, seem to be portions of the old work of the bishops of Durham, whose town residence was fixed here as early as the reign of Edward I. Stow says it was built by Bishop Hatfield in 1345. Bishop Tonstal surrendered it to Henry VIII., who converted it into a royal palace, giving in exchange the building known as " Cold Harbour," in Thames Street. During a great tournament given at Westminster by that monarch in 1540, and which continued for six days, the challengers lodged at Durham House, where, Stow tells us, "they not only feasted the king, queen, ladies, and all the court, but also they cheared all the knights and burgesses of the Commons House in the Parliament; and entertained the Mayor of London, with the aldermen and their wives, at dinner." Edward VI. granted Durham House to his sister Elizabeth as a temporary residence. It afterwards became the residence of John Dudley, Earl of Northumberland; and here was solemnized, in May, 1553, the ill-starred marriage of his fourth son, Lord Guildford Dudley, and the Lady Jane Grey, eldest daughter of Henry, Duke of Suffolk; a political alliance which ultimately brought both to the scaffold. On the death of Edward VI., the plot for making Lady Jane Queen of England was carried out in this house; and here the crown was forced on her which so speedily became a crown of martyrdom. Mary, on her accession to the throne, returned the mansion to the see of Durham. Elizabeth afterwards gave the use of the house to the great Sir Walter Raleigh, but he was obliged, after her decease, to restore it to the episcopal see. The mansion was not long tenanted by the bishops, but was purchased in 1640 by the Earl of Pembroke. It was pulled down in the early part of the last century, and the ground covered with houses.

SALISBURY HOUSE was separated from it only by a small garden, and was built in the reign of James I. by his treasurer and secretary, Robert Cecil, Earl of Salisbury. It was a massive rectangular building, with turrets at the angles, and presented an imposing frontage to the Thames. After the earl's death it was divided into two mansions, and then subdivided; ultimately converted into an Exchange, but having no "success" it was purchased by builders, and Salisbury and Cecil Streets were erected on its site.

Close beside Salisbury, stood WORCESTER, House, which, in the reign of Henry VIII., belonged to the see of Carlisle, but then passed into the hands of the earls of Bedford, and from them to the earls of Worcester, the last of whom died here in 1627. His son being created Duke of Beaufort, it changed its name to Beaufort House; and the space of ground it once occupied is still marked by Beaufort Buildings

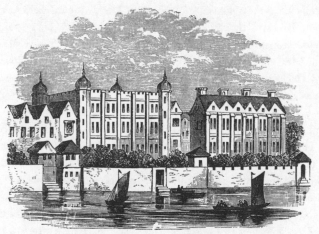

SALISBURY AND WORCESTER HOUSES.

in the Strand, erected after its destruction by fire through the careless-ness of a servant. Pennant informs us that the great Earl of Clarendon lived in it before he built his celebrated mansion in Piccadilly, paying for it at the extravagant rate of £500 per year, a sum fully equal to £1200 at present.

The old palace called the SAVOY was the next important residence on the river-bank. It was a fortress-like building close upon the stream, and without the intervening garden which characterized the others. It was originally founded by the Earl of Savoy in the reign of Henry III., and rebuilt by Henry, Duke of Lancaster. Here was imprisoned John,

King of France, after he had been captured by Edward the Black Prince
at the battle of Poictiers, in 1356. He was honourably and courteously
lodged here, and his imprisonment made as light as possible ; the king
and queen frequently visited him, and "made him great cheer." He
was released in 1360; but, having returned to England on a visit, he
died within the walls of this old palace, which had been assigned to him
as his temporary residence while he remained in London. It afterwards
passed into the possession of John of Gaunt, Duke of Lancaster, and during

THE SAVOY.

that time was burnt by the "rabble rout" who followed Wat Tyler.
It lay in ruin and neglect for a long time after that event. In 1505
it was restored as a hospital by Henry VII., suppressed by Edward VI.,
re-endowed by Queen Mary, and continued as a hospital and sanctuary,
"a nursery of rogues and masterless men throughout that century." It
recovered some degree of respectability at the Restoration, and within its
walls the meetings of the commissioners for the revision of the Liturgy
were held, in 1661, known as "the Savoy Conference." It consisted of

twelve bishops and several Presbyterians.   At this time Fuller, the author of the "Worthies," was lecturer here; and Charles II. promised the place of "Master of the Savoy" to the poet Cowley; he, however, ultimately gave it to Dr. Killegrew, which occasioned Cowley to write his poem, "The Complaint."   The same sovereign established the French Church here, first opened in 1661.   Strype describes the old building as "very ruinous" in 1720; but he adds, "in this Savoy, how ruinous soever it is, are divers good houses: first, the king's printing-press for proclamations, Acts of Parliament, gazettes, and such like public papers; next, a prison; thirdly, a parish church, and three or four of the churches and places for religious assemblies—viz. for the French, for Dutch, for High Germans and Lutherans, and lastly for the Protestant Dissenters.   Here be also harbours for many refugees and poor people."   The right of sanctuary was so strenuously upheld, that there is a record of one man who went, in 1696, to demand a debt from one who had taken sanctuary there, when the inhabitants rose *en masse*, tarred and feathered him, then carried him in a wheelbarrow to the Maypole in the Strand, and so bound him to it.   The modern Londoner can scarcely believe that these lawless doings were practised in the very heart of civilization not more than a century and a half ago!   The building then going gradually to decay, was patched up, and chiefly used as a barrack for soldiers and a prison, it was ultimately destroyed in 1816, to form the approaches to Waterloo Bridge.   The chapel, once within the walls, remains, and is a curious relic, containing many old monuments.   It was built in 1505, and has a fine old ceiling, and a beautiful altar-screen, said to have been designed by Sir Reginald Bray, and recently restored by Sydney Smirke.   The reparations were executed at the expense of Her Majesty in 1843.   Several noted men are buried here—the poets Gawin Douglas and George Wither, the African traveller, Lander, and the historical painter, Hilton.

The Surrey bank of the river between Westminster and Hungerford Bridges comprises the district known as " Pedlar's Acre," a piece of ground given to the parish of Lambeth, and situated on the verge of the Thames.   Popular tradition asserts the gift to have been made by a pedlar, who owned the land, on condition that himself and his dog should be commemorated on one of the church windows. We engrave this far-famed piece of glass-painting, which is certainly of the time of Elizabeth ; but there is no record in the parish accounts to justify the old tale.*

A PEDLAR.

The Lion Brewery and the great Shot Tower are the most conspicuous objects past Hungerford Bridge. The latter is of cylindrical form, a hundred feet in height. The shot is formed by pouring molten lead from the upper part through small perforations, the drops rounding as they fall to the bottom in water. The whole of this district was formerly known as Lambeth Marsh, an unwholesome and unprofitable locality, frequently overflowed in high tides. The buildings on this bank have all been erected since the opening of Waterloo Bridge in 1817.

WATERLOO BRIDGE, long celebrated as the finest over the Thames, and praised by Canova as "the noblest bridge in the world," was constructed by Rennie, at the expense of a public company. It cost £400,000 ; the approaches, &c., making up the sum to nearly a million.† Close to the foot of the bridge, on the City side, is SOMERSET HOUSE : it is a noble pile, now entirely devoted to government offices. ‡ It was built by Sir William Chambers, and is his finest work. The Thames front is 800 feet in length, and is provided with a terrace, supported on arches, 50 feet above the bed of the river, and is the same number of feet in advance of the main walls. This terrace forms a noble promenade ; it is much to be regretted that the public are excluded from what was once

---

* Some writers believe the glass is a rebus on the name *Chapman*. " Pedlar's Acre " was not called by that name till the end of the seventeenth century : its old name was Church Hopes.

† Owing to the heavy rate of its tolls, it was for a long time unprofitable to the shareholders. So great was its loneliness, that it was almost unsafe at night, and the scene of frequent suicides.

‡ Except the rooms granted to the Antiquarian, Astronomical, and Geological Societies.

an agreeable airing-place for London.   Immediately adjoining Somerset
House is the modern building, King's College.

The old palace of the Protector Somerset, uncle to Edward VI., stood
upon this site, and gave name to the present structure; it was a picturesque brick and stone edifice, erected for him from the designs of
John of Padua.   When the "proud Somerset" was beheaded, in 1552,
the house devolved to the crown; Edward VI. assigned it to his sister,
the Princess (afterwards Queen) Elizabeth; and James I. settled it on his
queen, who named it Denmark House, in compliment to her native country.

WATERLOO BRIDGE, AND SOMERSET HOUSE.

Inigo Jones added new buildings to it, and this is the condition of the
building as exhibited in our view on the opposite page.   The great
architect died within the walls of this building in 1652.   Here lived
Henrietta Maria, queen of Charles I., and here she founded a convent, and
publicly performed the most slavish rites of the Catholic church; on one
occasion her confessor enjoined as a penance that she should walk from
hence to Tyburn barefooted.   Cunningham says, "a few tombs of her
French Roman Catholic attendants are built into the cellars of the present

building, immediately beneath the great square." Here Oliver Cromwell "lay in state;" so also did General Monk. Catherine of Braganza, queen of Charles II., took up her residence here, at the Restoration. It seems to have been considered the private property of the Queens Consort of England, and was during the last century chiefly used, as Hampton

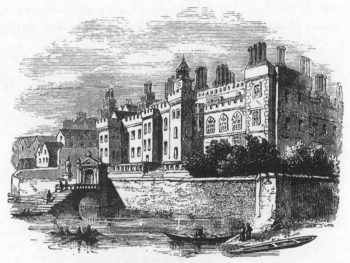

OLD SOMERSET HOUSE.

Court was used, for lodging the aged or poor retainers of the Court. In 1775 Buckingham House was given to Queen Charlotte in lieu of it; and it was soon afterwards pulled down.

Between this place and the Temple there is now nothing of importance to arrest the attention of the voyager. In the old time the ground was chiefly occupied by two noble mansions and their gardens; the first being ARUNDEL HOUSE, the home of Thomas Howard, Earl of Arundel, whose classic tastes made the mansion celebrated in the days of James and Charles I., for the rare collection of marbles and gems of all kinds he gathered here. He was "the greatest patron of literature and the fine arts of his own, and we might also add of any other, time. Inigo

Jones first rose into notice under his countenance; he brought Hollar from Prague, and established him in London; Francis Junius and Oughtred were received into his family; Cotton, Spelman, Camden, and Selden were among his intimate friends. It is only to be regretted that at his death the splendid collections he had amassed should have been so much dispersed as the state of the times, and perhaps more particularly the limited, if not distressed circumstances of the countess, his widow, occasioned. The marbles, embracing the ancient inscriptions,

VIEW FROM ARUNDEL HOUSE.

and among them that invaluable monument of Grecian history, the Parian Chronicle, were presented to the University of Oxford, in 1677, by his grandson, Henry Howard, Earl of Arundel and Surrey, and afterwards Duke of Norfolk." * They are now kept in the quadrangle of the Oxford Divinity School. It was at the instigation of Evelyn that the marbles were sent there, and the library to the then recently founded Royal Society, in which he also took a warm interest. Evelyn describes his visit to Arundel House in 1667, and says of the marbles: "When I saw these precious monuments miserably neglected, and scattered up and down about the garden, and other parts of Arundel House, and how

---

* Parker's "Handbook to Oxford."

exceedingly the corrosive air of London impaired them, I procured him
to bestow them on the University of Oxford.  This he was pleased to
grant me, and now gave me the key of the gallery, with leave to mark
all those stones, urns, altars, &c., and whatever I found had inscriptions
on them that were not statues." The donor died 1677, and in the
following year the old mansion was pulled down, and Arundel Street,
Surrey Street, Howard Street, and Norfolk Street, were erected on its site.

While Hollar resided in Arundel House, he made the curious engravings which are so well known to London topographers, preserving

ESSEX HOUSE.

as they do the peculiar features of the assemblage of old buildings of
which the mansion then consisted.* The curious view of London from
the roof of this house we copy from Hollar's careful etching.  It is of
peculiar interest, and was executed about 1646.  Looking toward the
city, the large building in front is ESSEX HOUSE, and over it we see old
St. Paul's Cathedral, after the spire had been destroyed by lightning.
The view of the group of houses and churches beyond is bounded by
the Tower and old London Bridge, with its numerous arches and houses

---

* It was originally the town residence of the bishops of Bath, and passed from them, in the reign of
Edward VI., to Lord Thomas Seymour, brother of the powerful Protector, Somerset.  After the execution of Seymour, the property was purchased by Henry Fitz-Alan, Earl of Arundel.

thereon. It is a faithful and curious picture of "the princely city" before the Great Fire.

Essex House, adjoining, obtained its name from Queen Elizabeth's unfortunate favourite; and from it he made his unsuccessful attempt to excite a revolt in the city, which led him to the scaffold. It has been well described by Pepys, as "a large, yet ugly house;" but it was continuously inhabited by a series of noble residents until the close of the seventeenth century, soon after which period it was taken down. It stood on the site of the present Essex Street.

We now arrive at the Temple Stairs, and admire the group of trees which still surround the little fountain that inspired the muse of L.E.L.; whose tastes were essentially those of a lover of London and its associations. As her graceful little poem is but slightly known, and few London scenes have inspired poets with a theme, we reproduce it here; it is one of Miss Landon's latest works :—

### "THE TEMPLE GARDEN.

" The fountain's low singing is heard in the wind,
Like a melody bringing sweet fancies to mind ;
Away in the distance is heard the far sound
From the streets of the city, that compass it round,
Like the echo of mountains, or ocean's deep call :
Yet that fountain's low singing is heard over all.

" The turf and the terrace slope down to the tide
Of the Thames, that sweeps onward, a world at its side;
And dark the horizon, with mast and with sail
Of the thousand tall ships that have weather'd the gale ;
While beyond the arched bridge the old Abbey appears,
Where England has garner'd—the glories of years.

" There are lights in the casements,—how weary the ray
That asks for the night-time the toils of the day !—
I fancy I see the brow bent o'er the page,
Whose youth bears the paleness and wrinkles of age :
What struggles, what hopes, what despair may have been,
Where sweep those dark branches of shadowy green ! "

Close to it is the noble old hall, remarkable as the only building remaining in which a play of Shakspere's was acted by his contemporaries,* as part of their Christmas revels. The fine old garden on

---

* It is recorded in the Diary of John Manningham, a student here, as follows :—"Feb. 2, 1601. At our feast we had a play called ' Twelfth Night; or, What you Will.' "

the river's bank has been a garden from the days when the chiefs of
the White and Red Rose factions plucked their flowers here as badges
for their adherents—a scene so vividly rendered in Shakspere's
"Henry VI." The present gardener has restored the glories of the old
garden, as well as such glories can be restored to a place in " populous
city pent." The show of summer flowers is generally good, but that of
chrysanthemums at the close of each year attract and gratify thousands—the beds being masses of variegated flowers. The picturesque
group, called "New Paper Buildings," of red brick and stone, forming
so striking a feature at the eastern side, was erected by Sidney Smirke,
A.R.A., in 1848. The memories that are associated with this spot, the
early home of the Knights Templars of London, the solemn old church,
where their effigies still lie, and where such men as Selden and Oliver
Goldsmith repose, demand a volume for their due description. Between
the Temple and Blackfriars Bridge, was the old lawless district known
as "Alsatia," celebrated by Scott in his "Fortunes of Nigel;" he there
gives a vivid and true picture of the loose characters by whom it was
inhabited. Its proper name was "Whitefriars," from the church of the
Carmelites, originally founded in the thirteenth century, which, with the
monastic establishment, were destroyed at the Reformation; but the
privileges of sanctuary continued until it became a nest of ruffians,
fraudulent debtors, and the worst members of society, who crowded into
the narrow lanes, where the law had no power. It ultimately became
so dangerous a nuisance that its privileges were abolished, and the
district is now principally occupied by factories and gas-works.

The Southwark side of the river, originally low marsh land, is now
thickly covered with houses; the river-bank presenting a continued
series of wharves, where may be constantly seen groups of barges, such
as are depicted in our cut. They have discharged their cargoes, and are
waiting for high water, to be "off" with the next ebb. The principal
vessel in the cut is one of the old-fashioned, square bowed, flat-bottomed
barges, having a large hatchway in the centre for the cargo, with the
small bunk, or cabin, for the crew. She also carries ingenious weather-
boards, to prevent the great amount of lee-way a vessel without a keel

would make, beating in a fresh breeze. The sails consist of a sprit, foresail, and mizen, and her mast lowers down by the forestay when the vessel is passing under bridges. The crew consists of a captain and three or four men.

On the Surrey side of the river, and exactly opposite Somerset House, was a celebrated old place of amusement, known as Cuper's Gardens. It was formed by a gardener of that name, who had been servant to the

BARGES AT BLACKFRIARS.

Earls of Arundel, and was laid out in shady walks, arbours, and flower-beds, the whole being decorated with such antique fragments as the earl was willing to spare him: some few of these were afterwards found in the Thames, and excited much curiosity. This garden was opened in 1678, and Aubrey, in his account of Surrey, says, "the conveniency of its arbours, walks, and several remains of Greek and Roman antiquities, have made this place much frequented." Early in the following century, an attempt was made here to rival Vauxhall, by the erection of an orchestra, and the exhibition of fireworks.   The gardens ultimately obtained a bad repute, and were closed in 1753.

Blackfriars Bridge, the third bridge built in London, was erected by Robert Mylne, and opened for general traffic in 1769.   The bridge and approaches cost the city £273,000.   It has been since repaired at a cost of £74,000.   Close beside the bridge (on the west of the London end) is a large arched sewer, which is all that now represents the old river Fleet, thus converted into an immense drain ; but in the olden time it

FLEET BRIDGE.

was a stream wide enough to allow barges to go inland as far as Holborn, and spanned by a bridge near the Thames, "after the manner of the Rialto, at Venice."   There is preserved in the library at Guildhall a curious painting, executed in the early part of the last century (attributed to Canaletti, but most probably by Hogarth's friend, Scott), which preserves a view of the "River Wells," as it was anciently called, but which had obtained an unsavoury reputation at that time, not a little aided by the severe lines of Pope, who summoned the heroes of his "Dunciad"—

" Where Fleet ditch, with disemboguing streams,
Rolls the large tribute of dead dogs to Thames."

3 L

This little river, in its days of purity, obtained its name from the *fleetness* with which its waters ran toward the Thames. The stream comprised the waters of certain "wells," or springs, to the northward of the city, and obtained a large accession about Clerkenwell; thence they continued down Turnmill Street, a name very simple in its etymology, and derived from the mills on the banks of the rivulet, which widened at Holborn (literally "old bourne," or "old brook"), where a bridge was erected; another was opposite Fleet Street; and a third nearer Bridewell, which is that represented in our engraving.

ST. PAUL'S CATHEDRAL.

The Fleet river became a nuisance in the days of Elizabeth, when it was little better than an open drain. Occasional attempts were made to improve it, particularly after the Great Fire, when it was railed off, and wharves constructed, so that vessels might come again up to Holborn, and unload their cargoes. This good intention failed from want of patronage; the wharves became ruinous, the trades carried on in them still more objectionable, and the nuisance increased till 1765, when the stream was arched over, and Fleet Market, a lane of shops and sheds, erected over it. In 1829 the market was removed. The "river" still runs down Farringdon Street, invisible in its course.

The number of church steeples that now appear above the city wharves, compared with the few seen farther west, recalls to memory the remark of Sir Roger de Coverley, who argued therefrom on the morality of the two districts. Grandly above all rises St. Paul's Cathedral, the noble work of Sir Christopher Wren, to whose genius we are also indebted for the greater number of the churches whose steeples

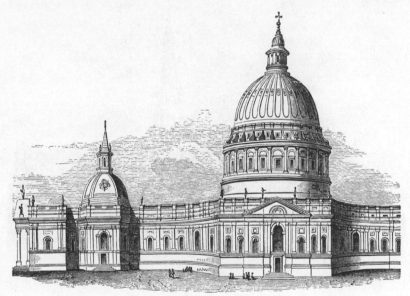

WREN'S ORIGINAL DESIGN FOR ST. PAUL'S.

are so conspicuous. Unfortunately we do not look upon the great metropolitan cathedral as Wren designed it. His first plan did not include the long aisle and side chapels now a part of it, and which are more fitted for the Romish ritual than our own. Wren had determined to omit them, and so construct the only great Protestant Cathedral; but the Duke of York, afterwards James II., obliged him to alter the design,

which caused the great architect many bitter tears. Thus, to gratify the
wish of one who sat upon our throne but two short years, and was then
banished for ever, we lost a magnificent idea, peculiarly fitted for us
of England. Wren's original design we here engrave. The dome is
much more graceful than that we now see completed; the architect
made his entire design converge to that grand centre. The wooden
model is still in the possession of the Dean and Chapter of St. Paul's;

OLD ST PAUL'S CATHEDRAL.

and such are the grandeur and beauty of its arrangements, within and
without, that all who study it must deeply regret to find that Wren's
ideas have been so unfortunately rendered inoperative.

The older cathedral, "the great glory" of ancient London, we also
picture from Hollar's careful view. It shows the steeple entire, before
its destruction by lightning in 1561; it was never afterwards restored.
In the days of James I. its great state of decay obliged some

measures to be adopted to preserve the building. It was patched up in a slovenly manner, and so remained till Charles I. set a vigorous example of restoration, and built the famous portico from the design of Inigo Jones. The royal example was followed by the noble and wealthy, and in 1643 the renovation was completed at a cost of one hundred thousand pounds. Desecration damaged it in the civil war, and the good work had to be done over again at the Restoration; but it went on slowly, and the Great Fire completely destroyed the ancient edifice.

Wren furnished a noble plan for the restoration of London after this event. His mode of operation is detailed by his son in his "Parentalia." He says, that after his appointment as surveyor-general and principal architect for rebuilding the city, he immediately "took an exact survey of the whole area and confines of the burning, having traced over with great trouble and hazard the great plain of ashes and ruins; and designed a plan or model of a new city, in which the deformity and inconveniences of the old town were remedied, by the enlarging the streets and lanes, and carrying them as near parallel to one another as might be; avoiding, if compatible with greater conveniences, all acute angles; by seating all the parochial churches conspicuous and insular; by forming the most public places into large piazzas, the centre of six or eight ways; by uniting the halls of the twelve chief companies into one regular square annexed to Guildhall; by making a quay on the whole bank of the river from Blackfriars to the Tower." In his clear-sighted plans and useful improvements he designed "the streets to be of three magnitudes; the three principal leading straight through the city, and one or two cross streets to be at least ninety feet wide; others sixty feet; and lanes about thirty feet, excluding all narrow dark alleys without thoroughfares or courts." An examination of his plan (engraved in page 446) will make these improvements apparent, and show how much London has lost by not adopting Wren's views. They were opposed by the vested interests of the citizens, which then, as now, too frequently deprecated changes that were evident advantages. They had insurmountable prejudices in favour of rebuilding in old localities and in old styles, and hence the architect lost the opportunity of rendering London "the most magnificent as well as

WREN'S PLAN FOR REBUILDING LONDON.

commodious city for health and trade of any upon earth." A glance at his plan will show how well he had laid out main streets, and studied the proper position of public buildings, with an eye as well to utility as to architectural effect. A shows the position of St. Paul's, which would have been the first grand object that claimed attention when the western side of the city was entered. At B is Doctors' Commons, in close and proper proximity. The letter C refers to the piazzas with which Wren intended to ornament London where the principal streets met. At D we have the principal buildings sacred to trade and commerce ; E is the Post office ; F, the Excise office ; G, Insurance office ; H, the Mint ; while at I are the Goldsmiths' shops. K shows the position of Guild-hall ; L that of the Custom House. At M are the public markets ; N, the strand entrance to the city ; O is Smithfield ; P, the Temple ; Q, a quay along the entire bank of the Thames ; R is the *débouchement* of the Fleet river at Bridewell ; S, Queenhithe ; T, Dowgate ; U, London Bridge ; and V, Billingsgate. W shows the position of the Tower ; X, that of Moorfields ; and Y, the circuit of the City Walls. The small black blocks, which are isolated, represent churches which he had intended to place in prominent positions in the main thoroughfares, but always free of the houses. It is only necessary further to remark, that that portion of our plan which is covered by lines of tint represents that part of London which was destroyed by the Great Fire.

The river-banks at "Paul's Wharf" are now lined with tall ware-houses, where once stood BAYNARD'S CASTLE, an antique edifice, so called from a follower of William of Normandy, its original occupant. It was a strong but gloomy pile, the occasional residence of many remarkable people, and the scene of some few historic events, one of which is immortalized by Shakspere, in his " Richard III.," and in which he has closely followed the narrative of Sir Thomas More. The Duke of Gloucester was residing at that time in Baynard's Castle, and here his creature, the Duke of Buckingham, induced the citizens to visit him and offer him the crown. On many occasions of formality it was used as a royal palace, until the reign of Queen Elizabeth ; and was ultimately destroyed in the Great Fire of London. It still gives its name to the Ward in which it stood. The City of London is divided into twenty-six Wards, each governed by an alderman and one or more deputies; the mayor is chosen from the aldermen; he must be a member of one of the twelve great livery companies of merchantmen or traders; and if he be not a member of any of these companies, he is chosen into one of them. Until recently he had the uncontrolled conservancy of the river Thames and the waters of the Medway, from London Bridge

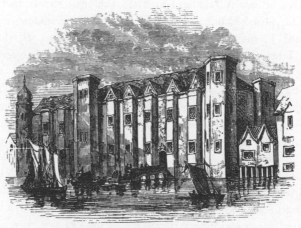

BAYNARD'S CASTLE.

to Rochester down the river, and from London Bridge to Staines up the river. He held Courts of Conservancy whenever he saw a necessity for them, and had the power of summoning juries in Kent and Middlesex, whose business it was to go on the river in boats to view the state of it, make their presentments, and furnish their report to his lordship. On some occasions these courts were held in the state barge, which was brought to that spot in the river with which the inquiry was connected, for the convenience of witnesses attending from the neighbouring villages. The Lord Mayor's and Companies' barges are the last relics of the old water-pageantry of London. In the olden time each noble who resided on the banks of the river kept his state barge, and had watermen, dressed in the livery of the family, bearing its badge on their sleeve. On the 9th of November it is the custom of the Mayor and citizens to go, in their gaily gilt and decorated barges (generally from Blackfriars Bridge), to the Court of Exchequer, in Westminster, and take the necessary oaths. The effect on the Thames is singularly picturesque.

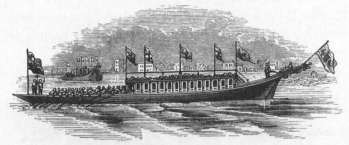

THE LORD MAYOR'S BARGE.

A short distance onward, and we arrive at the old haven, known as QUEENHITHE.* It retains more of the characteristic features of the Thames bank during the last century than are to be seen in any other part of London. The old wooden wharves, the boats in the little dock, the high steps leading from the water, and the picturesque tree over-shadowing them, seem to belong to the days of Anne, when the traffic in boats on the river was considerable, and the rich citizen and his wife would "take water" here for Vauxhall or Ranelagh. It probably obtains its name from the gift of it by King John to his mother, Eleanor, queen of Henry II.; but it was known in Saxon times as "Edrid's Hithe," and has been a common quay for nearly nine hundred years.

Immediately after passing the Hithe, we reach Southwark Bridge; it

---

* We engrave a penny of Alfred the Great, found in the mud of the Thames near this spot, and which is of immediate interest here, as it is his "London type," and contains on the obverse the monogram "Londinium," the letters forming part of each other — a convenient mode of getting a long name in a small compass. These early coins, though excessively rude, are of value in history, and tell of the very low state of general art at the era when they were executed. Many are remarkable for their rude imitation of the superior works of the Romans.

was designed by Rennie, and built by a company at a cost of £800,000. It has three cast-iron arches, the span of the central arch being 240 feet, that of each side being 210 feet; the piers and abutments are of stone. It was opened March 22, 1819.

We cross the river to visit the Surrey bank of the Thames, for the most interesting points of its early history are comprised between the two

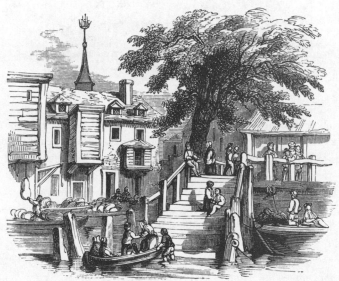

QUEENHITHE.

bridges—Blackfriars and Southwark. The Surrey side was "fashionable" in the reign of Elizabeth, the Londoners being ferried across to the places of popular amusement there thickly located. The Blackfriars Road now passes over the site of "PARIS GARDEN," where bear and bull-baiting rejoiced the citizens, the gala days being usually Sundays. Our print is copied from the rare woodcut map of London in the time of Henry VIII., now in the library at Guildhall; it exhibits in the foreground the kennels for the dogs, and the tanks in which they were washed. A graphic description of the place has been given by Paul Hentzner, a

German, who visited it in 1598. He says it was " built in the form of a theatre, for the baiting of bulls and bears : they are fastened behind, and then worried by great English bull-dogs ; but not without great risk to the dogs, from the horns of the one, and the teeth of the other ; and it sometimes happens they are killed upon the spot ; fresh ones are immediately supplied in the place of those that are wounded or tired. To this entertainment there often follows that of whipping a blinded bear, which is performed by five or six men, standing circularly with whips, which they exercise upon him without any mercy, as he cannot escape from them because of his chain. He defends himself with all his

PARIS GARDEN.

force and skill, throwing down all who come within his reach, and are not active enough to get out of it, and tearing the whips out of their hands, and breaking them. At these spectacles, and everywhere else, the English are constantly smoking tobacco. Fruits, such as apples, pears, and nuts, according to the season, are carried about to be sold, as well as ale and wine." The same writer mentions the theatres for dramatic representation on this side the water : the most westerly was the Swan, which seems to have gone to decay in the early part of the seventeenth century. Near that part of Southwark crossed by the road from the iron bridge, stood that most famous building—THE GLOBE, of which Shakspere was part proprietor, and for which he wrote his greatest plays. Its aspect will be best understood from our cut, copied from Visscher's map, 1616. Beside it were "the Rose" and "the Hope" playhouses, receiving their titles from the signs or figures painted or

THE GLOBE THEATRE.

sculptured over their doors. Rose Alley and Hope Alley still mark the sites of these theatres: the more celebrated "Globe" is believed to have stood where the ironworks of Messrs. Sheeres are now located, close beside the bridge.

The Globe theatre obtained its name from the figure which was placed over the entrance, and which represented Atlas supporting a large globe, under which was written, "Totus Mundus agit Histrionem" —a sentiment the great dramatist has finely worked out in one of his most famous soliloquies. Shakspere became part proprietor of the theatre soon after it was constructed, in 1593.* It was burnt down June 29, 1613, while Shakspere's play of "King Henry VIII." was being performed. In the scene of the masque at York Place, some of the wadding, shot from the cannon fired at the king's entry, set fire to the thatch of the roof, and so destroyed it. It was a mere framework of timber and plaster, open to the sky, and covered with thatch. Sir Henry Wotton, in one of his letters, describes the conflagration:— "It kindled inwardly, and ran round like a train, consuming within less than a hour the whole house to the very ground. Yet nothing did perish therein but wood and straw, and a few forsaken cloaks." In the year 1614 it was rebuilt of stronger material, as represented in our cut, and

---

* He is noted as " one of the inhabitants of Southwark " in a paper at Dulwich College, dated 1596 ; and in 1603 James I. granted him and his fellows licence to act " at their now usuall house called the Globe."

the fact is amusingly recorded in the following lines by Taylor, "the Water-Poet:"*—

    " As gold is better that in fire 's tried,
      So is the Bankside Globe that late was burn'd
    For where before it had a thatched hide,
      Now to a stately theatre 'tis turn'd:
    Which is an emblem that great things are won
    By those that dare through greatest dangers run.

It ceased to be popular after the time of James I., and was "pulled

THE " BILLY-BOY."

down to the ground by Sir Matthew Brand, on Monday, the 15th of April, 1644, to make tenements in the room of it." †

Crossing to the London side of the bridge, our attention is again directed to the busy wharves and the trading boats near them: one of these we engrave; it is of a peculiar kind, termed a "BILLY-BOY,"—the

* He was so called from having been originally a Thames waterman. Watermen at that time formed a numerous body: Stow says, in his " Survey of London," 1603, that " there appertained to the cities of London, Westminster, and Southwark, above the number, it is supposed, of two thousand wherries, and other small boats, whereby three thousand poor men, at the least, be set on work and maintained."

† Collier's " Life of Shakspere."

sailors' name for a round bow and stern coasting schooner : it is an
excellent sea boat, and, from its box-like form, carries a large cargo.
These vessels usually come from Yorkshire, but are generally found
on most parts of the English coast : their masts "lower," like the London
barges, for passing beneath bridges.

We meet with no important building until we reach the Fishmongers' Hall, at the foot of London Bridge, which is a modern structure,
built on the site of the old hall, in 1831. We engrave the original
stone-fronted hall that existed on the same spot before the Great Fire of

FISHMONGERS' HALL.

London, as depicted by Hollar, in 1647, including also some of the
wharves and buildings of that era, to complete as nearly as we can our
picture of the banks of the Thames. This view completely realizes
the idea we should form from D'Avenant's description of the aspect
of the Thames banks. It occurs in "The First Day's Entertainment at
Rutland House" (1656), in which a Frenchman and an Englishman dispute concerning the state of the rivers of Paris and London. The former
complains of the confused buildings on its banks—"Here a lord, there a
dyer, and places of the worst kind between both ;" but the Englishman
triumphs in asserting the Thames possessed greater purity than the Seine.

We have thus arrived at London Bridge, having been compelled to limit our descriptions to a mere enumeration of the various objects of interest the voyager will encounter on his way.

The various houses from Southwark Bridge to "the turn" leading to Barclay's brewery have nothing to recommend them to notice, but that they stand on the spot where the disreputable "garden-houses" of the Shaksperian era were located, and the "stews" that were rented from the Bishop of Winchester. Amid the wharves close to the river-side may still be traced some of the walls of the bishop's palace, which, with its gardens, occupied a large piece of ground: the old hall was burnt down in 1814; the gardens had been previously built upon. Along the banks are closely "congregated" the coal barges; and a busy scene is

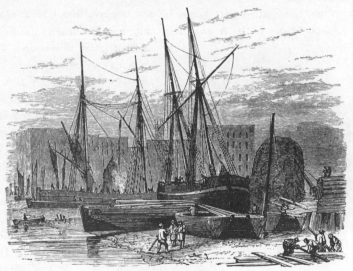

COLLIERS UNLOADING.

there when the colliers unload their freights, by aid of numerous "coal-whippers" employed by dealers. A small creek, called "St. Saviour's Dock," comes nearly up to the principal door of "St. Saviour's," or, as it is sometimes termed, "St. Mary Overy's church," one of the finest edifices on the banks of the Thames, but which has been unfortunately "restored," and partly rebuilt. Twenty years ago it was remarkable for the variety of its antique architecture, all of which has been destroyed : the Lady Chapel at the back would have suffered the same fate, but for the strenuous exertions of the parishioners. It has many curious monuments, the most remarkable being that of the poet Gower, the friend of Chaucer, and the favourite poet of the unfortunate Richard II. Here are also buried Edmund Shakspere, the youngest brother of the immortal William, and his friend Henslowe, the great theatrical manager; Fletcher, the ally of Beaumont; and, greater than all, Philip Massinger, who died poor, without a mark by which to know his grave, his interment being simply noted in the parish register as that of "a stranger."

A strongly-embattled gate protected the entrance from Southwark to Old London Bridge in the reign of Elizabeth, and was usually garnished

GATE : OLD LONDON BRIDGE.

with traitors' heads in "rich abundance," as may be seen in our cut, copied from Visscher's view, in 1579. The bridge was at that period covered with houses, a narrow road passing through arcades beneath them; and they abutted on props over the river on either side. The open spaces on the bridge were few; its general aspect is exhibited in our view, as delineated by Hollar, in 1647. It was proudly spoken of by our ancestors; thus, in the translation of Ortelius, published by J. Shaw, in 1603, he says of the Thames,—"It is beautified with statelye pallaces, built on the side thereof; moreover, a sumptuous bridge, sustayned upon nineteen arches, with excellent and beauteous housen built thereon." Camden, in his great work, the "Britannia," says,—"It may worthily carry away the prize from all the bridges in Europe," being "furnished on both sides with passing faire houses, joining one to another in manner of a street." Two of these buildings we may briefly describe: the first of these was a picturesque wooden gate and tower, erected in 1579; the second, a little further, on the seventh and eighth arches from the Southwark side, was the far-famed "Nonesuch House," a term applied to it from its supposed unique character; it was built entirely of

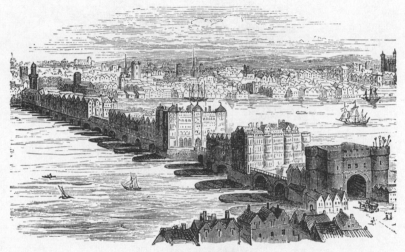

OLD LONDON BRIDGE.

wood, cut and carved in Holland, brought over in pieces, and fastened, when erected on the bridge, with wooden pegs only. The other houses do not demand particular notice; they were allowed to incommode the structure till 1758, when, for considerations of public safety, they were removed. In Scott's view of London Bridge, 1756 (now in the Vernon Gallery), we can trace the ruinous remains of the old Nonesuch House, as well as fragments of the Southwark Gate, and the squalid buildings that were heaped on the ancient structure. The arches were rendered still narrower by protecting them from the wear of water by wooden "starlings," which may be seen in our cut above. By this means many of them were impassable, and others only afforded passage for very small boats; this contraction produced a fall of water of several feet, and at every change of tide it rushed through with great noise and foaming velocity, carrying boats beyond Billingsgate.   Many lives and much property were lost yearly, and ultimately this bridge (erected by Peter

HOUSES ON LONDON BRIDGE, 1756.

of Colechurch in 1209) ceased to be used, after the opening of the new bridge in 1831; soon afterwards it was entirely removed.   In the process of clearing away the foundations, many antiquities were discovered; it had been the great highway over the Thames from the Roman era, and numerous relics were obtained, varying in date from that period to our own.*

Much of the ancient history of England is connected with this famed old bridge, which, for so many centuries, was a great highway over the

* We engrave such specimens of Roman coins found here as belong to the Britannic series.   The large central coin is one struck by Hadrian, and remarkable for the figure of Britannia, the first time

Thames. Its "Chronicles" have been written by Mr. Richard Thompson, of the London Institution, in a portly volume of nearly seven hundred pages. We cannot in our brief notice do more than point out a few of its suggestive "memories." The old inns that once lined the High Street of Southwark, and chief among them Chaucer's "Tabard," would alone furnish many pages of interesting narrative; we content ourselves with a brief notice of one which stood close to the bridge, and for which we are indebted to our friend, G. R. Corner, Esq., F.S.A.

The "Bear," at the Bridge-foot, was a noted house of entertainment during the fifteenth, sixteenth, and seventeenth centuries, and it remained until the houses on the old bridge were pulled down, in or about the year 1760. This house was situate in the parish of St. Olave, Southwark, on the west side of the High Street, and between Pepper Alley and the foot of London Bridge.\* The next mention of the "Bear" is in a deed in my own possession, dated 12th December, 1554, in the first and second years of Philip and Mary, whereby Edmonde Wythipolle,

impersonated as an armed female seated on a rock. It is the prototype of the more modern Britannia, reintroduced by Charles II., and which still appears on our copper money. The smaller coins

are such as were struck, during the reign of Constantine the Great, in the city of London, and are marked with the letters P. LON., for "Pecunia Londinensis," money of London.

\* For the earliest notice of the "Bear" at the Bridge-foot, I am indebted to the notes of Mr. Jacob Henry Burn, in his Catalogue of the London Traders', Tavern, and Coffee-house Tokens, current in the seventeenth century, presented to the library of the Corporation of London by Henry Benjamin Hanbury Beaufoy, Esq. Mr. Burn tells us that the "Bear" at Bridge-foot was a house of considerable antiquity, and that among the disbursements of Sir John Howard, in his steward's accounts yet extant, are noticed, "March 6, 1463-4. Item: payd for red wyn at the Bere in Sowthewerke, iijd." And again, "March 14 (same year). Item: payd at dyner at the Bere in Sowthewerke, in costys, iijs. iiijd. Item: that my mastyr lost at shotynge, xxd."

of Gwypiswiche (Ipswich), gentleman, conveyed to Henry Leke, of
Suthwark, beer-brewer (with other premises), the yearly quit rent of two
shillings, going out of a tenement, being a tavern called the " Beare," in
Southwark aforesaid, and in the parish of St. Olaf (St. Olave); and
another deed of the same date, and to the like effect, is witnessed by
" Roger Hyepy," who, I find by the parish books, was at that time
landlord of the " Bear," which was a house much frequented by the
inhabitants of Southwark.* It is frequently mentioned in the accounts
of the churchwardens of St. Olave's : for instance :—

> "1568 to 1570.
>
> Itm, for iiij dinners at the Visitations, whereof one at the } viijl. xiijs.
> Church hows and three at the Beare . . . . . . . }
>
> Itm, p'd for drinkinge at ye Beare, with Mr. Norryes, par- } ixs. iiijd.
> son, and certaine of the auncients of the parish . . . }
>
> Itm, p'd another tyme at the same place for the lyke } vs. vijid."
> drynkynge. . . . . . . . . . . . . . . . }

There are extant two tradesmen's tokens of the seventeenth century,
issued by occupiers of the " Bear." † One has on the obverse a bear
with a chain, and the inscription—" Abraham Browne, at ye," and on

the reverse—" Bridg foot, Southwark :"
in the centre—" His Halfpeny ;" and the
other has on the obverse a bear passant,
with collar and chain, and the inscription—" Cornelius Cooke, at the ;" re-
verse, " Beare at the Bridgefut ;" in the centre, C. C. A.

Cornelius Cooke was a man of some note in his time. I find him
mentioned in the parish accounts of St. Olave's, as overseer of the land
side, as early as 1630. He afterwards became a soldier, and was a
captain of the Trained Bands. He rose to the rank of colonel in Cromwell's army, and was appointed one of the commissioners for the sale
of the king's lands. After the restoration of King Charles II. he seems
to have settled down among his old friends in St. Olave's, as landlord of

---

* It may probably be shown in one of the three gabled houses to the left of our view of the Southwark Gate.

† Manning and Bray's " Surrey," vol. iii. Appendix. Akerman's " Tradesmen's Tokens."

the "Bear," at the Bridge-foot, where he doubtless frequently fought o'er his fields again, and told his tales of the civil wars.

Gerrard, in a letter to Lord Strafford (printed among the Strafford papers), dated January, 1633, intimates that all back doors to taverns on the Thames were commanded to be shut up; only the "Bear" at the Bridge-foot is exempted, for the convenience of passengers to Greenwich.* The "Bear," at London Bridge foot, is twice mentioned by Samuel Pepys in his amusing Diary :—" 24 February, 1666-7. Going thro' bridge by water, my waterman told me how the mistress of the 'Beare' tavern, at the Bridge-foot, did lately fling herself into the Thames, and drown herself; which did trouble me the more when they told me it was she that did live at the 'White Horse' tavern, in Lombard Street, which was a most beautiful woman as most I have seen. It seems she has had long melancholy upon her, and hath endeavoured to make away with herself often.

" 3 April, 1667. Here I hear how the King is not so well pleased with this marriage between the Duke of Richmond and Mrs. Stewart as is talked : and that he, by a wile, did fetch her to the 'Beare,' at the Bridge-foot, where a coach was ready, and they are stole away into Kent, without the King's leave; and that the King hath said he will never see her more : but people do think that it is only a trick." †

The "Bear" continued to afford hospitable entertainment to all who

---

* The "Cavaliers' Ballad" on the magnificent funeral honours rendered to Admiral Dean (killed June 2nd, 1653) while passing by water to Henry the Seventh's Chapel, has the following allusion—

"From Greenwich towards the Bear at Bridge-foot,
He was wafted with wind that had water to 't."

In another ballad, " On banishing the Ladies out of Town" by the commonwealth authorities, the notoriety of the " Bear " at Bridge-foot is again manifest :—

"Farewell, Bridgefoot, and Bear thereby,
And those bald pates that stand so high ;
We wish it from our very souls
That other heads were on those poles."
BURN's *Catalogue of Beaufoy Tokens.*

The allusion to bald pates refers to the traitors' heads exposed on the Bridge-gate.

† There is yet another poetical reference to the " Bear " at Bridge-foot, in a scarce poem entitled " The Last Search after Claret in Southwark; or, A Visitation of the Vintners in the Mint; with the Debates of a Committee of that profession, thither fled to avoid the cruel persecution of their unmer-

could pay, until the year 1761, when it was pulled down, on the bridge
being widened, and the houses thereon removed.    In the *Public
Advertiser* of Saturday, December 26, 1761, is the following announce-
ment:—"Thursday last the workmen employed in pulling down the
'Bear' tavern, at the foot of London Bridge, found several pieces of
gold and silver coin of Queen Elizabeth, and other monies to a considerable value." *

FRESH WHARF.

A group of clippers and sharp-bowed steamers, all busily taking in
cargo or passengers, arrests our attention on the left after passing the

ciful creditors: a Poem.  London: printed for E. Hawkins, 1691," quarto; in which the "Bear" is
thus mentioned by the author, after landing at Pepper Alley:—

> " Through stinks of all sorts, both the simple and compound,
>   Which through narrow alleys our senses do confound,
>   We came to the Bear, which we soon understood
>   Was the first house in Southwark built after the Flood,
>   And has such a succession of vintners known,
>   Not more names were e'er in Welsh pedigrees shown;
>   But claret with them was so much out of fashion,
>   That it has not been known there a whole generation."

* "Chronicles of London Bridge," p. 548.

bridge : this is at FRESH WHARF. The vessels are unloaded by porters, provided with a number of metal tickets, denoting the quantity each man brings as he delivers his load and his ticket to the warehouseman. By this means fraud is prevented, the work is fairly apportioned to each, and they are paid by reckoning the number of tickets delivered to the superintendent. These vessels present a strong contrast in their more graceful outlines to the bluff-bowed colliers and barges that lie so thickly in the vicinity, and serve to indicate the rapid improvement made in ship-building of late years.

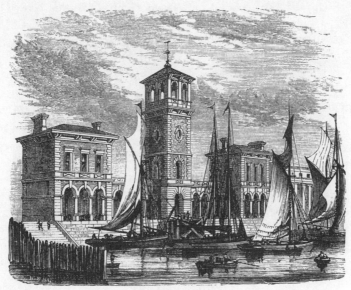

BILLINGSGATE.

A few hundred yards from this wharf, and we arrive at BILLINGSGATE, now a fine and convenient market, but a few years since a collection of dirty hovels and stalls, disgraceful to a civilized community : it was built and enlarged from the designs of the city architect, Mr. J. B. Bunning, between the years 1849 and 1853. It is a picturesque erection, in the Italian style, of red brick, with stone arcades and dressings. The central bell-tower is a striking feature of the design. The fishing-boats are moored to a floating quay in front of the market during the night, and the business commences every morning at five, by ring of bell. The fish is brought ashore in baskets, and sold by "Dutch auction" to the fishmongers, whose carts crowd Thames Street, and distribute their freight over London. It has been a market from the earliest times, and the toll on fishing-boats is noted in the laws of Æthelstan, who died A.D. 940.* It was first made a "free and open market for all sorts of fish," by an act of William III., bearing date 1699. Opposite the market, in Thames Street, is the New Coal

REMAINS OF ROMAN HOUSE, COAL EXCHANGE.

Exchange, a noble building, also erected by Mr. Bunning. The circular hall is decorated with figures of fossil plants found in coal strata, and the whole of the ornament is similarly appropriate; it is surrounded by three tiers of galleries, and lighted by a glass dome. In digging for

---

* The name is said to have been derived from Belin, King of the Britons 400 years before Christ; but upon no better evidence than that of Geoffrey of Monmouth, which is of not the slightest value: it more probably obtained a name from the spot being owned by some of the old Saxon tribe of Belingas, whose patronymic occurs in other localities.

the foundation in the month of January, 1848, the fragments of a
ROMAN HOUSE were discovered, about thirteen feet below the present
level of Thames Street; it was built upon piles, and provided with
drains to carry off the waste water. The portion of this house thus
uncovered consisted but of two rooms, the greater part of the building
running beneath the adjacent warehouses. The extreme length of the
ruins was about fifteen yards. The walls were composed of the ordinary flat Roman tiles in regular layers, varied occasionally by a course
of plain yellow tiles, and were about three feet four inches in thickness.
The rooms were on different levels; the square tesseræ which floored
the lower room (a portion of which is seen on the right of our cut) were
formed from fragments of the ordinary tiles used by builders at the
period of its erection, and were laid upon a concrete composed of quick-
lime, sand, and pounded tiles, with a mixture of small stones. The
upper floor is composed of concrete only; beneath the floor was a
hypocaust for warming the apartment, and open flues were continued
therefrom up the walls. This interesting fragment has been arched
over and preserved, and is the only portion of a Roman house existing
in London, though traces of many such have, from time to time, been
discovered. A descent of several stairs leads to the ruins now preserved,
which consist of the principal fragments exhumed, comprising parts of
the hypocaust and walls, and a seat formed of Roman tile. Other portions of the building have not been retained, as they consisted of walls
only. The visitor now treads upon the pavement where once the Roman
inhabitant walked. The hypocaust, supported by blocks of red square
tiles, firmly compacted with mortar, is nearly filled with pure spring-
water, for which a drain has been provided, so that the same necessity
for preventing an overflow is obliged to be adopted now as was adopted
in the days of the Cæsars.

The long façade of the CUSTOM-HOUSE next attracts the eye, with its
noble esplanade, adjoining Billingsgate Market. It is from the design
of Sir Robert Smirke, in 1825, the old Custom-house having been
destroyed by fire February 12, 1814. The long room is one of the
largest in Europe, being 199 feet by 66, and nearly 40 feet in height.

Here is transacted the principal business of our enormous London trade, and no more striking picture of the vast importance of our city can be given than this always busy scene presents.

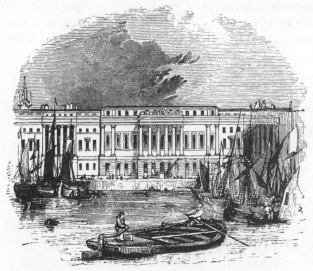

THE CUSTOM-HOUSE.

The TOWER OF LONDON is the next great feature on the Thames. The esplanade, now closed to the public, once formed an agreeable promenade. We see from the water the Traitors' Gate, with its round towers at each angle, and the deep stone stairs that led to the prison from the water. This gate exhibits a specimen of the most ancient part of the fortifications, being surrounded by a covered way, and provided with loopholes, by which archers might defend it from external assailants, or harass them within if they obtained entrance. Above it rises the Bloody Tower, so named from the traditionary story of its being the scene of the murder of the young princes, sons of Edward IV. It has no doubt been—

" With many a foul and midnight murder fed."

Above all rises the square mass of the White Tower, the oldest part of the buildings, and a conspicuous object from many points of the river.

It was erected by Gundulph, the clerical architect to the founder, William the Conqueror, and was begun in 1078; the walls are from ten to twelve feet in thickness. It has been occasionally repaired, and the external features somewhat altered by the insertion of windows, and the addition of cupolas in the time of William III.; but it is substantially ancient: the staircases and rooms are all antique. The council-chamber,

THE TOWER.

and the vaulted rooms on the first floor, are of much interest; but the great feature of the interior is the small CHAPEL OF ST. JOHN, the most perfect piece of Norman architecture the metropolis can show, and which was used for centuries by our ancient kings when the Tower was their chief royal London residence. It is supported by massive round columns, with capitals simply decorated, and has an ambulatory outside them; the end is apsidal, and it is lighted by deeply-recessed, round-headed windows. It was for a long time used as a repository for records, which have now all been removed.

The history of the Tower must be sought in the portly volumes which antiquaries of note have devoted to the important theme. It is not possible for us to descant upon the thick-coming memories which crowd the mind as we contemplate the old building. There is, however, one curious anecdote of its use in curbing insurrections, in the olden time,

CHAPEL IN THE TOWER.

so characteristic of the age, that we give it as narrated in "Hall's Chronicle." A cross fire of ordnance between the Tower and South-wark would be a startling occurrence at the present day. In the turbulent reign of Henry VI., in the year 1460, "on the news of the landing of the Yorkist army, commanded by the Earls of March, Salisbury, and Warwick, from Calais, which was afterwards joined by Lord Cobham and the Archbishop of Canterbury (Bourchier), Lord Scales was dispatched by the king, with the Earl of Kendal and Lord Lovel, and a considerable body of troops, for the protection of London; but the citizens being decidedly in favour of the opposite party, refused their assistance, whereupon Lord Scales entered the Tower with his forces, and omitted no opportunity to revenge the disloyalty of the citizens: but he was shortly afterwards besieged in the Tower by the Earl of Salisbury, Lord Cobham, and Sir John Wenloke; the latter carried on the siege on the eastern side of the fortress, Lord Cobham, with certain of the aldermen of the City, kept the west side, *and on the south artillery was planted on the opposite side of the river.* By these means the Tower was so vigilantly watched that no person could issue out or enter in, to the great displeasure of the Lord Scales and his company, who daily shot their ordnance, and had likewise great ordnance shot at them, to the hurt and no pleasure of both parties."* Some of the stone shot fired from the battery in Southwark against the Tower on this occasion were found in the Tower ditch a few years since, and were exhibited by Robert Porrett, Esq., F.S.A., to the Society of Antiquaries in November, 1843. A stone 8 lb. shot has recently been found at Mark Brown's Wharf, Southwark, which is immediately opposite to the Tower, and is now being rebuilt by C. Leach, Esq. This was doubtless one of those fired from the Tower against the battery in Southwark.

From the Tower Stairs the view, looking either way, is very striking; the river is crowded with shipping and steamers, and from this point begins that succession of vessels which affords the voyager so grand an idea of the vast trade of the British metropolis. There are, perhaps, few sights in the world more striking—certainly none more calculated to make an Englishman proud of his country. Here are not only the merchantmen of every part of the Queen's dominions, but the ships that bear " to and fro" the wealth of every civilized nation and people. " The Pool of the Thames "—for so is named that portion of our noble river that runs between the Isle of Dogs and the Tower—is truly a grand and glorious sight; the proudest " station " in the world : where gather vessels of all sizes, of every form and character, from every seaport of the globe.

The Surrey side of the river, from London Bridge to Rotherhithe, is now covered with warehouses and buildings : anciently it was open fields

---

* Brayly's "History of the Tower."

and grazing grounds; it is only in comparatively recent time it has
been densely populated. The Church of St. Olave, with its low square
steeple, is first noticed after passing London Bridge; the church at the
foot of the bridge on the City side is also dedicated to the same saint.*
Near it in olden time stood the mansions of the Earls of Warren and

SHIPS AT TOWER STAIRS.

Surrey, of the Prior of Lewes, the Abbots of St. Augustine's, Canterbury,
and other important personages. Then came an open space, still known
by its old name, Horslydown, where the parish butts were set up for
archery in the days of Henry VIII.; a mill belonging to the Knights of
St. John of Jerusalem was close by the river-side, and the large monastery of Bermondsey at about half a mile distant from it. Towards the

---

* St. Olave was the first Christian king of Norway, and was martyred by his rebellious subjects
A.D. 1030. He assisted King Ethelred, his godfather, in driving the Danes from London and Southwark, coming up the Thames with a strong fleet, and planning the destruction of London Bridge,
which thus cut off the two bodies of invaders, and made them an easier victory. The dedication of
these two churches, on the scene of his prowess, is generally thought to have originated in gratitude
for his timely aid. Tooley Street is a modern corruption of St. Olave's Street.

middle of the seventeenth century building commenced in this quarter; it has increased until Rotherhithe has been joined to Southwark by streets.

Rotherhithe is a town of very ancient foundation, and some etymologists derive its name from two Saxon words, signifying " the Sailor's Haven." It was originally part of the royal manor of Bermondsey, and the residence of some of our early kings. Edward III. here fitted out one of his fleets. It is now chiefly remarkable for the Commercial

ROTHERHITHE CHURCH: TUNNEL PIER.

Docks, which are said to occupy the trenches first cut by Canute in the eleventh century, and which extended to Battersea, thus turning Southwark into a sort of island, as a defence against attacks in that quarter. The docks are five in number, and comprise about sixty acres of water and forty of land, and they have immense granaries near them. Close beside ROTHERHITHE CHURCH is the entrance to the Thames Tunnel, which unites the banks of the river by an underground communication, consisting of a double passage, conjoined by a central arcade lit with gas, with footways on each side for pedestrians, and a carriage-way; but as it would require a very lengthy inclined plane to the mouth of the Tunnel on each side, that part of the scheme has never been carried out: foot passengers descend by a well-staircase. Each archway is about 20 feet in height; the entire width of the Tunnel is 35 feet, and at high water it is 75 feet below the surface. It was planned by the late Sir Isambart Brunel in 1823; and on the 25th of March, 1843, it was first opened to passengers. It is kept open day and night, the toll being one penny; and, on some occasions, a kind of fancy fair has been held in it.

From the Tower to the entry to this Tunnel, at Wapping, the Thames is lined with warehouses, wharves, and docks. Of the latter, the most important are St. Katherine's Docks, in close contiguity to the Tower. They take their name from the old hospital dedicated to St. Katherine, which once stood on this site, and which was founded by Matilda, the wife of King Stephen, A.D. 1148. When the old building was pulled down in 1827, the hospital and church were rebuilt in the Regent's Park. The docks were begun in May, 1827, and finished in October of the following year—a gigantic work, completed in an incredibly short time, by the continuous labour of 2500 workmen. The lock from the Thames has greater depth of water than any other dock-entry; it is 28 feet at some tides, and ships of 700 tons burthen can always enter. The warehouses surrounding it are on a gigantic scale, and are specially secure, owing to the lofty walls surrounding them. These docks were planned by the great engineer, Telford, and constructed by Hardwick, at a cost of £1,700,000.

The London Docks adjoin St. Katherine's, and have three entrances from the Thames. They were constructed by John Rennie, and opened in 1805. The larger docks can accommodate more than 300 vessels. There is warehouse-room for 220,000 tons of goods, and cellarage for 80,000 pipes of wine. These cellars are one of "the sights" of London, and a "tasting ticket" for wines is a privilege strangers are generally anxious to obtain through merchants who keep stock here. A small dock is exclusively devoted to vessels laden with tobacco, and a very large warehouse is consigned to its exclusive use, with a furnace near, where damaged or forfeited tobacco is destroyed. To a stranger there is no more curious and instructive sight than the London Docks, and nothing can give a better idea of the vast wealth and trade of the British Islands.

Wapping, Shadwell, and Limehouse (and the hamlets of Ratcliffe and Poplar) are the parishes in which these docks are situate. Their churches may be seen from the river, but they are comparatively modern, and call for no especial remark. The tower of St. Anne's, Limehouse,

ENTRANCE TO THE WEST INDIA DOCKS.

is most conspicuously seen where the river widens to the well-known "Pool of the Thames," and is crowded with craft of all kinds—a more striking scene than can be elsewhere viewed between London and the Nore. The river here sweeps round "Cuckold's Point," where the gates of the Regent's Canal may be seen; those of the City Canal, which cuts across the ISLE OF DOGS to save the circuit made by the

river opposite Greenwich; and the ENTRANCE TO THE WEST INDIA
DOCKS. These are said to be the largest in the world. They are nearly
three times as extensive as the London Docks, and include about 290
acres. The Import Dock, to the north, can accommodate 250 vessels of
300 tons each; and the southern, or Export Dock, can hold 195. They
were commenced in the year 1800, Jessop being the engineer, and
opened two years afterwards. They occupy the whole length of the
back of the Isle of Dogs, from Limehouse to Blackwall; their tall

ISLE OF DOGS.

warehouses and tiers of ships rise boldly above its level, and form a
striking background as we pass them on the Thames. The canal which
cuts across it is nearly three quarters of a mile long, with lock-gates at
each end 45 feet in width; it is now chiefly used as a dock.

The river bank of the island is generally known as Millwall, a name
derived from the embankment, once surmounted by windmills, of which
one still remains, and is seen in our engraving.

At Deptford, opposite, we arrive at the first town in Kent. Its name has little altered in the course of ages, so that its original meaning, *deep ford*, may still be traced. This manor was given by William the Conqueror to one of his followers, Gilbert de Maignent, who erected a castle here. It is chiefly remarkable as the place of residence * of Peter the Great, when he lived here to learn the art of ship-building;

DEPTFORD DOCKYARD.

and as containing the Royal Dockyard, established as early as the time of Henry VIII., and continued with improvements to the present day. The whole is immediately under the inspection of the Navy Board: about 1500 labourers are constantly employed here.† The

* Unfortunately, this interesting structure has been recently taken down, and no vestige of it now remains.

† Deptford Dockyard is famous for its bakehouses and biscuit factory, which are most admirably constructed, and make some of the best bread her Majesty's service is supplied with. It is considered as one of the chief victualing establishments for the navy; but has also some very large slips, where many of our finest vessels have been built. The whole is under the inspection of a captain superintendent.

whole extent of the yard includes about thirty-one acres. Many convicts are employed at the works, and the whole presents generally a very busy and well-ordered scene.

Queen Elizabeth visited the celebrated Captain Drake in his ship at Deptford, after he had completed his famous voyage round the world. She dined with him on board the vessel, and afterwards conferred on him the honour of knighthood, allowing him to assume the figure of a globe in a ship in his coat of arms, in memory of his having been the first circumnavigator of the world. The vessel in which he had performed the feat, and nobly entertained the Sovereign, was, by her Majesty's orders, preserved in the Royal Dockyard; and, when it went to decay, its timbers were formed into various relics. An elbow chair made of this wood is still preserved at Oxford.

The old church at Deptford is appropriately dedicated to St. Nicholas, the patron of seafaring men. The tower, of flint and stone, is embattled. In the church is the monument of Captain Edward Fenton, who accompanied Frobisher in his voyages, and was afterwards engaged in the action with the Spanish Armada. He died 1603. Another monument is to the memory of Peter Pett, master shipwright in the King's Yard here, who died 1652, and who first invented the war-ship known as a frigate. His family had long been distinguished for superior talent in ship-building, and his father, Phineas Pett, built, in 1637, the *Sovereign of the Seas*, the largest ship ever built before, and mounted with 160 guns. The meetings of the corporation of the Trinity House were originally held in Deptford; the hospital for old mariners still adjoins the church.*

---

* "The society of the Trinity House, founded by Sir Thomas Spert, Comptroller of the Navy to Henry VIII., was first established at this place, and incorporated by the name of 'The Master, Warden, and Assistants of the Guild or Fraternity of the most glorious and undivided Trinity, and of St. Clement, in the parish of Deptford, Stroud, in the county of Kent.' This company consists of a master, deputy-master, thirty-one elder brethren, and an unlimited number of inferior members, out of whom the elder brethren are elected. Among these are always some of the great officers of state; the remainder are captains either in the royal navy or of merchantmen. This corporation, having for its object the increase and encouragement of navigation, the good government of seamen, an the security of merchantmen on the coasts, is invested with the powers of examining the mathematica classes in Christ's Hospital; of examining and licensing masters of ships; appointing pilots both for the royal navy and for merchant ships; settling the rates of pilotage; erecting, ordering, and main-

At Deptford, if we are journeying by land, we have just passed the boundary of the county of Surrey and entered that of Kent, which we do not again leave, inasmuch as it continues to border the right bank of the river all the way to its junction with the sea. Deptford is made famous by its connection with many great men in naval history; but it boasts also of the residence of one philosopher. Sayes' Court (so called from the name of the family who long inhabited it) was once the residence of John Evelyn; and in 1598 he lent it to the Czar Peter the Great, at that time studying the art of ship-building in the dockyards of Deptford. It stood on the site of the old workhouse; it is now entirely gone: but tradition is yet active in the locality, and in the writings of "the lover of trees" may be found much curious matter concerning the Muscovite, who had sadly disturbed the harmony and tried the temper of him who, at all times and in all places, was a worshipper of Nature,— the czar was a "hedge-breaker," who ruined his garden,* and who had "a house full of people right nasty;" and it was a joy to the gentle old man when the time of imperial tenancy—and but a short time it was— expired, and he had again his garden, "most boscaresque, being, as it were an exemplar of his book of forest trees." A small river, the Ravensbourne, joins the Thames at Deptford.† Rising out of a pure stream on Keston Heath, it pursues its pleasant course,—

> "Wanders in Hayes and Bromley, Beckingham vale,
> And straggling Lewisham, to where Deptford Bridge
> Uprises, in obedience to its flood."

taining light-houses, buoys, beacons, and other sea-marks for the better security of ships; granting license to seamen to row on the Thames in time of peace, or when past service; licensing aliens to serve on board English ships; hearing and determining complaints of officers and seamen in the merchant service, subject to an appeal to the Admiralty. The revenue of the company, which arises from tonnage, ballastage, beaconage, &c., and from contingent benefactions, is applied (after defraying the expenses of light-houses, &c.) to the relief of decayed seamen, their widows, and orphans. The members of this corporation enjoy various privileges and immunities. The ancient Hall at Deptford, where their meetings were formerly held, was pulled down about the year 1787, and an elegant building erected for that purpose in London, near the Tower. The arms of this corporation are Argent, a cross Gules between four ships of three masts in full sail, proper."—*Lysons.*

* Evelyn laments most pitifully the damage done to his garden, and speaks of it as "my now ruined garden of Sayes' Court, thanks to the Czar of Muscovy!" Peter is traditionally asserted to have delighted in being driven through Evelyn's much-prized and neatly-trimmed hedges in a wheelbarrow!

† "The name of this place was anciently written Depeford, signifying the deep ford, where the bridge now is over the Ravensbourne."—*Lysons.*

In the river a little below was placed, as a hospital ship for all nations, the *Dreadnought*, which had been famous in many sea-fights of Nelson's era. It was used for a charitable institution, supported by voluntary contributions, and the old vessel, now broken up, was granted for the purpose to the Seamen's Hospital Society by the Government. Another

THE OLD DREADNOUGHT.

line-of-battle ship, formerly the *Caledonia*, has been lately altered at Woolwich, and admirably fitted to receive a larger number of patients. Here also is at present moored the great ship-building marvel of the age and the world,—the *Leviathan*, or the *Great Eastern*.

We now arrive at Greenwich : that town has been famous since the days of the Saxons, who named it *Grenewic*, a name it has retained, with very slight alteration, to the present day. Its park is a favourite resort for Londoners; its hospital the pride of England.

We have been voyaging among the ships of all nations, with huge store-houses, quays, and wharves on either side; the river now, however, widens out, and begins to clear somewhat; the steam-boat has a freer pathway, and may proceed with less hazard of running down some barge or row-boat, of which there seems to the inexperienced eye a peril perpetual, all the way from the Tower, through "the Pool," and in the over-crowded highway that leads from London downwards. A sudden turn brings us within view of Greenwich. Those who approach the hospital by driving through any of the pleasant villages that divide it

GREENWICH HOSPITAL.

from London—nominally so, indeed, for the road is now a continuation of houses all the way—will see with exceeding delight the glory of England,—the pride of every Englishman! Taken from any point of view it is "a palace"—beautiful in construction, graceful in all its proportions, as grand and imposing a structure as any nation of the modern world can show. But it is especially striking when seen as we voyage the Thames, either upwards or downwards; and dead must be the heart of him who does not share the sentiment—if he cannot repeat the lines—of the poet:—

"Hall! noblest structure, imaged on the wave!
A nation's grateful tribute to the brave:
Hall! blest retreat from war and shipwreck, hail!"

It is not because here many monarchs had their chosen seat, that as a "royal" palace it was famous for centuries—it is not even because it "gave Eliza birth" that we

"Kneel and kiss the consecrated earth;"

but because here three thousand veterans repose after years of tempest and battle—maimed many of them, aged all of them; they have done their work; they have earned repose as the right of toil, and honour as the meed of victory.

The Old Palace at Greenwich, commenced by Duke Humphrey, enlarged by the fourth Edward, added to by Henry VII., embellished by Henry VIII., by whom it was named Placentia, or "the Manor of Pleasaunce," * and subsequently a favourite residence of Edward VI., Mary, Elizabeth, and the four kings of the Stuarts, and one of the dwellings of the Lord Protector—that is not the palace our brave seamen inhabit as their own "for ever." The present hospital stands partly on its site, and during the reign of William and Mary it was dedicated to its high and holy purpose—the good and merciful suggestion emanating from the queen. Although principally the work of the architect Wren, it was added to by successive sovereigns, and finally completed by George II.—large sums having been supplied for its "finishing" out of the forfeited estates of the Earl of Derwentwater (in 1715), during the reign of George I. † From these estates, the hospital still derives a revenue, augmented from other sources—a small tax upon all seamen, duties arising from certain lighthouses, market-rents in the town, and forfeited and unclaimed prize-money.

The "old sailors" have their library, their reading-room, their picture-gallery (the famous Painted Hall, which contains a series of pictured records of glorious sea-fights), their walks in piazzas, under shelter in foul weather, and their park for promenade when the sun is shining;

---

* Henry VIII. made Greenwich, as Lambard says, "a pleasant, perfect, and princely palaice;" keeping his state here "with great noblenesse and open court," "with revels, masques, disguisings, and banquets royal."

† The hospital was opened for the reception of pensioners in the month of January, 1705.

their doctors, their nurses, their spiritual guides, and, above all, their memories of the victories they have aided to win, and the knowledge that duty and gratitude have provided for easing their ailments and comforting their old age.

At the entrance to the park, fronting it, and immediately behind the hospital, is the NAVAL SCHOOL, where numbers of happy boys may be seen

THE NAVAL SCHOOL, GREENWICH.

during play-hours. The long colonnade on each side was constructed for their use in wet weather. The whole was built in 1783, from the designs of "Athenian Stuart." The boys are fully educated for sea-service, and are bound to it for seven years on leaving the school ; many sailors have been trained here to fight their country's battles, and afterwards repose upon their laurels, in their old age, close to the scene of their earliest education.

The terrible experience of the past few years has taught us to esti-mate our soldiers almost as highly as they deserve : our "brave fellows" in the Crimea, our wonder-working troops in India, have aroused us to the necessity of a "standing army," as well as of a "floating armament."

The change, certain as unavoidable, that has followed our colonial increase, renders us no longer in fact an island; our head still wears the crown of Neptune, but our body and its members have continental requirements. The "tight little island" is not our boundary. Despite the well-intentioned but feeble remonstrances of the "peace party," and the ultra "moderation" that would govern and protect the people by the people, and make bonfires of gun-stocks, we are conscious that if we are to keep what we have got, we must be ready to fight for it on land as well as on sea.

It is somewhat remarkable that the two palaces of refuge—one for the worn-out soldier, the other for the worn-out sailor—should stand so bravely on the banks of our royal river. There is no need to tell John Bull he ought to keep up his navy, and provide "like a Briton" for his old Jack-tars when their

> " Last sea-fight is fought,
> Their task of glory done."

He is as proud of GREENWICH HOSPITAL as he is of his own estate, hereditary or acquired; or of his handsome wife, or half dozen or dozen of fair-haired children, or any particular happiness or glory that belongs exclusively to himself. There is something grand in seeing the way in which a regular Englishman wakes up after his "night's discomfort" in an Antwerp or Rotterdam boat when it comes in sight of Greenwich Hospital; he seems to have an instinctive knowledge of the fact, and you see his broad white forehead, and firm masculine features, at the right moment, as he thrusts himself among a troop of black-browed, pallid men, whiskered and bearded—the "*Mussoos*"—whose gaze is fixed on the solid, well proportioned, elaborate mass of masonry, with its lawns and its arches, its courts, its magnificent entrance, its comprehensive beauty and dignity, forming such a noble whole. Our genuine John Bull of the middle class does not speak French or German sufficiently well to be mistaken for a "native," but he gives forth the information warmly and gratuitously in a mingling of the three languages; he tells them that no continental king has so fine a palace as that, nor so fine a river to build it by: and he perplexes them by the assurance that, properly speaking, it is *not* a palace *now*, but a hospital—a home for the old sailor-men of England—the "Jack-tars" who man "the wooden walls" they hear so much—and *know* so much—about. There they are for the rest of their days—well taken care of—with goose at Michaelmas, and roast beef and plum-pudding at Christmas; and there isn't a man in England who would not spare sixpence out of his shilling to keep them there—such fine, brave old fellows! And the "Mussoos" wonder at his enthusiasm, and ask a few questions, which are willingly answered, for he loves the theme: he advises them to go and see Greenwich the first thing, for there is no home like it in the world for old sailors—nor any other old sailors that deserve such a home. About this there can be no dispute; and without bating an atom of our love for the sons of the ocean, we may surely hope that we are learning to legislate as well for our soldiers as we have done for our sailors. There is a better feeling also growing up between the two bulwarks of our safety and liberty: scenes of the most tender and affectionate brotherhood have passed between sailors and soldiers during the fearful wars of the last five years, and many a fine sailor now laid by remembers with affection the help rendered him by a soldier during dreary and disastrous sacrifices in the Crimea.

A friend of ours, who lives near Greenwich, and is as proud of the "Palace Hospital" as an Englishman ought to be, told us a little incident which it gratifies us to repeat. It is quite impossible not to observe that old Jack-tars have their favourite "runs" about Greenwich; you meet the same wooden leg at a particular corner, and at the same hour, almost (fair weather or foul) every day in the year, the same old trio "chaffing" and "yarning" on the same bench; the same "lot," with their pipes, of an afternoon in the park; their weather-beaten, broken-up faces, and their broken-up limbs, become *your* "familiars." They are not cordial at first with strangers, but our friend considers them worth knowing, and whenever he approaches a bench where trios or duos of the old fellows meet, there is immediately a courteous recognition of the "gentleman" who carries a snuff-canister always, and a roll of pigtail sometimes, for their especial comfort. You may coax a soldier with a cigar, but a sailor scorns it, and remains true as the needle to the pole to his "quid."

When the Crimean war was at the hottest, and hands trembled to unclose the lists of killed and wounded, our friend, on his morning walk down to "the boat," which he prefers as a mode of transit to the great Babylon, observed a somewhat stately old sailor walking by the aid of a wooden leg and a stick, sometimes beside the park wall when it was shady, at other times sitting on the grass in the sun. His habits were different from those of his messmates; he had no particular "run," but seemed to study the pleasure and caprice of a small Skye terrier, who was his constant companion. The dog was as shapeless and ragged as even "a Skye" can be; his large, bright, intense eyes glared from beneath his shaggy brows, and his short, stumpy legs were terminated by masses of blackish hair. He was what "the fancy" call "blue," and his broad black nose and sweeping tail constituted him a perfect "beauty." Sometimes he chose to walk by the park wall, and then his master followed; then "Skye" would take to the common, and, without a word, the obedient master would steer after him; then he would converse with other little dogs, and the old sailor would wait until the conversation was over. He never interfered except when "Skye" desired to attack donkeys or donkey-boys; then his protector would hook him up (he could not weigh more than four pounds) with his stick, tuck him under his arm, and disappear with him altogether. There was something so odd in the old sailor reversing the order of things, and following the dog instead of the dog following him, that our friend desired to make his acquaintance; but the old man evidently chose to keep out of every one's way. One evening, however, our friend suddenly came upon him at a turn in the park; the dog had taken a fancy to a tuft of *fiorn* grass, which dogs have the sagacity to know is good for them; and while he was picking off its long narrow leaves, the old man rested against a tree, patiently waiting the little beast's pleasure. Our friend opened the acquaintance by praising "Skye's" beauty; but instead of the courteous reply he expected, the old tar caught up the dog, and then turning sharply round, surveyed the gentleman from head to foot.

" You cannot suppose," said our kindly friend, "that I would deprive you of your dog?"

In reply to this he laid him gently down.

" No, sir, now I see you clear, I don't think *you* would; but you, as well as others, often cast an eye at him, and some come and offer me money for him, thinking that such as I would sell *love* for *money!* Why, bless your heart, selling that dog would be like selling my own flesh and blood!"

" It certainly is a beautiful little creature."

" Well, so everybody says. I wish it wer'n't, for the dog-stealers are after it, and if I lost it, it would kill me. It seemed to take a deal to kill me, too. I don't think there's six square inches of my body without a scar, and I wish I had a dozen bodies to give to the same service; but though *they* didn't send me to the locker, if I lost that dog I should never leave my bed again." He was about to follow the dog, who had finished his frugal repast, but our friend tempted him with a "quid." For once a low whistle intimated that he requested the dog's return, and Skye came, and laid him meekly down at his *foot*. A pinch of snuff cemented the acquaintance; and though they parted immediately after, at their next meeting he told our friend why he so loved the dog.

His grandson was a soldier in the 50th regiment: he would rather, he confessed, he had been a sailor, but his fancy was for the scarlet instead of the blue. No matter! his heart and his life were his Queen's, and a finer or handsomer lad was not in the regiment. He went out as lance-corporal. Before he went he brought him his little dog; and, though contrary to regulations, they let the old man keep his grandson's dog until his return—only, of course, until his return. No wonder he was so careful of Jamie's little dog. Here he paused: and then asked our friend if he saw the papers daily.

"Certainly."

The hard cordage of the veteran's face twitched and moved convulsively, and his hand appeared as if knotted to his stick. " Was there anything about the 50th regiment?"

" Nothing yesterday, but an engagement was expected?"

"Of course, sir, he knows his duty, and will do it, and has as good a chance of his life as another. I used always to spend an hour or two at the 'Anchor,' hearing the news, and the talk that followed; but now I can't bear it! The sight, sir, of a newspaper sets me all of a tremble! Isn't that quare for an old hulk like me, whose masts have gone by the board, and who hasn't a rag of canvas left? But it's true, sir. I steer clear of all my comrades, for it shakes me worse than the wind of a twelve-pounder to hear their talk. I have been ankle deep—ay, ankle deep in blood, sir, before now, on the deck of a 'seventy-four,' and never heeded it—the more death the less care;—and now——If I could read the paper myself I should not mind it, I think; but I am no scholar, and the dread of hearing——But I have one comrade who reads the news every day, and we hit on a signal. He comes over there, just at post-meridian, and as long as all's well, why, he steers up and down a bit, and then gets under way; but if there should be anything wrong —if the boy was badly hurt—he'd tie his black neckerchief to his crutch, and put it over his shoulder—a black flag, you know. There! he's heaving in sight! that's my old comrade."

The stick fell to the ground as he pointed him out; he threw back his hat, shaded his eyes from the sun, and, grasping our friend's arm, pointed to where his "comrade" moved slowly on—the black handkerchief floating behind him like a pennon!

What followed must be imagined, not described: it was too true—the brave sailor's grandson was returned amongst the list of "killed" as having "fallen in the trenches."

The old man remained rigid as marble, fixed in a state of coma long after he was laid on his bed, surrounded by his old comrades, and tenderly cared for by the physician. The first symptom he gave of returning consciousness was putting out his hand to feel for the dog. The fond animal was then permitted to follow its own will; it crept up and licked his face: this had the happy effect of causing a heavy burst of tears; and while he wept he pressed "Skye" closer and closer to his bosom.

There was no harm in suggesting that there might be an error; that men were frequently returned dead who had been only badly wounded or missing; that such had been the case even with officers. He did not seem to heed or to hear, but wept on.

In the strength and blessing of his hopeful spirit, our friend went to the Horse Guards, but there they could only refer to the list as it was in the last despatch. The next was long in coming: but when it did arrive there was more than usual excitement among the Greenwich pensioners; many of "the maimed and the halt" cheered as in the days of their youth; and as to the old bearer of the *black* flag, he see-sawed into the ward—which our friend's friend had never quitted since his bereavement—with a small snowy window curtain depending from his crutch; and then came a convulsed cry and trembling words—"He is not dead!" "Not dead?" "No; badly wounded—doing well—complimented—coming home!" And he *did* come home too, the brave gallant soldier, with three stripes on his arm; and his grandfather—ay, and his little dog—saw him receive his medal from the hand of his own honoured QUEEN.

The Observatory at Greenwich occupies the site on which formerly stood "a tower," which tower was "sometimes a habitation for the younger branches of the royal family, sometimes the residence of a favourite mistress, sometimes a prison, and sometimes a place of defence." It was founded by Charles II., for the benefit of his "pilots and sailors," "for the purpose of ascertaining the motions of the moon, and the places of the fixed stars, as a means of discovering that great desideratum, the longitude at sea."

The town of Greenwich * is busy, populous, and prosperous; its church contains many interesting monuments; it is, however, comparatively modern, having been consecrated in 1718, occupying the site of a very venerable edifice, the old Church of St. Alphege. Here, as will be supposed, rest many of our naval heroes. There is one object, fronting the palace on the waterside, that will attract the eye of all

---

* " Grenewic, or Grenevic, as this place was called by the Saxons, is literally the green village; meaning, perhaps, the village on the green."—*Lysons.*

passers; it is a monument, erected by public subscription, to the memory of a young and gallant French officer, Lieutenant Bellott, who died a volunteer in the service of England, the companion and friend of our Arctic voyagers.

While at Greenwich, we may visit Blackheath,—"so called, as some think, from the appearance of the soil, or, as others suppose, from its *bleak* situation,"—the picturesque villages of Lewisham and Sydenham, and the venerable mansion of Eltham, concerning which the history of many periods is full. Nor may we pass unnoticed an object seen from many parts of the river, and from the adjacent country, as well as from the heights and house-roofs in and about London, that wonder of the modern world, the Crystal Palace.

On the shore opposite to Greenwich, after passing the extremity of the Isle of Dogs, is Blackwall, famous chiefly for its fertility in producing the tiny fish known as whitebait, concerning which a few particulars will not be unwelcome to the reader.

There are few denizens of London unacquainted with this tiny fish,* as it appears daily during the season, dressed, at Blackwall and Green-

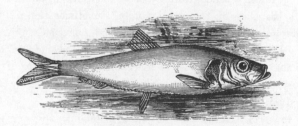

WHITEBAIT.

wich, where alone it is obtained "in perfection;" for unless "cooked" within a very brief space after removal from the water, it undergoes a change which the "nice" palate can at once detect. It would be curious to ascertain how many millions are taken daily during the

---

* It may be well to note here that our cut represents the "tiny fish" of its full size, the only instance in which that size has been adopted for the piscatory engravings of our volume.

months of June, July, and August of each year. It is unquestionably
a delicacy, and is relished greatly by tens of thousands who can afford
to buy luxuries; "a whitebait dinner" being a treat peculiar to the
metropolis, and enjoyed accordingly, even by those who believe and
maintain that the fish is engendered by London mud, and that, when
the Thames is cleansed and purified, the whitebait will vanish altogether
from the river.

An idea prevails that it is the young of some larger fish. Yarrell,
whose authority on such matters is universally accepted, says "it is a
distinct species," and in its habits differs materially from all other British
species of Clupea (*Clupeidæ*, the family of the herrings) that visit our
shores or our rivers. From the beginning of April to the end of
September they are caught in abundance; in April, they are small,
"apparently but just changed from the albuminous state of very young

FISHING FOR WHITEBAIT.

fry; in September specimens four or five inches long are not uncommon,"
but mixed, even at this late period of the season, with others of very
small size, "as though the roe had continued to be deposited throughout
the summer." Yet the parent fish are not caught, and are believed by
the fishermen not to come up higher than the estuary, where nets sufficiently small to stop them are not much in use. The largest whitebait

3 R

Mr. Yarrell had seen was in length six inches. "The colour of the sides is uniformly white;" "the length of the head, as compared with that of the body, alone is as two to five; the eye large; the irides silvery; the upper part of the back pale greenish ash." In their habits they appear to be similar to the young of the herring, always keeping in shoals, and swimming occasionally near the surface of the water. Mr. Yarrell thus describes the mode of fishing for whitebait:—"The mouth of the net is by no means large, measuring only about three feet square in extent; but the mesh of the hose, or bag-end of the net, is very small. The boat is moored in the tide-way, where the water is from twenty to thirty feet deep, and the net, with its wooden framework, is fixed to the side of the boat. The tail of the hose, swimming loose, is from time to time handed into the boat, the end untied, and its contents taken out. The wooden frame, forming the mouth of the net, does not dip more than four feet below the surface of the water." There is no doubt of their being found in other waters besides the Thames.

Passing the East India Docks, with another "forest of masts," we reach the estuary of the river Lea; here it enters the Thames, having, after its rise in Leagrave Marsh, near Luton, in Bedfordshire, adorned the lordly demesnes of Luton Hoo, Brocket Hall, and Hatfield, and watered and refreshed Hertford, Ware, Hoddesdon, Broxbourne, Ches-hunt, Waltham Abbey, Enfield, Edmonton, Tottenham, Walthamstow, and Bow. It is "the gulfy Lea, with sedgy tresses," of Pope; and "the wanton Lea, that oft doth lose its way," of Spenser.

The Lea is, and has long been, in high favour with the angler; it is the river made famous by honest Izaak Walton; all readers of his book are familiar with the places which adorn its banks, from "Theobalds" and Amwell Hill to Bow. Sitting here on one of its banks, arranging his hook or trimming his fly, the good old man may be supposed to have uttered that sentiment so dear to every brother of the gentle craft—"No life, my honest scholar, no life so happy and so pleasant as the life of a well-governed angler; for when the lawyer is swallowed up with busi-ness, and the statesman is preventing or contriving plots, then we sit on cowslip banks, hear the birds sing, and possess ourselves of as much quietness as these silent silver streams, which we now see glide so gently by us. Indeed, my good scholar, we may say of angling as Dr. Boteler said of strawberries, 'Doubtless God could have made a better berry, but doubtless God never did:' and so (if I might be judge) God never did make a more calm, quiet, innocent recreation than angling."

"The old course of the Lea affords many a charming picture. An old pollard willow, with an angler under its shadow, a few cows, perhaps, standing in the water, and enjoying with philosophic quiescence the cooling luxury,—perchance a punt in the middle of the river,—a bright blue sky overhead, reflected with a softened lustre in the clear stream, an abundance of yellow water-lilies at our feet, and the low banks decked with all gay flowers,—these are the materials of the picture; and he who has not his heart gladdened as he gazes on them, has yet to learn that there are things in Heaven and earth not dreamt of in his philosophy. Walton was not one of these :—

> " ' The meanest flowret of the vale,
> The simplest note that swells the gale,
> The common sun, the air, the skies,
> To him were opening Paradise.'

And only such as, in a measure, can participate in these feelings and sympathies, are fitted to wander along Izaak Walton's 'Lea.'" *

For a mile, and often more, in breadth, the river Thames in Essex is bordered by a low swampy plain; upon which, however, a range of small hills look down and form an agreeable background; but for beauty of scenery, and those interests which are derived from "history, tradition, and places populous," we must refer to Kent, which not unjustly claims pre-eminence as "the garden of England."

We must pass the somewhat distant village of Charlton, with its old manor-house of the time of James I.—keep in sight, as a most pleasant

---

* We extract this passage from the concluding volume of a very charming series of books, "Rambles by Rivers," by James Thorne, published by Charles Knight, whose name is so honourably associated with the highest and best order of English topographic works. To Mr. Thorne's volumes we have been often indebted during the course of our tour; we record our debt with gratitude. The "Rambles by Rivers" is the work of a scholar, a gentleman, a close observer, and an intense lover of nature.

view, the far-famed Shooter's Hill—and rest awhile at Woolwich, to visit, if we can and may, the noblest dockyard of the world,—its foundry, its arsenal, its schools, and its barracks.*   It is the most ancient of those magazines of our national strength and glory, and has furnished our country with most of its largest ships during the course of several reigns,—from that of Henry VIII., when the big *Harry Grace de Dieu* was launched here, to that of Queen Victoria, when it may be said to have achieved its highest glory.

It is not our purpose to describe Woolwich; to do so would require a volume, and not a page.   It is the great school of our artillery—a

WOOLWICH.

branch of the service in which officers and men are alike eminent for that educated intelligence which gives the soldier true strength.   The Arsenal is one of the chief wonders of England : science has here carried machinery to perfection.   The Academy is admirably governed : hence

---

* Woolwich is, in Doomsday, called *Hulviz*, or " the dwelling on a creek of the river. The records of succeeding periods mention it under the title of Wulewick, and afterwards Woolwiche."

issue the cadets, who obtain rank according to ability and desert. The dockyards give employment to thousands of artizans, shipwrights, and labourers. The war-ships here created bear the flag of England over the waters of every sea and ocean of the world,—

> " Far as the breezes blow, the billows roam,
> Survey our empire and behold our home."

From North Woolwich the DOCKYARD * may best be seen, with its long sea or river wall, extending from Charlton to the lower part of the

WOOLWICH DOCKYARD.

town; and this surface being covered with sheds, factories, and basins (containing many of our war-steamers, with several ships building of the first class), it assumes a singularly interesting appearance. The

---

* Visitors are admitted by signing their names in a book at the dockyard gates, and the wonders of the great steam hammer, and the interesting process of boring a cylinder for a steam engine, with the lathes, where metal shavings are cut twenty to thirty feet long, are certainly worth the trouble and expense of "a return ticket" from London.

river here is also dotted with picturesque hulks, reminding one of olden times and fights long past; they loom large against the departing sunlight, with the dockyard shears rearing up, endeavouring to compete with the great factory funnel for height. In the distance may be seen many of the numerous shipping dropping up the river with the last of the flood-tide.

Greenwich and Woolwich are neighbours. How large a volume of thought is suggested by the union of two such names!

The extensive marsh land at Plumstead, adjoining Woolwich, is now much used by the Military Academy for gunnery practice of all kinds, for which it is admirably adapted. The Thames partially encircles it, like a bent bow, and the chief roads cut it off from general traffic. It is a large tract of grass land, lying by itself in comparative solitude, used as grazing ground, or market gardens.

On the eastern side of the cheering village of RITH, the Darent contributes its waters to the Thames,—

> " The silver Darent, in whose waters clear,
> Ten thousand fishes play and deck his pleasant stream ;"

it is joined by the Cray, another " faire " river, in the marshes near the Crayford Saw Mills ; the former rising near Westerham, the latter near Orpington, in Kent, and both flowing through districts famous in the annals of the kingdom,—majestic mansions, picturesque churches, historic sites, fertile plains, quiet villages, and busy towns—the busiest of which is Dartford—happily intermixed. The conjoined rivers enter the Thames very near " Long Reach Tavern."

Our sketch of Erith was taken from the pier, looking up the river ; the limited space only represents the few houses nearest the water, with the pretty church and the rising woodland at the back. The sun was passing through a cloud, which cast a shadow over the background, giving all the near objects that glittering light so peculiar to the water. It is certainly one of the most charming spots on the river.

Nor is the coast opposite, low and uninviting and unhealthy as it seems, without its interest. Here the river Roding pays its tribute to the Thames; the spire of Barking Church is seen in the distance; Dagenham Reach, Hornchurch Marshes, and "the Rands," indicate the nature of the low-lying fields and sheets of water that skirt the great

ERITH.

river's banks. About Purfleet, however, there is a gradual rise of chalky cliffs, on one of which was placed the standard of England when our island was threatened by that Spanish invasion which Providence "set at nought." *

The once-renowned abbey of BARKING must not be passed without a word of notice, as it is now the parish church, and is a conspicuous object on the Essex side of the river, nearly opposite Woolwich, standing as it does on an elevation among the flat lands. It is of very ancient foundation, and was a monastic establishment well endowed in the middle ages. It was dedicated to the Virgin Mary, and is said

* At Purfleet is the great depot of gunpowder; and the voyager will observe several vessels moored in the river, which are also used as floating magazines.

to have been the first nunnery for women established in this kingdom. "It was founded about the year 670, by St. Erkenwald, Bishop of London, in compliance with the earnest desire of his sister, Ethelburg, who was appointed the first abbess." Many of her successors were of high rank, and some of them of the blood-royal. In 870, the abbey was burnt by the Danes, and the nuns were either slain or dispersed. About the middle of the tenth century it was rebuilt by King Edgar. The nuns were of the Benedictine order. It was surrendered to

Henry VIII. on 14th of November, 1539, "Dorothy Barley" being the last abbess. There is scarcely a vestige remaining of the once magnificent pile, which a succession of sovereigns delighted to honour. But at the entrance of the churchyard stands an ancient gateway, over which is "the chapel of the holy rood lofte atte gate edified [as is expressed in an old record] to the honor of Almighty God, and of the holy rood that is there, of right great devocion, as it sheweth by great indulgens graunted to the same chapel and place by divers of our holy faders, Popes of Rome." It is also known

CURFEW TOWER, BARKING. a

as the CURFEW TOWER :* and from thence the bell rang out at morning and evening, sometimes to the great safety

* The curfew bell was rung, according to ancient custom, as a warning for the inhabitants of towns and villages to put out their fires and retire to bed; it was a simple policy for general safety in ancient times; and though usually considered to be a vexatious law enacted after the Norman Conquest, is certainly as old as the days of Alfred. We have already noted it as still rung in some of the towns of England; and that the curfew, or *couvre feu*, used to extinguish the fire on the sound of the warning bell, was an implement of metal, which covered in the ashes raked together on the hearth, and brought them in a heap to the back of the grate, and so extinguished them. Our cut will fully exhibit its peculiarities.

of travellers in winter nights. There are records of gifts to the
monastery of many who were guided over the lonely marsh lands
through the winter fogs by
the tolling of the curfew
alone. In the old time, the
roadway between this place
and London was singularly
disagreeable : the land was
only partially drained ; the
pathways were bad, and they
were constructed on raised
embankments, which made
them dangerous to tra-
vellers in dark nights. The
parish church, dedicated to
St. Margaret, contains many
interesting and venerable monuments ; a singularly picturesque piscina we thought
it desirable to copy.

THE PISCINA.

Greenhithe and Northfleet
follow Erith, as we descend
the river, on the Kentish side. They are large and populous villages,
approaching the size and character of towns. On the high land above the
former are modern villa residences, commanding extensive views of the
river and the opposite county of Essex. Near it is Stone Church, one of
the finest and most interesting of the Kentish churches. It is in the
early English style, and abounds with beautiful architectural details. It
stands on a commanding eminence, and is clearly seen from the
Thames as we approach Greenhithe. At Northfleet is one of the
largest churches of the diocese of Canterbury, possessing some fine old
brasses, some ancient oak stalls, and other curious relics of ancient
date. The chalk pits, which first appear a little west of Greenhithe,
may be best studied at Northfleet.

While reverting to the many records of past goodness and past greatness which, in the course of our tour, we have noted as crowding the
environs of our royal river, we have a word to say concerning a daily
increasing evidence of the sympathy of the rich for the poor. We see,
at intervals not "far between," there a sanatorium, here an aged asylum
— a church — schools for the education of every denomination of
Christian childhood, hospitals for the cure of the sick, and dwellings for the protection of the helpless. These temples of charity
are erected by a liberal public ; and, from the stately building to
the humble almshouse, all tell of an earnestness in well-doing which
elevates England more even than her victories by sea and land, and
loudly proclaims that though great sins do spring up in her streets, like
foul weeds from a luxuriant soil—she makes great atonement !

They are glorious words we see so continually in England—producing
a just and holy pride, while exciting the admiration of all foreigners—
" Supported by Voluntary Contributions !"

But there are cases of individual charity standing forth in all their
dignity and purity, as incentives to others to whom God has given much,
to "do good and to distribute," which move us even more than charities
of association. It would be a singular record of well-doing, if a history
of the charities founded and endowed by persons *out of their own means*
could be compiled and published ; it would strengthen many a faint-
hearted worker, and stimulate still more the strong, to see what has been
thus effected for the good of suffering fellow-beings.

One of these " Rests" is remarkable even in this liberal age. A gentleman—whose name we do not mention, for we think it might be
distasteful to him to do so—has built a number of villa-homes adjacent
to Northfleet, where the waters of the Thames flow broadly on, and
where they may be seen by all voyagers, to shelter some of the helpless
many who, well born and well educated, have been beaten into poverty
in the great battle of life, and would have been prematurely crushed
into graves but for the generous protection afforded by these asylums,—
we use the plural, because each recipient of this good man's bounty has
a separate dwelling, where he or she may dwell, without being subject

to the interruption or observation that, to a certain extent, must be a restraint where numbers are collected into one common home.

We have not seen the internal arrangements of these "homes," erected at the sole expense of the gentleman we have alluded to, but we have heard one of the inmates gratefully describe their blessings. We know not how the beneficent "founder" has determined the "future" of his dependents, but in addition to the shelter he gives, he visits "his charges" once in each week, and bestows, delicately, with his own hand, the boon he knows will secure their comforts during the ensuing week.

If we could envy any living man, it would be the founder of such a true, high, and holy, charity. He did not wait, as many do, until he had "shuffled off his mortal coil," and then leave to his executors the task he has so happily accomplished : he felt it a privilege to do himself the work so emphatically "his own," and has thus raised a monument to his memory better than any ever built by human hands. His name may not be the most euphonious ; but it will be honoured as it ought to be wherever his good deed is known,—from the day on which his merciful task was a thought, to the moment when he hears the words, "Forasmuch as ye did it unto one of these my little ones, ye did it unto me."

Of this good and generous benefactor we know nothing but his name, —whether old or young, very wealthy or only comparatively rich, we cannot say,—but we may not finish our task without adding one blessing to the blessings of those he has healed, solaced, and comforted, offering, with them, a fervent prayer that God may lengthen his days in happiness and in health!

Between Greenhithe and Northfleet, on the Essex side of the river, stands the lonely CHURCH OF GRAYS, or Grays Thurrock. The river bends round here, and forms a reach known as South Hope. The marshy lands resemble the scenery of Holland; and the numerous ditches, pollards, willows, and groups of cattle, remind the spectator of pictures that have made the Dutch school of Art famous. This church stands close to the Thames, the marshes being protected from overflow by embankments. It is surrounded by trees, but no house is near it, and its isolation is very striking when approached over the dreary marsh land by which it is environed.

The embankments of the Thames, which prevent the water from overflowing the low banks on both sides of the river, are by some

GRAYS CHURCH.

authors attributed to the Romans, and by others to the Saxons; but the latest writer on the subject inclines to consider them a work of the twelfth century; and that before that time the Thames spread over the low lands to the hills on each side, among hillocks and sand hills formed from its own deposits.*   Lambarde relates that the abbot of Lesnes, in 1279, enclosed a part of these marshes at Plumstead, completing the rest in the course of twelve years; so that between 1279 and 1291 the wall of the Plumstead level, enclosing a large tract of good arable land, was rescued from the river, and so continues to this day.†   The importance of this work on the Thames banks, led to the employment

---

* The practice of draining is fully described during the Roman rule in other parts of England, particularly in the fen lands; such works are mentioned, A.D. 85, by Tacitus; and the severe labour exacted from the British serfs in their construction.

† The banks and ditches at the back of the Isle of Dogs, in what was then called Stebbenhethe Marsh, and which is now known as Stepney, are noted in very early records.   The whole of the island in the days of William the Conqueror was a woody marsh, upon which the Bishop of London fed more than five hundred hogs.   In excavating for the Blackwall Docks a large deposit of ancient trees, &c., was discovered, the remains of the wood which once thickly covered the island.   Lysons

of commissioners to superintend and keep them in repair; the earliest effort of the kind being in the eighth year of Edward III.

The rights and profits of the passage by water between London and Gravesend had been granted, from a very early period, to the inhabitants of the latter town. This water-passage was termed "the long ferry," and was under the management of a portreve, jurats, and barge proprietors, all the latter paying a fine of £5 yearly to the portreve for the use of the corporation. The fare for each person by the tilt-boats, from Gravesend to London, or *vice-versâ*, was settled, in 1573, to be "not more than sixpence;" but there was a cheaper conveyance by open barge without a tilt or covering, for which "twopence and no more" was to be charged. These more ancient barge-owners had exclusive rights, and no tilt-boat was allowed to take any passengers till they had secured theirs, and fairly started on their journey. Towards the end of Elizabeth's reign the covered boats gained a victory; and in the early part of the next reign a compromise of interests was effected between the owners of each kind. The open barges were disused in the reign of Charles I., and the tilt-boat became the ordinary conveyance. It was provided with loose straw under the tilt for passengers to sit or lie upon; and it was no unfrequent thing for them to be unable to reach Gravesend in one tide, when the passengers were landed wherever the boat might be, to shift for themselves. In 1737 it was enacted that no tilt-boat should be of less burthen than fifteen tons; and the passengers were limited to forty, including three chance passengers to be taken by the way. A bell was rung at Billingsgate to give notice of their departure at high tide, and another at Gravesend at low-water, when they proceeded to London. In 1738 five tilt-boats were licensed, and to this number they were limited until their discontinuance a few years afterwards, when larger boats with decks were

---

and other local historians allude to this covered forest : by one author this ancient deposit is described as being 8 feet below the surface, "a mass of decayed trees, leaves, and branches, accompanying huge trunks, rotted through, yet perfect in every fibre; the bark was uninjured, and the whole evidently torn up by the roots." This subterranean forest, which from time to time has been disturbed, is of considerable extent, and is traced from the river side opposite the dockyard at Deptford, across the East India Dock, and reappears in Essex.

employed; these were called by the old name of tilt-boat, though
without the tilt.  One of the last of the genuine old boats is represented
in our engraving, and very clearly exhibits its peculiarities, with the
steersman managing the principal sail, the captain and men in front,
and the passengers under the tilt or awning in the centre.  The last

GRAVESEND TILT-BOAT.

tilt-boat was named the *Duke of York,* and was withdrawn from the
service as recently as 1834, as its earnings did not pay its expenses.

Soon the spires of populous Gravesend come in sight; it is the first
port on the river, and directing the eye to the shore opposite, we obtain
a view of the time-honoured fort of Tilbury.

The threatened invasion by the Spanish Armada first led the government of Elizabeth to consider the necessity of fortifying the river here.
Hakluyt tells us :—" As it was given out that the enemy meant to
invade the Thames against Gravesend, a mighty army encamped there ;
and on both sides of the river fortifications were erected, according to
the prescription of Frederick Genebelli, an Italian, and there were
certain ships brought to make a bridge, though it were very late first."
A letter of the Earl of Leicester speaks of " lighters and chaynes that
sholde be provided and sent down to stoppe the river at Tilburye ;" but

the work seems to have been as badly done as any more recent govern-ment contract. The earl visited both places 23rd July, 1588; and his report, in a letter to Sir Francis Walsingham, states that at Gravesend, "I did peruse the fort, and find not one platforme to bear any ordnance, neither on the ground nor aloft. I went after to this fort at Tilbury, which I finde farther out of order than the other." By great exertions

TILBURY FORT.

the forts were put in order, and the vessels disposed across the river, and connected by chains to make a bridge or barrier. The Gravesend fort seems to have been the most important, and just beyond it was a block-house, which protected the river to the turn of the stream at Tilbury Hope; at the angle there, on the Essex side, another block-house commanded the river. The army was posted in the camp close to West Tilbury Church, as appears from a survey made at the time;* so that the popular tale of Queen Elizabeth reviewing her troops at Tilbury Fort is evidently a fallacy. "The fort seems to have been completed for defence upon future occasions of alarm and danger, rather than in time for defence against the Spanish Armada." The fort was

* Engraved in Cruden's valuable "History of Gravesend," to which excellent example of local litera-ture we have been indebted for these details.

then only a small earthwork; but there the Queen landed from her barge, and was escorted thence to the camp by a thousand horsemen; going there and back in a state-coach, staying the night in the camp, seeing a sham fight next day, and dining afterwards at noon, returning in great state to the royal barge. The fort, as completed, was small, but surrounded by ditches and outworks of some extent. In cases of emergency it was generally found to be in a very neglected condition, and was only properly attended to in the reign of Charles II., when the Dutch fleet entered the Medway, and burnt the ships at Chatham. The present fort was constructed after 1687, from the designs of the Engineer-General, Sir Bernard de Gomme; in which the newer principles of design introduced by Coehorn and Vauban were adopted; the cost of the stone gateway, the most striking feature of the edifice, is estimated at £634 in the contract then made.

The best spot to view Tilbury Fort is from a long wooden pier which runs some way out into the river; but the half-military-looking individuals located there (only recognised by their caps), appeared terrified at the bare idea of a pencil and paper—they have, we imagine, orders not to allow any one to sketch. The artist was therefore obliged to make his drawing from a green plat near the railway-station,* from whence he could just see the old gateway rising above one of the bastions, and a wooden pier, where some large flat boats were landing stores. The present fort appears to be a small military station, with a few guns mounted on the bastion, but it by no means conveys the idea of an important fortification. It is, however, much stronger than it seems to be; and commands the whole of the extensive turn of the river known as Tilbury Hope. Its form is pentagonal; and its outworks and ditches add greatly to its strength. The stranger who judges of it by its appearance as he passes on the river, without going over it, will form a very erroneous idea of its strength or utility.

While we are "putting" ashore at Gravesend, or at any of the landing-places below it, let us give a few minutes' consideration to the

---

* This is the terminus of the London and Gravesend Railway, which starts from Fenchurch Street; steamboats meet every train to cross the river to Gravesend with passengers.

only remaining object of the class to which we deem it expedient to direct the reader's attention.

Bare and unpromising as this region may appear in general to the naturalist, the conchologist may find an interesting field in the study of

GRAVESEND PIER.

the fresh-water shells which abound here, both in the waters of the Thames and in the adjacent marshes and canals. We figure three of the most noticeable species which are found associated together in great numbers, adhering to submerged piles, walls, &c. The most remarkable of these is the Zebra Dreissena (*Dreissena Polymorpha*), originally an inhabitant of the Volga and other Russian rivers; but having been imported with timber, it has propagated itself to an immense extent, and become completely naturalized in the Thames, and the specimens are even finer than those from the original habitat. In shape it resembles the marine muscles, and, like them, attaches itself to the surface of other bodies by a strong hemp-like "*byssus*." The colour of the shell is olive,

3 T

elegantly marked with brown and black stripes. The two smaller shells of the group are those of the fresh-water Neritine (*Neritina fluviatilis*), another shell seldom met with out of this district, but most abundant in situations similar to those of the last-described species; it is an extremely pretty shell, the surface being beautifully variegated with white and purple-brown markings.

The remaining species of our group, closely resembling in shape the common periwinkle, is the Marsh Shell (*Paludina vivipara*), found very generally with the last. It is especially interesting to the naturalist,

SHELLS.

from the fact of it being viviparous—the young shells being perfectly developed before quitting the parent shell, the mouth of which may sometimes be found crowded with minute shells about the size of peas.

The earliest notice of Gravesend occurs in Domesday Book, where it is termed Gravesham; but early in the next century it is termed Graveshende; the name is probably derived from the Graaf (Port-reeve, or Governor's) ham (or home). The port is of very ancient date, but its history is not fertile of incident. It has risen into its present importance very rapidly, and increased enormously within the last thirty years. Steamboats and railways have conspired to do this, and the cheapness and quickness of these modes of transit have made Gravesend a favourite place for Londoners to spend their leisure time. The fields in the neighbourhood of the town have been covered with streets, and Windmill Hill with houses; the old mill, however, remains, where a mill has been since the days of Elizabeth; before which time a beacon was placed there to warn the country—a use for which this hill was well adapted, as it is 179 feet above the level of the river at high-water mark.

In the fields, a little beyond the terrace-pier, are the fortifications constructed to aid Tilbury Fort in the protection of the river. They consist of earthworks and ditches of the form prescribed by Vauban, and are mounted with cannon; the fort is connected with the history of the last of the royal house of Stuart who ruled in England—King James II. During the reign of his brother, and while Duke of York, James was Admiral of England. The gateway of the old house in

FORTIFICATIONS AT GRAVESEND.

which he resided is still in existence, enclosed by a modern porch; it is of ornamental brickwork, and bears over it the date 1665, an anchor, and a semi-sphere above it.*

Milton Church is now in the suburbs of Gravesend; it is plainly descried from the river, and is a stone building with some few remains of the decorations of the fourteenth century, but having the prevailing characteristics of the fifteenth. It is supposed to have been constructed by the Countess of Pembroke, wife of Aymer de Valence, between the

* When James fled first from England, April 20, 1648, in the troublous time of the great civil war, he escaped from Gravesend in girl's attire to a vessel in the river, a short distance beyond the town.

years 1323 and 1377, when the manor of Milton devolved upon her as part of her dowry. In the village are the remains of an ancient chantry,

GATEWAY TO HOUSE OF JAMES II.

dedicated to the Virgin Mary and the Apostles Peter and Paul. It was founded and endowed in the reign of Edward II. by Aymer de Valence. All that remains of it now are a few ivy-covered walls near the road-side—the "Great Dover Road," which railways have now deprived of its largest amount of traffic.

At the "top" of the flood-tide many vessels usually accumulate at Gravesend, and anchor during the ebb; on the commencement of the next flood all are getting under weigh. This is a most animating scene, of which the artist has endeavoured to convey an idea in his sketch of GRAVESEND REACH. One or two of the vessels have fairly started, and are sailing up the river, heeling over to the breeze; others, with their sails braced in the usual manner for casting, while some have only just loosed the white canvas. The mist is rising off Gravesend, showing the town at the back of this collection of animated river life, and assisting to make up a most charming picture.*

---

* The water of the Thames at Gravesend is salt, but is turbid, for it is composed of the sea-water and water from the source, which is charged with the alluvial matter brought from the lands through which it runs, and with the drainage of the metropolis. The Thames water is preferred to purer spring water for use on board ships in long voyages; because it is believed to have a singular power of self-purification. Dr. Bostock has explained the process by which this is effected in a paper in the *Philosophical Transactions* for 1829, in which he shows, by an analysis of its component parts, that during a long voyage, "the more foul the water, the more complete will be the subsequent process of depuration;" and hence an explanation of the popular opinion that the Thames water is peculiarly valuable for sea-store, its extreme impurity inducing the fermentative process, and thus removing from it all those substances which can cause it to undergo any further alteration.

In the low lands at Milton is the entrance to the Thames and Medway Canal, which is now only navigable to Higham; it was continued thence for some miles through a tunnel opening to the Medway opposite Rochester. It is now drained, and used by the North Kent Railway. On the rising ground above the marsh lands we can distinguish Chalk Church, a lonely building in the midst of a few weather-beaten trees; it is chiefly remarkable for a curious sculpture over its door, representing a grotesque figure in a short doublet, holding a flagon of drink, and

GRAVESEND REACH.

gazing upward at a still more grotesque figure of a tumbler. It is supposed to commemorate the festivities known as Church Ales, in the olden time—annual feasts of ale and bread, bequeathed by some parishioner as a religious festival, and which was converted into a sort of county fair, or holiday, by the people.*

The high lands above are part of the woody domain of Cobham, and we can distinguish Gad's Hill, rendered memorable by Shakspere. There can be no pleasanter ramble than the few miles down green lanes to Cobham Hall, its fine collection of pictures, and the old church near it, containing the largest and most important collection of brasses in

---

* William May, of this parish, directed in his will (dated May, 1512) that his wife should make "in bread six bushels of wheat, and in drink ten bushels of malt, and in cheese twenty pence, to give to poor people for the health of his soul" every year on the anniversary of his decease.

the kingdom. The views of the Thames, and the variety of hill, dale, wood, and water, which meet the eye on all sides, make the road between Gravesend and Cobham one of the pleasantest in England.

That part of the Thames known to seamen as "the Lower Hope" is formed by the Gravesend and Milton marshes, and those of Higham and Cliffe, and the Essex shore.

The bold promontory stretching forth on the Kentish shore beyond these marshes is Cliffe, or Bishop's Clive, as it was anciently termed.

CLIFFE CHURCH.

The village and church occupy the summit, and the view of the winding of the Thames from Gravesend to the sea is very striking from this point; a long tongue of marsh land is at its foot, which causes an extensive curve in the river. The turn is known as Lower Hope Point, the water beyond as Sea Reach. This commanding height was rendered available in ancient times for "watch and ward" to the river. Beacons were ordered to be erected in the time of Richard II. at Cliffe, and the watchmen who were appointed to take charge of them were enjoined to light them whenever they saw hostile vessels approach, "and make besides all the noise by horn and by cry that they can make, to warn the country around, to come with their force to the said river, each to succour the other, to withstand their enemies." Our cut will exhibit their form at that period.

The village of Cliffe is a lonely primitive place. The church is a large and handsome fabric, dedicated to St. Helen, and stands on the brow of the chalk cliff. It is cruciform in its plan, having an embattled tower at its west end. In the windows are remains of the early painted glass which once filled them. In the chancel are three very elegant stone seats, and some very ancient monuments. Throughout it still retains many interesting vestiges of antiquity, one of which we engrave in a note. It is an enamelled patine of silver-gilt, part of the ancient church furniture in use before the great changes produced by the Reformation.*

BEACON.  a

The Thames now flows rapidly to the sea, passing between the flat lands of Essex, and the higher, but not more interesting, Kentish shore. Canvey Island, scarcely to be distinguished from the other lowlands of Essex, is on our left; it comprises about 3500 acres of pasture land, and is the "Convennos" of Ptolemy and the ancient authors.

---

* It was used to cover the chalice, and hold the bread at the communion; it is a work of the latter part of the fourteenth century, and in the centre is a representation of the crucified Saviour in the arms of the Father, surrounded by a glory. On the edge is inscribed, in old Gothic letters, separated by flowered ornament, "Benedicamus patrem et filium cum spiritu sanctu." It has been since used as an alms dish, and the ancient enamelling injured in consequence. It affords an interesting illustration of a passage in Shakspere's "Merchant of Venice," Act v. scene 1, where Lorenzo, in the garden at Belmont, directs Jessica's attention to the beauty of the stars :—

"—— Look how the floor of heaven
Is thick inlaid with patines of bright gold;
There 's not the smallest orb which thou behold'st,
But in his motion like an angel sings,
Still quiring to the young-eyed cherubim."

As an example of ancient Art, and church decoration, it is of considerable rarity, interest, and beauty.

As Sea Reach is entered—the last grand expanse of its waters—we notice the church and village of Leigh, a port much frequented by hoys and small craft, and used as a depot for lobsters brought from Norway and Scotland; and a little beyond is the stone, marking the boundary of the jurisdiction of the city of London. We then descry the rising town of Southend, situated at the debouchement of the river, and which is now united to London by a railway, a continuation of that at Tilbury. It is quite possible in little more than an hour to reach this pleasant spot, and it has, therefore, recently become much more largely populated. The

SHEERNESS.

houses are in many instances good, and the terrace commands a delightful and extensive view of the sea, the Nore, the Medway, Sheerness, and the ever-varying shipping of all nations so continually crowding the mouth of the Thames.

SHEERNESS, with its important dockyard, is situated at the mouth of the Medway, and is the principal town in the Isle of Sheppey.* It owes its greatness to the dockyard and fort erected there. The fort was established in the reign of Charles II., and due regard was given to its strength after the Dutch ships had entered the Medway. The fortifications were then greatly strengthened, and docks and storehouses were also erected. These occasioned the building of a large town, chiefly for workmen employed in the dockyard, now one of the most important

THAMES AND MEDWAY.

in the kingdom. At the mouth of the river here are generally moored many noble men-of-war, — "the fleet at the Nore" being always an attraction to steamboat voyagers. Sheerness is, however, only a chapelry to the parish of Minster, in which it is situate, and in which are performed all ecclesiastical rites of importance. It is estimated that there are more than three thousand inhabitants within the limits of the dockyard and town.

The Island of Grain, opposite Sheerness, is only kept from being

* The Saxon *Sceapige*, a name given it from the great quantity of sheep then constantly bred upon it. It is still a primitive agricultural district, and contains a few villages of very charming character.

submerged by strong embankments of earth. It is separated from the marsh lands of the Hundred of Hoo (which succeeds those at Cliffe) by a channel from the mouth of the Medway, named Yenlet (or the Inlet), or sometimes the Scray, and which was anciently of sufficient width to allow vessels to use it, as a short cut from the Medway to the Thames. The extent of the island is about three miles and a half in length, by two and a half in breadth. It contains only one parish, and a church dedicated to St. James. It consists chiefly of pasture land.

The neighbouring land is particularly low; and a novice in pilotage would hardly notice the junction of the Thames and Medway, sur-

NORE LIGHT VESSEL.

rounded as it is by low lands, were not his attention attracted by the masts of the guard and advanced line-of-battle ships, dockyard sheds, &c., rising above the projecting point that forms the entrance of the Medway. The water here is known as the Nore, and a vessel is moored in the centre, which bears a light to direct vessels at night, or during fog, into the Thames.

On reaching the NORE LIGHT we arrive at the principal anchorage for ships during the change of tide or wind, previous to advancing up the river. The old red light vessel is associated with many ideas of the best and happiest feelings of the sailor, on his arrival from abroad after a long cruise,—with his sadder sensations, also, upon his final departure from his native country. It has been the scene of many a wreck, and, in the old war time, of many a fight, when French privateers used to lurk about our coasts in foggy weather. In a picturesque point of

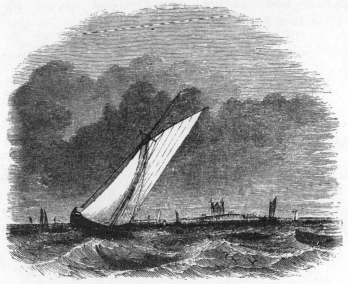

THE RECULVERS.

view it is most striking; the red sides of the vessel, pitching at her moorings, while the many different craft passing in every direction give variety and contrast.

After passing the Nore, there is one prominent object on the Kentish coast that will attract the attention of the voyager down the river before he reaches the open sea: two somewhat low square towers surmounted by spires, generally known as "THE RECULVERS," form a well-known sea-mark. They are all that remains of the ancient Church of Reculver, now an insignificant village, but formerly an important Roman station, called *Regulbium;* it is situated about three miles from Herne Bay, and ten from Margate. Owing to the constant encroachment of the sea, the church towers stand at the present time close to the edge of the low cliffs, and the bones of those interred in the old churchyard may be distinctly seen protruding through the earth by all who resort to the spot. The ancient Roman *castrum* surrounded the church; parts of the walls on the east, south, and west sides are yet to be seen; many Roman antiquities have been discovered here, and imperial coins are even now sometimes found after heavy rains.

The voyager is now on "the open sea:" he has left the Thames, but he is still, so to speak, on the territory of England:

> " Far as the breezes blow, the billows roam,
> Survey our empire, and behold our home !"

The ocean waves that roll around our coast are the fortifications that protect us:

> " Britannia needs no bulwark,
> No towers along the steep;
> Her march is o'er the mountain-wave,
> Her home is on the deep !"

Here, then, we close our pleasant task, trusting that our readers will be no more weary than we are of records associated with the bountiful and beautiful RIVER THAMES.

THE END.